PIRATES, PRISONERS, AND LEPERS

PIRATES, PRISONERS, AND LEPERS

LESSONS FROM LIFE OUTSIDE THE LAW

Paul H. Robinson and Sarah M. Robinson

Potomac Books
An imprint of the University of Nebraska Press

∞

Library of Congress
Cataloging-in-Publication Data

Robinson, Paul H., 1948–, author.
Pirates, prisoners, and lepers:
lessons from life outside the law /
Paul H. Robinson and
Sarah M. Robinson.
pages   cm
Includes bibliographical
references and index.
ISBN 978-1-61234-732-5 (hardback: alk. paper)
ISBN 978-1-61234-744-8 (epub)
ISBN 978-1-61234-745-5 (mobi)
ISBN 978-1-61234-746-2 (pdf)
1. Criminal law—Philosophy.
2. Criminal justice,
Administration of—Philosophy.
3. Punishment—Philosophy. I.
Robinson, Sarah M., author. II.
Title.
K5018.R6595 2015
340'.115—dc23
2014050161

Set in Lyon by Lindsey Auten.
Designed by N. Putens.

Dedicated to the 125,000 human generations,
and especially ours.
From
John Dale McAlpine
(born 1931)
to
Devlin and Austin Robinson and Charlie and William Hart
(born 2010 to 2013)

CONTENTS

ILLUSTRATIONS

ACKNOWLEDGMENTS

THIS PROJECT HAS BEEN IN THE WORKS FOR MANY YEARS, AND IN that time we have become indebted to many people. The book reveals the power of human cooperation and we found that and more in strangers and friends alike all over the world.

Our greatest debt goes to the staff and administrators at Penn Law, including Michael A. Fitts, dean; Merle J. Slyhoff, of library collection development and resource sharing; Edward Greenlee, associate library director for public services and adjunct professor of law; Silvana Burgese, manager of faculty support services; her deputy, the amazing Kelly Farraday; and the wonderful Jennifer Evans.

We have been helped over the years by a string of excellent research assistants, including Missy Kramer, Rebecca Blake, Brandon Kenney, Samantha Jacoby, Matt Majarian, Stephanie Wering, Daniel Wilson, Danby Kim, Aaron Ellias, Keenan Lynch, and Heather Blue.

Historians and curators from many corners have helped us find sometimes impossible sources. We are especially indebted to Pennie Moblo, instructor, Lane Community College, and curator of Molokai Archives; Anne Crawford, dean of Akitsiraq Law School, Netsilik; Colville Petty, curator of Heritage Collection Museum, Anguilla; Bob Conrich, a historian in Anguilla; Richard Featherstone, associate professor of criminology and associate dean of the college of social and behavioral sciences, University of Northern Iowa (for his materials relating to Attica); and Sylvia Garnet, mother of Ryan Holle.

Gathering the photographs for the book was another grand adventure. We received help from as far away as Australia with the Western Australian Museum providing the picture for the Batavia story. Rodrigo Dellutri, our Argentine visitor, was able to reach out to Nando Parrado for pictures from his time in the Andes. Closer to home, Richard Kallweit, formerly of Drop City, graciously shared some of his photographic memories. Sylvia Garnet, mother or Ryan Holle, and Mike Schafer, brother of Mary Ann, were also kind enough to help us tell our story with personal photographs of their loved ones.

Many of our friends have taken the time to read and comment on drafts of chapters as we shaped them for a general audience, including Reinheld Muenke, Nancy Bray, Carol Baker, Anita Friday, John McAlpine, George Sevier, Leo Katz, and Stephanos Bibas.

PART ONE

HUMAN RULES

CHAPTER ONE

WHAT IS OUR NATURE?

What Does Government Do for Us and to Us?

ON A SUNNY JUNE MORNING, THE PARENTS OF PRESCHOOLERS AT an elementary school in Los Angeles gather to celebrate the "graduation" of their twenty-three little ones. The cheery sky-blue walls of the classroom with its tidy bulletin boards welcome the parents, mostly mothers, to an endearing ceremony. It is followed by a photo session with each "graduate" posing in a cap and gown—a photo to memorialize the youngster's start down the path to what all hope will be a life of success and happiness.

But the mother of the most recently photographed child seems to be taking a bit too long removing the cap and gown from her child, at least in the view of the next mother in line. Mother Next comments on this, showing some frustration. Mother First responds with a less-than-sympathetic remark. Mother Next gives Mother First a shove. Mother First shoves back, and fists begin to fly. The mayhem quickly spreads into three separate fights, then into a general brawl. A few parents step clear of the brawl—and three take out their cameras to record the action.

A well-put-together young mother with a tight bun hairstyle runs toward the fight but is grabbed by a mother in a white blouse. Nice Bun breaks free by shedding her jacket. White Blouse is left holding an empty pink windbreaker as Nice Bun tackles Striped Shirt, who had been randomly pummeling those around her. The slapping and punching sounds are clear on the recordings, with children heard screaming in the background.

While Nice Bun and Striped Shirt roll on the floor, Long Legs reaches across the combatants to strike a different spectator. A small child dashes out from behind the new victim, her neat ponytail flashing. By now Striped Shirt is back on her feet, lunging at another new victim. An older woman, probably a student's grandmother, is pushed to the ground in the melee and struck her head on a bookshelf. When two mothers stepped in to help her, they too were attacked. The brawl spills out of the classroom and into the hall, continuing on past the maximum recording time of the cameras of bystanders.

The police are called. Several parents are arrested for assault. It is later determined that during the melee, purses and other property were stolen, presumably by those who had stepped out of the action. All school events involving parents are canceled for the remainder of the elementary school year.

This melee occurred among ordinary people—apparently loving mothers of preschoolers—walking through their everyday lives. It was not among some odd group of malevolent troublemakers or criminals, which seems to suggest that a mere scratch of the surface civility of ordinary people can reveal selfishness, meanness, and even aggression. Perhaps this incivility is always waiting to pop out as flashes of rudeness or worse over any of life's minor frustrations occurring millions of times a day as people react to the petty annoyances of life. Even the higher-profile breakdown of civility on display at the graduation brawl is hardly unusual. Consider a different group in a different context at the other end of the country.

FOR A NOMINAL FEE, A FRIENDS BASEBALL ASSOCIATION PROVIDES their offspring preschoolers with a full ten-game T-ball season, along with a baseball uniform, a team photo, and the right to march in the annual parade that begins the season. Every year, a new generation of children get to enjoy their first taste of organized sports.

On this August evening, the Florida weather is summer perfect. Earlier in the day, it had been ninety-one degrees, but a cooling rain has brought the evening temperature down to a more comfortable level. The night's game is between the Yankees and the Tigers, all preschool and kindergarten boys. The coaches are dads giving up their time for the youngsters. It is the end of summer and the start of the long Labor Day weekend, so lots of parents are in attendance. By this time in the season the boys have had some playing experience, so it promises to be a good game.

Late in the six-inning game the umpire makes a call that one of the dad-coaches disagrees with. An argument ensues. The argument spreads to other parents, then to parents from the other side. Tempers and voices rise. Soon the shouting turns into hitting, and before long the sidelines empty as twenty men, mostly dads of the two teams, charge the field. The four- and five-year-old boys stand watching as their dads swing at one another with wild punches and tackle each other to the ground. The umpire backs out of the melee, which continues without him.

The police are called. They are able to stop the brawling, take names, and begin interviewing the fighters and the bystanders, with the interviews continuing off the field the following day. A coach from each team is suspended, and at last report the police are still deciding whether and with what to charge the brawlers.

California and Florida. Moms and dads. It seems that even ordinary people today can easily misbehave over minor disappointments or frustration—and even in public, and in front of their children.

THERE EXISTS A COMMON WISDOM OF SORTS THAT HUMANS ARE inherently bad and government and law is the essential feature that saves us from ourselves. Founding father James Madison put it this way: "What is government itself but the greatest of all reflections on human nature? If men were angels, no government would be necessary."[1]

Think the postapocalyptic marauding bands of thugs attacking Mel Gibson in *The Road Warrior*, or Denzel Washington in *The Book of Eli*, or Kevin Costner in *Waterworld*. For centuries this has been the common view of man's natural state. According to philosopher Thomas Hobbes in his 1651 classic work *Leviathan*, without the restraining influence of governmental law, "every man is enemy to every man."[2] There is no right or wrong, only power and weakness. It is only government and its laws—the "Leviathan"—that restrains people from destroying one another.[3] "Law was brought into the world for nothing else but to limit the natural liberty of particular men in such manner as they might not hurt, but assist one another."[4] Governmental law, then, is the wellspring of all social order.

Many of us rarely see a policeman in our daily lives, but our conduct is nonetheless highly influenced, consciously or not, by the knowledge that an entire criminal justice machine is waiting at the end of a 911 call. We rarely even think about the possibility of making the call. The existence of government, laws, courts, and the police has created a cocoon in which most of us enjoy a degree of safety. We follow the laws most of the time, and life goes on. The imperceptible hand of criminal justice is always there to keep the wolves among us, or hidden within us, away from the sheep.

The problem with this humans-are-devils-and-only-government-can-save-us view is that, if it were true, we as a species would have gone extinct several million years ago. Our ancestors on the Serengeti Plain more than 125,000 generations ago were surrounded by predators that were stronger, faster, and bigger than they. Yet the weak humans, who should have been easy prey, became the most successful species in the history of planet earth. And they did it without the restraining hand of governmental law.

This miracle of human success was not the product of a Hobbesian inclination to destroy others, but just the opposite. It was the product of our natural tendency to cooperate with one another as a cohesive group (and made possible by our luck in developing an ability to communicate through language). There was no government restraining these early humans—or even the concept of such an external "Leviathan" anywhere in their consciousness. There was instead a cooperative human nature that did not need governmental laws to be successful.

However, this does not mean that there were no shared understandings of how the group members should or would be made to behave. We know that social norms develop that can effectively guide conduct, even without governmental law at work. A famous study of ranchers and farmers in Shasta County, California, by Robert Ellickson, a professor at Stanford Law School, showed that groups commonly organize their lives through their own social arrangements rather than through legal rules, even for those regular points of tension among members that the law purports to control. Ellickson describes substitute social rules for situations as diverse as dealing with damage to adjoining property when livestock stray, deciding who should bear the cost of fences to prevent straying, and collisions with livestock that stray onto roads.[5]

Do cooperative ranchers prove that Hobbes was wrong? Do they show that man does not need law to gain social cooperation? Not really. The social accommodations among the Shasta County farmers and ranchers are made possible only because they are made within an existing legal system—the 911 cocoon, if you will. No doubt the ranchers and farmers still call the police when needed, and knowing that help is just a phone call away creates a comfortable space within which they can make their social arrangements. Children at recess may play nicely when the playground monitor is standing nearby, but they might well revert to *Lord of the Flies* without her.

A true test of whether man needs laws would require dropping the Shasta County ranchers and farmers onto a large, uninhabited island. Absent a criminal justice system of laws enforced by police, courts, and prisons, would they show the same degree of social cooperation? Without that external restraint, would the strong bully the weak? The difficulty, of course, is that finding volunteers for such an experiment might prove difficult. (We set aside here the raft of reality television schemes that might seem to fit the bill. Besides the obvious sampling distortions—what kind of person volunteers for such wacky public exposure?—there still exists in such schemes the "playground monitor" being represented in the person of the producers, commercial sponsors, and the FCC, all of whom are watching carefully to be sure things don't spin too far out of control.)

DO WE REALLY NEED GOVERNMENTAL LAW TO COEXIST, AS HOBBES assumes? Could the cooperative nature displayed by the humans of the Serengeti Plain make government and law unnecessary? Indeed, need-for-law skeptics might go further to suggest that not only is governmental law not essential to our social organization and well-being, but that it affirmatively hurts us. It is not something to be celebrated and revered. Rather, it is only to be tolerated and continuously scrutinized. It may help us as a society in some ways but it hurts us in others.

The graduation brawl and the T-ball melee may actually illustrate the skeptics' point. This level of conflict upon trivial provocation is what we get when we rely on governmental law rather than on the interdependence and shared responsibility that marked early humans' social cooperation. The Serengeti humans would never have done something so silly. If they had, they would not have lasted long.

Has the advent of governmental law really saved humans from ourselves, or has it created a disconnect among us and stoked a selfishness that makes us less cooperative with one another? By inserting itself between people, by breaking the bonds of direct interdependency and the personal accountability that it brings, has governmental law created humans who have little interest or need to develop a habit of cooperation?

Clearly, the existence of governmental law has not made us a pleasant and cooperative society. The United States has more than one hundred thousand criminal provisions. Every state has its own criminal code, typically containing about two thousand provisions. Layered over this is federal criminal law, with another five thousand criminal statutes and many thousands more regulatory provisions that have been made federal crimes (three hundred thousand, it has been estimated). Because legislatures love to pass crime-related legislation, the number of criminal laws is increasing. Indeed, in some states the pace is accelerating, with the number of newly created criminal statutes increasing each year. We are the most legally controlled people in all of human history.[6]

Yet all this criminal lawmaking has hardly done away with crime or even reduced it to a minor problem. More than twenty-two million crimes are committed each year in the United States, and six million of those are violent crimes. But Americans are not the only ones to experience the limits of modern law's effectiveness. As bad as U.S. crime is, most of the world is worse. The U.S. murder rate of 4.2 per 100,000 people, for example, is lower than that of most countries in the world and is only about 60 percent of the world's overall murder rate (almost 7 per 100,000). Compare the U.S. rate of 4.2 to Africa's average murder rate of 17, South America's 20, and Central America's 28.5. Even many countries in the world's lower-crime regions have noticeably higher rates: Indonesia has a rate of 8.1, Russia

10.2, North Korea 15.2, and Greenland 19.2. Indeed, many countries have murder rates in the 30s and 40s, or higher. Honduras, the record holder, has a rate of more than 91 per 100,000.[7] It is hard to see governmental law as a roaring success in this respect.

Would governmental law do a better job if it sought to cherish and enlarge upon the human nature seen in the cooperation of humans on the Serengeti, rather than attempting to stamp out the evil human nature of the Hobbesian bad man? What should be the fundamental goal of governmental law: to constrain and reform our nature or to build upon and encourage it? The answer depends in large part on exactly what our common nature is today. Perhaps it is not just that government has changed our existence but that our existence under government has changed our nature. Perhaps the passing of the 125,000 generations since the original people of the Serengeti has changed us—we are no longer who we once were—and governmental law may now be, as Hobbes believes, essential.

Distilling the answer to this fundamental question—What is our basic nature today, if one removes the influence of governmental law?—seems nearly impossible. In a world so dominated by government and law, how could we even imagine a life without it? The Shasta County farmers and ranchers are not volunteering for the uninhabited island experiment. Luckily, the accidents of history and the unpredictability of life give us some enlightening instances in which we can glimpse humans living beyond the law. Our world and our history are rich with such natural experiments, most of which no one would volunteer for, but survivors of such events can tell us the data-rich tale.

A plane crashes on a remote mountain or a ship wrecks on an isolated island. If there is no prospect of rescue, how do the survivors deal with one another? If the group thinks it might soon be rescued, this is no true test. While no policeman is at hand, people might still conform out of fear that later they will be called to account by the law. A true test occurs only when the people of the group think they will never return to the control of governmental law, or if the situation is such that they no longer care about such a possibility. Once they feel completely free of legal constraints, how do isolated individuals behave toward one another? Perhaps they will continue for a while in their lawful ways out of habit or momentum. What happens when those habits are long washed out by the threat of extinction every day, like the humans on the Serengeti Plain? Do the strong maximize their chances of survival by victimizing the weak?

Such absent-law situations have occurred in a wide variety of settings beyond plane crashes and shipwrecks. A group may be forced into permanent isolated exile, as with the forced creation of leper colonies in the middle of the nineteenth century. A group may choose to isolate itself, as with groups of escaped slaves or pirates at the start of the eighteenth century. Members of these groups no longer see themselves as under the influence of governmental law. Indeed, for some groups the absence of governmental law is the primary enticement, as with the American hippie anarchist communes of the 1970s.

One can be in an essentially absent-law situation without even being in an isolated or remote locale. Prisoners in POW or concentration camps have their dealings with guards strictly controlled, but the guards often have little interest in the behavior of prisoners among themselves. How do such inmates deal with one another? Or how do residents in occupied areas during wartime behave when their occupiers forbid any police involvement and take no interest in what residents do to one another? If governmental law is the wellspring of social order, does its absence mean inevitable chaos and a state of war in which "every man is enemy to every man"? Or does the sudden absence of governmental law return the group to a natural state of cooperative action brought on by a shared situation and interdependence? Or is it something else altogether?

THE FOLLOWING CHAPTERS EXPLORE THE EVENTS AND RESULTS in a host of absent-law natural experiments. Some strikingly similar patterns appear across strikingly different situations. Barricaded prisoners, crash survivors, gold miners, Eskimos, pirates, lepers, hippies, and many others all show common inclinations. It turns out that we are not the selfish devils that Hobbes assumes, but neither are we selfless angels either. The reality is more interesting and the implications speak to how we should use criminal law today.

CHAPTER TWO

COOPERATION

Lepers and Pirates

IT IS EASY ENOUGH TO BE COOPERATIVE WHEN IT DOES NOT COST you anything. We are polite and congenial to one another much of the time. It takes minimal effort and gives us the benefit of enjoying each other's civility. We do sometimes put ourselves out for others, perhaps skipping a planned outing to instead babysit a friend's child, but this, too, makes good sense. We get not only the benefit of a return favor in the future but also the good feeling of friendship. Some people go much further, making dramatic contributions to others—such as the successful entrepreneur contributing a million dollars to his alma mater—with no expectation of a return other than the admiration of others and the good feeling that comes with generosity. Of course, he is not likely to be suffering any diminution in his level of luxury living. The cost to him is experienced as a pure abstract.

Would the same generous spirit survive if what you were giving was your own time on this earth in order to lengthen someone else's? Would you put your own life at risk to save another's? Of course we have examples of people who regularly do just that; the most storied are police and firemen. But even a policeman has only a 0.000186 chance of being killed in a given year, so twenty years on the job means a 0.00372 chance of death. Trashmen have about twice that risk of death. (Firemen are actually below the population average and have only a slightly greater risk of death than cashiers.)[1]

What if the risk of death is immediate and significant? What if you could extend your life and the chances of surviving by eating the only available food, or you could give it to another, sicker person and improve that person's chances of surviving. Assume there is no hero's parade to look forward to, because civilization is not part of your foreseeable future, and assume it is a stranger who needs the help, not a friend or relative. You are in an absolute state of nature and beyond worrying about what the law or society expects of you. What would you do? We know you would, of course, be a grand hero. What about the ordinary person and not the ordinary person as portrayed on television, but the real ordinary person sitting across from you on the bus? Be realistic. What would he do? Consider the situation in 1860s Hawaii.

HAWAII HAD A LEPROSY PROBLEM. THE DISEASE WAS HIGHLY CONtagious and lethal, they believed (a belief now known to be false). Citizen and business groups were alarmed and demanded action to protect them from the growing danger. Urged on by King Kamehameha, the legislature had the solution: they would buy a large section of a remote island, Molokai, and simply ship all lepers to it.[2]

On the morning of January 6, 1866, the sailing ship *Warwick* landed on the northern coast of Molokai. In a driving rain and choppy surf, the ship's cargo of sixteen people were put ashore on the beach—lepers brought here for forced exile. With an official on horseback leading the way, the group was marched single file up a rugged mountain path. They had not slept in twenty-four hours and had been given only meager rations of bread on the daylong voyage to the island.

Partway up the mountain they reached some abandoned huts in a small valley, which stood in the shadow of a towering cliff. Because it was nearly always in shadow and endured daily rain, the place never really dried out. The huts were damp and rotting, as were the taro and sweet potato crops abandoned in the nearby fields. Upon reaching the huts, the exhausted group dropped and slept.

As they slept, the official rode off without telling the group when or if he would return. He left a blanket for each person and some farm implements.

1. Boys with leprosy living on Molokai, ca. 1890. Courtesy National Park Service.

None of the group were farmers. Drinking water was available only from a mountain creek more than a mile away. Firewood was available only on the beach, back down the narrow mountain trail they had just traveled. The damp and chilly conditions were ideal for advancing leprosy.

The group awoke the next morning and found themselves alone. They were cold, hungry, and thirsty. Of the sixteen people, two were seriously ill and required considerable care and attention. Four were strong and healthy at this point. The remainder were somewhere in between. (Within days in the dampness, three more would become seriously ill and incapacitated.) There was enough food—salt pork and sea biscuits—to last only two or three days. If it were consumed only by the strong, it might last several weeks—perhaps long enough for the strong to locate more food and begin growing their own. Caring for the sick strangers would mean not only giving them a portion of the limited food but also diverting the time and energy needed to establish a sustainable existence for the healthy.

WHAT DO WE EXPECT THE HEALTHY LEPERS TO DO? WHAT WOULD the person sitting across from you on the bus do? Would they look to their own survival by taking what the weak have or by simply ignoring them? The incentives for the healthy to look out for themselves was great. There was no payoff in helping the sick. With fingers and toes rotted off from leprosy, the sick could not help plant crops anytime soon and instead would be an increasing burden. And the weak were strangers to whom the healthy had no obligation of family or friendship. For the most part the group had only met the day before, when they were all herded onto the same transport ship.

One might think that their common disease might provide a common cause, but think more about that. People of the time believed the disease to be contagious and fatal. By its nature, then, the disease trains its sufferers to expect alienation and shunning from those they meet. Their dehumanizing and embittering disease has made their lives miserable, full of revulsion and ostracism. Their government has declared them legally dead. They are living as legal zombies whose marriages have been annulled and whose property has been passed on. If the strong among these mistreated souls had some hope or positive expectation for the benefits of working as a group, it would have been the product of something other than rational calculation or life experience.

TWO WEEKS LATER THE *WARWICK* RETURNED TO MOLOKAI. THE official was delivering another batch of exiled lepers. The people who had been left sleeping two weeks before had not awoken to play out Hobbes's "every man enemy of every other," but instead had organized themselves into working groups. The two strongest had been given the task of nursing those who lay incapacitated. Others spent their days hauling firewood up from the beach and water down from the creek. The rest of the group scavenged for food and did the cooking. Banana and orange trees were located in the forest. To remove the damp chill that was so dangerous to the sick, fires were tended around the clock. Huts had been repaired and now offered dry shelter. From the rotting crops in the field, a store of salvaged food had been gleaned. There was a ready stack of firewood and a system for fetching and storing water. While the manual labor was difficult, several rows of sweet potatoes had been planted.

Without adequate food, water, or shelter, the weakest exiles certainly would have quickly died. Instead, all members of the original group were still alive and progress had been made toward creating better conditions. Why would this be so? If the healthy lepers had made a rational calculation on how best to survive the coming challenges, this would not have been the reasoned conclusion. But it seems highly unlikely that they or anyone else was doing much rational calculating. They were in desperate straits and probably running on autopilot as the vast extent of their misfortune became more evident.

One might assume that the lepers' is a unique and aberrational case, some odd quirk of a reaction. But that turns out not to be the case. When one looks at other human groups forced to make such difficult choices, this response is common. Certainly cooperation can be derailed, but cooperation is a recurring behavior among a great variety of human situations and seen in people from many parts of the world and at many points of human history.

IN OCTOBER OF 1972 A PLANE FLYING FROM URUGUAY TO CHILE crashed in the Andes Mountains. Those who survived the crash were stranded in snow at 12,000 feet without protective clothing, food, or even any certainty of where they were.[3] Clambering out of the wreckage, dressed in street clothes, the uninjured set to work freeing those who were trapped. After some initial chaos, task teams were formed. A medical group tended to the injured, another group converted the plane into a shelter, and a third group melted ice for drinking water and collected wreckage debris that could be useful.

Food was scarce. A distribution system was implemented with cups of wine, bites of jam for lunch, and squares of chocolate for dinner. Food was given to everyone capable of eating, not just those able to work. People too injured to feed themselves were fed, and water was dripped into the mouths of unconscious victims. Hammocks were constructed to keep the injured more comfortable. Because some parts of the plane were colder than others, a rotation system was introduced for the night hours.

After several weeks on the mountain, everyone's health was rapidly deteriorating from starvation. The survivors debated whether to begin eating the corpses of those who had died in the crash. One man proposed they eat the pilots, as they were the cause of the crash. Each survivor volunteered his or her own body to be eaten when they died. Eventually it was agreed that the existing corpses must be used as food.

Eating the human meat took some serious emotional adjustment for many but improved the health of all. A serious setback came, however, when an avalanche swept away much of the area and covered the plane in several feet of snow, trapping many inside and burying others in the snow outside. Digging furiously, the free members worked to save their snowbound compatriots. Those liberated joined in the effort to save those still buried. Despite the efforts, several died.

Only nineteen people now remained alive, and their situation was worse than before. Because the avalanche had swept away the bodies of the early crash victims, the group had as food only the flesh of the newly dead, who they all knew well. More important, it was now clear that no help was coming. The period during which authorities would search for them had long passed. (The plane had been well off its planned course when it went down, and the searchers had given up looking on the assumption that the plane must have disintegrated on impact or been buried in the snow, killing all aboard.) It seemed impossible that anyone, and certainly not any of these battered, starved, and unequipped survivors, could hike out of the snow-covered mountain range.

However remote the chances of success, the alternative was certain death. It was agreed that the five fittest men would be named expeditionaries and the focus of the group would be to build their strength for their expedition to bring help. The expeditionaries received larger quantities of food, were assigned the best places to sleep, and were excused from all camp labor. Two of the expeditionaries declined the special treatment.

On November 17 the five headed out, first attempting to find the plane's tail section, which might have important supplies, and then perhaps to continue on in the direction they believed lay Chile. They found the tail section, which had cigarettes, chocolate, some additional food, a thin fabric that could be made into sleeping bags, and, most important, batteries for the two-way radio. Believing the batteries would allow them to call for help, they retraced their path. But back at the plane they could not get the radio to work and were left as desperate as before.

The new food lasted only a short time. There remained few bodies to be eaten. Three more members of the group died, bringing increased urgency to a second attempt that was being planned. As November turned

2. Survivors from the Andes crash living in the fuselage of the wrecked plane, 1972. Courtesy Nando Parrado.

into December, four of the original expeditionaries again departed, but two soon turned back because they could not bear the cold and hardship. The other two continued on, without maps, adequate clothing, or ropes. As the period passed during which the last two expeditionaries could have survived, the remaining group faced the realization that they were probably going to die on the mountain as soon as the remaining bodies were consumed.

THE GROUP WAS NOW, AND PROBABLY FOR SOME TIME HAD BEEN, well beyond the reach of the law. If they had given it any thought they would have perhaps concluded that they were already breaking it by their daily cannibalism, but in truth the law had probably become irrelevant to them. Certainly now that they were facing death it had no hold on them even if they were to think about it. In other words, the law had nothing to do with why the healthy and uninjured had not and did not now promote their own interests at the expense of the injured and the weak. What explains this cooperative action of the survivors? And what can we expect of them now that it is clear that they will soon die on the mountain?

Under Thomas Hobbes's pessimistic account—without law "every man is enemy to every man"—the strongest survivors would have had little hesitation in killing others to preserve themselves, even if it was only delaying the inevitable, just as the man in the water after a shipwreck may instinctively pull the old lady off the ladder to save himself from drowning.[4] The Hobbesian bad man would have no inclination to tend to the injured. Indeed, this would only increase the number of mouths to feed and reduce the number of bodies to eat. Hobbes was not alone in his pessimistic view. Friedrich Nietzsche spoke of "man's innate 'will to power' [which] needs to be discharged through subjugation and exploitation." Man might become civilized but, as Henry David Thoreau put it, "The savage in man is never quite eradicated."[5]

Indeed, this is apparently how most people think others behave. Social psychology studies tell us that most people see others, especially strangers, as acting primarily in their own self-interests.[6] One set of researchers concluded that "only a minority of the American public cling to the belief that we are a people of compassion; the majority believe instead that we are driven by self-interest."[7] When the researchers asked subjects, "On the whole, do you think people in our country are genuinely concerned about helping the needy, or are they mostly concerned about their own activities and interests?" only a quarter expressed confidence in people's concern for others; more than two-thirds thought people were concerned only with their own interests.

And one would expect such natural selfishness to be all the more evident in desperate circumstances, such as the Andes plane crash. It might be easy to share with others when there is plenty, or at least enough. But when helping others necessarily hastens one's own death, it seems unlikely. Yet this is exactly what we see among the Andes crash survivors, not only immediately after the crash but even as their situation became clearly desperate. As the chance of survival faded, the strongest did not victimize the weak but rather continued to care for them, even though it was at their own expense.

Why would these survivors behave this way—in a way so contrary to their own self-interest? Law was certainly not playing a role. Law was irrelevant to their world. Something in their own character must have been at work.

THE STRONG SURVIVORS CONTINUED THEIR CARE OF THE WEAK during their entire time on the mountain. As it happened, the expeditionaries did not perish, as was reasonable to assume. Their trek turned into an astonishing tale of its own, with mind-numbing hardship after hardship. (See the postscript.) But one of the two, Nando Parrado, would not give up and pushed beyond the limits of conceivable human endurance. He brought the two of them out of the mountains on December 21, 1972, after eleven days of ceaseless struggles during which the other man had repeatedly pleaded with Parrado to let him just lie down and die.

Parrado led the rescuers back to the crash site by helicopter and brought out sixteen survivors. All of those who had been alive when he left the site thirteen days before, even the sick and injured, were still alive, thanks to the care of their comrades. In the end, every person who survived the plane crash and the avalanche was alive to be rescued. Ironically, Nando Parrado was one of the most seriously injured passengers after the crash. He suffered multiple skull fractures and lay unconscious for some time. Even though he was expected to die quickly, he was kept hydrated as long as he was breathing. He eventually regained consciousness, was nursed back to health, and went on to be the person who saved the group.

Nando Parrado nicely illustrates the long-term value of an instinct for social cooperation over individual selfishness. None of the survivors could have dreamed that by tending the unconscious Parrado they were in fact saving themselves. Yet while the individual person's perspective cannot see it, the bigger picture is one in which, over the longer course of human history, cooperative groups are likely to do better than groups of selfish individuals.

ARE THE ANDES SURVIVORS AND THE MOLOKAI LEPERS UNIQUE stories of exceptional people? No. The same pattern of social cooperation appears regularly in a wide variety of Hobbesian "state of nature" situations—and not just in cases of isolated groups in remote locations. In the gold rush mining camps of California, the territory was not governed by any law and each camp was a transitory group. A camp would disappear overnight if the gold ran out. Yet in each camp the miners formed a set of social norms and sufficiently powerful enforcement mechanisms to allow each miner to leave his tools, provisions, gold, and other worldly goods unattended all day while he mined.[8]

During World War II, as the SS hunted Jews hiding in the Warsaw Ghetto, the refugees hid in cellars, attics, and behind false walls. One woman described one such scene:

> The bunker grew increasingly crowded and stuffy. Anyone who went to the water-tap or toilet collided with others or stumbled over their neighbors in the darkness. There was no end to the disputes and squabbles, fights over nothing, insults, name-calling. Exhausted by the want of fresh air and the most elementary facilities, tortured by incessant fear and uncertainty, people began losing their self-control. The bunker became a real hell. . . . Yet, in the midst of this suffering, there grew up a solidarity, a mutual understanding and sympathy. It was no longer necessary to shout for quiet, lest the SS track us down, nor ask too long for neighborly help. People helped one another, even shared the last drops of medicine, without caring whether someone was a relative or a stranger, a friend or unknown, poor or rich. The differences between us disappeared. In the end, our mutual and tragic fate had united us into one great family.[9]

At the conclusion of the war the ordinary citizens of Berlin had been forbidden to leave the city in advance of the Russian Army. Trapped beneath the shelling were thousands of hungry and cold civilians who knew that their leaders had fled or killed themselves. Yet, despite the desperate and chaotic circumstances, the residents did not become Hobbesian "bad men" but instead maintained a state of social order in which people cooperated with one another in adhering to social norms. When Russian bombs were falling around them, it was clear that no authority was present, yet the strong waited in line with the weak. A female journalist waiting in a food line among the shelled-out buildings talked of her life in a nearby basement:

> We're no longer being governed. And still, everywhere you look, in every basement, some kind of order always emerges. When my house was hit I saw how even those who'd been injured or traumatized or buried in the rubble, walked away in an orderly manner. The forces of order prevail in this basement as well, a spirit that regulates, organizes,

commands. It has to be in our nature. People must have functioned that way as far back as the Stone Age. Herd instinct, a mechanism for preservation of the species.[10]

As outside observers with perfect hindsight we often can see that group cooperative action may be better for the group in the long run, but how realistic is it that the individual person in difficult circumstances can see this wisdom and be willing to act on it, especially when doing so often carries immediate personal costs? Cooperation often seems at best an unjustifiable risk, requiring an immediate sacrifice for a longshot payoff. Indeed, it is more likely that no such calculation is even made. Landing upon Molokai island or recovering from the Andes plane crash or hiding in a Warsaw Ghetto basement: few are probably reasoning at all. They are just responding instinctively to the immediate threat. Yet, despite the shock and the fear, their instincts commonly lead them to cooperation.

This tendency toward cooperation, apparently an innate human characteristic, has been seen not only in anecdotal illustrations but also in a large number of controlled empirical studies. People think that others act out of self-interest, but research suggests they "overestimate the power of self-interest" in others' conduct. While people think others are purely self-interested—which would give them every reason to act so themselves—in fact they still do not act that way themselves.[11]

Consider, for example, what are called "public goods" experiments. Participants are given an amount of money. They can either keep the money for themselves or contribute it to a group coffer. The money added to the group coffer adds value (similar to accruing interest) that is then divided equally between all members of the group, *whether or not they contributed to the group coffer*. Thus, one would guess that a rational, self-interested actor would keep all his or her money, contributing nothing, yet would get the benefit of the community coffer distribution on top of his or her original money.

In the controlled experiments, however, people typically do contribute to the group coffer, which thereby increases overall group welfare. In fact, participants on average will contribute up to 60 percent of their allotment to the group, even though they know that others may contribute nothing.[12] This suggests that humans commonly take cooperative actions they know can be costly to them personally.

As the social science studies make clear, a lot more than self-interest is going on in humans. They will invest in cooperative acts that benefit the group at their own expense, even when interacting with complete strangers and even when there is no possibility they will have an opportunity to interact with the same people again, just as subjects cooperated on Molokai, in the Andes, or hiding from the SS. This is so even if the subjects have no possibility of repayment and no expectation of gaining personal benefit, such as improved social status or reputation, and even when there are strong incentives for self-interested behavior.

WHAT IS DRIVING THIS APPARENTLY WIDELY HELD INCLINATION toward cooperation? People are not cooperating because they calculate it will benefit them nor because governmental law is telling them they must. Rather, cooperation seems to be their default setting. People can be dissuaded from cooperating—studies tell us they won't be "suckers" for those who won't reciprocate—but it seems to be people's inherent first inclination. Why might this be?

Reconsider the early human groups on the Serengeti Plain. They have been prey animals for thousands of years. Among their predators are a short-faced hyena, the Pachycrocuta; a huge saber-toothed cat with fangs twelve inches long, the Smilodon; crocodiles; and, in Australia, a giant predatory kangaroo with six-inch fangs.[13] Alone, even with tools or weapons, an individual human was seriously disadvantaged against these predators. On the other hand, a group of humans—especially with stout clubs—could become the predator rather than the prey. So, too, the group offered a chance to recover from a broken arm or a stomach virus, when a lone individual might have been fatally disadvantaged.

The benefits of cooperation are most clear when a threat exists, but a threatening situation is also when it is most evident that the benefits of cooperation are not assured. If the threat is not overcome—if the group loses its battle with the beast—the risks taken produced no reward. Worse, others could make this same calculation and decide to not risk themselves if a threat presents itself. They might be cooperative but then run off when a hungry tiger appears, leaving the others exposed. Better to hang back and let others take the risk and see what happens, like the person who contributes nothing to the group coffer yet looks to share in its distribution in the "public goods" experiment. The greater the number of such "free riders" in a group, the greater the likelihood that the threat will not be repelled and that those who risk themselves will be killed or injured. This would certainly weaken the group, and surely even the "free riders" would suffer as part of the weaker whole. But this is a distant, longer-term danger that is not likely to be at the forefront of an individual's mind when confronting the Smilodon with twelve-inch fangs. Better to run now and worry about the group's long-term interests later.

It is at the times of greatest need for cooperative action that the disincentives to act in concert are the greatest. Yet from the long-term perspective—like the longest-term perspective of evolution—it is also apparent that the group that tends toward cooperative action even in the most difficult situations will do better than the group that does not.[14] Are we surprised, then, that when the natural selection process is applied to the hundreds of thousands of generations of human history, it tends to favor human groups whose members have an innate inclination toward cooperative action—a group whose members are likely to cooperate even if the calculation of the immediate cost and benefits suggests cooperation is not the smart thing to do?

The early human groups that maintained effective cooperation even in the face of adversity were better able than their less cooperative peers to gain and keep the advantages of cooperation. Groups with more-cooperative inclinations thrived, while groups with less failed. Eventually only human groups with cooperative traits remained, which helps explain the natural tendency of humans to think in terms of cooperation even if a rational calculator in their situation would not.

Hobbes may think that governmental law is the source of social order, that law is here to "save men from themselves," but the truth is that man's natural inclination toward cooperative action saved our species long before governmental law was a thought in any human's head.[15] The earliest governmental law, ancient Egyptian law of 3000 BC, came only in the last miniscule portion of human history. The early human groups on the Serengeti had nothing but themselves: no governmental law, no government, no social institutions. Yet they became highly cooperative, and that trait more than any other made them the most successful species in the history of the world.

HUMANS WERE NOT THE FIRST SPECIES TO SHOW COOPERATIVE tendencies. As the anthropology curator for the American Museum of Natural History recently concluded, "Modern human beings are cooperative; and they would certainly never have become so had the biological underpinnings not already been present—not just in the hominid ancestor, but in a succession of precursor species among which, on average, behaviors we can at some level call cooperation had become more complex over time."[16] Thus, our instinct toward cooperative action traces back far beyond the 125,000 generations of humans. It was built upon a foundation of successful cooperation in social animals that had been developing for eons, likely before humans ever appeared on earth.

Compared to genetically similar species such as apes, humans display a much stronger penchant for cooperation, even at very early ages. Even social chimpanzees do not compare to humans, who have been shown to cooperate with non-family members, with people they are not likely to encounter again, and even with nonhumans. In many ways cooperation became the defining human trait that has brought our species to its unique evolutionary destiny.[17]

IN HIS CLASSIC BOOK ABOUT THE BRUTAL REALITIES OF THE Holocaust, *The Survivor*, Terrence Des Pres beautifully describes the organic nature of the human dynamics of cooperation:

Nature itself—by which I mean the system of living creatures—guards against dissolution and chaos; not through control by government, nor even by rational adherence to "laws of nature," but through the emergence, during times of prolonged crisis, of structures of behavior whose purpose is to maintain the social basis of life. Order emerges. That, as biologists like to observe, is the first and most striking fact about life, since entropy or the tendency to dissolution characterizes all inorganic kinds of organization. For survivors this is crucial. Uprooted and flung into chaos, they do what they must to stay alive, and in that doing achieve enough society to meet the crisis humanly, together. After the period of initial collapse comes reintegration, a process which usually occurs gradually, in accord with the fact that all things human take time. In some cases, however, it can happen remarkably fast.[18]

Des Pres describes the process by which ninety-six people jammed into a railway boxcar during the mass deportations to concentration camps dealt with their situation. One can imagine a similar human dynamic at work in the desperate situations of the Andes plane crash survivors and the Molokai-exiled lepers. As Des Pres describes, at one point quoting one of the survivors,

The "veneer" of cultivated behavior, which served well enough in normal times, was not equal to such stress. Fear and panic were the initial response, and for a time all was chaos. But then, as necessity bore down and hysteria gave way to realism, a more elementary kind of order, or at least a readiness, began to function. A condition came into being which allowed the "cooler heads" to be heard. Amid the mess they held an election; they came to agree on basic responsibilities, and settled down to face their common plight. This achievement may have been but a "semblance" of past order, but it was sufficient to keep the ninety-six people in that boxcar sane and alive and above the threshold of brutality.

Civility disintegrates and disorder prevails. Then slowly, in sorrow and a realism never before faced up to, the mass of flailing people grow quiet and neighborly, and in the end rest almost peaceful in primitive communion. In this and other instances,

The simple, shapeless agglomeration of human beings assembled by chance reveals a hidden structure of available wills, an astonishing plasticity which takes shape according to certain lines of force, reveals plans and projects which are perhaps unfeasible but which lend a meaning, a coherence to even the most absurd, the most desperate of human acts.

Order emerges, people turn to one another in "neighborly help." This pattern was everywhere apparent in the world of the camps.[19]

SINCE THE INCLINATION TOWARD GROUP COOPERATIVE ACTION is an innate human characteristic, it may reveal itself in unexpected situations and even in people for which it will seem out of character.

Even before Hurricane Katrina arrived in New Orleans at 3:00 a.m. on August 29, 2005, the city's protective canals had flooded and Lake Pontchartrain had overflowed its banks. Conditions deteriorated rapidly. Clean water was unavailable. Safe shelter was scarce. Officials encouraged people to congregate at the Morial Convention Center, a mile from the Superdome, but things were little better there. Bodies of the dead lay undisturbed, thieves openly robbed people who had come to the facility for shelter, and there was no food or water.[20]

In a somewhat different role than their usual, the street gangs brought order. The well-organized gangs did much to reduce the suffering (but only after negotiating the boundaries of each gang's turf within the Convention Center, of course). Like "Robin Hood," as one person put it, they patrolled the sometimes desperate crowd, keeping order. One witness remembered the gangs' actions this way:

They were securing the area. . . . These guys were criminal. They were. But somehow they got together, figured out who had guns, and decided they were going to make sure that no women were getting raped . . . and that nobody was hurting babies [children]. . . . They were the ones getting clothes for people who had walked through that water. They were the ones fanning old people, because that's what moved the guys.[21]

Clearly the gang members had a history, and probably a habit, of doing bad things and purely self-interested things. What seems so odd is that they would not take the opportunity of victim vulnerability to do more bad, self-interested things. Yet we see them move toward positive cooperative action. Why would such a thing even come into their heads? Why would it ever occur to them to change their normal pattern, to protect rather than victimize the survivors at the center? Whatever the reason, it was not governmental law at work but something in human nature. The pirates of the eighteenth century provide an even more revealing example of the strength and complexity of the cooperative phenomenon.

ON APRIL FOOL'S DAY 1696, THE GOVERNOR OF THE PORT CITY OF Nassau, Bahamas, was expecting a French fleet to arrive at any moment to burn his British-held town. He had no force with which to repel them. A man arrived bearing a letter, but the man was not a Frenchman. The letter explained that if the good governor would allow anchorage, shore leave, and time to unload, the captain of an unnamed ship would give a reward of twice the governor's annual salary plus a well-armed ship with which to defend his port. The governor agreed, and shortly thereafter the *Fancy* arrived, captained by Henry Avery, who with the others aboard had mutinied their British privateer, the *Charles II*. They had stolen the ship and rechristened her the *Fancy*, with plans to capture other ships for their own gain rather than for that of any crown or owner. Hence was born the age of piracy.[22]

Their exploits prompted a wave of other crews to do the same and drew sailors from many ships to join in the pirate life. Avery's pirates soon moved on, but their free-spending ways had made them and others like them welcome among the local citizenry. (Only later did word return of the terror that the pirates had spread.)

In 1704 a French and Spanish force did finally set fire to Nassau, devastating much of the port city, which was then largely abandoned. Benjamin Hornigold arrived with a group of sailors to use the forgotten town as the base for their pirating operations. The local waters were the only route by which to reach the rich trade of South America, the Greater Antilles, and Cuba, and the city offered an excellent base for interdiction. After fitting out several large rowing canoes, they went off in search of ships to seize.

When they returned six months later they brought loot far in excess of the wealth of the entire region. The richest resident of the island acted as a "fence" for selling off the goods. The port came back to life when other pirate crews soon joined Hornigold in using the port as a base of operations. Eventually it became a thriving port again, as a pirate colony from which sorties were launched and to which prizes were returned. The new wealth attracted commerce to support the lifestyle of the pirate class.

In 1716, using salvaged cannons from seized ships, various pirate crews collaborated to fortify the port against any attempt by a government to take it back. They solidified their hold as the only authority in port but never created a port government. They were content to operate under broadly agreed-upon collaborative understandings.

They were a brutal bunch who deserve a reputation more horrifying than the modern romantic view gives them. A "woolding" was a rope that was tied around the mast to give it extra support against breaking under strain. It also became the name of a type of common torture. Woolding a person was to tie a rope tightly around his skull, then slowly tighten it further. The force produced unbearable agony and caused a person's eyeballs to pop out like boiled eggs. The famous Captain Morgan used fire as a form of torture, tying a victim spread-eagle then placing burning fuses between his fingers and toes. It was common to have victims "strappadoed" (hands tied behind their backs and then made to bear their weight), hung by their thumbs, stabbed repeatedly, and left to die. Some prisoners were crucified. On at least one occasion a man was hoisted up on a rope by his genitals, which were then sliced off. Bartholomew Roberts, a pirate captain know for his unbending will, burned a slave ship with its human cargo because the captain of the ship would not pay the ransom that was demanded. When a ship was taken, they often killed many, raped female passengers, tortured those who would not give up personal goods, and left crews marooned. When they attacked towns they commonly set fire to the entire place, kidnapped the wealthy for ransom, and stole everything they could.

Yet it was in this bizarre and horrifying world that genuine democracy flowered, far beyond what existed in the budding democracy movement of the day. Pirate crews operated under principles of strict social cooperative

3. Pirate offender walking the plank, ca. 1710. Prints and Photographs Division, Library of Congress, LC-USZ62-63388.

action. Ship officers were elected and could be recalled at any time (other than during active battle). Each ship's company agreed beforehand to the rules that would bind them all, including formulas for the distribution of loot, compensation payments for injuries suffered, and punishment for crimes. Pirate captains who did well and earned a reputation for treating their crews fairly easily attracted skilled crews. Captains with questionable reputations for fairness had a more difficult time finding crews.

It was not the case that pirates were brutal to others but comradely among themselves. Just as offending officers could be fired, offending crew members were disciplined, often with the same brutality visited on captives and prisoners. It was common for offending crew members to be permanently marked—as by slicing them from nose to ear—to leave a distinctive scar that would make future hirings more difficult.

In other words, the pirates' cooperative social action was not part of a package of fuzzy humanist empathies that they had somehow suddenly and bizarrely adopted. Rather, it was for them a form of organization that valued every member equally even though it did not spring from a notion of intrinsic human value.

THE PIRATES, THEN, OFFER YET ANOTHER EXAMPLE TO CONTRA-dict the Hobbesian view of governmental law as the source of social order. Social cooperation was instead the product of an innate human inclination.

Nor were pirates simply applying lessons of government they had learned in their earlier lives. Just the opposite. They had no experience with self-government and none with democracy, and especially not in running a ship. Their experience was one of tyrannical captains and ships run under a tightly controlled hierarchy. Rather than being the product of government or its law, their democracy was prompted instead by the *disappearance of governmental control* over their lives. Democracy was not for them a "form of government" as modern commentators commonly define it, but rather a form of social organization. How could such democratization have happened so quickly and universally among pirate ships unless the model of organization was something natural to human groups, like those on the Serengeti Plain, rather than something taught to them by government example or political theory?

It does not seem likely that the pirates' organization was a matter of calculation of self-interest. Who would have calculated that the democratic organization of a ship would win more prize ships? If that were so, it would have been tried by owners wanting to maximize profit. It seems more likely that the pirates, left to their own devices, reverted to cooperative action as the default to which human groups naturally tend.

It cannot be denied that our tendency to look beyond ourselves and to identify with a larger group has caused its own set of miseries in the world. Human history contains an unbroken string of wars and conflicts inspired by group identification with religion, nation, ethnicity. But this same tendency has the potential for powerful human good. Perhaps most important, it accounts for why we exist as a successful species in a brutal world. In our modern existence it probably helps explain the rise of democracy and the continuous march in the improvement of the human condition, an advance fueled by the efficiency and creativity that comes with the power of working in groups. We are not selfless angels, but neither are we Hobbesian devils. Instead we come packaged with a predisposition toward cooperation with others without which we would not exist as a species and with which we are likely to bring enormous good to the human project.

CHAPTER THREE

PUNISHMENT

Drop City and the Utopian Communes

IF THE DISCUSSION ON THE HUMAN INCLINATION TOWARD COOP-eration has you feeling all touchy-feely, with the urge to sing "Kumbaya," hang on. The feeling may soon go away. What happens when a group member refuses to join in the group's cooperative spirit and instead seeks to take advantage of others? What is the group to do—ignore? persuade? punish?

The use of punishment has been energetically opposed by a host of modern scholars and reformers. In expressing an increasingly popular view, one scholar has explained that "the institution of criminal punishment is ethically, politically, and legally unjustifiable. . . . [A] society concerned about protecting all of its members from violations of their claims of right should rely on institutions other than criminal punishment."[1] Indeed, one of today's most influential penal policy scholars, David Garland, a professor of sociology and law at New York University, echoes this philosophy: "It is only the mainstream processes of socialization (internalized morality and the sense of duty, the informal inducements and rewards of conformity, the practical and cultural networks of mutual expectation and interdependence, etc.) which are able to promote proper conduct on a consistent and regular basis." Thus, "punishment is never fated to 'succeed' to any great degree." A society that "intends to promote disciplined conduct and social control will concentrate not upon punishing offenders but upon socializing and integrating young citizens—a work of social justice and moral education rather than penal policy."[2]

In the magical years of the 1960s social revolution, groups of people not only talked about the destructive effects of punishment but put their beliefs into action by establishing antipunishment communes. By their actions they hoped to prove the power of noncoercive means of living together, a demonstration that could inspire and lead the rest of the world.

IN MAY 1965, SIX ACRES OF SCRUBBY LAND OUTSIDE TRINIDAD, Colorado, were purchased for $450 by three recent college graduates. The trio envisioned a utopian community where everyone would "be allowed to do what they wanted."[3] The land became home to Drop City, a commune whose philosophy was anarchy—not the anarchy of "bombing and terrorist practices" but rather one that "opposed external authority, power, and coercion in favor of voluntary cooperation and self-imposed restraints"—a living form of the scholarly urgings described above.[4] Any action designed to collectively coerce individual behavior, such as punishment, violated the Drop City philosophy of permitting "unrestricted individuality."[5] Members believed they rightly could and should individually complain to a person about objectionable conduct. It was through the cumulative effect of these personal expressions of disappointment or displeasure—the application of social pressure—by which a wayward member could be educated and corrected. Coercive sanctions imposed by the group—the imposition of punishment—were prohibited.[6]

This did not mean, however, that the assemblage had no common understandings or agreements about how communal life was to be lived. All property was to be held communally among all residents. In fact, the deed to the land stipulated that it was "forever free and open to all people." No attempts would be made to limit who joined the commune. All members were to help all others with their projects, be it building new structures or constructing art displays. Meals were communally cooked and eaten. All assets and earnings of individuals were deposited into a commonly held bank account. Food, building materials, personal needs, and utilities for all were paid out of the common account.

In the first few weeks of working together the group built a rough geodesic dome as a shelter, planted a garden, began raising chickens, and started several art projects. Visual excitement mattered to the group; art was important. Even the refrigerator became a sequin-encrusted beauty.

Arriving after the completion of the first dome, an inspired, self-taught engineer directed the group in a revolutionary new method of dome construction using reclaimed car tops, an approach that yielded sturdy homes for less than $200 each. Many exciting variations on the domes were ultimately constructed; the commune became world famous for them. Drop City was a dynamic and inspiring community.

The Drop City commune was ahead of its time. Its members not only talked about the rejection of punishment but indeed lived it. They were demonstrating the practical power of the antipunishment model for the rest of the world and affirmatively hoped that the larger society would come to see its value and follow their lead.

IN THE SUMMER OF 1965 A MAN CALLING HIMSELF PETER RABBIT (most residents took on fantastical new names when they joined) came to live at Drop City. From the beginning he displayed no interest in the communal activities. He did not contribute to the routine communal work tasks, did not contribute to communal art or building projects, was combative, and would not share the supplies he had, as the commune's rules required. While the group was very unhappy with him and told him so, they concluded that their nonpunishment philosophy prohibited them from officially sanctioning him.

Drop City was located near a small town. The members had regular dealings with the people and businesses there. When Peter Rabbit stole tools from the only lumberyard in the town—a business that heretofore had been good to the group—the members were particularly upset. They feared it would damage their relationship with both the lumberyard and the town. Again, however, they concluded that their philosophy did not allow them to sanction Rabbit.

Rabbit spent his time in the Rabbit Hole, as it was called, a dome that the community had built for him and his family. His main activity was to write about Drop City in articles that were widely published. His writings upset most members. They believed much of what he wrote was untrue;

4. A group of "Droppers" sitting around, 1969. Courtesy Richard Kallweit.

he wrote as though he were the leader of the commune, and because some writings defamed specific members and some were obscene and racist, some material was seized by the U.S. post office. Despite their being upset, however, the members felt they could not sanction him. On the contrary, their philosophy obliged them under their communal project rules to help him disseminate the writings that they so abhorred as false and malicious.

In early 1967 Peter Rabbit came up with the idea of holding a "Joy Fest," an event the commune would host for whoever might want to come and listen to music, learn the Drop City message, and discuss art. The majority of residents opposed the idea, pointing out the potential for disaster if hordes of people arrived at their subsistence-level encampment. Even if they gave up all of their own resources, Drop City simply did not have the means to feed or shelter a large group of people. Many members saw the plan as threatening the very existence of the commune they had devoted two years of their lives to build. They tried individually to convince Rabbit to change his plans, but he would not. Failing to persuade him, they pitched in to dig latrines and purchase extra food.

The announcement of Joy Fest brought hordes of new arrivals, far outnumbering the small number of long-term residents. The residents spent their time trying to keep things working, but disorder reigned nonetheless. Sanitary facilities and drinking water were seriously insufficient, chaos took over the kitchen, and families no longer felt safe. The Drop City banner had been one of people coming together for community and art, but Joy Fest produced a new banner. As one member described it, it had become "a place to pursue perpetual fun, where a person could get high, maybe get laid, and feel no responsibility."

The scheduled end of Joy Fest came and went, but large numbers of people stayed on. The members decided that perhaps they needed a policy that limited the size and membership of the commune. Many of the new arrivals were unstable people with drug and other problems, including underage teenage runaways. The group decided it needed to adopt formal conduct rules that prohibited illegal drug use. However, just as the old understandings and agreements were ignored because of the no-punishment policy, the new rules were also disregarded.

The drug problem became worse. The stream of new arrivals continued. As one original member commented:

> There's just so many people coming through here all the time. We used to have some rules, but they never worked out. Right now there aren't any. We used to have rules about dope and like that but they just . . . they just never worked out.[7]

About this time, some members went into town to buy the group's groceries. By chance, they happened to see Peter Rabbit at a local restaurant, eating a steak. Drop City had always required that all money held by commune members be placed in the common bank account. It now became clear that Peter Rabbit had been getting money but not contributing it. When challenged, Rabbit confessed his deception but refused to change his ways and to contribute in the future. Despite this, the group concluded, as they had many times before, that they could not sanction him. Discontent grew, along with a growing reluctance of others to continue contributing to the communal fund, a fund from which Rabbit drew support.

Not long after the steak incident, a marine deserter named Jethro joined the commune. Here is how one commune member described the ensuing events:

One day a vehicle roared past my dome. I hurried out and saw [Jethro] and Mantis riding in circles about the property on a new little motor scooter. Everybody was taking rides on it, whizzing around, falling off.

"Who does it belong to?"

"Us."

"Great. Where did it come from?"

"I bought it." Jethro skidded off down the road.

Clard [a community founder] was standing there, looking glum. "The money to buy that scooter came from our bank account. He cleaned us out."[8]

Jethro had been put on the account only days before. The communal bank account instantly went defunct. Nobody was willing to put more money into it. With no one any longer willing to contribute to the common account and without any means of controlling misbehavior, it became clear that the possibility for cooperative action had been essentially destroyed. Soon after, the founders abandoned Drop City.

FRIENDSHIP AND SHARED VALUES WILL TAKE A COMMUNITY ONLY so far. Inevitably people develop personal conflicts or their differences in values surface. Some people will occasionally, or even regularly, promote their own views at the expense of others, as Peter Rabbit did at Drop City. In many such instances, "reeducation" through individual conversation or through social pressure won't do the trick of developing more group-oriented thinking. Only coercive sanctions—punishment—will have an effect. Such sanctions are most effective in gaining compliance and least disruptive to a community when enforced by the community as a whole, when contrary actions are restrained and legitimized by the group's collective judgment rather than imposed ad hoc by one or several individuals.

Social pressure and the influence of social norms can be important and powerful forces but they also have important limitations. For them to be effective, the person to be influenced must care about what other people think of him and must think such opinions more important to him than his other needs and wants. That was never the case with Peter Rabbit, and every community no doubt has some people for whom this often will not be the case. Given the natural differences in opinion and interests among people, strong conflicts will inevitably arise and every society must have a mechanism that will effectively deal with those conflicts by setting and enforcing some basic rules.

Presumably one could carefully screen membership, to permit into the group only those who are generous and like-minded in all important respects. One could exclude from the group any member later found to be lacking in this respect. Such membership restrictions are obviously inconsistent with the principle of "forever free and open to all people," however, which was so proudly proclaimed on the Drop City deed. More important, membership screening and exclusion is not feasible for general society—the population for which the scholars quoted above press their no-punishment regime. General society must deal with every person no matter how troublesome. The only means of excluding someone from the larger society would be to, say, put him or her in prison—but that would be the use of punishment, of which these scholars would disapprove.

One would want rules and a system to enforce them that is fair and just and would want the system to impose the minimum suffering possible to achieve its goal. (The general level of punishment severity in the current American criminal justice system is probably far beyond what it needs to be.) Such a punishment system is not an option but rather an essential precondition to achieving effective social cooperation. The community's core shared values must be respected and those who will not defer to them must be sanctioned, not only to compel them to respect the community's values but also to assure others that those values are indeed important and do deserve their continuing deference.

The Peter Rabbit story makes this point. Once it became clear that he would not defer to the values of Drop City—that he would not contribute his money to the communal coffers from which he drew—the communal fund and the commune itself collapsed. Only a sucker would continue to contribute to an enterprise that supported those who rejected its core values of social cooperation and its shared judgments of unacceptable conduct.

The real puzzle of Drop City is why its members repeatedly chose to be the easy suckers that Peter Rabbit exploited from the start. When he would not contribute to communal activities, they overlooked it. When he stole from the local lumberyard who had helped them, they did nothing. When he published writings abhorrent to them, they helped distribute them. When he arranged Joy Fest over their objections, they hosted it. It was only the final indignity of confirming his permanent refusal to contribute to the communal coffer—after he had been caught eating steak while they lived at subsistence level—that brought down the curtain on this tragic comedy.

The story is painful to follow—like watching a trusting and gentle dog get repeatedly kicked by its abusive owner. One may wonder how Peter Rabbit in good conscience could have so regularly taken advantage of people so obviously trussed up by their own misconceptions and so help-less to deal with the reality around them. Even more puzzling is how these people could be oblivious for so long to their role as professional suckers and how they could keep themselves so ignorant about the dynamics of human nature. The commune members were not stupid people. Perhaps they simply could not emotionally bring themselves to admit that the principle driving their project was so seriously flawed, perhaps like Soviet agricultural practices under Stalin, which allowed thousands of people to starve to death rather than admit that the principles of effective farming did not track with approved communist ideology.[9] The Drop City members stuck to their misguided principles in the face of an increasingly obvious reality until that reality bit them in the ass.

Perhaps today's antipunishment scholars have a similar road of discovery to follow. But it would be best if we did not travel it with them. One can feel admiration for the idealism of the Drop City members and even agree that informal social pressure ought to be the preferred reaction to minor social deviations. But, at the same time, one can only be astonished by their naive folly and wonder whether it was some form of pathological arrogance: For 125,000 generations humans have relied upon an effective sanctioning system to assure social cooperation, yet the people of Drop City somehow did not need one? Is it that they thought themselves a special breed of human? Probably not—after all, they initially sought to include all comers in their project. It seems more likely that they simply suffered a blind commitment to a false principle they could not bring themselves to admit was false.

The real tragedy of Drop City is that if the members had taken their early experience to heart—as an education about how human groups can and cannot work together and the essential role of an enforcement system in maintaining cooperative action—they could have saved Drop City and its important, inspiring marriage of art and community. Their initial ignorance eventually combined with their arrogance to destroy what they had created and what it could have been.

The modern abolitionist movement, opposing all forms of punishment, and much of modern penal theory seem to be playing out the Drop City tragedy. Luckily, it is at the moment primarily an academic game (as much of modern academia is); it is not currently doing much real-world damage but it also will probably live on forever in the ivy towers because reality cannot reach it to bite it, too, in the ass. We need to remain aware that this dangerous ignorance is afoot and to make sure it remains locked away in the ivy towers forever.

THE PEOPLE WHO REMAINED AT DROP CITY AFTER THE COMMUNE leaders gave up lived on their own terms. The "UFO Marine" went everywhere with a loaded gun, constantly threatening to kill people. Violent motorcycle gangs and methamphetamine addicts moved into the artistic domes, which gradually fell apart or were destroyed by vandals.

Peter Rabbit persuaded a well-to-do benefactor named Rick Klein to purchase land on which Rabbit started a new commune, named Libre (Spanish for "free"). But life at Libre was not exactly "free." It was strictly regulated, with rules and with sanctions for rule violations. Libre did not admit new members without a close examination of them and their motives for joining. Membership required the unanimous approval of all existing members and proof of self-sufficiency. Each family lived separately in its own structure and had to receive community permission to build any new structure. Further, "Libre quite deliberately never built any central facility, any common building, where crashers might land."[10] When a member of Libre was arrested and spent time in a local jail for growing marijuana on the property, upon his return to Libre he was informed that he had been expelled. He was obliged to leave the community and the home he had built there. Libre grew and still exists today. Peter Rabbit lives there with his two wives.

Drop City, in contrast, became a "hobo camp" with overflowing latrines, hepatitis, violence, and drugs. Ultimately, the "forever free" clause was removed from the property deed and the land was sold to a neighbor as a pasture for goats. The dynamic at work in Drop City is not unique to that particular utopian experience but rather is the standard form of such no-punishment experiments.

IN 1968, AS COLORADO'S DROP CITY BEGAN TO FADE, ANOTHER attempt at a punishment-free community was just beginning in a remote part of California.[11] Black Bear Ranch was intended to be a radical new model community in which no central authority would compel a particular code of conduct by anyone. The founders wondered: "What would happen . . . if we threw out all the rules and started over?" One of the founders dreamed "that I would find and establish a community—of artists, I thought—who would live and work together in harmony with nature." Following the dream, the founding group purchased a piece of property that had once been a gold mine, on which stood a house and a barn. The group raised funds, bought supplies, and prepared for the utopian life they envisioned. The commune's slogan was "free land for free people."[12] (For readers who can only too easily guess what is coming next, our apologies. Being mesmerized by a slow-motion train wreck may not be admirable but, let's admit it, it's hard to look away.)

Upon arriving at the property after their fund-raising and supply-purchasing mission, it was apparent that the word had already gotten out about the planned commune: the house on the property was already occupied. The founders moved into the barn. No one in the group had any knowledge of wilderness survival or even of how to perform simple outdoor life tasks such as chopping wood. They divided into work groups but then did little work. After four feet of snow fell and the group ran out of kerosene for the heaters, one man had to hike eighteen miles on homemade snowshoes to bring in more fuel. The commune was free of

5. A group of "Bears" enjoying the sunshine, 2005. From *Commune*, a documentary film by Jonathan Berman.

restraints but also free of food, warmth, and sanitation. During the bitter winter, the free-sex policy was suspended when the women began to withhold sex to protest the lack of heat. Rather than freeze and starve, the group decided they needed some rules after all. One member recounted later that "using a combination of revolutionary rhetoric, blandishments, and threats, they organized."[13]

But while they created a set of binding rules, they did not adopt a system for sanctioning violations of those rules (oops). Thus, many members still refused to work. When one man's "lack of physical labor and ceaseless sermonizing" frustrated the others, another resident broke a glass jar of honey over the man's head.

The official policy of not punishing wrongdoing applied not only to adults but also to children. The children quickly learned the lesson and regularly undertook outrageous conduct, such as ransacking or burning the homes of people who would not do as the children demanded. The adults, caught by their no-punishment rule, thought it best to comply with the children's demands. In one instance, the children wanted Easter candy and demanded that a man who owned a working car go into town to get it. The man understood that by refusing this demand to be the Easter Bunny meant his house would be burned, so he went.

In the fall of 1969 a group of black militants moved into a cabin and began to transform the place into an armed fortress, a guerrilla base. The land was, after all, "free to all." The militants carried loaded guns at all times and followed their own agenda, with little interest in the larger group. Although the commune's principles made all private property communal, the militants would not share their supplies. While the commune's principles required that everyone work to support the commune, as in tending the common garden, the militants worked only for themselves. It was eventually concluded that their conduct was not consistent with the commune's principle of "internal harmony," and commune members therefore undertook to use dialogue and social pressure to reeducate the militants. They were told to "mind your own business."

One morning, about a month after arriving, Roy Ballard, the militant leader, forced all of the commune members out of their houses at gunpoint and had them line up out in the open. Another armed militant was positioned on a knoll aiming his weapon at their backs. Ballard demanded to know what the community was angry about, a question that the commune members did not quite understand. One commune member stepped forward and tried to persuade Ballard to put the gun away. Ballard raised a 30.06 to the man's chest and told him to be quiet or he would be shot. After a few minutes of tense silent confrontation, and for reasons not apparent to the group, Ballard lowered his gun and walked back to his fortress. When the commune members awoke the next morning, the militants were gone. The strange confrontation ended for reasons as mysterious as why it had occurred.

After the militants left, Hells Angels arrived. But the commune members had now been scared into a slightly different view of the world. The bikers were informed that the land was no longer "free to all" and that they could not stay. They stayed anyway.

Perhaps because of the scarcity of free food and beer, the Angels eventually did leave. The commune members quickly installed boards full of sixteen-penny nails sticking up—a "wicked, tire shredding barricade at the gate"—to keep out any new residents.[14] The land "free to all" was now officially closed to all.

With outsiders excluded, the commune settled down to tend to their own private utopia. But utopia remained elusive. A group of adults charged with child care decided instead to drop acid. When the neglected children were discovered, their parents took up sticks and started to search for the tripping child-minders, to beat them for their lapse. It was determined that the commune's system for regulating conduct among its members needed to evolve. Perhaps rules and sanctions for violations were desirable after all.

Under new rules, no person could join the community without first being a guest for a set time period—a probationary period—and then getting a large majority to agree to extend an offer of membership. Only two licensed guns were allowed on the property, and those weapons were to be kept by the community, not by an individual. Failure to keep public areas "restaurant clean," with dishes washed according to an exact protocol, or any other violation of numerous rules would lead to verbal reprimand. Subsequent violations of the rules would require an appearance before "the circle"—a mandatory group meeting where the violations would be publicly discussed. Repeated violations meant permanent expulsion, with forfeiture of whatever the person had built or contributed.

While it can hardly be considered a model for the larger society, as was hoped—and, as noted, there is no "excluding" people from society, unless by that one means life in prison or the death penalty—the Black Bear Commune, with its written rules and sanctions for violations, continues to exist today. (A change in track avoids the train wreck. Aren't you glad you kept reading?)

TOLSTOY FARM, ESTABLISHED IN WASHINGTON STATE IN 1963, was another communal experiment of the antipunishment model that sought to follow the standard counterculture values of peace, love, and noncoercion.[15] The group rejected all regulation and tolerated all forms of thought and behavior, including drugs, nudity, and free sex. Its only rule was that no one could be forced to leave. Tolstoy Farm was to be a place where members worked for the common good and the desire for acceptance by the group would alone be enough to persuade members to act cooperatively. It was an experiment "to prove that man could live noncompetitively without private ownership and the external compulsion of law."[16] (Again, the reader can no doubt predict the coming difficulties. We'll keep it short.)

The lack of restraint resulting from the lack of sanctions made life increasingly difficult. All purchases were made using the communal funds and required a majority vote, but many members preferred not to use such things as toothpaste, tampons, soap, or laundry detergent, so they refused to vote for such things, thereby forcing their own (un)sanitary habits on others. There was also an arson problem, as some members would simply burn the possessions of people who offended them. Soon the commune began to slide into dangerous disarray. Something had to be done.

When a resident began shooting at the communal house, he was put in a car, driven off the property, and told not to return—violating the only fixed rule the commune had set for itself. But this incident did not prompt a reevaluation of the group's philosophy, so things continued to deteriorate.

The founding members quickly built private homes in order to move out of the communal house. Hart House, as that was called, continued to house newcomers, whose numbers included runaways, drug users, and mental patients—the "crashers and the crazies"—from which the founders tried to distance themselves. In the spring of 1968 Hart House mysteriously burned to the ground. One account of the story claims a mentally unbalanced girl had set the fire; another that the founders had done it.

The founding philosophy was eventually replaced. Rules were imposed and sanctions introduced, with the ultimate sanction being expulsion. Drugs were forbidden, and underage people without parents at the settlement were barred. Even people who did not manage their personal trash properly were found to be unsuitable and told to leave. The Tolstoy Farm commune continues to exist today.

This pattern is repeated in every known no-punishment experiment: after an initial period of delight runs into the realities of life and human nature, the cooperative action fails and the group either disbands or adopts rules and sanctions (commonly using the threat of exclusion as the ultimate sanction).

TO SOME READERS, ALL OF THESE STORIES HOLD NO SURPRISE. The dynamic that played out seems entirely predictable and a matter of simple common sense. How could a society deal with serious wrongdoing other than by punishment? If the offender is sufficiently indifferent to others' interests or sufficiently convinced of the importance of his own interests over those of others, why would such a person change his ways simply because of others' complaints? In most instances the offender knows he is injuring others, or at least knows that the victim and general community will disapprove, yet does what he wants anyway. Social pressure might work for some offenders some of the time, especially for children being disciplined by parents. But why would one think that social pressure would be sufficient to get all offenders to comply all the time? The puzzle for some people will be: what were these commune founders—or the punishment abolitionists of today—thinking? Although there have sometimes been claims to the contrary, we know of no society that has existed without some kind of punishment system.[17]

THE REPEATING PATTERN OF THE STORIES, ALL OF WHICH SHOW the importance of punishment to maintaining effective cooperation, has been confirmed by a variety of social science studies. The studies conclude that people are predisposed to cooperate with others but only as long as the others in their group do not behave selfishly. When others violate shared group norms, cooperation breaks down and eventually members stop cooperating.[18] Yet the introduction of punishment can resurrect cooperation.[19]

Recall the "public goods" experiments discussed in the previous chapter, in which each member of a group is given an allotment of money that he or she can contribute to a group fund or keep for themselves. The money added to the group fund gains "interest" and is then divided equally among all members, whether they contributed to the group fund or not. Most people contributed to the group fund, even though they could not be sure that others will do the same.

A variation of the experiment is relevant here: the experimenters conducted repeated rounds of the process among the same group. As the rounds went on, it became clear to members that some were not contributing to the group fund yet were still receiving an equal portion when the fund was divided at the end of each round. This is like the Drop City members discovering Peter Rabbit eating steak at a restaurant in town rather than contributing his money to their communal fund.

As the experimental subjects noticed the lack of contribution by others, most stopped contributing, just as the Drop City common fund collapsed. In other words, even people who are inclined to be highly cooperative will stop cooperating when faced with persistently selfish group members. Being cooperative is one thing; being taken for a fool is another.

Another variation of the "public goods" game is even more illuminating for our purposes. In this version, group members are given the opportunity to punish those who refuse to contribute to the group fund even if they will share in its distribution. The imposition of punishment is personally costly—the punisher must contribute part of his or her own money to do it. For every dollar a punisher contributes, the offender will be penalized three dollars. Despite the personal cost, cooperators still punish noncooperators.[20]

Even more illuminating is what happens next. Once punishment is allowed, the cooperators, who otherwise would have quit, begin contributing again.[21] Indeed, nearly everyone begins contributing, thereby yielding the greatest benefit to the group and all individuals in it.[22] In other words, the utopian communes could have advanced their agendas of promoting love, peace, art, community, or whatever else they were interested in if they had understood that the one thing they had to do—the one thing that was essential to maintaining cooperation within the group—was to provide a system for sanctioning those who violate important group norms. A group can dispense with many of the standard norms and restrictions—it can promote free love and communal property—but it cannot forego a system of punishment for those who refuse to defer to the norms the group needs to remain cooperative (such as norms against physical aggression or risk-creating conduct). Informal persuasion is a useful first response to a violation if the offender perhaps did not appreciate the seriousness of the wrong he was doing. But it must be backed by fair and just punishment if group cooperation is to survive.

Social scientists once described humans as operating in rational self-interest, but studies like these have revealed a more nuanced picture. Humans are not motivated by pure self-interest.[23] In fact, people have a strong predisposition toward cooperation. But they are sensitive to being taken advantage of and are willing to incur costs to punish others who do not similarly cooperate.[24] Some describe humans as "wary cooperators."[25]

ONCE THE ESSENTIAL CONNECTION BETWEEN COOPERATION AND punishment can be seen, it should be little surprise to find that humans, as a species with a natural predisposition to cooperate, also are a species with a natural predisposition to punish wrongdoers. Cooperation confers an important evolutionary benefit on humans. It helped early humans survive in a hostile world characterized by fierce competition for resources, elusion of predators that were stronger and faster, and dealing with natural threats like drought and famine. Cooperative groups also benefited from the efficiency of division of labor, shared resources, and the spoils of group hunting. It was punishment of wrongdoing that allowed humans to maintain their evolutionary advantage through cooperation, and thus it was punishment that was the key to our success, and probably our very existence, as a species.

Evolutionary scientists have puzzled over one aspect of punishment apparent within early human groups. While punishment might have been essential to the success of the group, who in the group would have been willing to take on the personal risk that came with being the one who actually imposed the deserved punishment? As in the "public goods" game, it only takes one person in the group willing to punish to maintain cooperation, but why would an individual take that risk? Why not let someone else do it? Of course, if all members took this view, the entire group would suffer, but it is easy to imagine that each individual might focus only on the immediate personal risk rather than the long-term detrimental effect on the group. We are not selfish devils but neither are we all angelic heroes.

The long-term benefit to the group requires that someone take on the risk of being the one to impose punishment. If an individual needs to intellectually reason out the long-term cost-benefit analysis of the choice to impose punishment, would anyone make that choice? On the other hand, if the felt need to punish was instinctually driven, the chances increase that at least one individual would take on the job. Some evolutionary scientists argue that it would only take a few individuals willing to do the punishing, even if a large numbers of rule- breakers are involved. They point to the use of tools and weapons that the group together controlled. A single person could inflict heavy punishment at reduced risk on even a physically stronger violator. Others in the group might join in to defend a member against an unjustified attack, but not in this instance, where the attack is seen as just punishment for the violation of a group norm.[26] Thus, a few group members willing to inflict punishment could maintain a group's cooperative dynamic. That cooperation helps to ensure a greater survival rate for the group as compared to groups without punishment, with that willingness to punish being passed through natural selection to future generations and ultimately becoming part of human nature.

HUMANS DID NOT INVENT THE USE OF PUNISHMENT. THEY DEVEL-oped and refined a practice that existed in a more rudimentary form in pre-human species that similarly depended on cooperative action for their evolutionary success. We see rudimentary forms of punishment for "norm violations" in other species, especially our close primate relatives and especially among socially cooperative animals. Even nonvictim members of a group act aggressively against violators, such as those perpetrating aggression or theft in violation of group norms and expectations.[27]

Indeed, punishment behavior is not limited to primates. Within the highly social naked mole rat communities, for example, queens appear to focus attacks on lazy workers. And wolves apparently refuse to play with those who violate the social rules governing play fighting, and violator wolves leave the group and die at higher-than-average rates. Behavior akin to theft is also a common target for punishment. For example, elephant seal pups caught trying to nurse from a female who is not their mother are not just shooed away. They are often bitten severely and sometimes killed. Young male deer attempting to sneak copulations with females belonging to adult males are not just shooed away but commonly attacked.[28]

The larger point here is that wherever long-term cooperation within a group is observed, a system of punishment for the violation of important group norms is also observed—regardless of which norms are essential to continued cooperation. The more essential cooperation is to the survival of the group, the more deep-seated will be the commitment to punishment. With cooperation at the root of human success as a species, a deep commitment to punishment among humans is exactly what one would expect. The utopian communes, or any other human groups, are free to explore any and all variations of lifestyle, but they cannot escape the fundamentals of human nature. Bring on the free spirits, free love, free lunch, and whatever else human creativity might invent, but be warned that it will all collapse if you do not also bring on a system to punish violations of the norms essential for social cooperation.

CHAPTER FOUR

JUSTICE

1850s San Francisco and the California Gold Rush

PUNISHMENT IS NOT THE EVIL THAT SOME ACADEMIC ELITES would paint it. Rather, it is the linchpin to the benefits of social cooperation that are at the root of human success. To follow the lead of the antipunishment fantasizers is to invite collapse like that we see in every antipunishment community in chapter 3. But that is only the starting point of punishment's interesting story. Giving violators more punishment than they deserve also can undermine the benefits of cooperative action. Overpunishment converts the noble imposition of justice into an unprincipled mugging. Chapter 5 will illustrate and explore this dynamic. At the same time, imposing markedly less punishment than what a violator deserves creates disaffection and acrimony that also can subvert cooperation. In other words, it is not punishment that is needed to maintain social cooperation, but justice. That is the subject of the present chapter.

Punishment requires only the imposition of suffering for a rule violation, but justice requires much more: a sanction must reflect the extent of the offender's moral blameworthiness for the violation, taking account of both the seriousness of the offense and the violator's culpability and capacities in committing it. It requires an assessment of what reasonably could have been expected from this person in this situation. Could this person, should this person have avoided committing the offense?

While the nuance required by such an inquiry may be possible to obtain in the quiet and safety of a modern courtroom, is it realistic to think that those caught in the often impossible circumstances of absent-law situations could be expected to show such subtlety in judgment? Perhaps justice is a luxury that an absent-law group cannot afford; perhaps punishment is the best they can do. That is, perhaps the nicety of tying the amount of punishment to the degree of the offender's blameworthiness must await the civilizing influence of governmental law?

Or perhaps the reality is just the reverse: left to their own devices, human groups naturally insist not only on punishment but on just punishment. It is modern governmental law that has lost its way and disconnected punishment and justice—in the name of efficient crime control or some other utilitarian interest—in order to impose punishment that is not deserved and forgo punishment that is.

THE 1800S WERE A POLITICALLY TURBULENT TIME FOR THE CALIfornia region.[1] It had been a Spanish colony but was now a state in the Mexican Republic. Seeing an opportunity to gain control of much of the North American continent, President James Polk in 1846 sent a small force to claim "the West" for the United States. Fearing British retaliation, Polk needed the action to appear as the will of the locals, so on June 14, the force arrived at the home of California's leading citizen, Don Mariano Vallejo. Vallejo, a Mexican general out of favor with the Mexican government and in command of no troops, remained the nominal military authority in this northern frontier. (What troops there were in the region were elsewhere and under the command of a rival general.) The party informed the general that he was a prisoner. Vallejo, who had been asleep, "had difficulty understanding what war he was a prisoner of." The group sat in Vallejo's home, drank local brandy, and wrote a formal statement of terms, and "by its third paragraph, the product of good native liquor, the California Republic was born."[2]

While President Polk had put the takeover in motion, the region could not be admitted into the United States without congressional action, and this was a touchy issue. California was already a free state. An additional free state would numerically put the slaveholding states at a disadvantage.

The result was an awkward limbo and Congress was reluctant to vote California into the union, but it was thought too vital to American interests to let others control the area.

Soon after, in 1848, the discovery of gold brought three hundred thousand men to California from all over the world. Yet this sudden mass of humanity lived without a functioning legal system. There were no licensing procedures, fees, or taxes to regulate gold prospecting. No miner worked land that he owned and any prospector could join any mining camp at any time. Had there been a legal enforcement system, it was unclear what law it would enforce. Richard Mason, who had been appointed governor of the few permanent inhabitants, described the situation when he wrote to an *alcalde* (the local magistrate):

> Having only been two days in office as governor, I am not at this time prepared to say what are the extent of your powers and jurisdiction as alcalde; you must, for the time being, be governed by the customs of laws of the country as far as you can ascertain them, and by your own good sense and sound discretion.[3]

Without a functional government there were no licensing procedures, fees, or taxes to regulate gold prospecting. No miner worked land that he owned. Any prospector could join any mining camp at any time.

Camp populations were a heterogeneous mix of "puritans and drunkards, clergymen and convict, honest and dishonest, rich and poor."[4] There was no common language, culture, or legal experience. The system of law an individual miner lived under prior to the camps' existence was now only a privately held memory. Previous life credentials, whether social, educational, moral, or economic standing, were now irrelevant. No one worked for anyone else, and no one needed anyone else's permission to mine a location.

The men shared a common set of needs, however. Each miner needed to be able to leave unguarded whatever he owned while he worked his claim. A miner who found gold needed to protect his find until he could convert it into cash or goods. Mary Floyd Williams, who was born in California to a father who worked the mines, described the common scene:

Thousands of gold seekers, constantly keyed to the highest pitch of excitement, gather in mountain camps far from the nearest office of government, generally unacquainted with the customs prevailing in the older settlements, and perfectly aware that there was no executive strong enough to enforce order, no police empowered to make arrest, and no jails where the lawless could be confined.[5]

As the camps sprang up in the hills of the Sierra Nevada, a set of community norms commonly emerged, much as occurred among Bob Ellickson's farmers and ranchers of Shasta County (chapter 1), but here they did so without the cocoon of a functioning criminal justice system. There was no one beyond themselves to deal with violators of those norms, even when the conflict escalated into violence.

In one camp, for example, it was agreed that each person was entitled to a ten-foot-square claim upon which to work. One miner accused another of encroachment and "appeal[ed] to the crowd." The group measured off the claim and agreed that there had been encroachment. It was determined that the encroachment was accidental, hence no punishment was given.

Tools left at a site stood as notice that the claim was active. In one instance, an Irishman and a Dutchman were accused of stealing an old shovel and pick that they thought abandoned. As it happened, the tools were marking a claim and by taking them, the two were effectively depriving the miners of their claim. As with the encroachment case, however, the group judged that intent mattered: the offenders honestly believed that no claim had been marked. The two were expelled from the camp rather than killed—the usual penalty for tampering with another's claim—and the owners of the claim were advised to leave better marks of their claims in the future.

The evolved norms included rules of property ownership over complex issues. Howard Shinn, a reporter whose beat was the mining camps of the region, explained:

Labor serves as the title of ownership in the gold mines. If men combine their labor to turning the course of a river, and "their intentions

6. Miners work at a sluice at Sutter Creek, California, 1849. Courtesy Wells Fargo Archives.

are made known, and the improvement staked out, no person intrudes upon the ground. . . . The adventurers, therefore, hold their rights as securely as if they were protected by a charter from the Government."[6]

Justice by necessity operated quickly, with "no lawyers to delay—no petty technicalities to obstruct the course."[7] Prompt adjudication of criminal cases was important for several reasons: there were no jails or guards, thus suspects could not be detained, and any camp might disappear overnight if gold was located elsewhere. Trials often occurred within moments of the discovery of a crime. The accused was guarded by men with revolvers or was tied to a tree. Sentences were executed immediately. "If it was considered safe to give the guilty man another chance, he was punished, usually by whipping, and driven from the camp with the warning that reappearance would mean death."[8]

The seriousness of an offense determined the size of the group that would hear the case. The members of a camp adjudicated small crimes by themselves: "The case was submitted to the assemblage without argument, and irrevocably decided *viva voce*."[9] But "in matters of greater moment the halloo was sounded from ridge to ridge, and a general gathering from a larger district was summoned for careful discussion and deliberation."[10]

With a problem that could not be resolved easily, a "presiding officer and a judge impaneled a jury of six or twelve persons, summoned witnesses, and proceeded to a trial forthwith."[11]

With time, life in the mining camps became more formalized. The camps often elected alcaldes—borrowing the word from the old Mexican system—who served as a first resource in settling disputes. In one instance at Jackson Creek, a man named Sim ejected another named Sprenger, his mining partner, from their claim when an injury left Sprenger temporarily unable to work the claim. Sim did not compensate Sprenger for his half of the claim, his half of the tools, or the work he had done. When Sprenger objected, Sim took the case to Rogers, the local alcalde, and paid him a bribe to decide the case in his favor.

Upon hearing of the unfair verdict, Sprenger appealed to the group for justice. Despite the cost to them in taking time away from their mining pursuits, the camp sent word out across the hills calling other miners to their camp. The miners gathered and demanded that the alcalde hold a jury trial for Sprenger. When he refused, saying his ruling was final, the miners asked: "Who but the people made this damned scoundrel [the] alcalde anyhow? We can organize our own court of appeals." Word was spread over a greater area that "a great wrong had been done, and that it was desired to examine the entire subject with all fairness and deliberation, sustaining or reversing the former judgement as the evidence should warrant."[12] Shinn reports,

> Every man of them all suffered a loss, by his day's idleness, of whatever his work that day would have earned—perhaps five dollars, perhaps fifty dollars; but the miners of Jackson Creek were willing to suffer the loss if justice, as between man and man, could thereby be established.[13]

The group elected a miner named Hayden to the position of chief judge. Hayden asked that a clerk and a sheriff be elected as well. When Alcalde Rogers refused to provide the court records of the case, it was decided that the case would simply be heard again—this time before a jury. The judge instructed the jury that "they must strip the case of technicalities, regarding no law but right and wrong, no test but common-sense."[14] The jury decided the case for Sprenger. Sim was required to pay the costs of Sprenger's illness, was forced to restore Sprenger as a full partner, and had to let him move back into their cabin. Sim was convicted of bribery. A mob formed around Alcalde Rogers's cabin. Judge Hayden convinced the miners to spare Rogers's life, but the corrupt alcalde lost his job and several tools, which the court seized.

Richard J. Oglesby, who worked in several mining camps, later recalled:

> There was very little law, but a large amount of good order; no churches, but a great deal of religion; no politics, but a great deal of politicians; no offices, and, strange to say for my countrymen, no office-seekers. Crime was rare, for punishment was certain. . . . I now remember Charley Williams whack three of our fellow-citizens over the bare back, twenty-one to forty strokes, for stealing a neighbor's money. The multitude of disinterested spectators had conducted the court. My recollection is that there were no attorney's fees or court charges. I think I never saw justice administered with so little loss of time or at less expense. There was no more stealing in Nevada County until society became more settled and better regulated.[15]

When the men of the mining camps faced a world without governmental law, they made their own. They had little choice. They could not proceed with their daily lives without some cooperative system of agreed-upon rules and a mechanism to enforce them. Yet what they invented was not just a system of punishment for violations but one that sought, within the terms of their situation, to do justice. While they all had given up their former lives to come to the mining camps to search for gold and become rich—at the exclusion of nearly everything else in their lives—they nonetheless made time to do justice, even in a case that had nothing to do with them and outside their own camp.

As the miners labored in the hills, the residents back in San Francisco, the point of entry for most of the miners, were having to deal with a similar but slightly different problem.

SAN FRANCISCO WAS THE BASE CAMP FOR THE GOLD RUSH. MORE
than 150,000 men passed through San Francisco on their way to the mountains. The city's dynamic, chaotic population was beyond the control of
the few existing officials. In 1846 the town had had a population of only
200. and had neither law nor the capacity to enforce order among the
passing horde.[16]

Understanding the city's vulnerable situation, a criminal gang calling
itself the Hounds began raiding stores and restaurants, which were "forced
to supply their demands and 'charge it to the Hounds.'"[17] One Sunday in
July of 1849, the Hounds were especially violent in their activities, beating everyone they robbed and shooting one victim. Several townspeople
called for a meeting to deal with the violence. Within days a self-formed
committee of citizens took most of the Hounds into custody. A second
meeting was called to decide their fate. During this meeting, a court and
a grand jury were formed, and the Hounds were "indicted, and charged
with a conspiracy to commit murder, robbery, etc."[18] The court, consist-
ing of a judge, a jury, and attorneys to prosecute and defend the Hounds,
ultimately convicted the men, sentenced them to exile, and threatened
with execution any who returned.

Such mass meetings and popular tribunals became the accepted means
of criminal justice in San Francisco. The citizens appointed an alcalde, as
the miners had done in their camps. And, just like in the camps, justice
was swift. In a common sort of case in 1850, a "burglary occurred at four
o'clock on an April morning. The alcalde issued warrants for the thieves.
They were pursued, arrested, indicted by a grand jury, convicted by a petit
jury, sentenced, whipped, and turned out of town within twelve hours."[19]
No doubt errors were made under such procedures, but with no effective
alternative, to the citizens the system seemed better than either rampant
lawlessness or outraged lynch mobs.

On October 18, 1850, California was officially admitted as a state. In
consequence, a number of political offices were created. Those who ran
for office in the first election commonly had little interest in staying in the
West, as was true of many if not most people there. Many sought to use

the "position solely as a means of obtaining money for a speedy return to the East."[20] Before these government officials appeared on the scene, the "courts of the people" were rough justice but difficult to manipulate on a large scale because judges and attorneys appointed by the group changed from case to case. The new courts, however, filled with men of dubious history, had not oversight and little motivation to serve the community. They became "notorious for their failure to convict and punish criminals, especially those who [could] pay for skillful defense. . . . This immunity [was] almost universally attributed to flagrant corruption within professional circles."[21]

Before statehood, a trial would have been held by interested neighbors soon after a crime had occurred. The new system transferred the responsibility for meting out justice to a physically and emotionally remote authority, usually long delayed from the offense. By 1851 the crime rate had skyrocketed. In response, citizens returned to what they knew worked and formed the Vigilance Committee. Every man in the city was invited to join. The group elected officers, kept records, and placed police on the streets and patrol boats in the harbor. Members also acted as detectives, jailers, lawyers, judges, and juries.

The Vigilance Committee heard hundreds of cases and eventually hanged four men, all of whom were convicted of, at minimum, murder and robbery. Persons convicted of robbery and some lesser crimes were transported on ships out of the area or simply banished. The committee confronted innkeepers who were known to aid criminals and warned them to stop giving quarter to such persons or they would be shut down. One man convicted of possession of stolen property was whipped.

In openly working against what they saw as corrupt authorities, the committee soon found its own members on trial by those authorities. Several were convicted by the official courts, but the enormous public uproar that followed caused the authorities to back down and the convicted men were never sentenced. Their convictions served only to draw hundreds of new members to the Vigilance Committee and its work. With the committee back in action, the crime rate again dropped. New elections were held,

7. San Francisco vigilante committee's anti-opium squad, ca. 1850. Courtesy California State Archives.

and with the election of men who were more invested in the long-term good of the community, the Vigilance Committee was disbanded.

THE EXPERIENCE OF THE GOLD MINERS AND THE SAN FRANCISCO residents nicely illustrates what we have seen elsewhere: in the absence of governmental law, people naturally organize themselves, they create their own group norms, and then they establish mechanisms to enforce those norms. The shared norms can include complex and nuanced matters—recall the group's rules governing the rights of miners who join to move a stream in order to mine its bottom, or the rules governing the proper treatment of a mining partner temporarily unable to work because of an injury.

These natural experiments also illustrate some new principles, such as the importance that people place on doing justice. Everything else in a gold miner's life was set aside—family, friends, romance, career, education, leisure—yet it was understood within the camp that all mining would be set aside to do justice, even when the wrongdoing did not involve the entire group and even if it involved another group entirely. Miners from a large surrounding area would lay down their tools to join in an assembly adjudicating a serious case. The same devotion to doing justice is apparent in the San Francisco experience. In the pre-statehood absence of governmental law and in the face of post-statehood ineffective or corrupt government, people joined to form vigilance committees to do justice even though it exposed them to a risk of physical harm and legal prosecution. They did this even when they were not the victims of the crimes or even likely to be.

In other words, doing justice is not just another mild preference that people have. And failures of justice are not just another point on the long list of minor disappointments that people have about their lives—which is the way many intellectuals seek to characterize it. For laypersons, failures of justice can cause deep disappointment and even dramatic upset. The woman outraged by the light sentence for her husband's killer reported that it made her physically "sick to my stomach."[22] People shocked by a justice failure have complained that it is "absolutely unconscionable,"[23] that it "keeps me up at night,"[24] that "it's a travesty,"[25] that "it's unbelievable. . . . [and they are] devastated,"[26] and that "it's insanity."[27] The upset over a justice failure may be even more exaggerated for a victim: as one stated, "I will forever live with this shadow."[28] Another said, "There's a sea of emotions I've had since this happened. . . . I find [the sentence] very insulting."[29] A rape victim explained she will "be forever marked" by the crime and the case's "embittering conclusion."[30] To laypeople, justice is not just one more policy preference but rather a necessary prerequisite for having their world be right.

THIS INHERENT HUMAN VALUING OF HAVING JUSTICE DONE CAN be seen in the social science laboratory, even when the testing involves only the mildest norm violations. In a type of experiment called the "ultimatum game," participants are paired and one person is given a sum of money. The person must give some portion of the money to the other but has complete discretion as to how much. But if the amount offered is rejected by the receiver, then neither person gets to keep any of the money. If the amount is accepted, then both people get to keep their respective agreed-upon amounts.

A purely efficient calculation presumably would lead the "recipient" to accept any amount offered—something is better than nothing. But this is not the typical pattern of response. The recipient is making a fairness judgment. Offers of less than 20 percent of the total are typically rejected.[31] Offers of a third of the total are rejected by a majority of receivers, even when large sums of money are involved.[32]

The attitude may be that there is no reason why the first person should get more than the second—it was just by chance that the first person was selected to be the giver rather than the receiver—so the proper and fair division should be equal, perhaps with some adjustment to acknowledge the "luck" of the person picked to be the giver. However, an attempt by the giver to "take advantage of the situation" by offering an unfair share too far from an equal division is seen as wrong.

People do not just feel that small offers are wrong in some intellectual sense. They feel strongly enough about it that they are willing to sacrifice their own money to deprive the wrongdoer of his. That is, they are personally willing to sacrifice to have the wrongdoer suffer for his wrongdoing.[33]

Somewhat more remarkable is the conduct of third-party observers of these interactions. Third-party observers—who have nothing at stake in the transaction—are inclined to punish those who they think are acting unfairly. Even more striking, third-party observers are willing to punish the wrongdoers even if it means that they, the observer, must bear the cost of the punishment!

This dynamic is shown in a variation of the game in which both persons are given an initial allotment and both can give any portion of it to the other. In this variation, each person can keep any portion not given away, but each person gets three times any amount given by the other person. Thus, they all can maximize their takes by giving their full allotment to the other person, in which case each will get to keep three times his or her initial allotment.[34] But the players must make the allocation decision without knowing whether the other person will reciprocate. Can the other person be trusted to contribute a full allotment? A person might give the other nothing, thereby keeping a full allotment and also collecting three times the allotment the other person gives. The safest course is to give nothing, which lets the person at least keep what he or she has. However, the studies show that people are in fact more likely to contribute than not, as our prior discussions on cooperation would predict. They choose trust and cooperation over pure self-interest.[35]

Our current interest in this experiment is in the reaction of a third-party observer. The observer is given her own allocation of money, which she can keep for herself or can use to punish one of the two people after she sees how they deal with the other. Every dollar she spends to punish a player causes the punished person to lose three dollars. A purely self-interested third-party observer would just keep her full allocation. She gains no tangible benefit from imposing punishment and suffers a clear tangible loss by imposing it. The observer has no personal stake in the interaction between the two people she is observing.

Yet when third-party observers see one person taking advantage of another, they commonly pay to punish that person. When one person transfers his allotment to the other while the other keeps his for himself (thus getting to keep his own and three times what the other person gave him), almost half of the third-party observers pay to punish that selfish person. On average, third-party observers pay more than a third of their money to punish wrongdoers.[36] The results illustrate in a tangible way the common desire to punish what is perceived as wrongdoing, even if the person is not the victim and even if the punishment is personally costly and provides no present or future tangible benefit.[37]

The larger point is that human nature is to impose deserved punishment. People commonly act as if doing justice provides a benefit in itself, or as if seeing wrongdoing go unpunished imposes an intangible cost on them. The science suggests that in a sense it does impose a cost.

The human desire to impose on wrongdoers the punishment they deserve is more than just a social preference; it seems to have a biological component.[38] In an experiment similar to the "ultimatum game" variations described above, researchers used brain scan technology to see what areas of the brain are at work when participants in the experiments are making their decisions during the game.[39] They found that when people impose punishment on those who are perceived as having acted badly, an area of the brain called the caudate nucleus is activated. The area is associated with reward sensations and is also activated, for example, when processing visual beauty, experiencing romantic love, and during periods of cocaine or nicotine consumption.[40]

With brain scans we can witness the biological rewards from doing justice. Is it any surprise that we seek it out in plays, films, books, and all manner of entertainment? Clint Eastwood's *Dirty Harry* movies and Charles Bronson's *Death Wish* series, both wildly successful, are built around a plot that has the protagonist personally correcting the failures of an ineffective and unjust legal system. The delayed-justice-finally-done theme is also seen in classics such as Shakespeare's *Hamlet*, Alexander Dumas's *Count of Monte Cristo*, and F. Scott Fitzgerald's *The Great Gatsby*, as well as in modern books by many of today's most popular writers, including Tom Clancy (*Without Remorse*), Lee Child (*Die Trying*), John Grisham (*A Time to Kill*), and Stephen King (*Carrie*).

THE SAGA OF THE GOLD MINERS AND THE CITIZENS OF 1850S SAN Francisco holds another important lesson about human nature: it is not the simple punishment of wrongdoing to which humans seem devoted, but rather the *just* punishment of wrongdoing. It would have been easy enough to authorize some strongman to punish all violators, but the groups willingly incur the costs of group adjudication to assure that the punishment reflects their shared norms. In the camps, recall that the more serious the charge and thus the more serious the potential penalty, the larger the group that was called in to adjudicate the case—that is, the greater the costs willingly incurred to assure proper liability and punishment.

The adjudications commonly demonstrate a sensitivity to differences in an offender's degree of blameworthiness. Recall the mining claim encroachment that was judged not intentional. The encroachment was corrected but not punished. Similarly, the Vigilance Committee did not blindly punish all rule-breakers but rather shaped its punishments to match the relative seriousness of the offense: Murderers were hanged, robbers were permanently banished, and those who received stolen property were whipped but allowed to remain. It was not a desire for suffering of all rule-breakers that drove the adjudications but rather the desire to impose what the community saw as just punishment.

Modern studies confirm that it is moral blameworthiness—the relative amount of punishment an offender *deserves* for his wrongdoing—that people use in assessing the proper amount of punishment. It is not something else, such as deterring future crime or keeping dangerous people off the streets. Certainly people want to be safe, but that preference does not negate our innate belief that punishment be just. People's intuitive human rules call for wrongdoers to be punished according to their blameworthiness, not based on sterile crime control calculations.

In one set of studies, for example, subjects were asked to assess punishment for a variety of different cases with no indication of what principle they should look to in doing so. They were then asked to again "sentence" the same cases, but in the second instance to use specific principles: one principle based the punishment on the offender's moral blameworthiness for the offense (his "desert"), another on what would best deter others in the future ("general deterrence"), and another on an offender's dangerousness and what was needed to best protect society from the offender in the future ("incapacitation"). The subjects' undirected assessment of punishment matched their "desert" assessment and conflicted with their "general deterrence" and "incapacitation" assessments. That is, left to their own devices, people want to impose deserved punishment for a past crime not to gain efficiency in future crime control.

Other studies have looked at the kind of information subjects ask for or rely upon in making punishment judgments. As above, these studies have found that people seek and rely upon information relevant to desert, not information relevant only to deterrence and dangerousness. The seriousness of the offense is central to people's assessment of the punishment deserved, along with a wide range of other factors relating to an offender's culpable state of mind, mental capacities, and other mitigating circumstances under which the offender acted. People do not normally look to factors such as a perpetrator's prior record or likelihood of future violence (which are used to predict future dangerousness) or the detection rate for the offense, the frequency of the crime, or the degree of publicity for the case (all of which are used in setting sanctions that will more efficiently deter). Instead, the subjects rely on specific information related to how "blameworthy" an offender is.[41]

The human tendency to want justice done, apparent in the gold rush era of mid-nineteenth-century California, can be seen in how people handle themselves in a wide range of absent-law situations in different eras and different places.

DURING WORLD WAR II, THE NAZIS ROUNDED UP AND TRANSPORTED Jews from all over Europe into camps that had been built expressly for the purpose of annihilating them. Also taken to the camps were homosexuals, Jehovah's Witnesses, communists, and gypsies. Those who were not killed upon arrival fought to survive against disease, brutality, starvation, and overwork.[42]

Prisoners in the camps commonly hid away small scraps of bread among their possessions. The precious bread crusts could mean the difference between life and death if untoward events brought a person to the brink of starvation. A crust thief was seen by the inmates as equivalent to a murderer and would be killed if caught.

Knowing the risks, bread thieves targeted not the strong but the weak, who would be less likely to fight back or take revenge, or often a person who might die that day, leaving the theft undiscovered. Yet the entire group was sufficiently outraged by such theft that they would take turns staying up at night to stand guard. Such lookout duty had a serious cost because it meant that the person would be in poorer condition for the coming day's grueling work, and poor performance might mean execution. But the commitment to catching and punishing those who victimized the weak was thought to outweigh the personal cost.

There were some prisoners who for whatever reason mistreated their fellows or even actively participated in torturing them, sometimes to death.

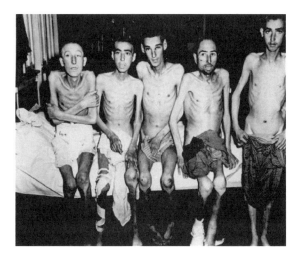

8. Emaciated prisoners of the Dachau concentration camp, 1945. United States Holocaust Museum, courtesy Tibor Vance.

The German SS who controlled the camps had no inclination to punish such acts. In fact, prisoners known to be cruel to their fellow prisoners were protected. Behind the scenes, however, prisoner justice was at work, and the protected "creatures" were often killed, commonly by prisoners who had not been their victims, had nothing personal to gain, and who put themselves at risk in doing so. One of the malevolent prisoners, Gregory Kushnir-Kushnarev, who claimed to be a former Russian general, was protected by the SS, but when he fell ill and went to the camp doctor (a fellow prisoner), the doctor by prearrangement declared him to be infectious and admitted him to the hospital, where other prisoners killed him by lethal injection. Why should these prisoners, typically the strongest with the best chances of survival, endanger themselves to punish wrongdoing to others?

IN 1719 CAPT. WILLIAM SNELGRAVE WAS IN CHARGE OF A MERchant ship that was captured by a band of pirates.[43] The quartermaster of the pirates interviewed Snelgraves's crew to determine whether Snelgrave had been a just captain, with plans to kill him if he had not been. By evening the crew had been interviewed and Snelgrave was found to be an excellent captain and was to be spared. The pirates' boatswain did not agree with the decision and during the night tried to kill Snelgrave himself. When the attack was reported, the pirate crew, all of whom liked the boatswain, "voted for his being whip'd."[44]

Captain Snelgrave, as their prisoner, was nothing to the pirates; he was someone they would never see again. The boatswain was a well-liked colleague, whom they would continue to live with. Yet the group chose to punish the latter because of his mistreatment of the former. He deserved it for his violation, and his punishment was the only way to set things right.

IN THE EARLY 1840S THE TANTALIZING PROSPECT OF FREE LAND, together with a stagnant American economy, induced thousands of families to travel across the continent along the Oregon Trail to California, Utah, and Oregon. Wagon trains formed in Independence, Missouri, during the winter, where they worked out agreements concerning leadership, supplies, and finances. The pioneers could not begin their trek until the grass that would feed the animals along the way began to sprout. At a rate of three miles per hour and with no delays, a wagon train could make the two-thousand-mile journey before the autumn snows blocked the mountain passes. Falling behind schedule could lead to disaster. People trapped in the mountains could die without food or shelter or be forced to retreat back across the prairie in hopes of reaching an army post, where they could survive the winter.

In the early weeks of the trip, some trains would try resting on the Sabbath, but the practice rarely lasted. Sunday travel was not optional if the schedule was to be kept. When people died on the trail, the bodies would roll along with the train until a long-enough stop gave time to dig a grave. When a person was too ill to travel, the group was forced to choose between abandoning the sick or delaying travel. Being separated from the train was a serious risk because it meant the loss of group contributions to everyday tasks, help with emergencies, and protection from attack. Yet the importance of moving was such that the sick were commonly left behind with only their family to stay with them in the hope that another train might come along soon. Sidney Smith, for example, was seriously

9. Wagon train navigating a tight mountain trail, ca. 1865. Lawrence and Houseworth Collection, Prints and Photographs Division, Library of Congress, LC-USZ62-22270.

wounded when he accidentally shot himself. "We were on the hunting ground of the Caws, the Pawnees were daily expected and the Cumanches [*sic*] were prowling around the neighborhood. To remain, therefore, in our present encampment, until Smith could travel without pain and danger, was deemed certain death to all." The train kept moving. Smith survived the first day of travel, but keeping him alive slowed the progress. The group finally decided to split up, with only a smaller group traveling at Smith's slower pace. (The slower group eventually gave up and returned east.)

With this understanding of the dramatic costs of delay, it is striking that one of the few things that would prompt a train to voluntarily stop was for the trial and punishment of serious wrongdoing. Each train made up its own rules. There was no U.S. legal authority present, and indeed the trains were not traveling across U.S. territory during much of their travel. They dealt with serious wrongdoing according to the group's own shared intuitions of justice.[45] It was not uncommon for a different train to stop to participate as the jury for a defendant who had nothing to do with them. Abigail Jane Scott recorded a case in which her train delayed for a day to participate in the trial of a man from a train ahead of them. The facts presented at the trial revealed that,

> Dunmore followed [Olmstead] and jumping upon him commenced beating him and endeavored to kick him in the face with his boots; Olmsted called upon the bystanders to take him off saying at the same time that he had a k[n]ife; As no one interfered he stabbed him in the lower part of the chest; Upon this Dunmore started back and exclaimed that he was stabbed. He fell and in twenty minutes was a corpse.[46]

The group judged Olmstead to be blameless and as having acted in proper self-defense, and no liability was imposed.

When James Reed, later to be a member of the infamous Donner Party (which resorted to cannibalism), beat another man over the head with a bullwhip, the leaders of the train convened a court and found him guilty of assault. Their choices for a sanction were limited. Rather than killing Reed, the makeshift court agreed to banish him. They decreed that he must travel alone and without firearms. Killing him outright seemed too severe, but sending him off with no weapon certainly put him at risk. While the company punished Reed, it also agreed to take responsibility for the welfare of Reed's family.

AGAIN, WE SEE PEOPLE UNDERTAKING ACTION, AT THE COST OF serious risk—be it delaying the train or incurring the wrath of the concentration camp guards—to do justice in cases in which they themselves were victimized and perhaps not even part of the victim's family or associates. Yet the people seem more than willing to make the sacrifice or to suffer the risk. Why would humans have such an inclination?

The evolutionary story of humans suggests an explanation. Recall the discussion of the serious hurdles that faced early human groups. At minimum, maintaining the all-important social cooperation required some sort of check on conduct such as physical aggression or taking of possessions without consent. A member who was regularly victimized would hardly be likely to be an enthusiastic contributor to the group's goals, which typically required not just cohesion but cooperation, whether in hunting or agriculture. A high level of cooperation had to be maintained if the comparatively small and weak humans were to survive their larger predators and nature's other hardships.

Some shared understandings among the members would have had to exist as basic rules of conduct. But even if a group came to agreement on rules of conduct, the real challenge would come when the group had to deal with a member who violated those rules. Where social pressures were insufficient to gain compliance, the most readily available means of punishing the improper physical violence or unconsented-to taking was, well, physical violence or unconsented-to taking.[47]

One can see the problem: how is a group to distinguish the "bad" beating or taking (of a rule violation) from the "good" beating or taking (of deserved punishment)? An effective enforcement system required not only a shared understanding of the prohibitions but also of the circumstances under which the prohibitions could be set aside in order to punish.

Often that was not enough. Cooperation was not likely to be maintained if trivial violations were punished brutally or particularly harmful violations were punished lightly. The punishment of any member held a potential cost to the group (for example, the violator who is beaten may for a time be a less effective hunter), thus there was value in punishing no more than was necessary. Yet it was also important to signal the relative seriousness of different sorts of violations. It was an important message, for example, to understand that the improper killing of another was worse than the improper beating of another. Thus, there had to be a shared understanding of both a continuum of seriousness among the violations and a corresponding continuum of seriousness of punishments, which then allowed the two to be matched.[48]

Although it is prehistory, we can guess that early human groups must have sorted out some such understandings, for we know that they flourished. Perhaps these shared understandings sharpened as their level of cooperative action heightened. It is hard to imagine a story by which such high cooperation could have developed and been maintained if there had been arbitrary punishment disconnected from the seriousness of the violation.

AS WE HAVE SEEN PREVIOUSLY, IT IS USUALLY NOT THE CASE THAT human traits pop out of nowhere. They commonly are built upon more rudimentary forms of the trait found in animals further down the evolutionary tree. This is true with regard to the use of punishment for harmful conduct and it is perhaps then no surprise to learn that many animals, especially the more social ones, also display rudimentary forms of a sense of fairness and justice. This is especially true of animals that live in cooperative groups.[49] Treatment perceived as unfair tends to provoke an unhappy response, one that one can easily imagine would undermine the animal's cooperative spirit within the group.

In an experiment with capuchin monkeys, for example, monkeys within sight of one another were regularly given cucumber slices in exchange for granite tokens. When the experimenter began to provide one monkey with a grape (a more highly valued food) in exchange for the same token that continued to yield mere cucumbers for the other monkey, the cucumber monkey often manifested considerable distress. It sometimes jumped up and down, even throwing the token or the cucumber at the researcher.[50] The cucumber monkey could see the disparity of value in its reward and was sufficiently upset by it to reject the "unfair" reward.[51] Similarly, chimpanzees often refuse to participate in an exchange once another chimpanzee is receiving a more valued reward for the same amount of effort.[52] Thus, both capuchins and chimpanzees behave in ways suggesting that they can perceive unfairness and that it often physically stresses them.

Behavior that suggests an ability to perceive fairness and unfairness underlies a great deal of social behavior in primates. Many primates regularly engage in sophisticated cooperation schemes ranging from simple reciprocal grooming and food sharing to complex tool using and coalition-building behavior, and an individual's participation in the activity is commonly dependent upon being perceived as making a fair contribution. In olive baboons, for example, there is a strong correlation between the support a baboon has given to another in an earlier conflict and the willingness of that other baboon to return the favor by giving support in a present conflict.[53] Similarly, macaques often support other macaques unrelated to them if those others have previously supported them in a conflict.[54] Vervet monkeys tend to prefer to groom individuals who have groomed them in the past.[55] When a chimpanzee grooms another early in the day, the other is more likely to share food with the groomer later in the day.[56] Chimpanzees engaged in tasks that require collaboration quickly determine which among different potential partners is the best collaborator and will recruit that individual for subsequent collaborative tasks.[57] Primatologists report that because sharing and other cooperative behavior exists in a "multi-faceted matrix of relationships, social pressures, delayed rewards, and mutual obligations," successful individuals are those who best distinguish good colleagues from bad and deal with each accordingly.[58]

Echoing the evolutionary speculation mentioned above, a failure to make a fair contribution to the group cannot just produce less help from others but also risks the imposition of punishment by the group, a fact that Alcalde Rogers in the mining camp might have been wise to consider before taking Sim's bribe. Rhesus macaques that discover food and are caught having failed to alert the group to the discovery, for example, often become targets of significant aggression.[59] In chimpanzee societies, those members reluctant to share their food are more likely to encounter aggressive responses when they later approach those who have food.[60] Chimpanzees will attack former allies who failed to assist them in conflicts with third parties.[61] And many primates, including chimpanzees, tend to intervene most often against those who have most often intervened against them.[62]

Among chimpanzees (who, along with bonobos, are the closest relatives of humans) such retribution is common enough that researchers consider it "an integral part of [a] system of reciprocity."[63] Frans de Waal, a prominent primatologist, describes the chimpanzee community as "a 'market' of reward and punishment,"[64] with "balance sheets" kept on social interactions.[65] The group's rules consist of "one good turn deserves another" and also "an eye for an eye, a tooth for a tooth."[66] "Not only are beneficial actions rewarded," de Waal reports, but "there seems to be a tendency to teach a lesson to those who act negatively."[67] Reward good deeds and punish bad. And not only do cooperative animals punish, but the intensity of the punishment often increases with the severity of harm caused by the transgressor, again echoing the evolutionary analysis above.[68]

To summarize, the leading animal researchers believe that evolution has supplied the "building blocks" of human morality.[69] The question is not whether biology has influenced the development of the human moral system, but rather to what degree.[70] "Evolution," they believe, "has produced the requisites for morality: a tendency to develop social norms and enforce them."[71]

THE LARGER POINT HERE IS THAT HUMANS' JUDGMENTS ABOUT justice are not just modern social preferences but an innate part of human nature. One of the most compelling demonstrations of this is found in scientific studies of child development. Children around the world in every culture and in every demographic cross-section within a culture follow a common path in the development of moral reasoning and an appreciation for basic principles of justice. Much of this occurs at an extremely early age, even before children have the tools to learn social norms (let alone governmental legal rules). Much of our intuitions of justice are the preprogrammed product of a process of development that largely transcends a human's environment.

There is a great deal of evidence, for example, in support of Lawrence Kohlberg's classic scheme describing a predictable sequence of stages in the development of moral thinking.[72] He suggests three discrete stages of development, each stage with two levels.[73] It is "the most widely researched description of moral development available," but it does not matter whether one accepts exactly his phase descriptions or even divides the development process as he does.[74] The important point is that there is general agreement across the entire field of child development that children everywhere progress through the same stages and at roughly the same ages.[75] This developmental flowering exists across all cultures, not just Western ones, including across cultures in which the existing legal regimes are dramatically different.[76]

Interestingly, while the early research suggested that children were precocious in their development of moral reasoning, in fact we now know that those studies vastly underestimated the sophistication of even the very youngest children. Indeed, many authorities suggest it is likely that research still has not fully revealed the precociousness of moral reasoning.[77] According to the recent literature, "moral capacity is well developed, although by no means completely developed, in the third year of life," when most children are barely verbal.[78]

In one early experiment, for example, very young children were tested to determine if they are able to make distinctions between violations of moral rules—that is, acts that are wrong and deserve punishment (for example, one child hitting another)—and violations of conventional rules—acts that deviate from a convention (for example, failing to say grace before a snack).[79] Using pictures of offending conduct and a pictorial scale of punishment (different-size frowns), the researchers showed that even children between two-and-a-half and three-and-a-half years old make such distinctions and would punish a moral offense more seriously than the violation of a convention, even if "there was no rule about [the moral offense]."[80]

In another study, four-year-olds, both middle-class European Americans and lower-socioeconomic African Americans, judged moral transgressions relating to physical or psychological harm and fairness as very serious, as deserving of punishment, and as generally wrong, and saw this as so regardless of whether they had ever been told of a rule that the conduct was prohibited.[81] In short, even young children seem to have textured and specific views and beliefs about deserved punishment, and those views are not simply derived from the dictates of authority.

The importance of these results should not be underestimated. The fact that such young children believe immoral acts are wrong even in the absence of known rules indicates a precocious, universalist view of morality.[82] Further, given that such conceptual distinctions are made by very young children, and universally so, it is not likely that they are acquired by social learning processes but rather as the product of an innate human developmental sequence.[83]

ANOTHER STRIKING ILLUSTRATION OF HOW MUCH HUMAN judgments of justice can transcend a person's situation and upbringing is found in social psychology studies showing people's shared judgments of justice. There is an enormous range in human condition and experience around the world. There is also an enormous range of governmental law and the ability of different populations (with dramatically different educational levels, for example) to understand that law, as well as enormous difference in the willingness of different peoples to give deference to and internalize governmental law (note, for example, that different governments have very different reputations with their people). Yet despite this wide range in human condition and experience and the wide range of governments and governmental law, the studies show that people across cultures and demographics share strong common judgments on many aspects of justice.

Cross-cultural studies have shown great similarity in ranking offense seriousness, for example. At the end of a particularly large cross-cultural study, one researcher concluded, "If one were to order the acts according to the proportions of each country sample criminalizing them, one would find a general consensus across all countries as to the extent that all acts should be tolerated."[84] And, "it is apparent that there was considerable agreement as to the amount of punishment appropriate to each act," and that looking at relative rankings indicates "general agreement in ranks across all countries."[85]

Indeed, the studies suggest that people are not simply looking to governmental law to form their judgments of justice, but in many instances are not reasoning out their judgments at all. The studies suggest that they commonly rely on their intuitions rather than on conscious reasoning.[86] That is, they are not calculating out the relative blameworthiness of the offender but rather are experiencing his relative blameworthiness as if it were a fact. (These studies show that these shared intuitions can be quite nuanced, taking account of a wide range of factors and even their interactive effect.) Intuitions of justice are widely shared across demographics especially in relation to the core of wrongdoing: judgments involving physical aggression and takings without consent.[87]

The claim is not that people agree on the precise amount of punishment that is appropriate for a particular crime but rather on the relative seriousness of one crime compared to another. In one study (by one of the present authors) researchers gave participants twenty-four short scenarios, each describing a different criminal episode (such as theft, assault, burglary, robbery, kidnapping, rape, manslaughter, murder, and torture). The participants were then asked to rank the scenarios in order of how much punishment was deserved for each.[88] Not only did the participants agree that serious wrongdoing should be punished and that minor infractions should not, they also showed almost unanimous agreement on the relative ranking of the blameworthiness shown in the twenty-four different scenarios.

This high level of agreement existed across all demographic differences among the study's participants. The level of agreement was strongest for crimes involving physical aggression, theft, and deception, which are the crimes most commonly committed. Unanimity is lost and the level of agreement decreases as the nature of the offense moves out from the core offenses toward a periphery of more culturally dependent offenses, such as those concerning religion, family, and some sexual practices.

The high agreement of intuitions across cultures and demographics for many aspects of core offenses makes it clear that people's intuitions of justice transcend governmental law. Even though laws vary across countries, people's intuitions of justice on many issues do not.

THAT MANY ASPECTS OF HUMANS' JUDGMENTS OF JUSTICE transcend culture and environment helps explain much of what we see in the absent-law cases. It should be no surprise that the California gold miners, the seventeenth-century Caribbean pirates, the Nazi concentration camp prisoners, wagon train members on the Oregon Trail, and residents of San Francisco in the 1850s all demonstrate a commitment to doing justice, even if it comes at personal cost to themselves and even when they are far beyond the reach of governmental law. Their commitment to doing justice is in large part what comes in the package of being human.

But some people will argue that what we see in absent-law situations is not a product of human nature but just the residual effects of what governmental law has taught. While the law itself may no longer have a direct effect, people in the absent-law situations are still carried forward by its momentum and, as if out of habit, act upon the norms that governmental law has taught and that they have internalized.

This view runs up against the scientifically confirmed reality just reviewed, however: the cross-cultural studies showing agreement on many aspects of justice judgments even though different cultures' legal rules vary widely; the child development studies showing a common path of moral development impervious to all environmental factors, let alone governmental law; animal studies showing the precursors to human notions of justice and fairness; and the evolutionary analysis showing the necessity for such shared intuitions for group success long before government or law was a thought in the human mind. How could one find such shared intuitions of justice around the world, a common path in the development of a child's moral views, and the precursors to justice judgments in our evolutionary predecessors if our punishment judgments are simply the product of what we have learned from a local governmental law?

Even the absent-law stories themselves refute the claim of governmental law's dominant role. Some of the absent-law groups, such as the Netsilik people (discussed in chapter 6), had no prior governmental law that could be learned and internalized. Nevertheless, they show the classic patterns of cooperation and just punishment. Other absent-law groups adopt norms dramatically different from those that their prior governmental law provided. The legal rules that governed British sailors, for example, were dramatically different from those that the pirates created for themselves—and, interestingly, the pirates' rules were much like the rules constructed by other absent-law groups in other centuries and in other parts of the world. Further, there is reason to doubt that some of the absent-law groups had ever internalized the prior governmental rules.

Certainly this is an open question with regard to such groups as those who chose to become pirates or the felons of Attica prison (discussed in chapter 5).

Perhaps the most compelling reason to reject the argument that the absent-law groups are simply carrying forward norms previously instantiated by governmental law is the enormous diversity of the situations from which the groups are drawn. They are from many different centuries across many parts of the world and drawn from demographics of every sort. The prior formal law for these varying groups could not be more different, yet we see common patterns of social cooperation and just punishment. If it was governmental law's prior normative influence at work, we would expect to see that same diversity in how the groups conduct themselves.[89] A more parsimonious explanation that fits the evidence, both scientific and anecdotal, is that the deep desire for doing justice is a basic human trait that is shared across demographics and cultures, as are many of the specific principles of justice that people use in assessing deserved punishment.

The nature of our judgments of justice is not just an academic question, but rather is at the crux of many of today's penal policy debates. If our interest in doing justice were just socially learned, then reformers need only reeducate us. Social reformers could make humans into any sort of creatures that they wished; they could create a population that does not care about doing justice and is happy to give up the institution of punishment. Good luck with that.

What the evidence suggests is that our interest in doing justice is an innate part of our character that has, over the course of generations, become a fundamental part of what it is to be human. Attempts at "reeducation" would be difficult and costly, if not hopeless. Our basic instincts of justice are likely so deep that they cannot be altered, at least not without using coercive indoctrination processes that no liberal democracy would tolerate.

Of course, understanding that the human inclination toward just punishment has an innate biological component does not in itself mean that we ought to follow that human urge wherever it leads. Things have changed for humans since our time on the Serengeti Plain. Its innateness does not make it right, or even good for us as a society. While we cannot change it, perhaps we will want to keep it within newly defined bounds. But as the second half of the book shows, it turns out that 125,000 human generations of evolution have given us some precious wisdom and there is a serious cost to be paid by ignoring the importance of our shared intuitions of justice.

CHAPTER FIVE

INJUSTICE

The Batavia *Shipwreck and the Attica Uprising*

SOCIAL COOPERATION REQUIRES PUNISHMENT, OR, MORE SPECIFI-
cally, justice, a point made clear by Peter Rabbit's case in Drop City and
many others. That is, failures of justice have costs, not just in an abstract
philosophical sense but in a practical, real-world sense: effective group
cooperation cannot be sustained without it.

WHAT ABOUT *INJUSTICE*—IMPOSING GREATER PUNISHMENT THAN
is deserved? Is doing injustice detrimental in a practical sense? Perhaps
doing justice is essential, but avoiding injustice is just a pleasant luxury.
Perhaps abhorrence of injustice is just a weak sister of the demand for
justice—purely a product of one's proper socialization? Or, have the
innumerable human generations that made innate the demand for just
punishment also made a human abhorrence of injustice innate? The absent-
law natural experiments again have much to tell us.

IN 1628 THE SAILING SHIP *BATAVIA,* WITH SLIGHTLY FEWER THAN
three hundred people aboard (in a mix of soldiers, sailors, and families),
set sail from Amsterdam on her maiden voyage to the spice ports of Java.
Navigation of the era involved a certain amount of guesswork, and when the
man navigating the *Batavia* guessed wrong, the ship got caught on a coral
reef off the coast of wild and unknown western Australia in June of 1629.[1]

The *Batavia* wrecked on an archipelago now called the Abrolhos. So flat and insignificant is its topography that at first it was unclear if the low, flat islands in sight nearby would even be above water when the tide came in. The strong winds that swept over the land for much of the year kept most of the spits of land utterly bare of anything other than piles of bird droppings. The strip of coral rubble on which they were caught, about five hundred yards long, was home only to seabirds and sea lions.

The captain rowed off toward the low islands to scout for options. In his absence things spun out of control. When it became clear that the ship would eventually sink, chaos reigned. Soldiers and sailors broke into the stores of wine and spirits and engaged in a wild orgy. As one account of the events reports, "Every taboo was swept away."[2]

When the captain returned he restored order, and the crew began the arduous process of rowing survivors and supplies to shore. After three days of work 200 survivors were ashore, but rescue efforts ceased when the remaining 70—some too drunk, some too terrified—refused to leave the perilous wreck.

The captain and crew took stock of the situation, and it became clear to everyone that no help would be coming. Their only chance of rescue was someone undertaking a seemingly impossible open-ocean voyage of two thousand miles to Java in an open boat to bring back help. With little other chance to save the 270 souls who had survived the wreck, the captain organized the attempt with a group of 40 volunteers. As they departed, no one expected them to survive for long.

The remains of the *Batavia* finally broke apart nine days after the wreck on the reef. The men still on the ship were cast into the sea. The last to wash ashore was Jeronimus Cornelisz, one of only two officers now on the island. In keeping with the policy of the Dutch East India Company, as ranking officer he was elected head of a committee, called the Raad, that ran the affairs of the sudden community. His exercise of authority did bring order to the group, as tasks were assigned and resources rationed, but his autocratic style rubbed many the wrong way. He increasingly lost credibility and respect by giving special privileges and resources to an inner circle of two dozen men whom he drew around him to do his bidding.

During this time another group was gaining in influence. A dozen soldiers

10. Mutineers attacking the other survivors of the *Batavia* wreck, 1629. Courtesy Western Australia Museum.

had organized themselves around a common soldier, Weibbe Hayes, who by his competence and fair dealings earned the allegiance of others, including those who outranked him. The cooperative nature of the group began to attract attention and admirers, and the Hayes group grew in influence.

Cornelisz saw this development as a threat to his control. His several-dozen-member inner circle was outnumbered on the island by the other survivors, so he ordered half of the people on the main island to be moved to smaller islands nearby while promising to bring them the supplies they needed. He kept on the main island useful artisans and the ship's doctor so his group would continue to benefit from their expertise. He ordered the Hayes group to search for water on a remote island of the archipelago and persuaded them to leave their weapons behind with a promise that the boats would soon return for them. The boats did not return. Cornelisz knew the other islands had no water and few resources, but the move extinguished what he saw as the primary challenge to his authority. Counting the exiles, the population on the main island was reduced to a hundred or so, a size he thought more manageable to control.

In one of the first disciplinary cases to come before the raad, a man had stolen food from the common stores and shared it with another man. He was convicted before the raad, and Cornelisz insisted that both men be killed. The committee objected that the punishment was too severe, especially with regard to the man who had only shared in the food. But Cornelisz wanted to make an example of the men to deter other misbehavior. With some arm-twisting, Cornelisz got his way. The harsh sentences may well have provided the intimidation that Cornelisz sought, but they also hurt his reputation and added to the population's increasing doubts about his fairness and judgment.

After the hesitations on the thievery case, Cornelisz engineered a revamping of the raad membership, substituting followers from his inner circle. The next case to come before the committee was that of two men who had been building a boat and were told by Cornelisz to stop. (He believed the boat could undermine the full control he needed.) When the men were caught working on the boat again, he ordered them killed and his new committee readily agreed. This served to further damage his reputation among the people on the island and only reduced the deference they were willing to give him. The reduced deference required him to be that much more autocratic and harsh in his judgments in order to maintain control.

During this time, the exiled Hayes group on the far island had survived, against Cornelisz's expectations. They had no weapons or supplies, but after twenty days they had in fact discovered water and sent up a signal to that effect. The group made the most of what they had and through their cooperative efforts were able to produce more. They built shelters, found food, and tended the sick.

The rest of the people who had been exiled to the other islands had chosen not to return to the main island, even though Cornelisz had never returned with the promised supplies. When they saw the Hayes signal, they were drawn by the Hayes group's good reputation for fair treatment and cooperative action. On the other hand, the trip to that farther island was dangerous, and not just because of the perils of the sea. When attempts at migration to it first started, Cornelisz was furious; he worried that the Hayes group might build enough strength to rival his own. He sent his henchmen in boats to interdict those trying to float to Hayes's island and had them killed. But everyone who successfully reached the island was welcomed.

That violence, for which there could be no pretense of legitimacy, sharpened the dilemma for those left on the main island with Cornelisz. Most had not been victimized by his group and indeed enjoyed a substantially higher standard of living than those sent to other islands. When pressured to do so, some people joined Cornelisz's mercenary band, but most refused. Indeed, some people on Cornelisz's island began defecting to Hayes's group despite the fewer resources they expected to encounter. Cornelisz posted guards on the boats. He demanded that all take an oath of loyalty to him. But still, most refused.

Cornelisz's increasingly autocratic rule only made the problem of defection worse for Cornelisz, who concluded that his only solution was an all-out attack on the Hayes group. He organized his remaining mercenaries in a series of assaults. The attackers possessed all of the swords and firearms, as well as the ship's cannon recently salvaged from the coral reef. It was expected to be an easy conquest but the conflict dragged out to a series of scrimmages when the attackers faced fortifications and weapons the Hayes group had fashioned by hand.

As it happens, in the midst of these attacks the captain appeared on the scene with rescuers! He had succeeded in making the astonishing two-thousand-mile open-boat voyage to Java, and returned to save his charges. The rescuers tried and convicted Cornelisz and his henchmen. Cornelisz and the worst of his group were executed, several were marooned on the coast of western Australia, and some of the younger ones were only keelhauled and whipped. (Chapter 12 tells the remainder of the *Batavia* story, and all of the stories in the book.)

IF PEOPLE WERE TRULY INDIFFERENT TO NOTIONS OF FAIRNESS and justice, the smart move would have been to sign on at the start as an enthusiastic supporter of Cornelisz, who had a monopoly on the existing resources and power. But, even at the start, when things remained relatively civil, most of the several hundred people on the island were put off by the injustice of Cornelisz's punishments and his unfairness in dealing with some situations. Most refused to join his governing group, even though by doing so they could have made their lives more tolerable and their long-term survival more likely.

Even when things became more threatening, most would not join Cornelisz. And even the well-treated artisans still refused to join his group or sign a loyalty oath, and many risked his wrath by their defection. Indeed, many well-treated people tried to join the Hayes group even though it put them at great personal risk. This illustrates the significance they placed on the unfairness and injustice they saw in the treatment of others and on how that treatment broke their interest in cooperating with the Cornelisz group, despite potential personal benefits.

Recall the ultimatum game experiments using a third-party observer (chapter 4). The third-party observers voluntarily suffered a personal cost to punish those who they thought deserved it, showing the importance that people place on doing justice. A part of those experiments is relevant here: recall that the wrongful conduct that the third-party observers were punishing was the unfair treatment of one person by another, the taking advantage of one by another.

This is the dynamic at work in the story of the *Batavia*. Even those not victimized by Cornelisz were alienated by seeing his injustice to others. They became willing to suffer considerable risk to themselves to avoid supporting such injustice—whether by refusing to join Cornelisz, to sign a loyalty oath, or slipping off to Hayes's remote island. They had no means to punish Cornelisz but they could at least deprive him of the benefit that he might have gotten from their support.

These people were probably not making a long-term calculation, saying to themselves, "Let me reject Cornelisz's group because groups with unjust treatment lack long-term cooperation and thus are inclined toward failure." Rather they were simply responding instinctively to their situation, giving expression to their natural abhorrence at seeing others treated unjustly. In that instinctive reaction is the wisdom of 125,000 generations of human evolution: cooperative groups do prosper, and stable cooperation does require avoiding injustice.

The point here is that cooperation can be as easily destroyed by *giving more punishment than is deserved* than as by *failing to give punishment that is deserved*. People may continue their membership in a group despite injustice if it is necessary for survival, but a weak bond will lead them to drop out when a viable alternative presents itself, such as an opportunity to join a more just group even if it has far fewer resources.[3] Even if they do not leave the group that tolerates injustice, they are not likely to share in its values, promote its goals, or defer to its authority.

GROUPS IN A WIDE VARIETY OF ABSENT-LAW SITUATIONS SHOW this same inclination to avoid injustice. The Vigilance Committee of San Francisco (chapter 4), in holding a trial for every person charged, let off more people than it punished.[4] Such behavior may seem quite odd at first glance. Given the difficult circumstances, why would the group even think to take account of the subtleties of blamelessness and mitigation when punishing one who has in fact broken the rules? It is a testament to the innate human inclination toward assessing blameworthiness that such subtleties are taken into account even in difficult circumstances.

It is common, for example, for groups to require proof of a violator's culpable state of mind, not just his violation, and to give a defense for an honest mistake. In the Andes plane crash (chapter 2), a man named Harley was discovered to have a private stash of toothpaste, which typically was part of the group's food stores (and coveted as a tasty dessert). At his "hearing" before the group it was determined that he was misled by another man, Delgado, who had told him that the toothpaste was not part of the group stores and thus he could properly trade it to Harley. Harley's plea, essentially one of honest mistake, was accepted and he was not sanctioned.[5]

Absent-law groups also commonly recognize both justification and excuse defenses. Justification defenses apply where a person violates a prohibition but does so because of special justifying circumstances:

something as common as self-defense or as rare as burning another's field as a firebreak to save a town from an approaching forest fire (called a "lesser evils" justification). Excuse defenses, in contrast, apply where a person does the wrong thing but they cannot be blamed for it because their conduct was the result of some cognitive or control dysfunction that caused their rule-breaking, such as insanity or duress.

Justification defenses, such as lesser evils and self-defense, are commonly recognized. Recall the wagon train case of the jury trial for a man who had stabbed and killed another man during a fight (chapter 4). At the hearing before the group it was determined that the dead man had unjustifiably provoked the fight and that the defendant had killed in reasonable self-defense. He was found not guilty.[6]

Excuse defenses also are recognized. In 1822, on the whaling ship the *Globe*, one of the officers, Samuel Comstock, had signed on with the intent of seizing the ship, sailing off to a Pacific island, and declaring himself to be a pirate king. Comstock recruited several other men, who joined him at the appointed hour in killing all the officers as they slept. One officer, Gilbert Smith, was not with the others, and before Comstock could bludgeon him to death he pledged allegiance to Comstock if he would spare his life, which Comstock agreed to do. Smith thereafter managed the sailing of the ship and even allowed a man to be hung for a crime Smith knew the man had not committed. Yet when the non-mutineers in the crew later took back control of the ship from Comstock, Smith was not punished, apparently on the theory that he had been coerced to participate.[7]

The absent-law groups also commonly limit punishment according to the relative seriousness of the violation, as has been previously illustrated with regard to the San Francisco Vigilance Committee and the pirates. To give another example, in the gold mining camps a minor infraction, such as deception in a horse sale, might be sanctioned with a fine. A more serious offense, such as theft of property, might prompt a whipping or banishment from the camp for a first offense.[8] The most serious offenses, large-scale theft or murder, were more likely to be punished by death.[9]

There are good crime-control reasons to punish anyone who violates a group rule. Letting a violator off can undermine the clarity or importance of the prohibition. Giving a defense advertises a potentially troublesome example of a person who is known to have violated a rule yet is not punished, a message that might well undermine the deterrent threat implicit in the prohibition.[10] Yet defenses are nonetheless regularly given.

That groups recognize defenses and mitigations in the absence of governmental law suggests that they are focused not just on effective prohibition and deterrence but, even in their difficult circumstances, also are concerned with avoiding injustice—avoiding punishing a person more than his moral blameworthiness deserves.[11]

In fact, it makes good long-term sense for humans to have an inclination to avoid injustice. Just as regular failures to punish violators can undermine a group's cooperative nature, so too can regular infliction of injustice. Third-party observers want to see justice done when they are not the victim, but so too third-party observers are likely to be alienated when they see injustice. This is apparent in the *Batavia* story, as Cornelisz's willingness to do injustice increasingly alienated the larger community even when they were not the victims and indeed benefited from his policies. His loss of moral credibility led to their loss of deference to him and ultimately to defections and resistance to his rule.

SO WHY DO PEOPLE ACT THIS WAY? WHY DO THEY CARE ABOUT avoiding injustice to others? Are people's abhorrence of injustice just a matter of proper socialization? Or does it have some innate component?

In many respects judgments about justice are simply the flip side of judgments about injustice, and answers to these questions are the same as the answers to analogous questions regarding the innate preference for having justice done. That human judgments about justice and injustice have an innate component is shown by cross-cultural studies showing agreement on many aspects of justice judgments even though different cultures' legal rules vary widely; by child development studies showing a common path of moral development impervious to all environmental factors, let alone governmental law; by animal studies showing the prehumans' notions of justice and fairness; by evolutionary analysis showing the necessity for such shared intuitions for group success long before government or law was a thought in the human mind; and by absent-law stories showing shared judgments even when the different groups have had very different life experiences.

In the child development literature, for example, recall the predictable passage of all children through the same process of moral development without regard to their dramatically different situations. The appreciation of the subtleties of justice and injustice are developed strikingly early, even before verbal communication. True sophistication in assessing blameworthiness begins around age seven. In one study, children aged four to seven were read stories about different crimes.[12] The offense described in each story varied in terms of whether it was intentional or unintentional and whether the damage was to a person or to property. The children then assessed blame and were asked about punishment. On average these young children viewed damage to property as less serious than injury to a person and judged unintentional damage or injury as less serious than intentional damage or injury.[13] Thus, children's intuitions of justice are sophisticated enough to include more than just an assessment of the seriousness of the wrongful conduct. They take account of a person's culpable state of mind.

They also consider various justifying and mitigating circumstances. For example, in one study children as young as seven years old recommended little or no punishment for a child who threw water on a child who was playing with matches. The children understood that acts do not occur in a vacuum and appreciated the tradeoff between present and potential harm.[14]

Children as young as five also take into account whether a rule-breaker is acting with a mistaken belief, and the nature of the mistake. The children's judgments are quite nuanced. If a person's belief is mistaken on a matter of fact—the state of the factual situation as compared to a mistake about what is morally right—then mitigation often is permitted.[15] However, if the mistake relates to what is right and wrong (for example, whether it is right for a teacher to discriminate against a student based on the student's gender), then the person's mistake does not exculpate in the children's view.[16] (Current criminal law incorporates this distinction, giving rise to the well-known legal maxim that "Ignorance *of law* is no excuse," even though ignorance or mistake *of fact* can be an excuse.) In other words, children have a sophisticated understanding of others' beliefs and the role they play in assessing blame for an offense.[17]

One final part of the answer can be found in the absent-law cases. What happens when a group of social misfits are left to govern themselves? Does their adjudication of violations reflect a concern for avoiding injustice, or are they deaf to such concerns?

IN 1971, ATTICA STATE PRISON IN UPSTATE NEW YORK WAS UNDER-staffed and overpopulated. On September 9, prisoners overpowered guards during breakfast and rampaged through the prison. For a time they had free run of the facility but later lost control of all but D Block and its yard. During the initial hours, all was chaos. Keys to the facility were seized, chair legs torn loose for clubs, previously fashioned homemade knives brought out, windows smashed, and fires set. Officer Mike Smith, a twenty-two-year-old guard, was beaten when inmates found him working in the metal shop. A short time later he was beaten again by another group. Officer Kenneth Jennings was struck eight times in the head with a weight-lifting bar that had been taken from the gym. One group of prisoners attacked guards with "burning mattresses, long poles, tear gas, lye soap, and streams of water from fire hoses."[18] Eventually forty-two guards and employees were taken hostage. The majority were stripped and forced to run a gauntlet of kicks, curses, clubs, and shovels. Several were injured but none were killed. Two days later, however, Officer William Quinn died from injuries.[19]

Despite the opening chaos, inmate leaders were able to bring order. A camp was set up in D Yard. (Camping outside would make tear gas less effective in an attempt to retake the prison.) Tents were constructed from materials taken from the prison, bedding was distributed, and a command station was set up. With medical supplies taken from the prison, an infirmary area was manned by prisoners with medical training. Men who could not deal with the stress were placed in a tent labeled "the mental ward." Racial tensions were understood to be divisive, and the group worked to avoid them. All racial groups were given a voice in the decisions. Scavenged food stocks were brought out and rationed. Tom Wicker, a *New York Times*

11. Elliot Barkley (*second from right*), the spokesman for Attica prisoners, during talks with New York State Commissioner on Corrections Russell Oswald (*foreground*), 1971. © Associated Press.

reporter present in the yard, observed at the time, "Alienated, angry men, many of them unschooled, violent and admitted lawbreakers," had put together a functioning society.[20]

An "open-mike" period was held during which any inmate could address the group. Out of this forum came a set of agreed-upon rules. Expressly prohibited were attacks on others, fighting, drug use, predatory sexual activity, and "selling out" (acting contrary to the group's interests in their dealings with authorities). All negotiations were to take place in full view of all inmates, ensuring transparency and preventing personal "sellouts."[21] Also prohibited was harming a hostage. It was agreed that the hostages would be kept safe as bargaining chips. Men were selected to guard the hostages and given instructions to protect them at all costs. Security personnel were appointed and wore distinctive armbands to signal their position. Their most common functions were to break up fights, confiscate weapons, collect drugs stolen from the infirmary, and bar a second helping of chow until all had been fed once.

A committee of inmates with representatives from each of the four cell blocks was appointed as the inmate leadership, to be the negotiators, spokesmen for the inmates, and judge and jury for any rule violators. The committee included three men who were serving terms for their third armed robbery, one man who had killed a store owner during a robbery, and one who had killed a man with a pool cue. Another inmate was recruited to act as their lawyer, and others to act as typists for the group's communiques.

In its role as a criminal court, the committee heard a variety of cases. Seven men were charged with violating the rule against selling out (they had flown a white towel over their tent, which the committee interpreted to be a signal to the authorities that they were not joining the uprising). Brought before the committee, the men were judged guilty, made to dig latrines, and otherwise placed under house arrest (i.e., confined to their tents). Other offenders brought before the committee were given punishments that varied widely, from clearing garbage to the death penalty.

In the latter case, the prisoners' security personnel saw Barry Schwartz and Kenneth Hess having a private conversation with a reporter and slipping him a note. Both were brought before the committee and found to be sellouts. They were taken to D Block and killed. From outside the prison many people saw what one witness described: Kenneth Hess as he "squirmed out an upper window, his throat already partly cut, wedging himself between the bars and the wall between the floors. He screamed for help, but the officers below could do nothing. Hands were seen clutching at his legs, and he was pulled back into the prison. His decomposing body was discovered in a closet after the retaking."[22]

Michael Privitiera, a.k.a. Crazy Mike, an inmate known to be unstable and violent, had been a problem for the security guards during the first day of the uprising. He was brought before the committee for attacking one of the hostages and assaulting an inmate in the process. The committee found that he suffered from mental illness or disturbance and, rather than punishing him, sent him to D Block for temporary preventive detention. He was not to be punished, but he was a disruption to the social order that the committee was trying to hold together. After a period of preventive detention he was allowed to return to the yard, presumably after he calmed down and seemed more stable.

DESPITE THE CHAOS, THE PRISONERS ORGANIZED THEMSELVES into a cooperative group and instituted conduct rules and punishments for violations, as we have seen groups do in other absent-law situations. This may seem a bit more surprising than in other cases, however, because these men were all serious lawbreakers. One might assume that serious criminals as a group were ignorant or indifferent to the intuitions of justice that others might have. Social science studies suggest otherwise, though, with substantial evidence that criminals share the society's intuitions of justice.

In one study a group of inmates were presented with a series of hypothetical crimes—including pickpocketing, burglary, mugging, robbery, and robbery with shooting—and asked what type and level of punishment the hypothetical offenders deserved, if any.[23] They were also asked what level of punishment they thought the courts, the public, and other inmates would impose and what criteria these others would use in judging (e.g., crime seriousness, prior criminal record, race, motivation). Nearly all of the inmates supported punitive sanctions, particularly incarceration. The criteria they used in imposing punishment matched that used by the courts and the public, and their level of punishment conformed much more to that which they expected from courts and the public than from other inmates. That is, not only did they in fact use the same criteria as the public but also saw themselves doing so—as sharing the punishment views of the courts and the public rather than what they assumed were the views of other criminals.

It may seem a surprise that in the midst of the Attica chaos the prisoners sought to and were able to establish their own order and that, despite their seriously difficult circumstances, the order included following some principles of justice in the adjudication of rule violations. The committee's judgments were not about punishment alone but about just punishment, including notions of proportionality, mitigation, and excuse. Getting people to follow the rules was essential at the time, and one can see the temptation to ignore proportionality, mitigations, and excuses. They needed people to take the rules seriously.

So it may seem odd that principles of justice had any role to play in the committee's adjudications. Why would these ideas even come into the heads of the vicious criminals in the midst of such chaos? In the Privitiera case, for example, an important rule had been violated. Why would it occur to the committee to do anything other than seriously punish the violator?

While this might seem puzzling, it is in fact consistent with a large body of research, some of which has been discussed previously, that essentially says that everyone has nuanced intuitions of justice, that doing justice is important to people, and that the concern for justice goes in both directions: not only do people want wrongdoers to be punished as they deserve, people also want to avoid injustice. Some circumstances can subvert these preferences, but the inclination toward justice appears to be a human default. This pattern of sensitivity to avoiding injustice, even among outlaws, is seen in other contexts as well. Recall the situation of the Caribbean pirates, for example (chapter 2).

IN THE LATE 1600S, MERCHANT SHIPS PRACTICED PRIVATEERING, whereby a merchant vessel could lawfully seize the ship of an enemy nation. The prize ship was sold and the proceeds divided between the government that had issued the "letter of marque" authorizing the seizure and the owners of the merchant vessel, who commonly gave a share to the captain, who in turn commonly gave a share to the crew. Such privateering was a means of extending naval warfare capability to nonmilitary vessels.[24]

Work at sea was abundant but treacherous, due not only to the dangers of the ocean and the common threat of disease but also to the often tyrannical leadership of merchant vessel captains, who had absolute authority. They legally administered harsh physical punishment, even death, and themselves suffered few legal restraints.[25] Captains were known to abandon sailors at distant ports, to beat them for using foul language, to fail to feed them, and to use their discretion to not pay them at the end of a voyage.[26] Veteran seamen would advise newcomers: "There is no justice or injustice on board ship, my lad. There are only two things: duty and mutiny—mind that. All that you are ordered to do is duty. All that you refuse to do is mutiny."[27]

It was in large part these conditions that created the institution of piracy. Recall Henry Avery, a sailor on the *Charles II*, a British vessel supposedly authorized as a privateer by Spain to hunt for French ships. After promising riches to induce service, the captain did nothing to search for prize ships because he had not in fact obtained the necessary letter of marque. Instead, month after month the crew was held captive on the *Charles II* at anchor. The captain refused the men's pleas to be set ashore, knowing he would lose his crew. With a family waiting for his earnings and outraged by the unfair system for the treatment of sailors, Avery led the crew to mutiny on May 7, 1694, as the captain lay drunk below deck. Flying a newly fashioned flag bearing a skull and crossbones, the mutineers sailed from the Spanish harbor of La Coruña and went into the prize-taking business for themselves, becoming the first crew in the new age of piracy.

Once they became outlaws, the crew of the *Charles II* (rechristened the *Fancy*) made up its own laws. The division of spoils was specified. Democracy was to be the guide to all decision making. Specific prohibitions and punishments were set out. Captains, and all other officers, were to be elected. Officers who failed to act as the majority willed were recalled and replaced. No officer had better quarters or better food than the ordinary sailor. The system became known as "Custom of the Coast" or "Jamaica Discipline."[28]

It was understood that a well-functioning ship had to have effective discipline. But a captain could keep authority and attract a crew for the next outing only if he were seen as fair and just in the discipline he imposed. An officer with a reputation for unjust punishment would lose his crew and his ship, or never be able to attract a crew in the first place.

In comparison to the unfair and brutal treatment of the seamen under the traditional naval system, the democratic approach of the pirates was extremely attractive and dozens of other merchant crews followed suit. When the crew of a merchant vessel faced a pirate attack, it often decided not to defend the ship but instead to join the pirating life.

The rules that these outlaws adopted for themselves had the degree of the punishment track with the seriousness of the offense. A pirate who did not keep his weapons in working order or "neglected his business" would be "cut off from his share." A man who endangered the ship by smoking in bed would receive "Moses law" (forty lashes). A man who stole from the group would be marooned on an uninhabited island, which was essentially a death sentence.[29]

Culpable state of mind was also judged relevant. In one case three officers were found to have taken clothing from the common loot storage area to make themselves more attractive to the women in town. Stealing from the common loot was a serious offense normally justifying a death sentence. Upon returning to the ship, the officers were put on trial before the crew to answer for the theft charges. The officers explained that their intention had been only to borrow the clothing for the night and not to keep it. The crew believed them but had to decide whether this undid the theft offense. They concluded that it had. As it happens, modern property law makes the same distinction: theft requires not just an intention to take but also an intention to permanently deprive the owner of the property (hence the need for a special "joyriding" offense).[30] The officers were discharged with only a warning.

For a group of outlaws, this would seem a fairly nuanced judgment to be making in assessing a violator's blameworthiness. Yet the evidence is that humans naturally make such nuanced judgments of justice, and those judgments are important to them in the imposition of punishment. The human inclination is not simply to punish but to punish as deserved. What the absent-law cases and the science suggest, then, is that not only is doing justice deeply ingrained in human nature but so, too, is avoiding injustice. A society must have rules and punishment to enforce them, but that punishment should be no more and no less than what the community sees as deserved.

MANY WRITERS AND POLICYMAKERS MAY AGREE THAT PEOPLE feel strongly about doing justice and avoiding injustice but they nonetheless argue that such feelings are unimportant or irrelevant. People may well have deeply felt judgments, but, first, their judgments are vague, and second, they are just the product of socialization and thus are entirely malleable.

The first argument is that people can only roughly distinguish between cases of "serious" and "not serious" wrongdoing, but no more. People's notions of justice are simply too vague to allow them to see injustice in other than the most extreme cases. This is the view of much of the current criminal law establishment: by its nature desert cannot really suggest any specific amount of punishment in a given case but, at best, can suggest only a wide range of proper punishment. It can only identify extremes that ought to be avoided. In the recent revision to the Model Penal Code's sentencing principles, for example, the American Law Institute explained that "few judges, philosophers, or other experts . . . can say that a particular offender who has committed a serious imprisonable crime . . . deserves exactly x years in prison." At best, "the imprecise dictates of moral judgment can, at some point in each case, tell us that a certain level of judgment is clearly too high and, at a different point, that it would clearly be too low."[31] Does it matter whether justice and injustice judgments are only vague? Yes. If it were true that they were only vague then reformers could enact whatever unjust criminal laws they liked with the assurance that people would not notice, except in the most extreme cases.

In the second argument, some modern criminal law scholars go further and suggest that, even if desert judgments are not vague but specific, they do not matter because they are malleable. If people at first might see something as an injustice, they can simply be resocialized to see it as just. "Democratic conceptions of desert are first, *elastic*: desert is hard to quantify and easy to stretch. . . . [D]esert is indeterminate and elastic, . . . an inherently 'mushy' concept . . . . too malleable to serve as a meaningful limiting principle."[32] In other words, people's views of what is deserved have no real content, but are simply a temporary present opinion that may change or be changed by others at any time.

Does it matter whether people's judgments of justice are entirely malleable? Yes. Modern penal policy commonly imposes undeserved or excessive punishment. (More on this in chapter 9.) Mandatory minimum sentences assure that legitimate mitigations will be ignored. "Three-strikes" statutes can double, triple, or quadruple punishment based strictly on an offender's prior record, which studies show assures punishment far beyond what the community sees as deserved. The age at which youth are charged and punished as adults has recently been lowered in many states, again regularly producing punishment in cases that the community sees as unjust. Narrowing or abolishing the insanity defense, adopting strict liability offenses that require no culpable state of mind, and a host of other injustice-producing reforms are increasingly common.

These and similar policies are commonly justified under various crime-control strategies—such as making "an example" of an offender or imprisoning him to prevent a minor risk of a future offense—but empirical studies of laypeople's judgments of justice show that these doctrines seriously conflict with what ordinary people think is just punishment. Yes, the policies have been democratically adopted. But that simply demonstrates the distorting effect of American crime politics. The studies show the conflict with community views of justice to be clear and striking.[33] Many people will support a political slogan on a bumper sticker but will have a very different view when faced with the sobering reality of a real case.

If people's inclinations to avoid injustice are simply learned preferences, then people can simply be trained over time to accept and tolerate these unjust legal rules. On the other hand, if people's judgments of justice are in some part innate and thus not easily malleable, then such unjust doctrines will continue as troublesome burrs that are not likely to fade with time but rather will grow and fester and produce increasing alienation and lost credibility for the system.

AS TO THE FIRST ISSUE: ARE PEOPLE'S JUDGMENTS OF JUSTICE vague? Not according to the available social science empirical literature.[34] On the contrary, studies show that people's judgments of justice are quite specific and nuanced. Small variations in facts can make large, predictable differences in what is seen as just punishment.[35] People make subtle distinctions among cases in judging relative blameworthiness, and people's judgments are sophisticated.[36] Ordinary people, even children, take into account a wide array of factors and the interactive effects among different factors.[37] Further, people have intuitions regarding all manner of potential injustices. The social psychology literature documents intuitions of justice by ordinary people on matters as varied as reduced culpable states of mind; coercion, mental illness, immaturity, or involuntary intoxication; threats to person or property or crime prevention; and reduced harm seriousness.[38] Indeed, ordinary people's intuitions of justice even recognize mitigations for factors beyond those of current criminal law, such as providing mitigations for remorse, public acknowledgment of guilt, and apology.[39]

People's most basic principle is that more blameworthy offenders deserve more punishment than less blameworthy offenders. Because people make many subtle distinctions among different cases when judging relative blameworthiness, they need a vast spectrum of different punishment amounts to give expression to the large number of distinctions they see. It turns out to be a bit of a challenge to construct a range of punishments with enough meaningfully different amounts to fully reflect the enormous number of distinctions people make. That is, people see a meaningful difference between one week and one week and a day, for example, but not between one year and one year and a day. As the punishment amount increases, the size of the meaningfully different punishment unit also increases.

Thus, the number of cases that people can distinguish from one another crowd the punishment continuum. Each case ends up sitting at a particular point on the continuum with a particular amount of punishment assigned to it. It is not that there is some magical connection between that case's facts and that amount of punishment. Rather, the amount of punishment assigned to each case is the amount that will put it in its proper ordinal rank among all other cases. If a society changed the high end point of the punishment continuum, say, reducing it from fifty years to twenty-five, as some Scandinavian countries might do, the punishments assigned for all cases would need to be reduced accordingly so that each case would keep its proper ordinal rank among all other cases.

The ultimate effect is that ordinary people's intuitions of justice require a specific amount of punishment for each case, not just some vague range of permissible punishments. As one researcher put it, "Virtually without exception, citizens seem able to assign highly specific sentences for highly specific events."[40] People's intuitions of justice are not simplistic or vague, but rather sophisticated and specific.

As to the second issue: are people's judgments of justice and injustice entirely malleable? Again, not according to the available evidence. A wide range of scientific evidence, such as the child development studies discussed earlier, show the universality of the human development of moral intuitions. Also relevant here are the studies of social animals, especially our evolutionary ancestors, that show rudimentary precursors to notions of justice and injustice. How could there be such a universal developmental path and such evolutionary precursors if human intuitions of justice were no different from the opinions that people have about which lawn mower is best or which country is safest?

Recall the studies showing the enormous justice-judgment agreement across all demographics and cultures, especially judgments concerning many aspects of the core of wrongdoing, physical aggression, and unconsented-to takings. This high level of agreement across demographics tells us that these judgments have withstood the powerful influence of life experiences, which are vastly different for different people. This suggests that these judgments can be changed only by something even more powerful than one's cumulative life experience. It might be possible to do this—perhaps through brainwashing techniques like that used on POWs—but it seems unlikely that such universally held judgments could be easily altered by any process that a liberal democracy would tolerate.

Indeed, we know from the absent-law cases examined here that even the extreme conditions in which many of these groups find themselves often have little or no effect in altering their commitment to doing justice and avoiding injustice. It is hard to see, then, that people's intuitions of justice are "elastic" and "malleable," as some scholars and policymakers claim. Rather, a society's planners must accept that people cannot simply be "educated out of" any intuition of justice that the planners find inconvenient. Some intuitions of justice are here to stay, and planners need to accept them rather than fight them.

The bottom line is that people's natural inclinations to avoid injustice must be respected. Reformers cannot plow ahead with unjust rules and assume that people will simply adjust to them and eventually accept them as just. Injustices will not fade—they will only fester.

CHAPTER SIX

SURVIVAL

The Inuits of King William Land and
the Mutineers of Pitcairn Island

SADLY, SOMETIMES THE CHOICE FOR A GROUP IS JUSTICE OR SUR-
vival. Doing justice, or avoiding injustice, could risk the group's viability.
If humans are naturally inclined toward doing justice, do they sometimes
follow those instincts blindly over the cliff? Presumably not often. The
desperate absent-law situations that modern man has endured (described
in earlier chapters) were routine for earlier humans. If humans had such
lethal irrationality they would have destroyed themselves as a species
many millennia ago.

If a group compromises on justice in order to avoid destruction, what
happens to cooperation, which we have seen depends on doing justice
and avoiding injustice? And once a commitment to justice is breached,
what does the future hold for the group? Is there any going back? These
are important questions for modernity because, given the relative safety
and comfort of modern man, doing justice comes at a cost and the commitment to justice can sometimes be broken. What happens then?

FOR CENTURIES THE NETSILIK PEOPLE HAVE LIVED IN A DESOLATE
portion of northern Canada now known as King William Land. Anthropo-
logical evidence suggests that they were cut off from other Inuit peoples
around the time of Columbus. In 1829 British explorer John Ross was

searching for the Northwest Passage when he unexpectedly made contact with this small population.[1]

The climate of King William Land is the harshest of any that human groups inhabit. The Netsilik had no wood, metal, or soil, yet they survived—on ten thousand square miles of ice. Food acquisition was the primary mover of the Netsilik world. All major decisions were made to maximize caloric intake. As the seasons changed these nomadic people inhabited different portions of the vast region to hunt seal or caribou or to fish salmon. Survival required close group action. During seal hunting season, for example, each hunter would remain silently poised for hours at a different seal breathing hole, not knowing through which hole a seal might appear. They could spend days on the ice floes and get nothing. When a seal was caught it was divided among all members.

The family, the primary social unit, was autonomous in its travel: would hunt when and where it chose and would leave a camp as it saw fit. However, within each camp, behavior was closely proscribed in many ways and usually in ways that promoted group cooperation. When a new person arrived in a camp, his obligation was to shake hands with every other person, including the smallest baby, flesh to flesh. The new arrival would then go to his own shelter—it took about an hour to build a decent-sized igloo—unpack his belongings and await the visit of each person. The new arrival was obligated to make everything he owned available to his visitors. Once in a camp, consumable supplies—whether food, tobacco, or tea—were shared. Stinginess in the sharing of food was a serious breach.

The Netsilik had no set leader or social hierarchy—the most successful hunter at the time enjoyed the greatest influence—and certainly they had no government or governmental laws. They did have, however, a set of shared social norms about how people should behave and shared understandings about how people should be punished if they violated those norms.

The level of punishment varied according to the seriousness of the violation. Mocking gossip was a common low-level sanction applied, perhaps used for a hunter who quit too easily. A more serious sanction would be something like having your frozen fish cache vandalized by anonymous children at the direction of their parents. This might be used, for example,

12. Inuit snow village during seal hunting season, 1800s. © North Wind Archives.

where a man who was asked for food to feed another man's dogs but gave only the bare minimum rather than the expected half. A man who killed another without cause or justification normally could expect to be killed himself.

The existence of such a system of social norms and the punishment of violations in proportion to their seriousness is similar to what we have seen in a host of other absent-law situations. Left to their own devices, humans tend to organize themselves along these lines in a fashion that will bring and maintain social cooperation. But the Netsiliks' experience illustrates another aspect of the human rules: not every violation was punished. In one instance, for example, a good hunter killed his hunting partner for a perceived insult. This was considered a serious wrong, but for the larger group to then kill him for his violation would mean losing not just the one hunter already dead but another as well, and during the vital seal-hunting season as well. Instead, the killer was resented and watched but not killed. Some months later, when he acted in a threatening way toward another hunter, a third man walked up behind him and stabbed him in the back, killing him instantly. This was accepted as appropriate, and the killer was not sanctioned in any way.[2]

In another instance of perceived insult among hunters, a pair of brothers were attacked in their tent as they slept. The younger brother was killed. The elder brother was injured but fled to his parents' camp some distance away, leaving his own family behind. His wounds eventually healed and he hunted caribou with his father. At the end of caribou season, his father presented him with a new bow and his mother remarked that she would like her daughter-in-law to help her make the caribou skins into clothing. All understood the meaning. The man returned to the camp where his brother had been killed and killed the men who had killed his brother. The people in the camp then invited him to visit, and admired his new bow. Justice had been done. The balance had been restored.

The special demands of survival meant not only that justice would sometimes have to be delayed, as in these cases, but justice permitted certain killings thought to be essential to survival. In times of shortage a family could and would kill an elderly member who could no longer contribute or a newborn infant who would be a serious burden to feed. If a man killed a family member without such justification, however, he himself would be killed by the group.

Doing justice and avoiding injustice were important to the Netsilik, but they were not everything. Survival trumped justice, especially in the desperate circumstances in which the Netsilik often found themselves. This same dynamic—forgoing what the group saw as just punishment if avoidance of it was necessary to survive—is seen in a wide variety of absent-law situations, including those involving modern and Westernized groups.

RECALL THE PLANE CRASH SURVIVORS TRAPPED IN THE ANDES Mountains in 1972 (chapter 2). The group's daily work tasks included melting snow for drinking water, tending the sick, preparing and rationing food, and cleaning the shelter. Yet several men were unwilling to contribute to the work. The shirkers were verbally reprimanded several times, to no avail. Some members then threatened to withhold food if they did not work, but this, too, had no effect. As food became more scarce, the group felt more of a pull to do something about the noncontributing members. They formally decided that they would withhold food from one particularly lazy man, but the man simply shrugged and still would not work. For two meals he got nothing. He agreed that they were acting fairly to withhold food from him. The group sensed that he was indifferent as to whether he lived or died, and understood that a loss of hope would threaten the group's survival; anything that might lower morale was dangerous. The group backed down and fed the man, keeping him alive.

Pilfering food was normally a serious violation, but there was a tacit understanding that cutting flesh off corpses was particularly unpleasant work. The group turned a blind eye to minor pilfering during this work. However, as food became more scarce the group decided that this accommodation would cease, and the new policy was formally announced and punishment was threatened. Yet the pilfering continued. The group again backed off in enforcing the threatened punishment, fearing it would be disruptive to fragile morale.

When the expedition to find rescuers had been gone for some time, morale was getting very low. One of the lazy men was caught stealing extra food. The group again hesitated to impose the agreed-upon punishment, fearing it would be disruptive, but it also became clear during discussions that the group was reaching a new point in its judgment: greater disruption would come in the future from not punishing food thieves rather than punishing them, so no further exceptions could be made. In other words, failing to do justice was sometimes necessary but it always had a cost, and that cost could outweigh any benefit from forgoing deserved punishment. (Before the group faced another incident to test its new resolve, rescue arrived.) The group understood that its survival depended upon cooperative action, that rules are needed to sustain cooperation, and that punishment is needed to enforce the rules. But while they felt the rule violations deserved punishment—and some violators were indeed punished—they were willing to forgo deserved punishment if doing so was necessary to preserve the social order upon which their cooperative action depended. Justice is important but, under the right circumstances it can be trumped by survival. Conversely, a failure of justice always comes with a cost that needs to be justified.

We can see the same dynamic in situations where survival is not so clearly threatened as it is felt among the Netsilik or the Andes plane crash survivors. A threat to the group and its social order might come in many forms that can be seen as grounds for forgoing deserved punishment.

IN 1790, A GROUP OF MUTINEERS FROM THE SAILING SHIP *BOUNTY* (of Captain Bligh fame) kidnapped twelve women and six Polynesian men and took them to make a new colony on remote Pitcairn Island.[3] Over the years, the island had a series of visitors. With the aid of a learned man who was a brief visitor, Pitcairn's citizens adopted a set of formal group rules in 1910. They sought the rules in large part to regulate the behavior of visitors and did not always think of themselves as bound by them. They had their own set of norms that in many ways appear to have transcended the formal rules they adopted. For example, the rules that prohibited adultery, fornication, thievery, and fighting were seldom enforced. A teacher who worked for a short time on the island reported, "Crime is of frequent occurrence; of Law there is almost none, every man does practically as he sees fit—while the idea of restraint in any form, is abhorrent to them."[4] (This may bring to mind the antipunishment communes described earlier, but the path down which the systems leads the Pitcairn group is somewhat different.)

In 1934 Pitcairn elected to come under British control. Starting in the 1950s the residents became increasingly exposed to the outside world through visitors and media, which began to affect the expectations of some residents. In the 1970s one mother came to a council meeting with her young daughter's bloody underwear and accused a powerful man of raping the child. She was ignored and her family ostracized and denied their fair share of the goods coming onto the island.

British police officer Gail Cox was on the island in 1999 to investigate theft charges. Near the end of her stay the mother of a fifteen-year-old girl, Belinda, informed Officer Cox that her daughter and two friends had been raped by twenty-three-year-old Ricky Quinn.[5] Quinn admitted to the assaults. Officer Cox attempted to pursue the case, but it was explained to her by people on the island that Quinn was a hard worker and therefore "above the law."

13. Descendants of Matthew Quintal and John Adams, two of the *Bounty* mutineers, 1862.

Receiving little cooperation from the locals, Cox talked with her superiors in Britain and was given additional manpower to investigate. As the police interviewed former female residents who now lived in New Zealand and Australia, the allegations multiplied. Another series of rapes had occurred two years previously. Another man, Shawn Christian, was named as the perpetrator. A fourth girl then told of being raped at age ten. As the investigation continued, the extent of the problem finally became clear. As one of the investigators explained, "Every Pitcairn girl, and I mean every single one, a 100 percent hit, had been a victim of sexual abuse."[6] Most females reported more than one attacker and many reported assaults starting at preschool age.

Belinda, whose allegations had started the investigation, took seven hours to recount all the assaults she had endured from just two men. The attacks started when she was ten and included gang rape by the two men. As with Quinn, the men they questioned did not necessarily deny the charges. Denial would have been difficult because at the time of the investigation, the average girl living on Pitcairn was expected to be a mother by age fourteen. It also became apparent that starting in the 1960s, when women had more opportunities to leave, many left the island as they approached their teens—after being raped or fearing they would be—and did not return until they were middle-aged or married.

When the investigation was complete, the British government began the prosecutions that the locals had failed to undertake. Although initially angry at the rapists, when it became clear that the British were seeking to punish the men, most parents of the raped children stopped cooperating. Belinda's father was angry at her: "It'll be all your fault if the islanders are arrested and this island breaks apart. If you go ahead with this, you'll never be able to come back to Pitcairn and you'll be out of this family."[7]

Over her parents' objections, Belinda continued cooperating with prosecutors. She was disowned by her parents and made to leave the island. Many other girls, including a woman named Catherine who reported that she had been raped by Belinda's father, recanted their testimony under heavy pressure from their families; they were welcomed back into the community.

The police then got a new set of stories from people who had already given information. Belinda, they were told, had fallen down a well as a child and was a mental defective. Another woman, who had her first child at age nine and a second at age eleven, told investigators that the British were using the men as a means by which to depopulate the island so the British would no longer have to fund Pitcairn.

Despite the ever-shrinking witness pool, the case nonetheless went to trial. Even as the residents of the island denied wrongful behavior, their testimony often pointed to unequivocal guilt. One man claimed the seven-year-old girl he raped was flirting with him. When asked whether he had ejaculated into a girl who was nine years old, one defendant answered, "At that age, what's the chance of pregnancy? Why should you worry at that age?"[8]

Some islanders, especially the women and the elderly, spoke openly of their fear of what would happen to the island if the men were incarcerated. The men performed the necessary manual labor on the island, including running the longboats that hauled tourists and cargo from passing ships. Because a large portion of the island's income came from the tourist trade, convictions for pedophilia could serve a lethal blow. The women had survived a culture of rape but they now feared a destruction of the order they knew and depended on. The threat that derailed justice in this instance was not the serious threat of starvation faced by the Netsilik or the Andes plane crash survivors, but it was serious enough in the minds of many of the women of Pitcairn to justify not punishing the serial rapists.

Survival demands, or what are perceived as such, also can create situations in which groups in absent-law situations tolerate deviations from justice of the reverse sort—imposing much more punishment than is deserved. Consider the case of the Maroons.

THE ISLAND OF JAMAICA WAS SETTLED BY THE SPANIARDS DURING the sixteenth century and by the British beginning in 1655. In need of cattle herders, the Spaniards brought the first African slaves to the island. Many of the slaves fled captivity and, using their special knowledge of the local terrain, were able to remain free. These transplants succeeded in forming new communities with other escaped slaves that became known as the Maroons.[9]

They colonized the steep, heavily forested terrain because such areas were uninhabited and more easily defended. The Maroon economy was a mixture of self-sufficient agriculture and plantation raiding. During their raids, the Maroons stole slaves, livestock, ammunition, and anything else of use. Information from newly escaped slaves allowed the Maroons to more effectively target a plantation. Fear of the raids and the resulting loss of profits deeply eroded the ability of the British to develop a plantation economy on the island.

When the Maroon communities were still small, their night raids targeted marginal estates. As their numbers and experience grew, however, even the largest estates were open to attack. The costs to the British owners increased, and efforts to eliminate the Maroons also increased, but the Maroons remained a serious threat.

The Maroons were in a vulnerable position, however, because if the British could find their settlements, their weapons would easily overwhelm them. It was the Maroon ability to remain undetected that kept them safe. That meant that a single disaffected individual had the power to destroy the community by providing information to the British. It would be a simple matter, for example, for a person who might be angry about having been whipped for a rule violation to inform the British about where and when

14. The government of Jamaica declared Queen Nanny a national heroine in 1975. Her portrait appears on the Jamaican 500 dollar bill.

a raid would be attempted or the location of the settlement to which the raiders would return. And such information would be well rewarded.

In the absence of the ability to indefinitely imprison a violator, the Maroons adopted a practice of using death as the punishment for most violations. An individual who spoke in any language other than English was killed. A person who sought to join the Maroons but failed a loyalty test was killed. Adultery was a capital offense. All members in the community had a specific job—as a land clearer or an animal tender, for example—and anyone who failed in his or her job without reason was killed. Few would believe that death was an appropriate sanction for such minor violations, nor would people normally think to punish both serious and minor offenses in the same way. But it was a practice that was tolerated because it was thought to be necessary.

Another example of this dynamic—imposing more punishment than is deserved in order to protect the viability of the group—is the Attica prison case (chapter 5) in which mentally ill convict "Crazy Mike" Privitiera was segregated and detained after assaulting a hostage and another prisoner. The group's rules called for the death penalty, yet Crazy Mike's obvious mental illness was taken into account as an excuse for his violation.

To pick up the story where we left off, Crazy Mike was subsequently released from detention but he then immediately assaulted another inmate.

He was brought before the committee again. His conduct was likely as much a product of his mental illness on this occasion as it had been on the previous occasions, but the committee did not have the resources to provide the kind of long-term supervised preventive detention that Crazy Mike clearly needed. He was taken to D Block and killed.

THESE EXAMPLES OF ABSENT-LAW GROUPS COMPELLED TO DEVI-ate from desert—to either give more or less punishment than is deserved—reveal the limits that people in absent-law situations sometimes place on meting out justice. On the other hand, the more revealing aspect of these situations may be how they illustrate the resilience of the commitment to justice. When the distorting conditions recede, these groups typically reverted to doing justice as if it were their natural default position.

After their contact with British explorer Ross, life for the Netsilik began to change. Sled runners that traditionally had been fashioned out of salmon frozen in a line were increasingly made of metal obtained from traders. The sled bodies made of bone and tusk were now made of wood. The people gained access to metal knives, fishhooks, spears, and sewing needles, all of which made daily life and survival easier. Firearms, steel traps, canned food, and other technology soon followed. As the Netsilik moved back from the brink of starvation, their willingness to tolerate failures of justice similarly diminished. Insult killings were no longer tolerated, even by good hunters, nor was the killing of infants or the elderly. With the introduction of a criminal justice system, revenge killings also were forbidden and punished.

Unable to check the growing power of the Maroons through military force, the British in 1738 negotiated a peace agreement. The treaty brought an end to the military conflict and allowed open trading between the British and the Maroons. The British deeded land to the Maroons for permanent settlements. With the treaty, the Maroon community no longer needed absolute discipline, and at the same time they gained greater flexibility in the range of punishments they could impose. They then reverted to the use of prison and other nonlethal punishments, including whippings, exile, demotions, assignment of women's work, and ostracism. The Pitcairn residents, as of this writing, live under the same conditions described above, although the construction of a planned breakwater harbor might change this by eliminating the island's dependence on the men who run the longboats.

THIS PATTERN OF REVERSION TO JUSTICE WHEN THE SURVIVAL-threatening conditions recede is consistent with what we know from empirical studies. In one study, for example, subjects were asked to "sentence" an offender who had assaulted another and, in some of the variations presented, remained dangerous because of a brain tumor. Seeing the subjects' reaction to the different variations allowed the researchers to tease out whether the subjects looked to desert criteria or to incapacitation-of-the-dangerous criteria in deciding sentences. The authors concluded that the subjects' default judgment was to look to desert.[10]

Some subjects could be diverted from desert, however, to take some account of dangerousness in sentencing if they were made to feel sufficiently at risk by the dangerous person's release from all control. But the subjects promptly reverted to pure desert criteria when the dangerousness threat receded, either because of a successful operation to remove the brain tumor or because they were told of the availability of civil commitment to detain the person.[11] That is, they saw the criminal justice system and the imposition of punishment to be properly and exclusively focused on desert, even though under the right circumstances, they could be diverted from pure desert, at least temporarily, if there was no other way of detaining a person who posed an immediate danger.

THE PATTERN OF DEVIATION AND REVERSION COMMONLY REPEATED in the absent-law cases only confirms how serious is the human commitment to doing justice. It is not mere inconvenience that is required to divert groups from justice; it is what they perceive as a threat to survival. The Netsilik, the Maroons, and the Andes crash survivors all faced death had they not compromised on doing justice or avoiding injustice, each depending on their particular situation.

It is not that these groups are unaware or indifferent to the failures of justice or the injustices they do. Rather, they see them but judge (rightly or wrongly) that it is a cost they have no choice but to suffer. The important point is that there is a cost, a serious cost, to deviating from justice, which, of course, explains why the groups tend to revert to justice when circumstances change.

The existence of such reversion is quite striking. Once a group has habituated itself to certain conduct and has established certain habits in dealing with (or ignoring) wrongdoing, one would expect some significant force is needed to change those habits. It was not that the Netsilik who enjoyed a less threatening life were reverting to some prior set of customs when they changed their practices. Their embrace of more just practices was something different from what they had historically done, yet the change was brought about internally and not forced upon them by an outside world. That is, even during their earlier practices, they carried with them an inclination for justice that often could not be expressed. This inclination survived the bad times.

In other words, the occasional survival-induced deviations from justice are in fact a useful demonstration of the depth of the community's commitment to justice. The reversion to justice when a survival threat recedes publicly demonstrates how serious a threat must be to justify the deviation. The cycle publicly reaffirms that justice will be honored in instances short of survival threats. Unfortunately, modern American criminal justice has lost its way on this issue and regularly demonstrates its willingness to trade away justice in order to promote minor interests and sometimes for administrative convenience only.

CHAPTER SEVEN

SUBVERSION

Prison Camps and Hellships

HUMANS MAY HAVE AN INCLINATION TOWARD COOPERATION, BUT the world is full of examples of just the opposite. War and conflict continue unabated—an obvious challenge to any illusions we may hold about a cooperative human nature. Some of this conflict is an unfortunate by-product of the inclination toward group cooperation: it is the tendency to see one's group against other groups, a tendency that has helped give rise to the nationalism, religious intolerance, and other group allegiances that have produced much human misery.

Within groups chaos and disorder can exist, sometimes with devastating consequences. One need look no further than today's crime rates and, on a larger scale, failed states like Somalia and Haiti: obviously something has gone badly wrong for cooperative action. How can this be our modern existence when cooperative tendencies in absent-law situations are equally apparent even in the absence of the organizing influence of government and law? Some absent-law situations in the laboratory of human history suggest some possible explanations that have implications for modern institutions, including criminal justice.

AFTER THE BOMBING OF PEARL HARBOR, AN ILL-PREPARED AMER-ica entered World War II. Thousands of Americans, mostly reservists, together with Allied troops from the Philippines, England, Australia, the Netherlands, and elsewhere gathered at American bases in the Philippines.

The initial thought was to push toward Japan, but the realities of a two-front war became apparent. The war in Europe was given priority, leaving little support for the Pacific forces. Perhaps not surprisingly, things went badly and the Philippines were unconditionally surrendered in April 1942.[1]

The Japanese marched 75,000 prisoners across the length of the Bataan Peninsula—an event aptly called the Bataan Death March—to prison camps in the southern part of the country. According to a *Congressional Record* account, during that time,

> they were beaten, and they were starved as they marched. Those who fell were bayoneted. Some of those who fell were beheaded by Japanese officers who were practicing with their samurai swords from horseback. The Japanese culture at that time reflected the view that any warrior who surrendered had no honor; thus was not to be treated like a human being. Thus they were not committing crimes against human beings. . . . The Japanese soldiers at that time . . . felt they were dealing with sub-humans and animals.[2]

After six days the march ended but the dying did not. Within weeks of reaching the camps, an additional 22,000 Filipinos and 1,500 Americans died. One prisoner did the math: "If I'm the last dog to be hung, I've still got nineteen days to go. But it will sure be lonesome here on that last day."[3] The Japanese soon relocated the non-Filipino prisoners to new camps with slightly less treacherous conditions.

The Japanese were firmly in charge of many aspects of life within the camps, including the daily schedule, the assigned work details, and whether officers and enlisted men were housed together. But the captors left the prisoners to sort out for themselves most other things about how the camps would be run.

Most American troops, assigned to Camp 1, were reservists with little military training or experience and typically these men were strangers to one another. (Other forces, such as the Australians, were primarily professional soldiers organized in familiar units.) All contingents were trying to figure out how they could survive. June saw 503 more deaths, July 786. The officers were able to avoid the heavy labor endured by the enlisted men. By pooling their resources they obtained some basic necessities, carved out a separate fenced compound, and got access to bathing water. Because of the better conditions, the officers died at a tenth the rate of the enlisted men.

A Camp 1 soldier noted, "Without leadership, American soldiers turned on each other. The strong preyed on the weak, stealing food from the sick, the dead or the distracted prisoners."[4] Resentment grew in the enlisted part of the camp. One master sergeant positioned himself next to the officers' compound each day at mealtimes and wrote down what the officers ate, reporting it to the enlisted men. The officers court-martialed him. The enlisted men became unwilling to follow orders from officers, whom they viewed as purely self-interested. One enlisted prisoner put it this way: "If the Last Supper were held in prison camp, a general would be seated above Jesus, not enough so that people could criticize him for being ostentatious, just enough to let everyone know he was God."[5]

Filth, mud, and black-market dealing ruled Camp 1, and the men continued to die at alarming rates. In October, men from Camp 3, located ten miles away and where the death rate was less than one per month, were transferred to Camp 1. One of the new arrivals was a career marine colonel, Curtis Beecher. He was not the highest-ranking officer at the camp but he was a military professional and others deferred to his obvious competency and natural leadership.

Colonel Beecher began a campaign to "turn a cesspool into a place of survival."[6] He ordered waste trenches dug, put adequate latrine facilities in place, built walkways to keep soldiers out of the mud, and found personnel with expertise to build a functioning waste disposal system. Flies were also targeted. One prisoner recalled:

They lived and bred in the open latrines and small garbage dumps. Fly killing campaigns were introduced and prizes of an egg or a few cigarettes were offered to prisoners killing a hundred flies or more. Eventually, an Engineers officer, Lt. Col. Frederick Saint, by using scrap lumber and salvaged tin, built an experimental septic tank. With its success and the building of these tanks throughout the camp, the fly

15. This drawing, showing prisoners being used as slave laborers by the Japanese, was drawn with a piece of charcoal on the back of a salvaged Japanese ledger page and smuggled out of the camp. Courtesy Montana Museum of Art & Culture Permanent Collection, University of Montana.

population was reduced to the vanishing point. After the septic tanks, what flies there were came from the Japanese side of the camp, where similar sanitary conditions did not exist.[7]

Beecher also ordered that everyone, including officers, must work. As the camp became cleaner, the men were required to start cleaning themselves. Clothing was boiled and sleeping mats were laid in the sun to kill body lice. The men cut their hair and made the effort to wash themselves. By January, the dying among Camp 1 prisoners had stopped. Soon there was more than just not dying; there was living. The men built a baseball diamond and a library. Classes were taught on many subjects.

THE EXPERIENCE IN CAMP 1 ILLUSTRATES HOW EASILY COOPERA-tion can be undermined by the existence of leadership that is not seen as having the group's interests at heart. Groups with no formal leader may function well, as the Andes plane crash survivors, the gold miners, and the Molokai island lepers did, for example. But when a leader is specially authorized, as in the military situation—where the enlisted men and their officers are trained to see themselves as followers and leaders, respectively—the existence of cooperative action seems in part dependent on the nature and quality of the leadership. Self-interested or perhaps just incompetent leadership can lead to a serious breakdown in cooperative action, and disastrous consequences, as in Camp 1 before the arrival of Colonel Beecher.

The selfish officers in the camp might normally have been simply ignored, with the group's deference going to a group-minded person. But a badge of authority can override that normal dynamic. Recall the shift of deference from the selfish Cornelisz to the group-minded Hayes in the case of the *Batavia*, which Cornelisz tried to override by use of force (chapter 5). Although the *Batavia* and the Japanese prison camps were three hundred years and three thousand miles apart, human nature is the same. The soldier Hayes gained influence, while ranking officer Cornelisz had to fight to keep control. Colonel Beecher was not the ranking officer in Camp 1 but he became the camp's de facto leader. Hayes and Beecher were successful because they put the group's interests first, as compared to Cornelisz and the original officers in Camp 1, all of whom put their own interests ahead of the group's. The latter's lack of credibility and legitimacy cost them their authority and cost the group the benefits of cooperative action. Yet the natural inclination toward cooperation was not destroyed during the bad times of selfish leadership. Cooperative instincts lay dormant, only to be quickly resurrected when more credible leadership emerged.

Is this dynamic simply a result of the particular situation in which these groups found themselves? Would different dynamics result if the absent-law situation differed slightly? The vagaries of history give us a compelling natural experiment involving these same people—POWs of the Japanese—but in a different problematic situation, that is, the Hellships.

WHEN THE ALLIES WERE FINALLY ABLE TO FOCUS THEIR RESOURCES on the war in the Pacific, the Japanese lost ground quickly. Back on mainland Japan, labor shortages were hurting the war effort and it was decided that prisoners from the camps would be transported by ship to work as slave laborers on the mainland. The initial transports were mostly of enlisted personnel loaded by the thousands into the holds of freight ships.

Baking in the tropical heat without adequate oxygen, water, food, and sanitation, some men cracked under the strain. One man recalled the first night in the hold:

> As a guy goes crazy he starts to scream—not like a woman, more like a dog. We were locked in a hold together, 500 of us. We're in solid, wall to wall. Tight, so you couldn't put your feet between people when you tried to walk. I don't know how to describe the heat, there was no way we measured temperature. We were practically naked by that time, because we had taken off everything in order to cut down on the heat. It must have been 120 or 125 degrees in that hold. . . . I went back to my group and told them the officers were all gone and would be no help. We were on our own.[8]

An officer on deck shouted down to the men that they must stop the screaming or the Japanese would close the hatch. Closing the hatch, the only source of air, would have meant the suffocation of everyone in the hold, so any men who continued to rant were killed. A small towel was the weapon of convenience. "A guy who had worked in a mental institution in Pennsylvania knew how to do it. If they howled, they died."[9] The hatch was not closed. "Just one man near us questioned what was done. When he was invited to come a little closer to discuss it, he stopped talking and turned his head the other way."[10] Only Americans killed others during the nightmare on the transports.[11] Those who survived put the blame on their absent officers. Had there been leadership, they felt, there might have been other choices.

As more POWs were moved from the camps, more officers, who had used their own status to delay transport, began to be included, and the later transports were mostly of officers. By the time a ship named the *Oryokko Maru* was loaded, the 1,619 men divided into the three holds consisted of over 1,000 officers. Would the different mix of officer-enlisted change the dynamic? Panic set in when the Japanese announced that there would be

16. Drawing of thirteen hundred thirst-crazed American prisoners using only one faucet with a trickle of water while being transported to Japan, 1945. Courtesy *Chicago Daily News*.

no more water. "Men began to attack each other. The *Oryokko Maru* was the ship where the worst, most uncontrollable madness broke out earliest, starting on the very first night and turning to killing by the second night."[12]

By the third day the men baking in Hold 3 were told that their screams were annoying the Japanese; the hatch was closed. Commander Frank Bridget, not the highest-ranking man in the hold, climbed halfway up the ladder and began to talk. Through the force of his voice, he calmed the men: "If each man remains calm and still, it will be better for all. The more you move, the more energy you burn."[13] Once his voice had quelled the immediate panic, he began to organize the men into working for the common good: "Now hear this. The men in the far corners are suffocating. Take off your shirts and fan the air towards them."[14] A survivor described Bridget's confrontation with the Japanese: "Climbing to the top of the stairs, under the very muzzles of Japanese rifles, he practically demands relief for his dying men." After a tense confrontation the hatch was removed, men were allowed up on deck four at a time, and the Japanese again began to provide food. Whenever the situation turned bad, Bridget confronted the Japanese and forced them to take notice of the humans suffering in their hold. The group in Hold 3 worked out a rationing system and a "mental ward" to keep under control those least able to cope with the stress.

An Australian private, Roy Whitecross, talked about his experience on the Hellships, which had similar conditions yet a different reaction to the American experience. The Australian officers, who tended to be professionals, stayed in the holds with their men. They were crushed together as in the other transports.

> Next day we sorted ourselves out, divided the space in the holds equally . . . at night the men slept so that the meager space was used to best advantage. But that way every man had somebody's feet resting on his shoulder, while his feet rested on his neighbors shoulders.[15]

No one died on Whitecross's transport.

On another transport, the *Noto Maru*, 1,035 men were locked in a hold that was a mere 70 feet by 140 feet. Though officers were allowed to be on deck, three chose to stay in the hold with the men. The senior officer of the group, who stayed on deck, upon occasion would come a few steps down the ladder and speak to the men. He always began with "Bear with me, men." The officers in the hold gave the men jobs and imposed discipline. "A big, tough army lieutenant" announced to his fellow prisoners that he was going to beat anyone who caused trouble. His weapon of choice was a bar of soap placed inside a sock. No one died on his transport. Instead of allowing the strong to grab what they wanted, men were rotated through the job of dividing the food.

The disciplinary lieutenant with the improvised club was separated from the group when they arrived in Japan. The loss of the "big-sock-and-soap-man" was keenly felt:

> I regretted losing him and wished he had remained with us; I felt so secure in his strength as a buffer between our captors and me. Men follow a leader; he was one. 'Bear with me' left obscurely, forgotten and unwept.

UNLIKE IN THE PRISON CAMPS, WHERE SOME MEN COULD MANIPU-late the system for their own benefit through bribery or rank, the Hellships, especially the later ships with a high percentage of officers, put the men in an intense closed system with little maneuvering room. The challenge was not the long-term goal of keeping one's health and building up calorie intake, but rather the immediate problem of suffocation, collapsing from the heat, or being trampled to death. Death was not down the street or around the corner; it was palpable. Yet the human dynamics were similar: cooperative action could save the group but it could be undermined by leadership seen as illegitimate or not acting in the group's interest. Nevertheless it could be quickly revived by leadership seen as credible. The prison camps and Hellships illustrate the dynamic at work among officially sanctioned leaders—here military officers—and groups trained to give them deference. Perhaps the dynamic is unique to these special situations and different for nonhierarchical groups?

RECALL THE LEPER COLONY ON MOLOKAI ISLAND (CHAPTER 2). We pick up the story where we left off, in January 1866, when the official supervisor of the colony returned to the settlement. (Recall that the original exiles had worked well together and survived.) The supervisor rode up from the beach to the settlement on horseback, leading eleven new exiles walking behind him.[16] The new people obviously had done nothing to start the crops, collect the firewood, haul the water, or repair the huts, but they required food and shelter. The supervisor simply dropped them off, expecting the original group to take care of them. That original group was hesitant to share the subsistence living they had scratched out and demanded that the supervisor provide the resources needed for the new arrivals. The supervisor refused. When the hungry new arrivals began helping themselves to the food, the two groups came to blows.[17] The supervisor simply turned his horse and rode off.

When he was not off getting new exiles, the supervisor generally kept away from the lepers, both because he feared catching the disease and because he feared their wrath over their miserable conditions. (It probably did not help that he spoke only German and the exiles spoke Hawaiian.) While he was the official authority on the island, he left the lepers to manage their own affairs. Fights erupted over everything, even the possession of a bowl. Factions grew up according to past residency or family ties.

The weaker residents often were denied shelter, instead living in gullies between rocks with palm fronds or tree branches for a roof. If they had shelter, eight might live in a hut twelve feet square.

Soon all manner of civility broke down. One writer describes it as a "great change in their moral and mental organization. . . . So far from aiding and assisting their weaker brethren, the strong took possession of everything, devoured and destroyed large quantities of food on the lands, and altogether refused to replant anything."[18] The strong simply took what they wanted. Eventually criminal activities made their way to the island, including building a liquor still, running gambling operations, and setting up female exiles as prostitutes. Without protection, private property was stolen and good shelter was usurped. Unaccompanied women and children were at greatest risk. "Children were valuable commodities, as servants and sexual objects. Women could be taken for personal use, raped, or sold to another for food or a draw of liquor."[19] When a leper holding a store of food was threatened by exiles armed with clubs, he invited the men to kill him and put an end to his suffering. These people of Molokai, who had been declared legally dead, were now condemned to hell.

When the supervisor did venture into the settlement it was only with a loaded weapon. He soon quit the position but was replaced by a series of equally ineffective supervisors. The residents of the island reported the ghastly conditions to their families back home. One politician wondered, "alas, we dare not think what we might be or do, if we were confirmed a leper, sure to rot daily unto death."[20] Despite the complaints, little was done to provide either more resources or more effective leadership that could bring order.

In May of 1873 Father Damien, a young Catholic priest, entered voluntary exile to join the lepers on Molokai, which at that point numbered 749. Damien decided to visit each person in the settlement once a week, a task that took five days. He undertook a series of modest activities that he hoped in cumulative effect would improve the quality of life. He "played games with the children, and conducted lessons in carpentry. He gave detailed advice, often unwanted, about gardens and crops and the state of an exile's home."[21] Because animals dug up the graves of the newly dead, Damien built a fence around the graveyard. Leprosy tends to clog the throat, so Damien drilled holes in the church floor so people could spit as needed. He constructed coffins and presold them for the cost of the lumber. He soon built up a devoted congregation. When revolt was planned by a group of hungry young lepers (many such revolts had occurred earlier), Damien soothed the trouble by talking to the angry exiles.

As Damien's popularity with the people grew, he gained a degree of immunity and of authority. He was able to do things that others could not have gotten away with. He removed children from those who abused them and moved them to a group home he had established. (Many children were exiled to the island without parents or had become orphans when their parents died.) He also served as local disciplinarian. For those who were "poised to fall astray and possibly founder in drink and vice," he made extra visits and would threaten "terrible punishments, which often produced a good effect."[22] Damien used church funds and money donated to him personally to construct housing. Those who behaved would get good housing; those who misbehaved would not. As Damien made his rounds through the settlement, if he came upon misbehavior, "he entered the spiritual 'battlefield' swinging his cane, breaking cups, smashing gourds and bruising flesh. He made it crystal clear that his love for them was not of the sentimental type."[23]

Under Damien's influence, life on Molokai became safer and more tolerable. Good and bad (and some criminal) supervisors came and went, but the colony was no longer dependent upon them. The officials might have held official governmental authority, but Damien's moral authority became the real source of power on the island and brought an ever-improving cooperative existence. In time, the settlement became a community. (In 1889 Father Damien, who had contracted leprosy, died on the island.)

THESE LATER EVENTS IN THE MOLOKAI LEPER COLONY CONFIRM the now familiar pattern: poor official leadership undermines cooperative action and can be disastrous; cooperation can be resurrected when credible leadership emerges. The failure of leadership is not only in the malicious actions of a Cornelisz or the selfish actions of the original officers in Bataan Camp 1, but also in the failure of action by the person holding official authority.

This second act of the Molokai story also affirms another theme of earlier chapters: the saintly Father Damien understood that one cannot have a cooperative community without rules or without discipline to enforce the rules. Punishment was not the act of barbarity that today's abolitionists make it out to be but an act of love by which Father Damien taught and condemned. Because it was done justly, however, ultimately it created a community.

The leper colony story also illustrates a new point: the kind of leadership that can effectively bring cooperation and survival is not necessarily "leadership" at all. That is, it need not be hierarchal, as with the group pledging allegiance to and informally coronating Hayes leader of the *Batavia* group, or Beecher leader of Camp 1. Father Damien never wanted such a role. Indeed, he took views that were unpopular with many, such as smashing the stills, taking child slaves from their keepers, and ensuring that cooperative people received better resources. He pushed people when they needed to be pushed. While he never sought leadership status, his works earned him sufficient credibility and people deferred to him. That individual deference was enough to promote the cooperative action that the colony needed to succeed.

This is significant in part because it confirms the idea that hierarchical government is not necessary for cooperative action, as Hobbes and others claim (chapter 1). Cooperative action can be a naturally occurring dynamic among human groups without a formal leader. And cooperative action is the way humans are built; it is not a lesson taught by modern institutions. Indeed, one may wonder whether the advent of modern institutions has dulled individuals' instincts toward cooperative action. Modern life commonly organizes people into large institutions in which an individual is not likely to even know most of the other people involved in the same enterprise. One may wonder whether such institutionalization short-circuits the natural cooperative inclinations of humans because it takes them out of the personal groups that seem to trigger the instinct.

These stories of subversion of cooperative action give another reason to perhaps be pessimistic about man's cooperative future. The lepers were lucky that an extraordinary man like Father Damien appeared; he fostered cooperation and brought peace and safety, as was similarly true of Colonel Beecher in the Japanese camps and Weibbe Hayes in the *Batavia*. In each instance, the leader harnessed the group's cooperative inclinations and the group survived. But these stories of subversion might lead one to worry that cooperative action is fragile or that it can be easily subverted. There will not always be a Father Damien or a Colonel Beecher waiting in the wings.

But there is also reason to be optimistic, for the stories illustrate that the cooperative inclination remains intact despite chaotic times, and it will grow whenever it is nurtured. No matter how terrible the past experience—what could be worse than slowly roasting while screaming men around you are being choked to death to keep them quiet?—the human character remains open to cooperative action. Cooperation can be stomped down with brutal enough treatment but it remains like the seed in the crag waiting for fertile ground.

The reader may still have a nagging suspicion that these absent-law stories are each a product of their special circumstances with little reason to draw from them general conclusions about the importance of cooperation and the dynamics of its subversion and resurrection. But history has provided us with yet another useful natural experiment: two ships wreck on the same island at the same time but the groups never learn of one another. The prison camps and Hellships showed us the same men in different situations. This story shows us different men caught in the same situation, where the stories of the two ships play out quite differently and the reasons for that difference are now likely to be quite predictable.

ON MAY 10, 1864, HUMAN ERROR COMPOUNDED BY A FIERCE STORM brought the sailing ship *Invercauld* to a reef off the Auckland Islands, a volcanic archipelago of the New Zealand subantarctic islands lying 290 miles south of the mainland. For several hours the fate of the ship was clear: she would sink. Capt. George Dalgarno and some of the other officers openly wept. They issued orders that could not be followed. Nothing was done to

17. The remains of the wrecked *Invercauld*, 1864. Courtesy Alexander Turnbull Library, National Library of New Zealand, Wellington.

prepare for the coming catastrophe. The *Invercauld* sank during the night. Six died in the following chaos, but mercifully nineteen reached shore.[24]

The captain and his officers survived the wreck but they did nothing to lead the group. The conditions on the island were harsh. The climate was cold and stormy to the degree that the unceasing wind forced trees to grow nearly parallel to the ground. A crude shelter of planks was built. The men ate only water-sodden food that washed up on shore. For five days the majority of the men and all of the officers sat on a narrow beach under a steep cliff. A few men had earlier climbed the cliff and caught and killed a pig. Smelling the cooking pork, the group decided to scale the cliff, abandoning one man who was too weak to follow. After eating, the men wandered off in different directions. When they gathered again it was reported that the ship's cook, who had wandered off with one group, had been left behind when he said he was too tired to move. No one chose to look for him.

Robert Holding, a common seaman, tried to motivate the others to organize but got no support from the officers. When Holding left in search of food, two men agreed to go with him. That evening Holding's partners suggested drawing lots for who would be killed so that the other two could eat him. Fearing where this kind of thinking would lead, Holding escaped during the night. The would-be cannibals were never seen again.

Upon his return, Holding found that the group had done nothing while he was away. He convinced the remaining nine men—all suffering from malnutrition and frostbite—to move to another beach, where he had found an abundant supply of shellfish. When that food ran out Holding left to find more food. By the time he returned three more men were dead. Two of the dead were the shipboys whom the first mate had continued to order about despite their weakened state. Holding came up with several more schemes to organize the group toward survival efforts but with limited success. Each time he would return to the group from an expedition, he would find that more had died in place. Soon only Holding, Captain Dalgarno, and the first mate remained alive, and the other two were wholly dependent on Holding. For a time the two officers insisted that Holding, not being their equal, should not shelter or speak with them, although they continued to eat the food he brought. When Holding made plans to shift to an offshore island that had seals on it, the two officers concluded that they could after all live with Holding. In May of 1865 they were rescued by a passing ship.

THE *GRAFTON* ARRIVED IN THE AUCKLAND ISLANDS ON NEW YEAR'S Day of 1864 (four months or so before the *Invercauld* would wreck there). The ship had five men aboard who were thrilled to find seals, which they planned to kill for profit. The seals were spotted lying on the beach of a large interior bay, but before the ship could navigate out of the bay the wind died and they were trapped until the wind returned. The barometer showed that a storm was coming, so they secured the ship in place. But the hurricane-force storm snapped the anchor cables and it became clear that the ship would be pushed by winds onto the rocky shore and wreck. Using the little time they had, the men planned their survival. Alick Maclaren, a

Norwegian who was the only one who could swim, swam a line from the ship to the shore. The men loaded equipment and supplies onto a small boat and guided it through the rocky surf onto the beach. Capt. Thomas Musgrave tied the grievously ill first mate, Francois Raynal, to his back and, hanging from the rope, tried to make the crossing to shore. The combined weight was too great, and both men started to go under. Maclaren swam to the rescue. Within minutes of landing the castaways set up a tent using sailcloth. They started a fire, prepared a hot meal of food salvaged from the ship, and drank tea while their clothing dried.

In the morning Raynal, who was too sick to walk more than a few feet, began to instruct his fellow survivors in the construction of a hut. In short order the men had a fine weatherproof shelter complete with a stone chimney built with cement made from seashells. When tension arose about the captain being in charge, given that they were no longer seamen, it was agreed that they would adopt their own set of rules and manage themselves as a group. A journal entry explained, "It was evident that we had no strength except in union, that discord and division must be our ruin. Yet man is so feeble that reason, and self-respect, and even considerations of self-interest, do not always suffice to keep him in the path of duty."[25] The rules were recorded on paper and each Sunday they were pulled out and read aloud.

During the day the men worked to acquire food and fuel. At night they took turns teaching lessons in English, Portuguese, Norwegian, French, and mathematics. Raynal relates:

> From that evening we were alternately the masters and pupils of one another. These new relations still further united us; by alternately raising and lowering us one above the other, they really kept us on a level, and created a perfect equality amongst us.[26]

In time they built a forge. Using the forge to make metal parts, they built a boat. Using the boat, the men eventually rescued themselves, sailing across 250 miles of open ocean through a raging hurricane to New Zealand. It took nearly two years but all the men of the *Grafton* arrived to safety in good health.

18. 1863 drawing of Francois Raynal, too ill to save himself, tied to his captain's back. As their combined weight began to pull them under, seaman Alick Maclaren jumped in to rescue both men. Courtesy Alexander Turnbull Library, National Library of New Zealand, Wellington.

THE MEN OF THE *GRAFTON* AND THE MEN OF THE *INVERCAULD* were stranded on the same island during the same period under the same conditions, yet only three of the *Invercauld*'s twenty-five survived to be rescued by a passing ship while all of the *Grafton*'s crew survived, in good enough style to rescue themselves. Clearly, group dynamics that promote cooperative action win the day, but those dynamics can be undercut by malicious, incompetent, ineffective, or indifferent leadership.

BEYOND A CATALOGUE OF THE WAYS IN WHICH POOR LEADER-ship can subvert cooperative action, the cases in this chapter illustrate several other points, such as the importance of cooperative action. In dangerous circumstances cooperative action can mean the difference between life and death. Indeed, the dynamics of cooperation turn out to be more important than the dangerousness of the conditions.

In 1789 nine mutineers from the *Bounty* made it to Pitcairn Island with the twelve women and six Polynesian men whom they had kidnapped.

There was tension and conflict among the men, especially over the women, and after two years on the island the men began killing one another, sometimes with help of the women. When only one man remained alive, peace returned.

Compare the outcome of the Pitcairn mutineers to the outcome of the crash survivors in the Andes (chapter 2). Pitcairn has a pleasant tropical climate with all the resources the group needed to survive, but internal strife led the group to near destruction. The frozen Andes offered nothing but danger and death, yet through cooperative action all who survived the crash and the avalanche came home safely. The difficulty of the circumstances is obviously important, but not as important as the dynamics of cooperation.

Indeed, one might argue that difficult circumstances can increase rather than undermine cooperation. The absent-law cases suggest that one factor that can help insulate a group from cooperation-subverting forces is the demand of a common goal. The gold miners simply could not mine without group cooperation because they could not leave their goods unattended unless they had some enforceable rules to protect them from theft. The challenging task demanded of a pirate crew—to take a prize ship—or that facing a wagon train—to cross a dangerous continent—could not have been achieved without cooperative action. The common mission is sometimes simply to stay alive, as with the Eskimos, the POWs held by the Japanese, the Maroons, and the wreck survivors, all of whom had to deal with life-threatening conditions.

Other things being equal, the more difficult the conditions, the more likely the cooperation.[27] Desperation breeds cooperation. It takes some special twist, like an unsuitable leader placed in a position of authority by an outside force—the special circumstances common to most of the stories in this chapter—to have group cooperation derailed in tough circumstances. This raises the interesting issue of the role of government in fostering cooperative action. "Government" in these stories is commonly the "outside force" putting a bad leader in place: the bad officers in the prison camps, the bad supervisors for the lepers, and the bad officers of the *Invercauld*. Does government then help or hurt cooperative action?

Certainly government allows the creation of the complex institutions that are the most dramatic examples of cooperative human action across countries and around the world. But has our increased reliance upon government to provide cooperative action through complex institutional-legal constructs diminished our capacity to cooperate within face-to-face human groups? When government takes responsibility for providing cooperative action it is easy to see how we individual humans might at least get out of practice. It is not a habit that we have developed and refined, as early humans must have done. One might wonder whether, within the cocoon of government oversight, the human inclination for cooperative action has atrophied. Perhaps humans have lost touch with that instinct as they became "civilized" into governmental control.[28]

The absent-law experiences reported here suggest otherwise. Most of these are stories of modern humans who have grown up with government yet clearly not lost their cooperative inclination, at least were able to bring it to bear when it is needed. We may not use it nearly as much as early humans once did, but the proclivity for cooperation lies within us and is waiting to be called into action.

The comparative safety that our modern existence gives us may mean that cooperative action is less likely to be called upon. The ironic corollary to the rule that "desperation breeds cooperation" is that "contentment breeds insulation." The more comfortable our existence, the less inclined we may be to see ourselves as dependent on others. It is the comparative safety of our modern existence, perhaps, that makes more likely the chaotic Florida T-ball brawl or the Florida preschool graduation melee.

Hobbes and others claim that government and law are essential to social order. But one may sometimes see less cooperation in the context of a law-present instead of a law-absent situation. The existence of a legal system can provide a level of complacency, contentment, and independence that may seem to dim the human practice of personal sacrifice in support of cooperative action. This development is not a bad thing in itself. It shows the success of government and law in making our lives better. But it may have implications for what we should expect of people and how we should formulate governmental law to get the best from people rather than the worst.

Certainly one lesson from the absent-law cases is that credible leadership will earn deference, support, assistance, and acquiescence; the members will make its goals their own. Leadership seen as misguided or as promoting goals that are inconsistent with what members see as their own, will prompt only resistance and subversion. This turns out to be a foundational lesson for anyone constructing a criminal justice system—the institution by which modern governments seek to control, on the most basic level, the interactions among their members. Like the authorities in the absent-law situations, a criminal law seen as conflicting with the community's sense of justice prompts only resistance and subversion. Only law that earns credibility within the community it governs can inspire deference and compliance.

PART TWO

MODERN LESSONS

CHAPTER EIGHT

CREDIBILITY

America's Prohibition

THE ABSENT-LAW CASES DISCUSSED EARLIER TELL US SOMETHING about how human groups behave when left to their own devices beyond the influence of government or law. Do these insights into human nature say anything about the proper formulation of governmental law today? The human situation is dramatically different today from what it was on the Serengeti Plain. But while our situation has changed, the basics about human nature have not. The predispositions we have inherited through 125,000 generations are still with us, and many of them are at work in modern absent-law cases. Do those predispositions suggest anything about formulating law for our modern world?

We might be tempted to respect the fact that long-term evolutionary processes have given us our present instincts. We have them for a reason. Human success has been in large part a product of the benefits of cooperative action fostered by the human inclination to do justice and avoid injustice. Do those inclinations hold a similar key to our future success? Should we cultivate or abandon our shared intuitions about doing justice and avoiding injustice?

Today's accepted crime control theories tell us we would be wise to abandon them. A system's reputation for justness—for doing justice and avoiding injustice—may have moral and even political implications but it has little or nothing to do with effective crime control. How could it? Potential criminals are moved by the opportunity to offend and by the danger of being punished, not by a system's reputation for being just. The addict contemplating a theft to buy drugs, the young man determined to rape his date, or the corrupt politician seeking to enrich himself with graft all want what they want. The criminal justice system's reputation for justness has little or no effect on the choice they make, right?

"I AM THE SWORN, ETERNAL AND UNCOMPROMISING ENEMY OF the Liquor Traffic. I have been, and will go on, fighting that damnable, dirty, rotten business with all the power at my command."[1] So preached Billy Sunday, a professional-baseball-player-turned-evangelist preacher at the end of the nineteenth century. Living in YMCAs all over the country while he played ball, Sunday had seen the way alcohol ruined many men. His anti-alcohol message began as a movement among rural women who sought to protect their families and obey their religious beliefs. Billy Sunday adopted their message and his populist style convinced many to leave drink behind and become workers for the cause.[2]

Sunday's efforts spurred big money to invest in a campaign for national prohibition. Sunday originally preached in Detroit, where powerful industrialists understood how alcohol abuse hurt their workers and their businesses. Many of Detroit's powerful businessmen, including Henry Ford, contributed to the movement. Dime-store king S. S. Kresge offered Sunday his palatial home to use as a headquarters. Automaker Henry M. Leland gave Sunday an $8,000 Cadillac as a "personal thanks offering." With their help, Sunday's charismatic preaching reached audiences all over the nation. He preached that "whiskey and beer are all right in their place, but their place is in hell."[3] He promised America that the removal of alcohol from America would cause the Devil to hang vacancy signs in hell and slums to fade into memory.

Sunday was passionate and persuasive, but it was Wayne Wheeler who brought the Anti-Saloon League (ASL) into play as a national political force. The head of the Ohio ASL hired Wheeler to organize political support for Prohibition. Under Wheeler, politicians who supported the ASL's "dry" initiatives received active support, but the ASL also worked tirelessly against any politician who opposed Prohibition. Wheeler made the case simple for voters: if a candidate did not support Prohibition, he was in favor of wife beating, prostitution, and sin. As a result, prominent politicians all over Ohio fell to Wheeler's single-issue campaign, and by 1908, 85 percent of Ohio was legally dry.[4]

As the United States edged closer to World War I, Sunday and Wheeler brought a new weapon into the fight against alcohol sales: anti-German hatred. While Sunday preached "I tell you it is [Kaiser] Bill against Woodrow, Germany against America, Hell against Heaven," Wheeler gave voters an easy voting reminder: Germans manufactured and drank beer. Money earned at German-owned factories bought the bullets used to kill American soldiers. Grain and other raw materials used to distill liquor was food otherwise taken from the mouths of American soldiers. Prohibition became patriotic. With the goal of saving women and children from drunk husbands and saving those husbands from damnation in eternal hell, all the while defeating Germany in the process, the national movement for Prohibition was unstoppable and culminated in the Eighteenth Amendment. In the process, Wheeler won a congressional seat.

Former president Howard Taft cautioned the nation that the law was against the "views and practices of a majority of people" and "the business of manufacturing alcohol, liquor and beer will go out of the hands of the law-abiding members of the community and will be transferred to the quasi-criminal class."[5] Woodrow Wilson, the sitting president, vetoed the Volstead Act, which was passed to enforce the Eighteenth Amendment, because he believed the government should not regulate private behavior, but his veto was overridden by a congress too afraid of being branded as pro-German or pro-sin.

The Eighteenth Amendment to the Constitution became law on October 28, 1919. At the stroke of midnight on January 17, 1920, the Volstead Act went into effect. Celebrations were held all over the country, but within an hour after the law had passed, while Billy Sunday stood preaching that prisons would now have to close for lack of inmates, armed men stole $100,000 worth of "medicinal" whiskey. Under the Volstead Act, a person could legally possess and consume liquor at home but manufacturing and selling liquor were prohibited. The Volstead Act carried very little enforcement weight, however; the reformers felt the law's prohibition itself would be sufficient to change behavior.

Lax enforcement of the law quickly gave way to corruption. What good did it do to arrest a bootlegger who was making $10,000 per month when he would simply pay a $100 fine and go back to work? Federal Prohibition agents were exempt from civil service requirements, so politicians awarded thousands of the positions as patronage jobs. Agents came and went quickly, with many caught in corrupt schemes. Because Prohibition agents who accepted bribes lived richer and safer lives, fighting corruption became a difficult battle.

The Volstead Act forced people to treat as a federal crime what they saw as ordinary, even desirable behavior: giving a champagne toast at a wedding or sharing a drink with friends. To most Americans the passage of legislation still did not make such appealing conduct condemnable. People began making their own brews from standard ingredients and some even created exotic new concoctions that included nitrous acid, peaches, or cactus plants. Stores hired lovely ladies to caution that "raisin cakes," a new product coming out of California vineyards, would turn into wine if one were to, by chance, be placed with water and yeast into a jug for twenty-one days. The new raisin cakes sold so well that several vineyards previously facing bankruptcy became successful.

While some people produced liquor for home consumption only, others brewed moonshine for profit. New local brands quickly became available, such as Yak-Yak Gin, Sugar Moon, or Old Stingo. The newly established black market for liquor also increased distribution of highly potent and sometimes toxic liquors. Of the 480,000 gallons of seized liquor analyzed in New York in 1927, 98 percent contained poisons of one kind or another. When denatured industrial alcohol was not sufficiently diluted or was consumed in large quantities, the result was paralysis, blindness, and often death. In 1927 almost twelve thousand deaths were attributed to alcohol poisoning, many of these among the urban poor who could not afford the imported illegal liquors. In 1930, U.S. public health officials estimated that fifteen thousand people suffered from "jake foot," a debilitating paralysis of the hands and feet caused by drinking denatured alcohol flavored with

19. New York City deputy police commissioner John A. Leach (*right*) watches as agents pour liquor into a sewer following a raid at the height of Prohibition, 1921. Prints and Photographs Division, Library of Congress, LC-USZ62-12357.

gingerroot. People who suffered from such maladies had no legal recourse, so the distribution of the poison went unchecked.

Long-standing, legitimate alcohol-related businesses that had earned good reputations could no longer operate and no longer paid taxes. In contrast, illegal speakeasies did not hesitate to serve minors or encourage prostitution and they certainly did not pay taxes. Some established bars, whose clientele included police and politicians, never bothered to acknowledge Prohibition and continued to do business as usual. Other establishments worked out payment schedules with local precincts and the police split the payments among themselves.

Harry Daugherty, U.S. attorney general under Warren Harding (a president who publicly drank while in office), made untold millions through his efforts to aid and abet bootleggers. One scheme took advantage of two of the Volstead Act's "loopholes." Selling liquor in drugstores to those who had prescriptions was legal. Also, millions of gallons of legally produced liquor were trapped in warehouses, unable to be withdrawn and sold. Congress had not established provisions to compensate the owners of that whiskey so the people who owned the liquor faced financial ruin. But Attorney General Daugherty was willing to sell the right to withdraw the warehouse liquor for use, on paper, as medicinal liquor.

George Remus had been a criminal lawyer who defended bootleggers in the early days of Prohibition. Seeing his clients, most of whom were fairly ordinary men, profit so greatly led him to conclude that he could run a better bootlegging operation himself. Remus arranged with Daugherty to buy withdrawal rights. After all, the Remus people said, "What was wrong with that? If anything was wrong it was wrong for the Government to destroy the value of [the owner's] property without compensating them for it. If the Government wanted to abolish whiskey drinking, why didn't it buy all this whiskey and dump it into the river?"[6] Remus bought hundreds of drugstores, then for an initial payment of $300,000, plus an additional $42,000 per certificate and about $2.00 per case, he was able to withdraw and resell the liquor using his stores. He also bought many famous distilleries, including Fleischmann, Jack Daniels, and Old Lexington Club, so he could control both the liquor stored within and the right to remove that liquor. Remus was careful to select the right kinds of business partners. As part of the deal to buy the Jack Daniels Distillery his syndicate included a congressman and the St. Louis director of the Internal Revenue Service. Remus took in $40,000,000 a year when his operation was in full swing, half of which went to buying protection from prosecution in one form or another.

On one occasion two Prohibition agents got lost on their way to an assignment and mistakenly arrived at one of Remus's storage facilities. They thought they had made the most spectacular catch of their careers but the man in charge of the facility made a phone call. After talking with their supervisor, the agents apologized, stayed to get drunk, and were driven back to town by Remus's people. On another occasion, when an extended gun battle occurred at the front gate of the facility between Remus's people and some would-be hijackers, several of the hijackers were killed but no police ever arrived. Remus was just one of Attorney General Daugherty's many bootleggers. Daugherty had many to protect. When a Philadelphia prosecutor decided to pursue a case against the local Prohibition director, Daugherty had the prosecutor fired.

The 1921 American Bar Association annual conference was held in Cincinnati, where the entire police force received payments from Remus. Harry Daugherty gave the keynote speech, reminding everyone that enforcement of national Prohibition was essential to national security. "Our safety and happiness lie in obedience to law by every man, woman and child."[7]

So much money was to be made in bootlegging and drinking seemed so harmless that many people thought it foolish to obey the law. For fishermen in Maine, for instance, a single smuggling run would pay more than a year of what fishing could bring in. It was easy to tell who had succumbed to the temptation if a fisherman's family had food all winter long without running up a bill at the local grocery and or if he could buy a new boat and new shoes for each family member. Sea shanties even came to include Prohibition lyrics:

Oh we don't give a damn
For our old Uncle Sam
Way, oh, whiskey and gin!
Lend us a hand
When we stand in to land,
Just give us time
To run the rum in![8]

Foreign governments, including Canada and England, made millions in revenue through hefty export taxes on illegal liquor shipments to the United States. When the American government asked the British to stop selling to bootleggers, the British refused: giving up the practice meant the operations would simply move elsewhere. During Prohibition, French champagne imports into Canada increased by more than 1,000 percent. These large-scale operations were possible because the illegal liquor trade had encouraged the growth of a much more organized sort of crime: criminal syndicates.

Small-time bootleggers merged or were muscled out. Al Capone was one of the good organizers and soon ran most of the trade in Chicago, having bought the mayor he wanted. William Hale Thompson, called "Big Bill," openly campaigned that he would flaunt the laws of Prohibition. He claimed, "I'm wetter than the middle of the Atlantic Ocean." Capone and his associates contributed more than $300,000 to Thompson's election fund. On voting day Capone's men—and their guns—were out in force so that all voters would understand his preference. Thompson served three terms as Chicago's mayor and the level of lawlessness skyrocketed.

After being elected to his third term, Thompson tried to reduce his dependence on Capone. He even backed a group of independent racketeers over Capone in a dispute over shares of illegal gaming proceeds. As a result, the homes of four of Thompson's associates were bombed. The 1928 Chicago primary became known as the Pineapple Primary, so named because of the hand grenades used to disrupt voters and intimidate candidates.[9] By April of 1928 sixty-one "pineapples" had been used against various Republican candidates. Thompson himself began to fear for his life. The police could not be trusted—the criminals were bribing the police—and the criminals were throwing bombs. Capone was firmly in charge.

After the bombings, the federal government began pursuing enforcement of Prohibition in Chicago with slightly more vigor. Thompson was none too keen on the perceived trespass by the federal agents, however. When a federal agent shot a municipal court bailiff who drew a gun on federal agents during one raid, the Chicago police demanded that the federal agent be released to them and they organized to storm the federal building to get him. There was no shoot-out, but Thompson did not back down either. He said:

> I will do all in my power to save Chicago citizens from any more suffering at the hands of the thugs and gunmen sent here by the Federal Government to further Deneen's [a United States Senator] political influence. Deneen is filling this town with dry agents from Washington, who run around like a lot of cowboys with revolvers and shotguns. Our

opponents would have us believe we don't know how to run our town. Vote for the flag, the constitution, your freedom, your property, as Abraham Lincoln and William Hale Thompson would have you do.[10]

Thompson also noted that warrants had been issued to "throw every dry agent in jail."[11] When federal agents later raided Capone's hotel room and confiscated his account ledgers, which listed thousands of names and payments, the local police got hold of the books and returned them to Capone.

In the Chicago suburb of Cicero, Capone had been promised free run of the city if he would arrange for a particular candidate to win. The mobsters kidnapped precinct workers, used hand grenades to intimidate citizens, stole ballots, and killed people on the day of the election. Capone's candidate won and the local court upheld the results.

While the thriving liquor businesses of the mobsters and corrupt politicians were often ignored, prosecutions of individual citizens went forward. A Michigan mother of ten got a life sentence for possession of a pint of gin. Inequitable and overzealous enforcement was reported by the press and eventually brought public anger over corruption issues. As public opinion turned, a movement arose attacking the government for its Prohibition efforts on many fronts. Much of the public came to see government malice in everything it did. For example, the government's practice had been to require that alcohol produced for industrial use be chemically denatured to make it poisonous if consumed. But if people were going to drink it anyway, it was argued, wasn't the government responsible for the resulting deaths? Wasn't it the government that was killing these people?

After ten years of Prohibition it became clear that the Anti-Saloon League's promise of empty prisons was pure folly. Crime had skyrocketed and the prison population was at an all-time high. Even with only casual enforcement, five hundred thousand people had been sent to prison for Volstead violations, and even non-alcohol-related crimes had skyrocketed. Meanwhile, uncontrolled alcohol was dangerous and expensive, creating even greater problems for families, and alcohol enforcement cost millions of dollars. Government tax revenues from alcohol sales had completely stopped, and Americans began to view government as hopelessly corrupt. These had not been the promises of the "Drys."

WHY DID THE NOBLE EXPERIMENT GO SO BADLY WRONG? THERE is little dispute that Prohibition not only did not stop the consumption of alcohol but in fact ultimately may have increased long-term consumption. Alcohol consumption initially dropped when Prohibition first took effect, likely the result of increased prices due to constricted supply rather than the result of a choice by people because they saw consumption as wrong or because they respected the law.[12] Instead of resulting in mainstream compliance or changing community norms, Prohibition led to "widespread public disenchantment" with the law and the criminal justice system more generally.[13]

Prohibition increased lawbreaking, even in areas unrelated to alcohol consumption. Violent crime increased every year from 1920 to the repeal of Prohibition.[14] Per capita homicide rates drastically increased as well, even when alcohol consumption was unchanged or decreasing in an area or when non-alcohol-related homicides increased.[15] A study of homicide rates in Chicago during Prohibition suggests that while the total homicide rate increased by 21 percent from 1920 through 1930, the rate of alcohol-related homicides remained unchanged.[16] In other words, the increase in homicides was due solely to an increase in non-alcohol-related killings. The researchers suggest that the rise in homicide was the result of "a general shift in the tolerance and opportunities for violence."[17] Prohibition created a culture of violence and lawlessness that was beyond the reach of the legal system.

The majority of Americans disagreed with the nationwide ban on alcohol sales. That disagreement contributed to a more generalized disillusionment with the criminal law and left people to start second-guessing its many other parts. As one writer put it, a "general tolerance of the bootlegger and a disrespect for federal law were translated into a widespread contempt for the processes and duties of democracy."[18] A federal government commission noted, "It is therefore a serious impairment of the legal order to have a national law upon the books theoretically governing the whole land . . . which public opinion in many important centers will not enforce."[19] Here is how the famous pool wizard Minnesota Fats recalled the period in his autobiography:

Back in the '20s, every living human was making what they call "whoopee" from morning to night. Whoopee meant a lot of different things in those days but mostly it meant doing exactly what the generals said you weren't supposed to do. . . . The big proposition was the Volstead Act, which said any sucker found belting the booze was a public enemy. So what happened was all the suckers wanted to be public enemies. They guzzled the bathtub gin like it was lemonade and cut up in those all-night speakeasy joints until the sun came up, even though that kind of action was against the law. The trouble was those generals never took human nature into consideration when they cranked out that kind of con. . . . That's exactly how it was in the '20s. People went crazy doing ridiculous things they never would have dreamed of doing if the generals in Washington hadn't put a contraband on the refreshments. . . . They knew it was against the law to drink, but everywhere they went they saw people guzzling the juice and when they got home at night, there was the old man sneaking in a couple more pints. Junior knew the old man wasn't obeying the law, so when papa told junior the pool room was out of bounds, the kid almost broke a leg getting there.[20]

THE DETRIMENTAL EFFECT OF A CRIMINAL LAW LACKING CREDIBILITY with the community it governs, so apparent during Prohibition, is affirmed in social psychology research studies. The studies show that people obey the law in large part because they see it as a moral authority to which they should defer. A criminal law that proves unreliable in assessing deserved criminal liability and punishment is a criminal law that loses this deference and is more likely to provoke resistance and subversion. And, the studies show, the system's credibility suffers even when the law's deviations from desert fall short of Prohibition's extremes. Any regular and intentional deviation appears to incrementally undermine the system's credibility and to produce corrosive effects.

In one study, for example, participants read accounts of real cases in which the criminal law, in pursuit of some goal other than doing justice, imposed what people saw as either too much or too little punishment. The cases of too much punishment included several "three-strikes" cases (in which, for example, the offender was given a life sentence for writing a $100 bad check because he had a prior criminal record), several cases in which a reasonable mistake of fact or law was denied as a defense, and a case in which an essentially regulatory violation was treated as a criminal offense—all real cases that are becoming increasingly common in modern American criminal justice. Also included were cases where, in the subjects' view, too little punishment was imposed, including a case of diplomatic immunity and a case of failing to help or notify authorities that a stranger needed medical care.[21] The study found that just learning about these injustices and failures of justice significantly disillusioned subjects and led them to believe that the criminal justice system was indifferent to the importance of just punishment.

The effects of such disillusionment are striking. In a further study, subjects were first tested to determine their views on a variety of issues related to whether they would defer to the demands of the criminal law or instead help investigators, report an offense, take criminalization to mean that the conduct really was morally condemnable, and so on. The subjects were then told of a variety of real cases in which the criminal justice system had done injustice or failed to do justice, not by accident but as the result of the liability rules formally adopted with the knowledge that they would produce such results, including the cases described above. This information had the expected disillusioning effect on the subjects and, when they were tested again, their views on their willingness to defer to the law in these various ways had all weakened.

This is actually a quite surprising result, if you think about it. When adult subjects are tested in a study like this they come to the laboratory with an already-formed opinion about the moral reliability of the criminal justice system. A researcher can do a limited amount in the lab to shift that preexisting view. But despite the fact that subjects' views can be only incrementally nudged, the study found a corresponding incremental shift in the willingness of subjects to defer to the criminal justice system. In other words, it is not just extreme situations such as Prohibition that will produce disillusionment and lead to reduce crime-control effectiveness. Any legal rule or practice that predictably produces injustice or failures of justice can incrementally undermine the system's moral credibility and its crime-control effectiveness.

A follow-up study used a slightly different methodology. Instead of asking the same subjects their views after being "disillusioned," the researchers used separate groups to determine their results: they mildly disillusioned some subjects, more seriously disillusioned other subjects, and did not disillusion a third group, then asked all the subjects the same questions to test their willingness to defer and comply. The study found again that the extent of the disillusionment determined the extent to which the subjects would defer to the criminal justice system.

Why should this be so? Why should an incremental decrease in credibility produce an incremental decrease in deference, even in a criminal justice system like that of the United States, which is generally well regarded or at least not so disparaged as that under Prohibition? Part of the explanation lies in the potentially enormous power of social influence and internalized norms.

A criminal law with moral credibility can, for example, harness the power of stigmatization. Many people will avoid breaking the law if doing so will stigmatize them and thereby endanger their personal and social relationships. Without moral credibility a system forfeits its power to stigmatize because it is no longer seen as a reliable moral authority.

A system with moral credibility also can help avoid vigilantism. The San Francisco Vigilance Committee (discussed in chapter 4), for example, showed that people will take the law into their own hands if they see a criminal justice system as regularly unable or unwilling to do justice. A system that has earned credibility can short-circuit that temptation toward vigilantism.

A loss of credibility also can provoke active resistance to and subversion of the system, as seen during Prohibition. Such resistance and subversion is evident in how people deal with the system: Do victims report offenses? Do potential witnesses come forward to help police and investigators? Do prosecutors and judges follow the legal rules, or do they feel free to make up their own? Do trial jurors follow jury instructions or do they substitute their own judgment of what they think the law should be? Do offenders acquiesce in their liability and punishment, or do they instead focus on the injustice they think is being done to them? Perhaps the most powerful force that comes from a morally credible criminal justice system is its power to shape societal norms and cause people to internalize those norms. If the criminal law has earned a reputation for doing justice, then when the law criminalizes a new form of conduct or determines that a conduct is a more serious offense, the community concludes that the conduct is in fact more condemnable. This dynamic can be seen at work in areas such as drunk driving, spouse abuse, and date rape.

A criminal law can maximize its moral credibility within the community it governs by committing itself to, above all else, doing justice and avoiding injustice—resulting in criminal liability and punishment that tracks with the community's shared judgments of justice and nothing more and nothing less (this has been termed "empirical desert," that is, what social science research shows to be the shared judgments of laypersons in a community).

Part of the attraction of this approach for assessing liability and punishment is that it continues to provide the opportunity to deter and to incapacitate or control offenders who might commit another crime in the future. In fact, the only way to obtain greater deterrence or incapacitation than is inherent in a just sentence is to give an offender more punishment than he deserves—but that is to do injustice. In such cases of injustice, the participants in the criminal justice system are most likely to subvert the rules in order to avoid the injustice. Even if the system is successful in implementing the unjust punishment, whatever crime-control benefit gained by doing so can be washed out by the crime-control costs of the resulting loss in credibility.

One could summarize the conclusions of the empirical studies in this way: legal rules that deviate from a community's notion of justice are not cost free, as many scholars and policymakers have generally assumed. Rather, when criminal law enforcement adopts rules or practices that produce criminal liability or punishment that is seen as unjust or as a failure of justice, the system suffers a loss in crime-control effectiveness. To be most effective the criminal justice system must do justice in accord with the shared judgments of justice held by the community being governed. In that way it can build moral credibility and harness the substantial power of social and normative influence.

THE DAMAGING LOSS OF CREDIBILITY AT WORK DURING PROHIBI-tion resulted from more than just punishing people for alcohol use that was not deserved or from failing to punish the corruption and criminals who did deserve it. The loss in credibility also was a product of an important signaling mechanism that seemed to reaffirm people's view that the criminal law might not merit their respect: each person saw many other people openly displaying their own disrespect for the law by openly disobeying it. Whatever loss of credibility might arise from the person's own perceptions justice failures, that disillusioning conclusion was affirmed and probably amplified by the realization that so many others felt the same way, as reflected in the popularity of lawbreaking: if others so disrespect the law as to violate it regularly, why does the law merit my deference?

This same signaling dynamic is the basis of some modern policing theories, such as the "broken windows" theory. The crime rate depends in part on how much respect people have for the law, which is based in part on how much respect they see others showing the law. According to the broken windows theory, when a community displays signs of disorder, such as litter, graffiti, or broken windows in vacant buildings, the people in that community engage in more acts of vandalism and crime because they view such acts as commonplace and more acceptable.[22] The corollary to this observation is that one can reduce the overall amount of crime in an area by eradicating signs of disorder and disobedience.

The hypothesis has been tested and confirmed in many studies. In one experiment, an envelope containing visible cash was placed in a mailbox so that anyone who walked by would see the money.[23] The mailbox was clean and located in an area free from litter. A mailbox in another location with otherwise similar conditions contained money but was covered in graffiti. A third mailbox in another location was surrounded by litter.

Only 13 percent of passersby stole the money from the clean and litter-free mailbox, while 27 percent stole the money from the mailbox covered in graffiti and 25 percent stole the money from the mailbox surrounded by litter. These results suggest that when signals of disorder such as graffiti or litter are present, people find it easier to ignore laws and underlying social norms. The disorder signals that others have violated the rules, making it more acceptable for the person to do so as well—which in turn increases the signals of disobedience. It all spirals toward greater lawlessness.

Such results also can be seen in studies of real-world crime policies. For instance, researchers examined the efforts of the New York Police Department to reduce violent crime by aggressively enforcing misdemeanor offenses such as public intoxication, prostitution, and vandalism.[24] Results showed that increased misdemeanor arrests significantly reduced the overall instances of more serious crimes, including robbery, auto theft, and grand larceny, which lends support to the theory underlying the broken windows approach: focusing on less serious crimes—the "signals" of disorder and disobedience—can reduce the prevalence of more serious crimes.

In another real-world study thirty-four crime-ridden areas of Lowell, Massachusetts, were selected for an experiment.[25] In half of the areas the police department cleared the area of trash, fixed streetlights, increased the number of misdemeanor arrests, and strictly enforced building codes. In the other areas the police did not change anything. The areas that received the special measures experienced a 20 percent decrease in calls to the police.[26] Furthermore, signs of social and physical disorder and disobedience also decreased. For instance, the number of loiterers decreased by 72 percent, the number of public drinkers decreased by 73 percent, the number of drug sellers decreased by 62 percent, the number of unrepaired buildings dropped by 63 percent, and the number of structures defiled by graffiti decreased by 23 percent.[27]

When people see evidence in their neighborhoods that others are disrespecting the law—be it by graffiti, vandalism, drug selling, or prostitution on the street—the fabric of social norms is altered and they come to view disorder and crime as more acceptable, and then they act in ways that contribute additional signals of disrespect. When signals of lawbreaking are eliminated, the downward spiral is short-circuited.

The larger point is that it is not just the system's rules that can undermine credibility but also the system's enforcement practices. They can either serve to reinforce the law's reputation as a reliable and effective moral authority or they can signal disrespect for the criminal law. (It should be noted that other aspects of enforcement practices, such as perceived professionalism and fairness of police in dealing with citizens, also contribute to the criminal justice system's reputation and thereby the deference that it is paid. Abusive or corrupt police may destroy credibility as do unjust laws and ineffective enforcement.) The relationship between a system's credibility with the community—the respect it has earned and the deference it is paid—works in both directions. Just as reduced credibility can reduce crime-control effectiveness, as occurred during Prohibition, an increase in credibility can increase deference and compliance.

AFTER WORLD WAR II A DEFEATED GERMANY WAS DIVIDED INTO four zones, with each zone to be temporarily occupied by a different Allied power. Berlin, the capital, was itself divided into four sectors. East Germany was occupied by the Soviet Union, including the eastern half of Berlin. The other three zones were occupied by the United States, France, and Great Britain. In 1949 the three Western zones were combined to form the Federal Republic of Germany, commonly known as West Germany. The German Democratic Republic, or East Germany, was established in 1949, thereby creating a Soviet satellite state under the Socialist Unity Party, which was fiercely loyal to Stalin.[28]

Many people in East Germany viewed the Soviet-imposed government as illegitimate, and 2.7 million East Germans expressed their frustration by risking their lives to flee to West Germany in the 1950s. In response, the government erected barriers—most notably, the Berlin Wall—to prevent people from fleeing, and threatened imprisonment or death to those who tried. For those who remained in East Germany, life was difficult, both economically and politically. Under the centrally planned economy, private ownership was essentially abolished. East Germany also had to pay enormous war reparations to the USSR. The Soviet army dismantled and carted away much of East Germany's infrastructure and industrial plants, extracting approximately $10 billion worth of industrial and agricultural goods by the early 1950s.

East German culture was strongly influenced by Soviet-style communism, which was characterized by meager food rations, hard labor, and fear of the military police. The East German Ministry of State Security, also known as the Stasi, was one of the most repressive intelligence and secret police agencies the world has ever known. The Stasi controlled East Germany starting in 1950 and by 1989 it had infiltrated nearly every aspect of East German life. The agency officially employed over 125,000 people and had another 100,000 informants. It became impossible for people to trust anyone because the Stasi had 1 informant for every 6.5 East German citizens. The Stasi's internal slogan was "We are everywhere."[29]

The Stasi kept records on a fourth of all East German citizens, and even on citizens of other countries. For example, Frederic Pryor was a student at Yale University who was living in West Berlin while writing his dissertation on foreign trade in the Soviet Union. Because of his work he spent six months in a Stasi prison for supposed espionage. After German reunification Pryor got access to his Stasi file, which contained five thousand pages of detailed information on his life and work.

The reputation of the criminal justice system with the community was at this point very poor, understandably. Hans-Joachim Jentch, the justice minister for the East German state of Thuringia after reunification, later explained: "It's a big job to reinstill respect for the law. For decades there was no real justice here, and people lost respect."[30]

Frustrated by political oppression and spurred by the weakening economy in the Soviet Bloc, members of the Eastern Bloc began insisting on reform. In 1988 Mikhail Gorbachev announced that the USSR would allow Eastern Bloc countries to freely determine their own affairs, which enabled a softening of state control; the new freedom allowed public protests in East Germany, along with similar protests in other Soviet Bloc countries, including Poland, Hungary, Bulgaria, and Czechoslovakia.

In 1989 Hungary, in a strong statement of state autonomy, opened its border with Austria. After the border opened, in one three-day period at least thirteen thousand East Germans used the opportunity provided to leave the Soviet Bloc. Citizens who remained in East Germany engaged in a series of peaceful protests. To combat the protests and the political embarrassment of the mass exodus, East German officials decided to allow citizens to travel freely through the Berlin Wall into West Germany, making the Wall instantly useless. Immediately, citizens on both sides began chipping away at the Wall and tearing down pieces of it. In one night, November 9, 1989, communist rule in East Germany symbolically and effectively ended.

Immediately after the end of East Germany's communist rule but before the process of reunification was complete, the country experienced a power vacuum of sorts—the police and other government institutions fell but there was nothing to take their place. Chaos reigned, causing a breakdown of social order. Without the coercive control of the Stasi, the criminal law itself had no credibility or influence with the citizens.

After the end of communist rule in East Germany, many people called for reunification with West Germany. Rather than creating a new joint government, however, East Germany was absorbed into the existing West German government, including all of its existing laws and political institutions. One benefit was quick political reunification, but along with it came culture shock for East Germans. In less than a year East Germany, which had been fully under communist rule, transitioned to a system of private ownership and full democratic rights.

The transition was not easy. Though East Germany was fortunate to be absorbed into prosperous West Germany, its citizens had to adjust to an entirely new system of government and a new social structure. There was a vast disparity in the economic health of East and West Germany, a disparity that most East Germans were not used to seeing after having grown up in a strict communist regime. At the same time, East Germans had no history of holding confidence in governmental authority or the criminal justice system, and no reason to trust the present system with which they had little experience. The situation led to noticeable increases in violence; homicide rates spiked in the years immediately following reunification. The number of bank robberies increased from six in the first half of 1990 to more than two hundred in the first half of 1991. The effects spilled into West Germany, as armed robberies in West Berlin neighborhoods swelled from 89 in 1989 to 156 in 1990.[31]

Even after political reunification was complete, social unification went unrealized. After forty years of radically different experiences, it took several more years before East Germans felt truly adjusted to and integrated with their Western counterparts. In 1994, more than three years after official reunification, East Germans expressed much lower levels of trust in government institutions than did West Germans. Only 27 percent of East Germans trusted the judicial system, as compared to 48 percent of West Germans. By 2000, however, East Germans' level of trust in the judicial system had risen.[32]

The noticeable increase in the credibility of the criminal justice system among East Germans was predictably matched by a noticeably lowered crime rate, as compared to the high rate immediately following collapse and reunification. From 1995 through 2005 the rate of theft, both serious and petty, dropped from approximately 6,000 to just over 3,000 per 100,000 inhabitants.[33] The total number of crimes reported in East Germany in 1995 was over 1.4 million—or 10,094 per 100,000 inhabitants—but by 2002 that number had dropped by 250,000 offenses—to 8,434 per 100,000 inhabitants.[34] The same dynamic can be seen on a smaller scale in the operation of criminal justice in a single city.

PAKISTAN HAS LONG STRUGGLED WITH POLICE CORRUPTION. THE Gujranwala Range region in the northern part of the country is no exception. By the 1990s it had "given birth to the present situation of social breakdown" and "a general sense of insecurity."[35] According to citizen surveys, the police were viewed as the most corrupt government body of all. To convince the police to investigate a crime a victim often had to offer a bribe. A person under investigation could pay to have his name removed from a list of suspects. A guilty party who was apprehended often could pay to be released. Crime rates were high and businesses had trouble functioning, especially because of unchecked kidnappings and thefts.[36]

When pressed to reduce crime rates but with no help from a distrustful community, the police had to consider unattractive measures:

> For efficiency, the necessary information has to be extracted out of the community, often by force. This is done by the field officers either through a network of 'paid informers,' payments being made out of money extracted from parties always willing to pay bribes to harass their opponents, . . or [through] high profile activities such as stopping people randomly in the streets, raiding premises, taking people in for questioning, not on the basis of information already received, but as part of an attempt to secure information. This stop and search method creates deterrence and gives information at the expense of public alienation.[37]

In Lahore the deputy inspector general settled on a plan to reduce crime: shoot criminals on sight. Lahore Deputy Inspector General (DIG) for Operations Ghulam Mahmood Dogar on Thursday warned all criminals to give up or flee the city, otherwise, according to the new crime-controlling plan, they would be shot dead on sight. Dogar said that the crime graph would be brought down by the new crime-controlling strategy and policemen would break into houses and dens of criminals and, if they resisted, all criminals would be gunned down.[38]

When Azhar Hassan Nadeem was appointed deputy inspector general of police for the Gujranwala Range, he decided to take a different approach. He set to work to combat the police's poor image and lack of credibility with the public. Nadeem understood that he had a tough job ahead of him; the citizens did not believe another round of "reforms" would change anything. He also understood that it was "the element of fear that keeps people at a distance from the police" and prevented them from cooperating with the police.[39] Removing the causes of that fear and skepticism was his goal. He labeled his new vision "community policing."

The first step involved acquainting elected officials with the police. It was hoped that having the groups interact would lead to better government coordination. The local police were also instructed to address problems that affected people's daily lives, such as street lighting, traffic control, and neglected infrastructure.

Nadeem also believed that the more police and religious leaders could communicate a single clear message, the easier crime prevention would become. In anticipation of the crime spike that inevitably accompanied every religious holiday, the police and Ulema, the local religious leaders, held meetings with young people about the dangers of criminal conduct and to enlist their aid. The police were also tasked with running neighborhood watch programs and getting to know their local citizens and the issues they faced. Nadeem believed that as long as the police abused their power, fear would continue to alienate the citizenry. The police had to abandon the practices that were "ill-mannered, corrupt and devoid of sympathy for their own countrymen."[40] While the police worked to implement Nadeem's initiatives, there was little public reaction, and the crime rate remained high.

One day a robbery was perpetrated on a local merchant, by which he lost 830,000 Pakistani rupees (Rs), or nearly US$9,000. The police stopped a rickshaw at 2:00 a.m., and upon opening the occupants' bags, found the stolen loot. The thief offered to split the take with the two police officers, both of whom made slightly over Rs2100 per month. They declined the bribe. They were then offered all the money if they would let the man go, but again they declined. All of the property was returned to the victim, which almost startled the town's citizens. The police made sure that news of the return made it on national television. As that case was followed by others like it, cooperation with the police increased and citizens even began to act on their own to identify offenders for the police.

When a group of *dacoits*, or armed robbers, broke into a family's home, the residents resisted and yelled for help. The dacoits began shooting and the neighbors "surrounded the accused and returned fire."[41] Two of the dacoits were killed and the third was remanded to police custody. The incident, where neighbors willingly entered into a situation where the police were certain to become involved later, was considered a large step forward.

In September of 1991 the police began working with various civil organizations to focus their enforcement efforts on specific warlords and influential criminals. By themselves the police had not made progress against these entrenched elements, but with a combined effort during a two-night operation, 526 different "protectors and patrons of dangerous criminals, dealers in narcotics, and gun runners" were arrested.[42] There was an immediate decrease in the crime rate.

The change in attitude toward the police, who sought to win greater respect among citizens, was contagious. Citizens who had lived among lawlessness their entire lives began assisting law enforcement. When citizens were surveyed in June of 1992, 95 percent said they would not give evidence against a criminal. By January of 1993 only 11 percent of those surveyed were unwilling to provide evidence. Before the community policing initiative, 53 percent of the citizens stated that they would not help a neighbor who was being robbed; six months later only 1 percent still said they would not help. Before the community policing effort only 5 percent of the citizens in the survey said they would give evidence against a criminal even when they themselves had been the victim. Six months into the new policing model, though, 87 percent were willing to give evidence, regardless of who the victim was.[43]

In time, the power of the community policing came to be understood by others. In July of 2010, one hundred admittedly corrupt police officers from Punjab districts took an oath on the Quran never to take another bribe, and their bosses agreed to be held accountable if they did. It was acknowledged that the source of the idea came from the success of the Gujranwala model.

The larger point here is that the relationship between a system's credibility among the community and its crime control effectiveness moves in both directions: reforms that increase credibility can increase a community's deference, as occurred in modern East Germany and Pakistan, and doctrines that decrease credibility (by deviating from deserved punishment, either because of legal rules indifferent to justice or corruption or incompetence) can correspondingly decrease deference.

TO RETURN TO OUR ORIGINAL STORY, THE REPEAL OF PROHIBITION was in many ways similar to the political path of its enactment. It was brought about not by a change in people's views of the condemnability of drinking but by the practical and political effects of Prohibition. Women seeking to protect their families from the dangers of unregulated alcohol demanded repeal. Businessmen began to see that the speakeasy had simply replaced the saloon, unleashing a vast army of lawbreakers on an unprecedented scale that hurt the productivity of workers to a higher degree than seen before Prohibition. Rural grain-producing communities, deeply hurt by the Depression that gripped America in the late 1920s, needed the income generated by a domestic alcohol industry that had moved abroad just when local governments needed the tax revenues of alcohol that criminal syndicates were collecting. On December 5, 1933, the twenty-first amendment was enacted and Prohibition ended.

Unfortunately, national Prohibition left a near-permanent legacy. The era had fundamentally changed the structural organization of crime. The high demand for illicit alcohol created organized crime rings that evolved into sophisticated and powerful organizations.[44] Though organized crime had existed in some form prior to the 1920s, it was not until the Prohibition era that organized crime became an influential part of American life.[45] Gangsters became more than mere criminals: they had evolved into businessmen with access to capital, ranks of employees, and influence in politics and government. Members of the organized crime community selected political candidates and funded their campaigns.[46] The corruption spread from the highest levels of government down to the rank-and-file police force, and these arrangements continued to be useful as the bootleggers transitioned to other businesses such as gambling, prostitution, drugs, "protection" rackets to bakeries, laundries, and others, and the running of labor unions.

NATIONAL PROHIBITION ERODED THE CRIMINAL JUSTICE SYSTEM'S credibility through its open hypocrisy—it criminalized conduct that a majority did not see as condemnable and failed to effectively rein in the corruption and crime that had been enacted. The detrimental effects of this reduced credibility should not be a surprise given human nature. Seeing justice done and injustice avoided is important to people, not just as a mild, learned preference but as a fundamental part of human nature and something for which people are willing to make personal sacrifices.

To be effective a system must not only work at deterring or incapacitating likely offenders; it must also more broadly address everything in the society that shapes people's internalized norms or that influences their conduct through social effect. Further, the successful system must look to its effect on all those people on whom it depends to operate and shape the criminal justice system: witnesses, victims, officers, jurors, officials, and even voters. Does their respect for the system cause them to defer to it and to follow its rules, or do they feel justified in resisting, subverting, and perverting it?

The criminal law's loss of credibility is not unique to cases like Prohibition or other instances of laws that criminalize what is seen as not truly condemnable. Any set of criminal laws that in the community's view regularly give undeserved punishment or fail to give deserved punishment can undermine credibility. Unfortunately, a pattern of such intentional deviations from desert is common in American criminal law, and increasingly so. Chapter 9 talks about the modern criminal law doctrines that intentionally give more punishment than is deserved; chapter 10 talks about those that give less than deserved.

CHAPTER NINE

EXCESS

*Committing Felony Murder While Asleep in Bed
and Life in Prison for an Air-Conditioning Fraud*

RYAN HOLLE, TWENTY, AND HIS SISTER, HEATHER, EIGHTEEN,
were raised by their single mother, Sylvia, while she served in the U.S. Navy.
Sylvia was engaged to be married. In anticipation, Ryan and Heather had
recently moved out of their mother's house and into a small bungalow in
Pensacola, Florida, near their grandparents. They shared the house with a
number of other young people, most of whom worked at a local restaurant
or grocery store.[1] After moving in, Ryan Holle met William Allen, twenty-
three, who also became a member of the household.

On March 6, 2003, everyone in the house attended Sylvia Holle's wedding, where Ryan gave the bride away and Heather served as the maid of
honor. At the end of the weekend, the young people hosted an informal
party where everyone drank and talked late into the night. Among the
guests was Jessica Snyder, eighteen, William Allen's girlfriend. Holle's
housemate Allen had known Snyder for quite a while and had been to her
house several times, sometimes to visit and sometimes to buy marijuana
from Snyder's mother, a well-known local drug seller. Also at the party,
at Allen's invitation, were three men whom Ryan Holle had never met
before: Donnie Williams, twenty, Jermond Thomas, twenty-two, and
Charles Miller, twenty-three.

Jessica Snyder, Allen's girlfriend, left the party about 4:00 a.m. At around
5:30 a drunk Holle (who drinks alcohol but does not use drugs) went to

bed in his own room, where two partygoers were already asleep. The only partygoers left awake were Allen and his three friends, Williams, Thomas, and Miller. The three men, all drunk and high, told Allen that they had been thinking of robbing Jessica's mother's safe of the drugs and money she kept there.

An hour after Holle had gone to sleep, Donnie Williams woke him and asked to borrow his blue Chevy Metro. Holle refused and went back to sleep. A short time later Holle was awoken again, this time by Allen asking to borrow the car. Thomas and Miller also came into the room and talked between themselves. Holle in the past had always lent his car to Allen whenever he asked and agreed to do so again. Holle was not told where the men were going or for what purpose and was not invited to join them.

In Holle's car the four men drove to Snyder's house, which was about a mile and a half away. Allen waited in the car, somewhere out of view, while the three men walked up to Snyder's house, apparently to size up the situation. Jessica's younger sister, Marcy, who knew Williams from his previous drug purchases from her mother, answered the door, then woke Jessica to come to the door. Marcy then went about getting ready for school, while Jessica and the men talked. The men appeared to want to argue with Jessica about a missing phone, but Jessica told them to leave because she needed more sleep before going to work. The men left. Soon after, Marcy locked the door and went to school.

After the men had left Holle's house, the sleep-alcohol haze began to lift from the now-awake Holle, who began to worry that something was not right about Allen having borrowed his car with the three men. He called Allen and asked what was going on. Allen gave a quick, cryptic response and hung up. Holle called him back and got another cryptic response and another hang-up. Holle called back several more times but Allen would not answer.

After Marcy left for school, the three unarmed men got out of the car and Allen drove away. The men forcibly entered the Snyder residence through the front door, finding Jessica Snyder in the house alone. They knew the safe was in the mother's bedroom. Thomas tasked Miller to keep Jessica quiet in her room while they took the safe. The men had not brought any

20. Ryan Holle, his mother, Sylvia Garnett, and her new husband at the Garnetts' wedding in 2003, which was held the night before the incident. Courtesy Sylvia Garnett.

weapons, but Miller found a shotgun. Either to keep her quiet or to try to get the safe's combination, Miller hit Jessica with the stock of the shotgun several times in the head and neck, swinging it like a bat.

Thomas and Williams found the safe too big to carry out of the house alone, so Thomas went to get Miller's help, arriving at Jessica's room as Miller was swinging the shotgun to hit her again. She died from her wounds. The three men then moved the safe to the living room and texted Allen to come and pick them up. When the car arrived, the three men loaded the safe into the car while Allen remained behind the wheel.

The next-door neighbor observed the three men moving what he thought was a television set into the car. He worked with Allen and recognized him sitting in the driver's seat. The neighbor telephoned Jessica's mother, Christine Snyder, about what he had seen, and Christine left work and arrived at her house to find the front door "busted off the hinges" and the kitchen water running. Jessica was dead on the floor of her room with splintered pieces of the shotgun stock scattered about.

Back at Holle's house, Holle was awakened when Allen drove the car through the fence to park it in the backyard. Williams entered the house crying, and Holle learned that they had stolen the safe and that Miller had beaten Jessica Snyder. Williams, crying and mumbling, feared that Snyder had been killed. Miller was yelling at Williams, telling him to keep his mouth shut.

Holle told the men to get out of his house and demanded that they get all their stuff out of his car. Holle yelled at the men for using his car to commit a crime. Miller reassured him that they had used a bandanna to cover the car's license plates, so no one would know it was his car. Miller told Holle they would open the safe and leave town. The three men took the safe to a shed in the backyard to try to open it. Allen left with the car to go to his parents' house.

As the three men were trying to force open the safe, Holle retreated back to his bedroom. The men used a blowtorch, sledgehammers, and other tools to try to break into the safe. They burned the clothes they had been wearing.

The police soon arrived and took Thomas and Williams into custody. Miller fled and was arrested the next day. Allen was arrested at his parents' house. The police came into Holle's house and rounded up everyone there for questioning. Holle volunteered to tell all he knew and consented to having his car searched. Upon its opening, the safe contained a cashier's check for $5,000, $40,000 in jewelry, and a pound of marijuana.

WE KNOW FROM EMPIRICAL STUDIES THAT DELVE INTO INTUITIONS of justice that people assess liability for a homicide based first and foremost on a person's culpable state of mind toward causing the death. Most blameworthy is a killing resulting when the person intended to cause death; he wanted or hoped he would cause it. Somewhat less blameworthy is the person who does not necessarily want to cause death but nonetheless knows that his conduct will cause it. (Both intentional and knowing killings are typically punished as murder.) Less blameworthy than either of these, from people's point of view, is a killing in which the person consciously created the risk of death, which eventually came about; he was not sure his conduct would cause death but he knew that it created a risk of death, and he disregarded the risk and proceeded anyway. (This is usually punished as manslaughter.) Finally, still less blameworthy is a killing where the person was unaware that his conduct created a risk of death, but he should have been aware. A reasonable person would have been aware. He should have been paying more attention to the possibility. (This is usually punished, if at all, as negligent homicide.)

On the facts of this case, average people are likely to see serious blameworthiness in Miller, who did the killing: his liability would be greater had he intended to kill Jessica rather than if he intended only to hurt her. Given the circumstances, people are likely to assess his liability as very high.

Previous studies of people's intuitions of justice also tell us that Thomas and Williams will be seen as deserving of serious punishment, certainly for the robbery and possibly with some liability for the homicide. Even had they not wanted or even known that Miller would kill Jessica Snyder, their robbery plan created a situation of confrontation and danger in which someone might well have been hurt. People's judgment on these circumstances will lead them to see that the men's deserved punishment would be serious, although not nearly as serious as Miller's.

Allen is a somewhat different case. He did not participate directly in the robbery, although he did give the men a ride presumably knowing that they planned to rob. That is, while he did not himself directly create the robbery situation embodying confrontation and danger, he must have been at least aware of the possibility that he was helping other people create such a possibility. Studies tell us that ordinary people are likely to see him as criminally liable but something noticeably less than that of Thomas and Williams.

Holle insists he never knew anything of the men's planned robbery. If this were true, the studies suggest that people would see no criminal liability in him whatsoever. The men might have used his car to get to the robbery, but this alone would be seen as insufficient for criminal liability if he did not know their plans. Yes, Holle's car played a role in the robbery, but lots of other things did too, and no one would think they would be grounds for liability. For example, the men probably would not have committed the offense had they not been drunk from the party, but that hardly makes host Heather liable for the robbery they later committed while drunk on her liquor.

Assume for the sake of argument that Holle had overheard the men talking among themselves about a robbery scheme. He says he would have paid no attention to it if there had been such talk; he would have dismissed it as the silly bragging of drunken partyers. If this were the case, the studies again suggest people would support little or no liability for Holle. Typically, criminal liability is reserved for people who are aware of at least a substantial risk of a crime or at least should have been aware of it. This is especially true of a person who does not commit an offense but whose conduct, like lending a car, only aids it.[2] Even if one assumed for the sake of argument that Holle was aware that the men might use his car to commit a robbery, he still would have no reason to suspect that there might be a killing. He had less reason than Allen to think that anyone would be hurt and had done much less than Allen to assist in the underlying robbery.

If Holle had known about the planned robbery, we would have preferred that he have done the right thing: challenged the men on their plan, insisted on getting back his car keys, and called the police. But it does not follow that Holle should suffer criminal liability for not doing the right thing. No U.S. jurisdiction criminalizes a person's failure to report another person's plans to commit a robbery.[3] Most people think it would be the right thing to do but would be hesitant to make it the basis for criminal punishment.

Thus, even under the harshest assumptions about what Holle knew about the robbery plans of the three men, the empirical studies suggest that few people would think Holle deserved much, if any, liability for Miller's later killing of Jessica Snyder.

AFTER THE POLICE ARRIVED AT THE HOUSE, HOLLE VOLUNTARILY gave statements to the officers. Ten days later, on March 19, Holle gave another voluntary statement. During this period, the police reported that Holle was very cooperative with their investigation.

On April 8, Holle was arrested and taken for an initial appearance before a court and appointed a public defender. He was charged with felony murder with a firearm, burglary of an occupied dwelling with assault or battery, and robbery with a firearm. Holle waived arraignment on the charges and pled not guilty. Prosecutors offered Holle a plea agreement: if he pled guilty to second degree murder he would be given a ten-year prison sentence rather than the life without parole sentence that he risked if he refused the plea deal. Prosecutor David Rimmer offered the deal to Holle because, he said, "he was not as culpable as the others." Holle refused to plead guilty to any offense, feeling that he had not committed any crime.

Miller confessed to the killing and on May 12, 2005, was sentenced to life without parole. Thomas and Williams claimed that they ought not be liable for the homicide because they did not know and had no reason to believe that unarmed Miller would kill anyone, but they were treated as if they were equal in blameworthiness to Miller and, under Florida's felony murder statute, they too were sentenced to life without parole. Allen, who was not present in the house and claimed he had no way of knowing of any possibility of a homicide by the three unarmed men, similarly was treated as if he were equal in blameworthiness to Miller; he too was convicted of felony murder and sentenced to life without parole.

Holle, refusing a plea deal, went to trial. The prosecutor's mantra at trial was "no car, no crime." But if that sort of causal connection were enough for murder liability, then presumably Heather also should be liable for murder if the men needed to steady their nerves with drink: "no alcohol, no crime." Or perhaps Jessica's mother should be held liable for Jessica's murder: "no safe, no crime." Indeed, Jessica's mother's drug dealing and her use of the safe to store her drugs produced a real danger to the people in her household and good reason to be aware of such danger—certainly a better reason than Holle having to worry that lending his car to his house-mate would lead to a murder. (Jessica's mother served three years for her drug dealing.)

For his decision that morning in his bedroom to let his housemate borrow his car, twenty-year-old Holle was convicted of felony murder and sentenced to life in prison without the possibility of parole. He is now serving that sentence in the Graceville Correctional Facility outside of Tallahassee.

IT IS PERHAPS NO SURPRISE THAT HOLLE REJECTED THE PROSECU-tion's offer of a plea agreement. From his point of view he had committed no crime. Regardless of what one thinks about whether Holle ought to have some criminal liability for his loan of the car, ordinary people generally agree that this most serious penalty, life without parole, is properly reserved for the most serious crimes and the most egregious forms of intentional killings, murder. How is it, then, that Holle was treated as such a murderer? What is this "felony murder rule" and how does it justify itself?

To be seen as guilty of murder, the criminal law typically requires that a person *intended* to kill the victim. The intent, the culpable state of mind, is the vital component that differentiates murder from lesser crimes. Manslaughter requires a lower culpable state of mind than murder: one need only *consciously risk* causing a death. Another step down in culpability is a person who caused a death by *creating a risk* of death but was unaware of the risk: a reasonable person would have been aware of the risk but this offender was not. This lower level of culpability produces liability for the less serious offense of negligent homicide, an offense that many states do not recognize.

The felony murder rule short-circuits all of these distinctions. The rule treats any killing caused in the course of a felony as a murder, even if the death was completely accidental. Further, the rule commonly applies this murder liability not just to the person causing the death but also to all accomplices in the underlying felony, no matter how trivial their contributions and no matter how unlikely any risk of a death. Miller probably would be liable for murdering Jessica Snyder even without the felony murder rule—he probably at least knew his beating would kill her—but Thomas and Williams were liable for felony murder only because they were accomplices with Miller in the underlying robbery, as was driver Allen.

The law's standard forms of criminal homicide—murder, manslaughter, and negligent homicide based upon intentional, reckless, and negligent killings—correspond perfectly with people's shared intuitions of justice. But the felony murder rule does not; indeed, it seriously conflicts with people's shared intuitions of justice. Studies show that when a person kills another accidentally during a robbery, ordinary people might support what one might call a "felony manslaughter rule" on the theory that the offender must have been aware that his commission of the felony risked creating a chance of causing death. But this applies only to the person actually doing the killing. Ordinary people generally do not hold accomplices to the same level of liability as the perpetrator of an offense, and ordinary people hold a person liable as an accomplice to a homicide only if the person has some culpable state of mind as to assisting the killing.[4]

The felony murder rule, especially in its broadest form, has left a trail of injustice. In one felony murder case that was studied, for example, Forrest Heacock supplied cocaine to people at a "drug party" that he attended. He was one of four people who were injecting cocaine when one of them overdosed and died. Heacock was convicted of felony murder for the death and was sentenced to forty years imprisonment.[5] When ordinary people later were asked to judge this case, they saw his role as much less blameworthy than murder and as something more akin to punching someone during an argument when the victim later requires stitches.[6] In other words, the offense was nothing like murder. Yet Heacock was sent away for forty years.

In another case that has been studied, a man named Jerry Moore agreed to help an acquaintance, Montejo, burglarize a house while the owner was away. Neither man was armed. When the resident returned unexpectedly, Moore was surprised when his partner shot and killed the owner with a gun—he apparently had found it in a nightstand at the house. Moore nonetheless was convicted of murder under felony murder for Montejo's shooting and was sentenced to life imprisonment at hard labor without the possibility of parole.[7] When ordinary people were given the facts of the case, their view was that Moore's liability ought to be something more akin to that of injuring someone by clubbing them during a robbery—nothing close to murder liability or the sentence of life without parole that the felony murder rule provided in the case.[8]

What do cases like Holle's, Heacock's, and Moore's do for the moral credibility of the criminal law? How could such perceived injustices help but have an alienating effect on the community's faith in and deference to the law? Studies put the lie to those scholarly claims that people's intuitions of justice are entirely flexible. As one scholar argues,

> The longer we live with a doctrine—and felony murder has been a companion for more than 150 years—the more familiar it becomes. And, if

I may corrupt a phrase, familiarity can breed content. Felony murder has been so much a part of our law for so long that the very thought of abrogation is discomforting.[9]

But it is simply not true that people interpret their judgments of justice from the law itself, as chapters 4 and 5 make clear. It does not matter that the felony murder rule has been around for so long; the rule still produces serious conflicts with people's judgments of justice and will continue to do so until it is abolished or narrowed.

There has been some movement in the past several years toward that end. The American Law Institute, in its Model Penal Code, recommends completely abolishing the felony murder rule, but only two states have followed that lead.[10] Some states have retained the law but have imposed important limitations on its use. In New York, for example, the rule would not apply if the person didn't believe his accomplices were armed and had no reason to think they would kill anyone. Note that under this formulation, felony murder liability would be inapplicable not only to Holle but also probably to driver Allen as well.[11]

Other states apply different restrictions. While ten jurisdictions still allow that the commission of any felony is a basis for applying the rule, most jurisdictions now limit it to inherently dangerous felonies (such as arson or robbery) to trigger the rule.[12] But this limitation does little to fix the rule's problems. Florida, where Holle was convicted, uses the "inherently dangerous" form of the rule. The inherently dangerous felonies Holle supposedly committed were burglary of an occupied dwelling with assault or battery while armed, as well as robbery with a firearm.[13] Of course, he never committed such offenses and is only being treated as if he had by a legal fiction that perpetuates the injustice of the rule.

Why would a rule that so regularly produces what people see as injustice be so commonly found in the United States? The underlying rationale for the rule is primarily one of general deterrence: seeking to prevent crime by the threat of punishment. By imposing murder liability on anyone who even accidentally causes a death during a felony the law hopes to signal to other potential offenders that they ought not commit a felony and, if they do so, they ought to be extremely careful in the process. Of course, that rationale doesn't have much application to Holle who, being at home asleep, didn't have much to do with whether the men borrowing his car would commit a felony or how careful they would be while committing it.

Perhaps the most obvious point of objection here is that the system is using the defendant simply as a vehicle to send a message to others. His unjust punishment is like hiring a billboard. He is to be punished more than he deserves because it is thought that such unjust punishment will send a useful message to others. Setting aside for a moment whether general deterrence theory really works in everyday practice, one may be troubled by this line of justification.

Doesn't fairness and justice require that people be punished according to what they did and their blameworthiness for it, and not according to their good or bad luck in making a good billboard message to send to others? The more media attention a case might attract, for example, the better it serves as a message-sending billboard. Should media attention then increase a person's punishment? The general deterrence approach would say yes.

If criminal punishment is about the deterrence of others, and not about justice, then presumably we should punish even an innocent person if it would provide a sufficiently useful deterrence message. Many general deterrence advocates concede that the logic of deterrence leads to this indefensible result, but nonetheless attempt to defend it.

> The more promising utilitarian response is not to attempt to deflect or avoid the conclusion that there may be some extreme situations where utilitarianism commits us to punishing the innocent, but rather to accept this outcome and contend that as horrible as this may seem on a pre-reflective level, on closer consideration it is not a matter that *really* insurmountably troubles our sensibilities to the extent that it entails that any theory which approves of such an outcome must necessarily be flawed. By drawing comparisons with other situations in which we take the utilitarian option it is contended that punishing the innocent is not a practice which is necessarily unacceptable.[14]

Beyond the potential immorality of the idea general deterrence, there is reason to doubt its efficacy because it rests upon some unlikely assumptions. First, to influence the conduct of the potential offender—the person we are trying to deter in the future—that person must know of the rule. Yet evidence shows that few people know the legal rules, especially rules that are inconsistent with people's normal intuitions of justice. We know from studies that people assume the law is as they think it should be—just. When an unjust rule is created for deterrent effect, people won't know about it unless they are specially educated. How many people know what form of the felony murder rule applies in their state, or whether it exists there at all?

Second, even if the target audience knows of the deterrence-based legal rule, the rule can deter only if that target audience has the capacity and willingness to alter their conduct as the rule directs. Evidence shows that many if not most criminals do not possess such rational decision making skills due to alcohol or drug use, impulsiveness, mental illness, or a host of other influences that undercut rationality. If they are not making rational calculations, the threat of the deterrence-based rule will be lost on them.

Finally, even if the target audience knows of the rule and is made up of all rational calculators, the deterrence-based rule would have no effect unless the target audience perceives the costs of the offense as outweighing its benefits. And that is not likely. The punishment rates for offenses in the United States, even serious offenses like homicide, are often so low as to be not meaningful to the target. Most offenses have a 50-to-1 or a 100-to-1 punishment rates for the offense; only homicide and aggravated assault approach anything like serious probability of punishment, albeit still often less than 50 percent. In any case, it is not the actual punishment rate that matters but rather the rate perceived by the target. Unfortunately for the general deterrence theory, most offenders think they can get away with their offenses. Even if they turn out to be wrong in believing they can escape conviction—and most of the time they are wrong in this—it does not matter. Their cost-benefit calculations will be based upon their *belief* that they will not get caught and punished.[15]

When his housemate woke Holle and asked to borrow his car, does anyone think that the felony murder rule ever came into Holle's head? Why would it? If it didn't occur to him, how could it have had any effect on his conduct? When Heacock decided to go to the drug party at which one of the partyers later died, or when Moore decided to help his unarmed friend burglarize the empty house, is it likely the felony murder rule ever entered their thinking? They had no expectation that anyone would die, so why would it have? Would they even have known whether or what version of the rule applied in their states? What are we achieving by punishing Holle and others beyond what ordinary people think they deserve—other than to hurt the criminal justice system's reputation for justness?

It should be no surprise, then, to find that in most instances in which doctrines are formulated to optimize deterrence, such manipulations have not been shown to work, and there are good reasons to believe that they are highly unlikely to be productive and in fact are likely to be counterproductive. For example, one recent study looked at the crime-reducing effects of the felony murder rule.[16] The study's results illustrate the complexity of attempts at such deterrence through legal rule manipulation and the study's author concludes, "States that punish robbery death more severely have [a] higher share of robberies that prove fatal. States that punish robbery death as either murder one or two even have higher numbers of robbery deaths due to guns. However one measures the felony-murder rule, states with stiffer penalties for this crime report greater numbers of victims of robbery-murder."[17]

A similar though less statistically significant result also obtains for rape: the felony murder rule may slightly reduce the overall number of rapes but it also correlates with an *increase* in the number of rapes resulting in death.[18] One can only speculate about what causes this complex result (that is, the apparent tendency of those who engage in robbery or rape, when a felony murder statute is in effect, to be slightly more likely to cause the death of their victim). But it obviously means that we ought not justify the felony murder rule on general deterrence grounds. Given the loss of moral credibility to the criminal justice system that the rule regularly and intentionally produces, it would seem that the rule cannot be justified at all.[19]

Given such problems, it is perhaps no surprise to find that the felony murder rule is rarely used in other countries and has been affirmatively rejected by most countries that had it at one time or another, including England and Wales, Northern Ireland, Ireland, Canada, and India.[20] A lawmaker faced with this reality ought to conclude that the best way to fight crime is to simply do justice, nothing more and nothing less. Imposing the deserved punishment already provides a deterrent threat. Trying to punish more or more heavily to increase deterrence is likely to fail.

Unfortunately, deterrence arguments have been used to support all sorts of rules and doctrines in American criminal law: in support of "strict liability" offenses (liability without proof of any culpable state of mind), in support of vicarious liability, in support of broad complicity liability and in support of abolishing or narrowing the insanity defense. Deterrence rationales also influence the grading and sentencing of offenses.

The deterrence-based agenda of modern criminal law has simply failed, on both moral and practical grounds. It fails to give defendants what they deserve—and admits this. But, as is becoming increasingly clear, it also fails to achieve its own goal of controlling crime. The evidence increasingly suggests that giving offenders the punishment they deserve, no more and no less, is not only morally preferable but also the better crime control strategy. As of this writing, Ryan Holle has already served eleven years for agreeing to let his housemate borrow his car (already more than the ten years the prosecutor offered to get him to plead guilty to murder).

WILLIAM J. RUMMEL HAS HAD TROUBLE HOLDING DOWN ANY KIND of job, more from laziness than incompetence. At the age of thirty he has no wife, no children, and few friends. His parents are both alive, but their health is poor and Rummel rarely sees them.[21]

Rummel has a string of criminal convictions, most minor opportunistic offenses. From age sixteen to age twenty he was convicted for four minor offenses, for each of which he got a minor sentence of a fine or thirty days in jail. When he was twenty-one Rummel was convicted of credit card fraud after he used a company credit card to buy two new tires for his car. The tires were worth a total of $80.00. Because of his earlier convictions, Rummel

21. William James Rummel, 1980.
© Bettman/Corbis

was sentenced to three years in prison, of which he served twenty-eight months.[22] Four years later, when he was twenty-five, he was convicted in a domestic violence case and was sentenced to thirty days in jail. On the day of his conviction for that offense he passed a bad check for $5.61 at a Gulf service station and was again convicted of swindling by check, for which he was sentenced to serve an additional thirty days. A year later he was convicted of forging a check for $28.36 and was sentenced to two to four years in prison, of which he served just over two years.

Two years after getting out of prison, on August 15, 1973, when he was thirty years old, Rummel walked into Captain Hook's Lounge in San Antonio. It was a hot day and the bar's air conditioning was not working. Rummel approached the bar's owner, David Shaw, and offered to fix it. Shaw agreed, and Rummel began his inspection. After a few minutes and a little tinkering he announced that the unit needed a new compressor. Cost: $129.75; labor free. Shaw quickly agreed and wrote Rummel a check for that amount. Rummel left, with no intention of ever making the promised repair, then cashed the check and never returned. Shaw filed a complaint with the police, who easily traced Rummel through the check, which he had endorsed with his real name.

Rummel's offense, theft by false pretext, would normally render him liable under Texas law for a sentence of no more than two to ten years, although violators typically receive a sentence of months, not years. Rummel, however, had a criminal record, and his earlier offenses in some ways made his latest offense more blameworthy. He was not taking seriously enough the criminal liability and punishments he had previously been given.

WE KNOW FROM EMPIRICAL STUDIES THAT ORDINARY PEOPLE DO see greater blameworthiness in repeated criminality. Repeated violations give the unattractive appearance of an offender thumbing his or her nose at the law and at the community's norms. The additional punishment that a repeat offender deserves for this nose thumbing is usually not as much as what he or she deserves for the offense itself—the thumbing isn't a greater violation than the offense itself—but it does aggravate the offense to some extent, as any of a variety of aggravating circumstances might.

People's judgments of justice on these matters and on the *Rummel* case in particular have been studied. Given Rummel's prior criminal record, people see the air-conditioning fraud as something more serious than just the unlawful deceit of the $129.00 scam; they see it as more akin to the blameworthiness of, for example, taking a microwave from a house.[23] Such a burglary is more serious than Rummel's simple fraud because it involves not just the unlawful taking but also the unlawful intrusion, in this instance into a house's kitchen. That is, people see Rummel's prior record as aggravating his offense to an extent similar to the way physical intrusion aggravates a theft offense. The people in the study sentenced Rummel on average to 3.1 years in prison. Several hundred law students also have read the facts of the Rummel case and suggested a sentence they believe Rummel deserved, given his past criminal record: two-thirds gave a sentence of 3 or 7 years, with the average of all of the students' sentences being 3.4 years, consistent with the view of the nonstudent subjects in the empirical study.

ON APRIL 11, 1973, A JURY CONVICTED RUMMEL OF THE THEFT. Because the $129.75 check was over the $50.00 statutory cutoff, the offense was classified as a felony. The next day, the state presented evidence of two prior felony convictions and asked the judge to declare Rummel a habitual criminal. That classification authorizes a dramatic increase in the prison term, under the theory that such is the only effective way of preventing habitual offenders from committing more offenses in the future. The declared purpose of this Texas sentencing statute was to deal "with those who by repeated criminal acts have shown that they are simply incapable of conforming to the norms of society as established by its criminal law." The prior felony offenses that qualified Rummel included the credit card fraud from nine years before and the minor check fraud from four years before. All totaled, the three felonies netted Rummel $215.36. Following the statute's direction, however, the judge sentenced thirty-year-old Rummel to life in prison.

Rummel, who grew pale and thin in prison, made something of his time there. In just over seven years, he earned 67 hours of college credit, spent 350 hours teaching other inmates, and took additional training in construction maintenance. His prison time passed unremarkably. Rummel was a "middle of the road type inmate," prison warden D. A. Christian said. "He don't cause any problems. He's not a ringleader or a big follower. In a prison, you know your troublemakers, your snitches. He's not any of these. He's not that violent. As a con man, he ranks low on the totem pole."[24]

"I'm not saying I should not be punished, but why give me a life sentence?" Rummel asked an interviewer. "If I had murdered seventy-five people or raped five women, something of that nature, I could see where I could become a potential threat to society. But who do I threaten? I don't threaten anybody. I don't use narcotics. I don't use alcohol to any extent."[25]

RUMMEL'S CASE IS NOT UNUSUAL. IN ANOTHER CASE, FIFTY-NINE-year-old Charles Almond was frustrated by the constant arguing of his two adult sons (who still lived at home) over which television program to watch. As the latest argument surged, he picked up a .22 revolver that his oldest son had left on the table and shot out the television screen. Several decades earlier, Almond had been convicted of "burglary of an unoccupied building; . . . throwing a missile (a rock) at an automobile occupied by his father-in-law; and . . . breaking and entering the office of Peeler Oil Company."[26] Because of Almond's decades-old felony convictions, a sentence of fifteen years without parole was imposed in his television-shooting case, for "possession of a firearm as a felon" combined with a "career offender" statute.[27] But the judgment of ordinary people in an empirical study was quite different. They judged the shooting of the television, even in light of the prior criminal record, as something more akin to (and indeed less serious than) taking a clock radio from the backseat of a car. On average, the subjects gave Almond a sentence of 1.1 years rather than the fifteen years without parole that he got under the three-strikes statute.

These and other studies expose the error of claims by some scholars that the community's intuitions of justice are unendingly flexible and that they will simply shift to accept whatever the legal doctrine provides. One well-known scholar, for example, argues that habitual offender statutes reflect community notions of deserved punishment:

> The point is . . . that conceptions of desert change over time. It does seem to have been a perceived need to incapacitate that prompted such laws—but once the public perceived this need to incapacitate, notions of deserved punishment quickly adjusted to accommodate the utilitarian demands. Our desert conceptions are not independent of utilitarian considerations, and hence we should not expect desert conceptions to constrain the pursuit of utilitarian aims.[28]

This line of argument seems to confuse political rhetoric with community views. The empirical studies show that people do not alter their judgments to match the law. On the contrary, people have independent judgments of justice and they are often quite durable and difficult for the law to change. The criminal law's several decades' use of three strikes and other habitual offender statutes has not altered ordinary people's judgments on the matter. No matter that the laws have been around for some time, three strikes continues to seriously conflict with community views. As other empirical studies have independently shown, ordinary people look to desert and moral blameworthiness—not to the need for incapacitation, or to general deterrence—in assessing punishment.

Habitual offender laws that conflict with ordinary people's sense of justice, as in *Rummel* and *Almond*, are common throughout the United States.[29] A majority of states and the federal system have "three-strikes" laws—so called because of the idea that you get "three strikes and you're out." As the nickname suggests, a third offense dramatically enhances the chance for punishment. There is some variation among the states as to what counts as a "strike" and what it means to be "out" (that is, what the enhanced punishment entails). All of the statutes include violent felonies such as murder, rape, robbery, or kidnapping as "strikes." Some states also include some nonviolent crimes as strikes, such as selling drugs (IN), treason (WA), escape (FL), or embezzlement and bribery (SC). There is wider variation as to how much additional punishment a repeated offender will receive under a three-strikes rule. Eleven states impose a mandatory life sentence without possibility of parole: Georgia, Indiana, Louisiana, Maryland, Montana, New Jersey, North Carolina, South Caroline, Tennessee, Virginia, Washington, and Wisconsin). In some states parole is available but only after long periods of time served: New Mexico, Colorado, and California.[30]

Unfortunately, studies suggest that three-strikes laws have had virtually no impact on crime rates.[31] Many judges and prosecutors know injustice when they see it, and many will be inclined to subvert the system in such cases. But of course that subversion just introduces an additional source of arbitrariness in the system: a defendant's good or bad luck in the prosecutor or judge who happens to hear the case. Why keep the statutes in the first place? Why not just give offenders the punishment they deserve?

HOW CAN IT BE THAT THE CRIMINAL JUSTICE SYSTEM IMPOSES upon Rummel a sentence of life imprisonment knowing that it is far in excess of the three-year sentence that the community judge as the punishment he deserves? People think Rummel's case is akin to stealing a microwave from a house, while the law treats it as if it were murder. The short answer is that the system has stopped being one of criminal justice and has become instead, in somewhat cloaked form, one of preventive detention. It has stopped looking only to an offender's moral blameworthiness in assessing punishment and instead has switched its focus to predicting what a person might or might not do in the future. This shift in focus can be traced back to the early 1960s. The National Council on Crime and Delinquency's Model Sentencing Act of 1962 proudly proclaimed that the nature of the crime that has been committed ought to be of little relevance:

> The [Act] diminishes the major source of [sentencing] dispar-ity—sentencing according to the particular offense. Under [the Act] the dangerous offender may be committed to a lengthy term; the non-dangerous offender may not. It makes available, for the first time, a plan that allows the sentence to be determined by the defendant's make-up, his potential threat in the future, and other similar factors, with a minimum of variation according to the offense.[32]

But a system that looks to preventive detention must de facto assign liability and punishment in ways that are quite different from deserved punishment for past wrongdoing. Not all dangerous people are blameworthy and not all blameworthy people are dangerous. Severely mentally ill persons, for example, may need civil commitment but probably do not deserve punishment. A law-abiding citizen discovered to be a former Nazi concentration camp commandant deserves punishment even though he is no longer a danger.

A just punishment system focuses on what is deserved for a past wrong, while a preventive detention system has no reason to even require a past wrong. Assume a test could reliably predict who will commit a certain offense in the future (think Tom Cruise's movie *Minority Report*). Would it be just or fair to punish a person who fails the test? One can debate whether some preventive measures might be appropriate, but the prediction of future conduct offers no ground for imposing deserved punishment. To "punish" is "to subject to pain, loss, confinement, death, etc., as a penalty for some offense or transgression." One can "restrain" or "detain" or "incapacitate" to prevent a future crime, but the imposition of deserved punishment requires past wrongdoing.

The criminal justice system generally purports to be in the business of doing justice and giving offenders the punishment they deserve, no more, no less. It calls itself the criminal *justice* system, not a criminal *preventive detention* system. It describes its sanctions as *punishment*, and on this ground justifies punitive conditions of confinement. In cases like *Rummel*, however, the system quietly shifts from a justice rationale to a protection rationale without openly admitting the change. The system keeps the "punishment" label but uses it as a cloak for its preventionist agenda. It does not punish Rummel for what he has done; his current offense is minor—even taken together his string of offenses are still minor thefts. In reality, Rummel is being detained because of the offenses that he might commit in the future.

IMPOSING PREVENTIVE DETENTION UNDER THE CLOAK OF CRIMInal justice is a bad idea because it hurts both criminal justice and effective preventive detention. It is not good for the criminal justice system because the unjust sentences, like those imposed on Rummel and Almond, conflict with the community's view of justice and undercut the criminal justice system's moral credibility and accompanying detrimental effects (as discussed in chapter 8). Applying preventive detention under the guise of criminal justice also is bad for fair and effective preventive detention.

In a prevention system, the detention ought to be periodically reexamined to determine whether the detainee remains dangerous. To keep him longer than is necessary wastes resources and infringes on his liberty for no benefit. But when preventive detention is used as part of a criminal justice system, it is stuck with the procedures that are designed for determining deserved punishment. Normally a court has at the time of sentencing everything it needs to know in order to determine deserved punishment; there is no reason to delay the decision or to reconsider it again later. But in fact, the "Truth in Sentencing" movement—which seeks to avoid the "deception" of publicly imposing a sentence in court but then having a parole board reduce it later out of the community's view—has moved many states and the federal system away from allowing parole boards to alter a court's publicly imposed sentences. Under the reforms, a sentence announced in court is the sentence that generally will be served. This makes good sense for doing justice but not for preventive detention.

Another problem with trying to provide an effective preventive detention system under the cloak of criminal justice is that efficient and fair preventive detention requires an inquiry into how likely it is that the offender will commit another offense, how serious that probable offense might be, how reliable is the prediction being made, and other such inquiries. One would not want to expend the thirty thousand dollars per year on preventive detention to avoid a fifty-dollar credit card fraud that an offender has a 20 percent chance of committing sometime in the next decade where even that prediction has only mixed reliability.[33] Yet when preventive detention is used under the guise of criminal justice, none of those kinds of inquiries are made because they are all irrelevant in assessing deserved punishment.

Preventive detention also affects the conditions of confinement. Imprisonment as punishment is meant to be odious—and cause suffering (consistent with human dignity). Conversely, when preventive detention causes intrusion on liberty that is not deserved punishment, the detained person—like the person civilly committed because of mental illness or a contagious disease—ought to suffer the least amount possible yet protect society. This may mean not only nonpunitive conditions but also the least intrusive form of custody, such as house detention or electronic bracelet surveillance if such would provide adequate security. Further, a prevention rather than punishment rationale logically would mean that if something can be done to reduce or extinguish the detainee's dangerousness, it ought to be done. For example, a detainee ought to have an absolute right to any treatment that can reduce the need for or the extent of the loss of liberty imposed upon.

Using the criminal justice system for preventive detention is not only unfair to detainees but also wasteful and ineffective in preventing future crimes. The three-strikes and habitual offender statutes at work in *Rummel* and *Almond* are not only bad because they do injustice but also bad because they do not lead to efficient prevention. They turn good prevention on its head by detaining offenders only after their criminal career is sufficiently advanced to have accumulated the necessary three strikes, while failing to detain potentially dangerous criminals during their more crime-prone teens and twenties.[34] We spend potential preventive resources housing geriatric former offenders who present little danger rather than on those who are presently dangerous. Yet these sorts of inefficiencies are unavoidable if preventive detention is not conducted out in the open where it will attract the scrutiny that it deserves; it should not be dressed up as if it were deserved punishment.

Some studies conclude that three-strikes laws do not achieve significant crime reduction, while others suggest that if they have any effect it is a very modest one and not worth the expense.[35] Even in situations in which studies suggest that a three-strikes law does have some preventive effect, it seems likely that the same resources could have an even greater preventive effect if they are used more directly, openly, and effectively.[36]

Whether three-strikes statutes could clearly show a crime-control benefit, however, it does not necessarily follow that they are a good idea. If the criminal justice system stuck to giving offenders the punishment they deserve—no more and no less—the punishment already provides an opportunity to restrain and to rehabilitate an offender. The additional sentences provided by giving offenders more punishment than they deserve undermines the system's moral credibility and hurts crime-control effectiveness. Even if additional unjust punishments actually provide some useful detention goal, the crime-control benefit from it might be outweighed by the crime-control cost of the lost credibility. To the extent that effective and efficient preventive detention is possible, it ought to be done openly within the construct of a civil detention system that is explicit in its goals and criteria. It ought not be done under the guise of criminal justice because it undermines that system's credibility.

No one can dispute that a society must be able to and inevitably will do what is necessary to protect itself from dangerous persons. Any democratic government that does not do so loses its political power. But while the protection of society from dangerous persons is legitimate and inevitable, the use of the criminal justice system to do it, as with the Texas three-strikes statute in *Rummel*, creates serious complications. If we are to engage in preventive detention we ought to do it openly, in a civil commitment system like the one we now use for detaining or otherwise controlling people with a contagious disease, with drug dependencies, or with serious mental disease who present a danger to themselves or others. Pursuing preventive detention cloaked as criminal justice leads to ineffective and overly intrusive preventive detention and undermines the criminal justice system's reputation for being just.

Fairness and efficiency suggest that if the system is to shift from punishment to prevention it logically must change the way it operates: it must provide periodic reviews, nonpunitive conditions, the least intrusive restraint, a right to treatment, and minimum requirements for the seriousness of the danger threatened and the reliability of the prediction. A criminal justice system designed to give offenders the punishment they deserve typically does not, and often should not, do these things.

HABITUAL OFFENDER STATUTES ARE ONE OF A HOST OF MODERN American criminal law rules designed to incapacitate suspected dangerous persons rather than punish offenders as deserved. For example, a prior criminal record often has an enormous effect on sentencing guidelines—sometimes doubling or tripling the sentence for an offense because of an offender's prior record.[37] In these cases no claim is made that the punishment is deserved; rather, only that the offender should be detained longer to prevent future offenses. The United States Sentencing Commission, whose guidelines influence criminal sentencing in all federal courts, explains the rational in its *Guidelines Manual*: "[T]he specific factors included in [the calculation of the criminal history category] are consistent with the extant empirical research assessing correlates of recidivism and patterns of career criminal behavior."[38] Almond was sentenced under the commission's guidelines.[39] Even the sentencing judge thought that Almond's sentence under the federal guidelines was "unfairly harsh on its face, given Almond's conduct and record."[40]

The expansion of criminal law rules designed to prevent rather than punish is not limited to habitual-offender statutes or to recidivist-enhancement guidelines, but has begun to appear in a wide range of other criminal law rules. For example, recent reforms have decreased the age at which juveniles may be tried as adults.[41] They ignore the lesser blameworthiness of children, who may not yet fully appreciate what they do, and focus instead on using the criminal justice system to gain greater control over persons who may be dangerous in the future. Another is the introduction of criminal code provisions that set the grade for an incomplete offense (attempt) to the same grade as the completed offense.[42] Thus, rape and attempted rape are to be punished the same; aggravated assault and attempted aggravated assault are to be punished the same. Such provisions clearly conflict with ordinary people's judgments of justice. Their view is that, when a rape actually occurs, it demands noticeably greater punishment than where no rape has occurred; the failed attempt deserves serious punishment but not the same as when a rape has in fact occurred.[43] From a prevention point of view, treating rape and attempted rape the same makes good sense if the goal is to maximize the system's control over dangerous people rather than do justice.[44] The offender who fails because police are lucky enough to interrupt his crime may be as dangerous as the offender who completes the offense, making both equally attractive candidates for preventive detention.

If the criminal justice system is to be returned to a focus on deserved punishment, it will require reforms in a variety of areas without which the system will continue to generate liability and punishment that undermine the criminal law's moral credibility and undermine its crime-control effectiveness. If we are to have preventive detention, which every society will demand in one form or another, let it be done openly, under the scrutiny that it merits, and not cloaked as criminal justice. The next chapter examines deviations from desert of the reverse sort: criminal law rules that predictably and regularly produce gross failures of justice.

CHAPTER TEN

FAILURE

Getting Away with Murder
Beyond a Reasonable Doubt

LARRY EYLER, THIRTY, WAS A MAN OF CONTRADICTIONS. HE HAD a big, round baby face and a shy, quiet manner, but his six-foot-one-inch body was all muscle. His behavior was childlike and naive but he could be cunning when necessary. Eyler's greatest inner conflict, however, revolved around his sexuality. Though attracted to men for as long as he could remember, he could barely talk about the subject. Probably as a consequence of his strict religious upbringing, he was terribly ashamed of his sexual orientation. This shame translated into violence. When he engaged in sex he was brimming with rage. He was into bondage and enjoyed tying up his partners and cursing at them.[1]

By day Eyler led a seemingly regular life in Terre Haute, Indiana, working in the Vigo County government offices and sharing an apartment with David Little, a middle-aged library science professor, who also is gay. Eyler had had a steady romantic relationship for the previous year with John Dobrovolskis, a married man who lived in Chicago. (Dobrovolskis's wife, Sally, was aware of his homosexuality but she preferred to live with him nonetheless.) The relationship between Eyler and Dobrovolskis was not always calm and involved frequent heated phone arguments. Housemate Little's undisguised hatred of Dobrovolskis added tension for Eyler.

Eyler sometimes tied up Dobrovolskis during their sexual sessions but did not hurt him. Eyler reserved his violent tendencies for other people.

He liked to drive to uptown Chicago to cruise near the gay bars late at night, carrying in his pickup truck a "torture kit" that included knives, a metal-tipped whip, a sword, handcuffs, and paralyzing tear gas.

On December 19, 1982, Steven Agan was hitchhiking in Terre Haute when Eyler picked him up. Agan had previously met Eyler because he worked at a car wash that Eyler frequented. But it was a different Eyler that Agan encountered in the pickup truck—one with a butcher knife and anger. Eyler drove north on Route 63 to an abandoned farm near the tiny town of Newport. At knifepoint he ordered Agan to take off his shirt, then handcuffed him, gagged his mouth, and dragged him into a shed. He tied the terrified Agan to a beam, unbuckled Agan's belt, and pulled his pants down. Eyler brought equipment from his truck and meticulously set a stage for ritual torture: flashlights to make dramatic light and his torture kit laid out in order. He then slowly stabbed Agan in the chest. Agan, unable to scream because of the gag, struggled and squirmed, which only excited Eyler further. In an increasing frenzy Eyler made deeper and deeper horizontal gashes on Agan's abdomen and throat. Agan bled to death but Eyler continued to mutilate the dead body. After he calmed down, Eyler dragged the body into a wooded area and drove away. Agan's mutilated body was found nine days later but the police had no clue as to the killer's identity.

By early 1983 more bodies of young men were found along the highway routes between Chicago's northern suburbs and Terre Haute. Most of the men were gay; some were hustlers. All were found mutilated in a similar fashion. Indiana police suspected a serial killer and set up a special multiagency task force. Lt. Jerry Campbell was appointed commander of the task force, with Sgt. Frank Love in charge of daily operations.

Among their leads, an informant called in and identified Eyler as the murderer. He told Sergeant Love that Eyler was into bondage, that he was violent during sex, and that he regularly cruised the routes where the bodies had been found. The informant added that Eyler was involved in a stabbing in Terre Haute in 1978. (Eyler had picked up Mark Henry and, at knifepoint, had driven him down a deserted side road then began to sexually abuse him. When Henry tried to run away, Eyler stabbed him and

22. Larry Eyler at the Indiana State Police post in Lowell after being stopped for a traffic violation, 1983. Courtesy Indiana State Police.

left him in a field to die. But Henry managed to stumble to help and was taken to a hospital. Eyler was apprehended, and the police searched his truck and found his "torture kit" then charged him with aggravated battery. But when it came time for the trial, Eyler's lawyer offered Henry $2,500 to drop the charges, which Henry accepted because he needed the money.)

The task force put Eyler under intermittent surveillance. He was observed cruising the Chicago routes late at night and entering gay bars. He sometimes picked up hitchhikers, but there were no murders while the task force was trailing him. Unaware of the ongoing investigation, Eyler continued to prey upon young men. At midnight on August 30, 1983, he picked up Ralph Calise near Chicago's lakefront. Calise, young and poor, lived on welfare and sold small quantities of drugs. With Calise in his pickup, Eyler drove north at a high speed, then pulled over and dragged Calise into the woods just south of Lake Forest. Eyler handcuffed and gagged his victim, unbuckled his belt, pulled down his pants, and began his torture ritual. Eyler slowly inflicted seventeen deep cuts to Calise's chest, abdomen, back, and neck, cutting deeper and deeper as he went. He punctured Calise's lungs and cut his liver. The blood splashed onto Eyler's pants and ran into his boots. By the time Eyler was done and Calise was dead, loops of small intestine were protruding from the abdomen of Calise's body.

This time, though, Eyler did not make a clean getaway. The earth was damp and his boots and his pickup's tires left impressions. Investigators from the Lake County Sheriff's Office in Waukegan, Illinois, found the body the next day and made cast prints of the boot and tire marks but still had no clue as to the murderer's identity.

Eyler spotted his next victim in the early hours of September 30, 1983—Daryl Hayward, a young drifter from Arkansas—hitchhiking on the Dan Ryan Expressway on his way to a funeral in Indianapolis. The surveillance team had been following Eyler earlier that night but had lost him in traffic. Eyler told Hayward that he could take him where he wanted to go and Hayward said, "Tonight's my lucky night."

After some time Eyler whispered, "I have a fantasy."

"What is your fantasy?" Hayward asked.

"Tying people up," Eyler answered, and added, "I'll give you a hundred dollars if I could tie you up. I get off like that. It's just someone being helpless for a while, being tied up, that gets me off."

Eyler promised that he would not hurt Hayward and would untie him after the act. Hayward refused at first but was swayed by the offer of money. Eyler headed south on Interstate 65 and pulled over near a ditch. They got out of the truck and Eyler handed Hayward a plastic grocery bag with ropes and tape. Once in the ditch, Eyler asked Hayward to take off his shirt. The loud noise of the highway traffic made Hayward uneasy so he asked, "Why don't we go where nobody can see us?" Eyler agreed and suggested that they go to a quiet barn he knew.

Just as the two men emerged from the ditch, around 7:00 p.m., Indiana state trooper Kenneth Buehrle passed by in the opposite direction. Parking along the interstate was prohibited, and Buehrle made a U-turn to check the truck. He saw that one of the men was carrying a bag, which made him suspicious. Eyler and Hayward got into the pickup and drove away, but Buehrle followed and pulled Eyler over. He checked Eyler's driver's license and wrote him a warning ticket for illegal parking on the interstate. When the trooper asked Eyler what they were doing in the ditch, Eyler said, "I was taking a shit"; when he asked to see the bag Hayward was carrying, Hayward tried to deceive him by handing him his personal toiletries bag instead of the grocery bag with the ropes and tape. Buehrle knew the bags were different and his suspicions intensified. He radioed Max Hunter, the dispatcher at Lowell police post, to check the truck's registration.

As Hunter heard the driver's description he realized that it matched the "wanted" notice of "Larry Eyler—wanted for possible suspect in murder cases," which was posted on the clipboard of the day's assignments. Hunter excitedly informed Buehrle of the match and called Det. Sgt. John Pavlakovic, the shift supervisor, for instructions. Pavlakovic, caught in the middle of his morning shave, said to detain Eyler and Hayward long enough to investigate further at the station.

In the meantime, two other officers joined Buehrle on the scene. Eyler and Hayward were patted down for weapons, handcuffed, and placed in different police vehicles. Upon questioning, Hayward revealed that Eyler had offered him money for bondage sex. Eyler and Hayward were read their *Miranda* warnings and Hayward repeated his description of Eyler's offer of sex for money. One of the officers searched the pickup and found the bag with the ropes and tape, which Buehrle identified as the one he saw the men carrying.

At the station the local officers did not know what to do with Eyler and Hayward. The "wanted" notice about the "possible suspect" did not include any orders or directions about what to do with the suspect, so they put Eyler in a cell then urgently asked the task force to come and deal with the situation. At about 12:15 p.m. a police helicopter landed at the post, flying in Love and two additional task force officers. Around 1:30 p.m. Love started questioning Eyler. Eyler refused to talk about his sexual preferences but he was otherwise cooperative, answering all questions and agreeing to virtually all of the officers' requests, including a search of his pickup truck. Eyler denied any involvement in any murders.

An officer from the post came in to return to Eyler the belongings taken from him before he was put in the cell, which included his boots. One of the task force officers saw the boots and suspected that they matched the footprints taken by Lake County detectives at the Calise murder scene. Pavlakovic asked Eyler if the police could keep the boots, and Eyler agreed.

In the meantime, police technicians were searching the truck. They looked for fingerprints and took ink impressions of the tire treads. They found Eyler's knife with blood on it. When Eyler heard about it, he said, "If it's got human blood, it's mine. I cut myself and went to County Hospital."

Love was concerned about Eyler's being held for so long without being charged. "You've got to charge him," he told Pavlakovic. "Soliciting for prostitution isn't much, but it's all we've got." Pavlakovic refused to do so, saying, "Bond's a hundred dollars, and Eyler's got a one-hundred dollar bill. What would be the point?" As tension built up between the local police and the task force officers time dragged on, and still no charges were filed. Eventually, at about 7:00 p.m., twelve hours after Officer Buehrle stopped him, Eyler was told that he could take his pickup truck and go. Shortly after Eyler left the Lowell post, the officers from Lake County arrived and were angry to hear that Eyler had not been charged but instead released.

The task force put renewed efforts into the investigation. The next morning, October 1, 1983, Love and another officer came to the apartment that Eyler shared with David Little holding a search warrant. Eyler and Little, both of whom were in the apartment, were cooperative and agreed to the search. The officers took many of Eyler's personal items, as well as telephone bills and credit cards.

At police headquarters a careful study of the bills revealed that Eyler had made phone calls to Little and Dobrovolskis at odd hours from faraway pay phones located near at least nine of the crime scenes of murders that had been attributed to the person who had come to be called the "Highway Killer." The calls were each made just a short time after a murder had been committed. Likewise, a study of the credit card records revealed that Eyler had purchased gas near some of the murder scenes at times consistent with the murders.

On October 3, Lake County officers appeared at Dobrovolskis's house in

Chicago, where Eyler was at the time. The officers informed him that the earlier ink impressions of his tire treads were not suitable and got Eyler's permission to take new ones. In the following weeks three additional searches of Eyler's and Little's apartment in Terre Haute were made, and the police took blood and hair samples from Eyler.

Eyler's boots, knife, and pickup tires were sent to police and FBI crime laboratories. The FBI lab found that the human blood inside Eyler's boots was the blood type of murder victim Calise, which was a different blood type than Eyler's. The specialist at the Indiana State Police crime lab got the same results for the blood on the knife. In addition, Eyler's boots and pickup tires exactly matched the prints taken from where Calise's body had been found. In October 1983, Assistant State Attorney Raymond McKoski filed charges against Eyler for the murder of Ralph Calise. Eyler later confessed that he had engaged in more than twenty other murders of the same sort.

IT IS HARD TO IMAGINE MORE EGREGIOUS CONDUCT THAN WHAT Eyler had done. To satisfy his own perverted desires he took the lives of others; he was a pitiless predator putting his own sexual delight ahead of the value of human life. No doubt common people's intuitions of justice would find this to be an appallingly egregious case, which is a conclusion supported by the fact that of the hundreds of test participants who have read the facts of *Eyler*, essentially all of them found that he deserved the most serious punishment available, whether life imprisonment or the death penalty. What would a community think of a criminal justice system that adopted rules that it knew would protect Eyler and offenders like him from any punishment for their hideous crimes?

EYLER'S FAMILY HIRED DAVID SCHIPPERS, A CHICAGO ATTORNEY, to represent Eyler. Schippers filed pretrial suppression motions based mainly on a contention that Eyler was illegally arrested on September 30. Among other things, the motions sought: (1) to suppress the evidence seized, and the statements made in the Lowell police post, on September

30; (2) to quash the search warrant of October 1 and to suppress the evidence seized based on that warrant; (3) to suppress evidence seized on October 3 from Eyler's pickup truck; and (4) to quash three other search warrants executed in October and November under which the samples of Eyler's hair and blood, among other things, were taken.

The pretrial hearings began on January 21, 1984, before Judge William D. Block of the Nineteenth Circuit Court in Waukegan, Illinois. The hearing revolved around whether the warrantless search and seizure conducted on September 30 were lawful under the Supreme Court's 1968 decision in *Terry v. Ohio*. Under *Terry* police can briefly detain and search someone based on a reasonable suspicion of criminal activity—a lower standard than the "probable cause" usually required for arrest. Such brief detentions have come to be known as "*Terry* stops."

At the hearing, Prosecutor McKoski contended that the searches were all legal. The police officers acted in good faith and indeed had obtained Eyler's permission to conduct the initial searches. Buehrle had justifiably stopped Eyler for a parking violation, and during the valid stop the defendant was recognized as a suspect in the murders of young gay men, which allowed for a *Terry* stop so the police could further investigate Eyler's conduct on the current facts. In any case, Eyler's consent to the searches avoided any illegality. Further, while Eyler was not officially arrested at the scene for solicitation, the police had grounds to do so based on Hayward's report in the back of the squad car; the searches could have been authorized as incident to such an arrest.

Judge Block ruled that although the original stop was valid under *Terry*, Eyler's subsequent detention went beyond what the *Terry* decision authorized. While the officers subsequently found probable cause for an arrest—based Hayward's confession in the back of the squad car that their intention was to have sex for money as well as the evidence connecting Eyler to the murders—they had not seized the evidence they did because of that offense but rather had seized it in their investigation of the murders. *Terry* only allowed a stop for a limited time, and that period expired before the officers had obtained the probable cause to arrest him.

The decision that Det. Sgt. John Pavlakovic, the shift supervisor, had made in the middle of his morning shave, to have Eyler and Hayward detained for further investigation, turned out to be in error, in the judge's later view. All of the evidence found during and after that invalid detention was excluded from consideration.

Further, all subsequent searches in the days following the invalid arrest were also excluded—as "fruit of the poisonous tree"—because they were based in part on evidence obtained from the invalid arrest and search. This included even the searches based on evidence that Eyler had given permission to seize, because that permission was given during what was technically an illegal detention. The judge rejected the state's arguments that even if the officers' conduct had been technically in error, they had not intended or even realized that what they had done would violate Eyler's Fourth Amendment rights. Under the law, their lack of bad intention did not matter; they had violated the judge's view of Eyler's rights.[2] The judge granted Eyler's motions to suppress all the evidence gathered on September 30, as well as the evidence seized in the October 1 search and all of the later searches—ruling that those searches were based on now-suppressed evidence from the earlier search.

When Judge Block gave his decision, Prosecutor McKoski was stunned. The compelling evidence—the knife and the boots with Ralph Calise's blood on them found in Eyler's truck and the phone and credit card bills found on October 1—was all excluded and could not be used. Following the decision, Schippers requested Eyler's immediate release on bond. Eyler was still technically charged but everyone understood that those charges could never be pursued now that all of the evidence had been suppressed. Eyler was a free man. (Several months later attorney Schippers forced the police to give Eyler back his pickup truck, which he continued to use to troll for victims.)

This was no rogue judge gone crazy. Judge Block's decision was affirmed by the appellate court in Elgin, Illinois, on April 26, 1985. According to the decision, this was how the exclusionary rule was intended to work. As he watched Eyler get into a car and drive off after being released by Judge

Block, outraged Lake County Sheriff Robert Babcox complained to the press who were gathered: "He's freed to kill. Hell, it's only a matter of time."[3]

WHY SHOULD THE DETECTIVE SERGEANT'S MIDSHAVE ERROR IN allowing the detention of Eyler mean that Eyler should escape all liability for his horrendous crimes and be free to go? Even under the judge's later studied assessment, the sole infringement on Eyler's rights was his being detained too long. When Hayward confessed to their sex-for-money plan, the police could have arrested Eyler for that offense alone. The real infringement on Eyler's rights, then, was being held past the time normally allowed for a *Terry* stop. How does that intrusion on Eyler's civil rights—holding him for several hours—compare to what he did to the young men he had tortured and murdered in his gruesome ritual? What do legal rules—the kind that would let an Eyler go free—do to the moral credibility of the criminal justice system with the community it governs? Such a result could occur in no other country in the world. How did American criminal justice come to this odd state?

There can be little argument that our society is better off with the Bill of Rights, including the Fourth Amendment protection from unreasonable searches and seizures, the Fifth Amendment protection against compelled self-incrimination, and the Sixth Amendment right to a speedy trial. These rights are meaningless unless there exists some effective means of enforcing them. What is striking about the U.S. approach is that the federal courts have chosen to enforce rights not through the usual method of sanctioning those who violate the rights, whether they are officials or private citizens, but rather by automatically excluding even reliable and compelling evidence from use in a prosecution, even for the most horrendous of offenses, like Eyler's.[4] A minor legal infringement can become a get-out-of-jail-free card. The courts don't claim that the constitution requires this odd enforcement arrangement; other enforcement mechanisms exist and are constitutional.[5] Rather, the courts have simply decided on their own, without legislative agreement, that this is the best way to proceed as a matter of policy.

One may wonder about their choice. As the late Stanford scholar John Kaplan notes:

> [T]he United States is the only nation that applies an automatic exclusionary rule. . . . [T]here are many other countries which do not have a mandatory exclusionary rule but which seem to be at least as able as we to prevent their police from intruding upon the rights of citizens. In fact, their leading legal representatives express in private, and occasionally in public, a complete mystification that the United States would adopt a rule which deprives the prosecution of reliable evidence of guilt. In other words, the exclusionary rule is hardly a facet of American jurisprudence which has aroused admiration the world over.[6]

There is some question about whether this exclusionary rule approach is even effective. It has the effect of protecting the rights of guilty offenders but offers no protection for honest citizens being illegally searched or seized, nor protection for anyone if the police have no interest in using the evidence in a subsequent prosecution.[7] Empirical studies seem to confirm this. There has never been a clear demonstration that the exclusionary rule reduces the number of unconstitutional searches and seizures.[8]

This should be no surprise; the cost of violating civil rights, under this approach, is borne not by the police who err but by the society as a whole, which must suffer the effects of letting guilty offenders go free. Under these conditions, why would we expect it to significantly alter police behavior? We could get much more compliance from something as simple as an automatic suspension without pay for an officer who performs an illegal search or seizure. Even if it were for just a day, it would likely provide more deterrent effect on police than the current system, for which infringing police suffer little or no cost.

Even if the exclusionary rule approach does have some deterrent effect on police, that effect comes at a serious cost to society. It affects not only the horrendous cases like *Eyler*, where an egregious harm goes unpunished, but thousands of other less serious cases by which courts in every city in the country let guilty offenders go free.

The devastating impact of the rule comes in part because it is applied not just to searches or seizures that are in violation of the rules but also to the evidence that is obtained *within the rules*—even evidence obtained under a judicial warrant—the result of which relies in some part on evidence that was later suppressed. This is the so-called fruit of the poisonous tree aspect of the exclusionary rule. Thus, just like a line of dominoes waiting to fall, once the *Eyler* judge declared the initial stop illegal, the whole chain went over. Even the evidence that was obtained under a court-issued search warrant was excluded because the warrant was based in part on evidence obtained after the detective sergeant's ill-fated decision to have Eyler detained for a period that the judge later determined was too long. To many people this expansion of the exclusionary rule to include "the fruit of the poisonous tree" is its most damaging and least justifiable element. It allows the most trivial early error to set off a chain reaction strong enough to destroy an entire mountain of compelling evidence later collected under warrant, just as occurred in *Eyler*.

The next time you see on television or in the newspaper a person being arrested for a horrible offense—be it serial murder or rape, or swindling thousands of people—understand that no matter how clear and compelling the evidence, that offender may simply walk away free. After arrest, a lawyer will compel the system to go back and examine every search, seizure, interrogation, and other decision police ever made in the case, even if one of those was done years earlier in the investigation. If the police ever made any mistake, it might mean the exclusion of evidence which, like the falling dominoes, could lead to the exclusion of all subsequently obtained evidence. That possibility hangs over every prosecution for every offense.

The costs of the exclusion of reliable evidence is not just in the lost prosecution of guilty offenders but, perhaps more important, in the lost credibility of a criminal justice system seen as willing to let obviously guilty offenders go free. This loss of credibility can seriously undermine the criminal justice system's crime-control effectiveness: by inspiring resistance and subversion rather than assistance and acquiescence; by provoking vigilantism; by undermining the ability to get compliance in instances where the condemnability of conduct is unclear; and by subverting the power of criminal law to harness the forces of social influence to shape societal norms and to inspire people to internalize those norms.

Some defenders of the exclusionary rule offer another argument in its support, beyond the goal of controlling police and prosecutors: it is needed to promote the legitimacy of the criminal justice system. That is, they argue that it does not look good for the system to be using evidence seized in violation of the rules. But this legitimacy claim must be weighed against the corresponding loss of credibility that comes from letting an obviously guilty offender go free. And empirical evidence shows that the loss of the system's moral credibility in the failure to imposed deserved punishment is significantly greater than the perceived illegitimacy resulting from error in adjudication procedures.[9]

Further, it is not clear that the people of the community would see application of the exclusionary rule as enhancing the system's legitimacy. On the contrary, for all of the reasons noted above, it is as likely that ordinary people see the rule as evidence that the system is caught up in game playing rather than in seriously and thoughtfully trying to protect citizens from serious governmental intrusions on liberties. Consider a recent poll concerning the operation of the *Miranda* rule, which excludes incriminating statements, no matter how reliable they are proved to be, if the suspect was not first told of his *Miranda* rights.[10] The poll found that nearly 40 percent of the public believe the rule has caused too many offenders to escape punishment.[11] A justice system can scarcely claim legitimacy if 40 percent of its citizens believe it adopts rules that will regularly produce failures of justice. Studies also show that people think the exclusionary rule should take account of the reason the police performed an illegal search in the first place. They are much less likely to accept exclusion of evidence if it is out of inexperience than if it is out of racism, for example.[12] Yet the rule is applied without regard to the officer's motivation.[13] Indeed, most factors that one might think relevant, such as the seriousness of the offenses at issue, are deemed equally irrelevant.

One might conclude that sacrificing the ability to prosecute a minor drug offense is a tolerable price to pay to sanction police for an error, but sacrificing punishment of Eyler for his multiple murder-tortures is not.

What does it say about the importance the system places on doing justice when it completely disregards the seriousness of the offense as it lets offenders go free under the exclusionary rule?

If the goal is to protect the civil liberties of all citizens, a better approach would be to use mechanisms such as administrative or criminal sanctions against officials who intentionally violate rights or easy and automatic civil compensation for those whose rights are violated, or both. This approach would show a true commitment to protecting liberties while simultaneously working to build the system's legitimacy. There is little "legitimacy" to be earned by an approach that focuses not on the rights of honest citizens but rather seems intent on helping the torturer-murderers of the world, like Eyler, win the excluded-evidence lottery.

While some scholars have been intent on pressing the American view on other countries—more on this in chapter 11—those efforts thankfully have been generally unsuccessful. As Chief Justice Warren Burger said in dissent in *Bivens v. Six Unknown Agents of Fed. Bureau of Narcotics*, "This evidentiary rule is unique to American jurisprudence. Although the English and Canadian legal systems are highly regarded, neither has adopted our rule."[14] Of the few countries that have any sort of exclusionary rule, the rule is typically applied discretionarily and often is designed to serve some interest other than deterring police conduct, such as protecting privacy.[15]

Even countries likely to be influenced by the U.S. practice reject the American approach. The Canadian system, for example, rejects automatic exclusion in favor of a selective discretionary approach that looks to the effect on the system's reputation. Section 24(2) of the Charter provides: "Where . . . a court concludes that evidence was obtained in a manner that infringed or denied any rights or freedoms guaranteed by this Charter, the evidence shall be excluded if it is established that, having regard to all the circumstances, *the admission of it in the proceedings would bring the administration of justice into disrepute*" (emphasis added). As the Canadian courts explain, "The main purpose of s.24(2) is to protect the reputation of the administration of justice," hardly a purpose that would be achieved by letting the Eylers of the world commit repeated murders with impunity.[16]

The United Kingdom also rejects the American form, which would allow the suppression of "the very body of a murder victim," and adopts a noticeably more limited rule, showing a greater concern for the importance of doing justice.[17] English law does not apply the "fruit of the poisonous tree" doctrine when the "fruit" is reliable evidence. For example, when a coerced confession leads to recovery of stolen property, the confession will be suppressed but the property will be admitted in evidence. Under the U.S. approach, the reliability of the evidence is irrelevant. The English exclusionary rule as applied to the fruits of excluded confessions is tempered by a reliability principle.[18]

The European Court of Human Rights also rejects the American automatic exclusion in favor of an overall assessment of what is fair:

> It is not the role of the Court to determine, as a matter of principle, whether particular types of evidence—for example, unlawfully obtained evidence—may be admissible or, indeed, whether the applicant was guilty or not. The question which must be answered is *whether the proceedings as a whole, including the way in which the evidence was obtained, were fair* [emphasis added]. This involves an examination of the alleged "unlawfulness" in question and, where violation of another Convention right is concerned, the nature of the violation found.[19]

This approach rejects the American obsession with the violation of any of its detailed and fixed rules and asks the larger question about fairness. Criminal justice should not be a game; it should be a search for fairness and justice. Under this approach it would be hard to find that detaining Eyler for that extra time was so unfair as to demand his impunity for multiple torture-murders.

UNDER THE TERMS OF HIS BOND RELEASE EYLER COULD NOT LEAVE Illinois to return to his apartment in Terre Haute, so David Little helped Eyler rent an apartment on West Sherwin Avenue in Chicago. Attorney Schippers offered Eyler a job painting his offices, at which Eyler did a good job and received other painting opportunities. However, he soon returned to his old habits. His relationship with Dobrovolskis started up again, and had the same friction as before: the telephone "screaming sessions," the jealousy, and the animosity between Little and Dobrovolskis, with the attendant anxiety for Eyler.

In early April 1984 a teenage drifter called Cowboy disappeared from the streets of uptown Chicago. Sometime after that a homeless person found a pale human hand while going through a trash dumpster behind Eyler's apartment. He ran to the nearest phone and called 911, but he sounded sufficiently unstable that the police dispatcher thought he was a lunatic or a joker and hung up on him.

In July, after Schippers successfully forced the police to return Eyler's pickup, Eyler returned to his nightly rides. On Friday, August 17, Little came for a weekend visit to Eyler's West Sherman apartment, which set off a series of fights between Eyler and Dobrovolskis. Dobrovolskis threatened to begin seeing someone other than Eyler. After Little left, an infuriated Eyler got in his pickup to cruise the night. Dobrovolskis was waiting for his new date at the corner of Western and Montrose when Eyler passed by. Dobrovolskis shouted to Eyler, but Eyler ignored him.

Searching the streets for prey, Eyler found Danny Bridges, a fifteen-year-old prostitute working the street. Eyler picked him up and they went back to Eyler's apartment. He promised Bridges extra money for bondage sex, and Bridges agreed. Eyler tied Bridges with a rope and then forcefully gagged his mouth. Becoming scared, Bridges began to resist. Eyler hit him hard in his right eye and stunned him. Eyler finished tying Bridges up and unveiled his torture kit. He took out a newly added awl and used it to puncture Bridges's breast, making blood spray all over. This excited Eyler, and he started using his butcher knife to make cuts on Bridges's abdomen and back, going deeper and deeper until he perforated Bridges's heart and left lung, killing him.

Shortly after the killing Eyler received a phone call from Dobrovolskis, who persuaded him to come over for a few hours. Eyler went. When he returned from his visit, Eyler used a hacksaw to cut Bridges's already mutilated body into eight pieces, which he then put in separate large gray garbage bags. This task took him until the afternoon, when he carried the bags out to the dumpster of the next building over, 1640 West Sherwin. The bags were heavy and it took him several trips. Both the janitor for

Eyler's building, Al Burdicki, and the janitor for a neighboring building saw Eyler carrying the bags past the dumpsters for his own building to throw them into the dumpster behind 1640.

Back at the apartment, Eyler continued the cleanup. Because of the blood, he had to repaint the walls. Dobrovolskis came over late Monday night and noticed that the apartment was unusually clean and freshly painted. When he found that the drain in the kitchen sink was plugged, he used a plunger to unclog it and suddenly blood, white pieces of flesh, and black material came up. He thought it was probably chicken fat or something like that.

Early Tuesday morning, the janitor at 1640 West Sherwin saw the heavy gray bags in his dumpster and, knowing they did not belong to his tenants, ripped one open. Inside he found the upper part of a human leg and called the police. Officer Michael Zacharski responded. He talked with the janitors, who identified Eyler as the one who had dumped the bags. More officers arrived, and one of them remembered that Eyler was a serial killer who had been let loose. The officers asked Burdicki to open Eyler's apartment, where they found and arrested Eyler and Dobrovolskis.

The apartment looked clean and tidy, but a methodical search by a forensics team produced abundant evidence. The body was identified and traces of its blood were found all over the apartment. The hacksaw and awl were found, and the pathologist concluded that these tools were consistent with those used to torture Bridges and cut up his body. He also determined that Bridges was tied up before he was killed. Two of Eyler's fingerprints were found on one of the bags, one of them on the inside. On his attorney's orders, Eyler gave no statement and offered no explanation for the evidence found by the police. Prosecutor Mark Rakoczy charged Eyler with five offenses: murder, kidnapping, aggravated kidnapping, unlawful restraint, and concealment of a homicidal death. The charges meant that under Illinois law Eyler could face the death penalty.

At Eyler's trial for the murder of Bridges, Little testified for the state. Eyler did not testify. The jury convicted on all counts and Eyler waived his right for a jury to determine whether the death penalty should be imposed, electing instead to have the judge determine it. On October 3, 1986, Judge

Joseph Urso sentenced Eyler to death, telling him, "If there ever was a person or a situation for which the death penalty was appropriate, it is you. You are an evil person. You truly deserve to die for your acts."[20]

Yet, if his crime was so horrendous, how could he be allowed to kill many other young men with impunity simply because he was held too long during a *Terry* stop? One can believe in the importance of the Bill of Rights yet also see that there are ways of justly enforcing it that are both more effective and less damaging to the criminal justice system's moral credibility than the shameful exclusionary rule that American courts have forced upon us. The exclusionary rule is only one of many American criminal justice practices that reflect an apparent indifference to the importance of doing justice and maintaining the system's credibility.

AFTER HIS DIVORCE, MELVIN IGNATOW BECAME SOMETHING OF a flashy dresser and lived a flashy lifestyle. He wore expensive jewelry, had his hair permed and dyed, drove a Corvette, and joined singles clubs. He met Mary Ann Shore at work, and they became a couple. They dated for ten years.[21]

Brenda Schaefer, who lived in the same area, married Charles Van Pelt in December 1971, but the marriage had been unfulfilling, in part because of problems with physical intimacy. Schaefer liked to kiss and hug but she was uncomfortable with having sex. Money was also a problem: Van Pelt complained that Schaefer was too materialistic and Schaefer complained that Van Pelt was financially irresponsible. They were divorced after four years.

Schaefer, then a thirty-four-year-old X-ray technician, worked in the office of Dr. William Spalding. She met Melvin Ignatow, who was then forty-eight, through a mutual friend who was dating Schaefer's best friend, Joyce Smallwood. The two couples went on double dates, including a river cruise on Ignatow's thirty-two-foot boat. Ignatow and Schaefer's relationship became serious, and on Valentine's Day 1987 Ignatow proposed, giving Schaefer a custom-designed 2.3-carat engagement ring. The couple did not set a wedding date.

Ignatow was thrilled with his relationship with Schaefer, whom he saw as young and beautiful. He described it as an "ego trip." "I couldn't imagine what she would want with an ugly guy like me."[22] Schaefer's coworkers and friends believed that her relationship with Ignatow might well be driven by her material desires but with limited emotional attachment. Schaefer and Ignatow only saw each other on weekends. Ignatow continued to have sex with his previous girlfriend, Mary Ann Shore, even after his engagement to Schaefer, but he no longer dated Shore. Shore felt hurt and bitter about being "dumped" for the younger woman.

Coworkers at Dr. Spalding's office began to notice that Schaefer's work was suffering and that she seemed increasingly nervous. Schaefer told her closest friends that she was coming to dislike Ignatow and even to fear him. She recounted one occasion on which she awoke to find Ignatow leaning over her holding a rag doused in chloroform. She had demanded an explanation, and Ignatow said that he was trying to help her sleep. Schaefer also confided that Ignatow occasionally forced her to take "sex drugs," and that after taking the pills she would awaken without clothing or any idea of what had happened to her. She reported that she had decided to break off their engagement.

Ignatow complained to Mary Ann Shore that Schaefer was "frigid." Ignatow wanted Shore to help him with a "sex therapy" session to be held at Shore's home in Louisville, Kentucky, "to bring [Schaefer] out of that." Shore agreed. The date was set for September 24, 1988. Ignatow also asked Shore to help him dig a hole behind the house. Telling Ignatow that she did not want to be part of whatever he was planning, Shore refused. Ignatow assured her that he just wanted to scare Schaefer. Shore acquiesced. Unsure how much noise the house would muffle, the pair tested Shore's house to gauge whether screaming sounds would escape to the outside. In preparation for the planned Saturday meeting, Ignatow brought to Shore's house a wooden paddle, a camera, film, plastic garbage bags, a vibrator, lubricating jelly, tape, a pair of gloves, rope, and a bottle of chloroform.

On September 21 Schaefer told the women at her office that she had ended her relationship with Ignatow. The next day Ignatow called her at work. Schaefer's coworker told him that she was busy, but when Ignatow became belligerent, Schaefer accepted the call, saying to Ignatow, "I told you never to call me again." After the call she reported that she agreed

23. Mel Ignatow, with fiancée (and his future victim) Brenda Schaefer. Courtesy Schaefer family.

to meet Ignatow the next day to return his gifts of jewelry and a fur coat. Schaefer confided again that she was frightened of Ignatow. Upon arriving home from work, Schaefer spoke with her sister-in-law, Linda Love, reporting that she feared that Ignatow had followed her home. She also shared that she had started to date an old flame, Dr. Jim Rush. She and the doctor had a date arranged for Sunday.

On Saturday afternoon Schaefer picked up Ignatow from his home. She had brought with her the items to return to him, and they went out to eat at Gold Star Chili. During the meal Ignatow suggested that they visit a friend of his who had expressed interest in buying the jewelry. By 6:00 p.m. Ignatow and Schaefer had arrived at Shore's home. Ignatow sat Schaefer down on the couch and explained his "sex therapy" idea. Schaefer attempted to leave but Ignatow forced her back down on the couch. Ignatow told her that "she needed to have this because she was just very cold-natured, and he needed that sex." Ignatow had made a checklist on a yellow piece of paper, listing all of the planned steps. He then forced Schaefer to stand against a wall and disrobe while being photographed. Ignatow then stripped off his own clothing and tied Schaefer to a coffee table. For two hours he sodomized her while she cried and screamed. Following Ignatow's commands, Shore acted as photographer.

Ignatow then moved Schaefer to the bedroom, where he began another round of torture. He tied Schaefer to the bed and ordered her to perform fellatio, then continued with various forms of torture for some time. Shore photographed the assaults. When commanded to do so, Shore stuck her finger in Schaefer's anus and then hit Schaefer. Schaefer cried during the assault and began screaming when Ignatow beat her with a wooden paddle. Shore, scared by Ignatow's continued attacks on the bound woman, fled to the kitchen, leaving Schaefer alone with Ignatow.

Ignatow poured chloroform onto a handkerchief and covered Schaefer's mouth and nose until she appeared dead. Uncertain whether she was dead, Ignatow tied a rope tightly around her neck and choked her. He emerged from the bedroom and announced that she was dead. Shore went into the bedroom and saw Schaefer on the bed with her hands tied and a rope tightened around her neck. Ignatow folded Schaefer's body into a fetal position, securing it tightly with ropes. With Shore's assistance the body was wrapped in garbage bags and buried in the backyard.

Ignatow then changed his clothes and threw away the soiled ones. He placed the vibrator, bottle of chloroform, camera, tape, and rope in the trunk of Shore's car. After using a nail to puncture the rear tire of Schaefer's car, he got into the car and drove to Interstate 64 with Shore following in her own car. They abandoned Schaefer's car on the roadside and Shore drove him home.

IGNATOW'S CONDUCT SEEMS TO JOIN EYLER'S IN THAT SPECIAL category of appalling-beyond-belief. It is difficult, and painful, to imagine things more depraved. People's intuitions of justice would see this as deserving the most severe punishment, a conclusion supported by the fact that, of the hundreds of test subjects who have read these Ignatow facts, essentially all of them believed Ignatow deserves the most severe punishment available, whether that is life in prison or the death penalty. What would a community think of a criminal justice system that adopted rules that it knew would protect Ignatow and offenders like him from any punishment?

AT 6:08 A.M. OFFICER TOM GILSDORF OF THE ST. MATTHEWS Police Department spotted Schaefer's white two-door 1984 Buick Regal on the shoulder near the Breckinridge Lane overpass. The car had a flat right rear tire, a broken rear window, a missing radio, and an unlocked passenger-side door. There was damage to the left rear corner of the trunk lid and the trunk lock had been pried. It appeared that the backseat and the exterior of the car were splattered with blood.

Schaefer's brother, Tom Love, and his wife, Linda, went to the police station and met with Det. Jim Wesley. Love told Wesley everything Schaefer had shared about Ignatow and his creepy behavior. Wesley and two other officers went and questioned Ignatow at his home. Ignatow carefully recounted the events of the previous day. In fact, he had made written notes that he referenced during the interview. He told the officers that Schaefer picked him up at 3:00 p.m. on Saturday afternoon and that they went for a drive. He provided lots of detail and mentioned every stop, but the officers left feeling unsatisfied. Ignatow seemed too cold and methodical, given the disappearance of his fiancée.

The investigation continued with little progress. Ignatow was asked to take a lie detector test but refused, claiming that such a test would put too much stress on his weak heart. Other people came forward with stories of Schaefer's whereabouts on the day of her disappearance that conflicted with Ignatow's story. Members of the Kentucky Rescue Association spent eighty hours searching for Schaefer's body in the Ohio River. Dr. Spalding, Schaefer's employer, started a reward fund for information on Schaefer's disappearance that grew to $16,000 in two weeks. Ignatow did not contribute to the fund.

While the investigation continued, Dr. Spalding, who suspected Ignatow's involvement in Schaefer's disappearance, sent Ignatow a letter threatening him if he did not disclose the location of Schaefer's body. (The letter ultimately led to a 1989 conviction of Dr. Spalding, for making "terroristic threats.") Joyce, Schaefer's coworker, eventually provided investigators with some key information. Joyce knew a hairstylist, Lauren Lechleiter, who had cut Ignatow's hair and reported knowing a woman named Mary Ann Shore, who had confided in her about Ignatow's control over her and her inability to get over her relationship with him. Robert Spoelker, who paid Shore $125.00 a week to babysit his children, told the authorities that Shore had taken Saturday, September 24, off from work. Suspicion of Shore began to grow. A background check revealed five outstanding arrest warrants for bad checks. Wesley and the FBI decided that the bad check charges could be used as leverage were Shore to refuse to cooperate.

Shore was questioned by the police and took a polygraph test, which she failed. When Wesley confronted her with her test results she became agitated and refused to say more. Wesley allowed her to leave and arranged for an officer to follow her. That night, Shore and Ignatow were watched as they walked in the rain. Detective Wesley was notified, and an unmarked police car pulled up next to the couple and asked them to come to the station. At the station Wesley grilled Shore, demanding to know the full story and telling her that Ignatow had no feelings for her. Shore refused. Wesley sensed that Shore had something more she wanted to say, so he pulled out all the stops, threatening her with prosecution for the bad checks. She still refused to talk, and at 12:45 a.m. on February 14, 1989, Shore was fingerprinted and put in jail on the outstanding bad check warrants. Later she was released on bail.

Some months later Shore was called to testify before a federal grand jury. U.S. Attorney Scott Cox asked Shore how many times she had seen Schaefer before her disappearance. Shore replied each time that she had seen Schaefer only once. When Cox later asked what Schaefer looked like the last time she had seen her, Shore responded, "You mean the last time?" When Cox pointed out the discrepancy in Shore's statements, Shore turned pale and left the jury room. On January 9, 1990, Shore confessed to the FBI and the police that she had been present when Ignatow killed Schaefer at her house. Leading the police into the woods behind the house, Shore showed police the area where the body had been buried. In return for her cooperation the authorities agreed to make tampering with physical evidence the only charge against Shore.

The following day, the police brought in a cadaver dog and within fifteen minutes the dog picked up a scent. Digging where the dog indicated, the police shovels hit a black plastic bag. The larger bag contained four overlapping plastic bags sealed in plastic tape. Before they were finished, a second smaller bag had also been unearthed; it contained Schaefer's clothing. Rot had erased the body's facial features, but a forensic odontologist identified the body as that of Brenda Schaefer.

While the police were digging up the body, Shore met with Ignatow wearing a concealed microphone provided by the police and talked of her fears of being found out. Ignatow ordered her to resist investigators' requests for a lie detector test and mentioned how unlikely it was that the body could be found, referring to Schaefer's burial site. Ignatow was then arrested and charged with murder, kidnapping, sodomy, sexual abuse, robbery, and tampering with evidence.

On December 3, 1991, Ignatow's jury trial began. The day before, Mary Ann Shore had pled guilty to tampering with physical evidence. Shore testified as to what had happened. Ignatow also testified, giving a very different story. At the conclusion of Ignatow's trial, on December 21, the jurors began deliberating. Most believed that Ignatow was involved somehow, but there were problems they couldn't get over. First, Shore did not seem to be a reliable witness. Ignatow's attorney had done a good job of portraying her as a jealous, vindictive ex-girlfriend. One juror said,

Mary Ann Shore's word, which we decided wasn't worth too much. . . . She seemed to have an awful lot of animosity towards Mel [Ignatow]. Because he never would marry her, that's what I thought. She just looked like she wanted to get even with him somehow.[23]

Second, the thirteen-minute taped conversation between Shore and Ignatow turned out to be less than compelling; the defense argued that Ignatow was talking about a safe that he had loaned to Shore. The jurors' view of the taped conversation between Shore and Ignatow was, "they didn't mention Brenda. They didn't mention a grave. They didn't mention a body."[24] The jury did not feel they had been given conclusive evidence that tied Ignatow to the crime. Ignatow was acquitted. As he walked from the courtroom a free man, he told the media, "This is the best Christmas present I ever had." On February 3, 1992, Mary Ann Shore was sentenced to the maximum allowable sentence of five years in prison for tampering with physical evidence.

On October 1, 1992, Ronald and Judith Watkins, who had moved into Ignatow's old house, were having new carpet installed. To do so they had to remove the vent cover on the heating duct. Behind it they discovered film and jewelry, which they turned over to the FBI. The film included one hundred photographs of "sexual acts, sadomasochistic bondage, disrobing, and torture of Brenda Sue Schaefer," providing conclusive physical proof of the horrendous things Melvin Ignatow had done to Schaefer. However, the double jeopardy bar was invoked by the defense to bar prosecutors from attempting to retry Ignatow.

CLEARLY THERE IS VALUE IN A RULE THAT FORBIDS PROSECUTORS from simply trying a case repeatedly until they happen to get a jury that will convict. The U.S. Constitution's double jeopardy clause stands as an appropriate bar to such abuse. But it does not follow that we ought to bar every retrial for any reason—and we don't. While the language of the Fifth Amendment's statement of a general principle—no person shall "be subject for the same offence to be twice put in jeopardy of life or limb"—the courts have always understood that the principle had exceptions. As they do with most constitutional clauses, the courts have interpreted the language to make sense of it given what the drafters were trying to achieve and, sometimes, in light of how modern life is different from that of the original drafters.

The courts allow, for example, the retrial of an offender if his conviction is reversed on appeal, although nothing in the language of the constitutional prohibition specifically authorizes this. If the trial was flawed in some way, why should that allow the prosecutor to do it again, to "twice put [the defendant] in jeopardy"? The courts have attempted to give the broad constitutional language some sensical meaning by saying, for example, that a defendant "waives" his right to avoid double jeopardy when he appeals his conviction. (One may wonder whether Ignatow similarly "waived" his right when he helped obtains an acquittal by perjuring himself under oath at his trial.)

Similarly, the courts allow a retrial if a first trial ends in a mistrial or a hung jury or if, even after an acquittal, the case is brought by a different state or by federal prosecutors, even if it is prosecution for the exact same conduct alleged to be criminal.[25] (Recall the federal prosecution for the beating of Rodney King after an acquittal of the officers in state court.)

Again, nothing in the constitution's prohibition of "double jeopardy" specifically authorizes an exception for such second prosecutions. Rather, they are permitted because the courts reason that this makes the most sense given the danger the amendment was sought to guard against. Using any number of arguments, a court might say, for example, that "jeopardy did not attach" because of some set of conditions, or that "jeopardy does not apply" because of some policy reason, such as the "independent sovereignty" of state and federal jurisdictions.[26]

These are all good reasons to limit or except the application of double jeopardy in some situations. If courts have the ability to determine the sensical application of the double jeopardy bar, why don't they similarly conclude in a case like Ignatow's that, for example, a defendant "waives" his right to avoid double jeopardy when he commits perjury under oath at his trial, thereby vitiating its legitimacy? Or courts might rule that anyone who unlawfully obstructs justice by illegally destroying or hiding evidence or engages in other criminal activity meant to pervert his trial—to render it unfair to prosecutors—similarly "waives" his right to avoid double jeopardy.

In fact, most countries in the world do not have a double jeopardy rule so strict and inflexible as the U.S. rule that barred the prosecution of Ignatow.[27] Even the country from which the courts took the rule, England, has abandoned it in cases like *Ignatow*. The United Kingdom has reformed its double jeopardy rule to permit retrial after an acquittal if there appears to be "new and compelling evidence" against the defendant and the retrial would be "in the public interest."[28] There is no indication that this reform has brought any abusive retrial practices.

The English reform came about after several high-profile cases brought public outrage when clearly guilty offenders who had committed terrible offenses were let go with no punishment. One case involved the brutal murder of a young woman, Julie Hogg, whose body was found in 1990 behind the bathtub in her home. The prosecutors accused Billy Dunlop, who at trial claimed innocence under oath. After two hung juries he was discharged. Later, while in prison for a separate assault conviction, Dunlop confessed to the murder and admitted perjury at the trial, yet because of double jeopardy he could not be convicted and punished for the killing.[29]

Without reform, the criminal justice system's moral credibility with the community would have been in serious danger.

Other British Commonwealth countries have taken a similar approach. In 2008 New Zealand created an exception to the double jeopardy bar for offenses whose maximum punishment exceeds fourteen years, where the defendant got an acquittal by committing an "administration of justice" offense—such as perjury, fabricating evidence, or corrupting witnesses.[30] Similarly, the Council of Australian Governments permits "retrial of the original offence or prosecution for a similar offence where the acquittal is 'tainted,'" as occurred when Ignatow perjured himself at trial.[31]

Countries beyond the British Commonwealth also reject or limit the prohibition against double jeopardy. Many countries allow prosecutors to appeal acquittals, i.e., a trial is not considered final, for double jeopardy purposes, until both parties have exhausted all appellate options. The Japanese constitution bars double jeopardy but permits prosecutors to appeal acquittals, which is also the case in some European countries such as the Netherlands.[32]

DESPITE CLEAR PROOF OF HORRENDOUS CRIMES, IGNATOW could only be charged with lying at his trial. Knowing that he was protected by the double jeopardy clause, Ignatow confessed to the torture-murder of Brenda Schaefer and pled guilty to perjury. Having earned a year off for good behavior, he served five years in prison and was released on Halloween 1997.

If Eyler had decided not to testify there would have been no offense for which he could have been convicted. On the other hand, if Ignatow had committed his offenses in England, or in most other countries in the world, he would have been liable for the torture-murder.

THE EXCLUSIONARY RULE AND THE DOUBLE JEOPARDY BAR ARE only two of a wide variety of American criminal law doctrines whose formulation reveals a sad indifference to the importance of doing justice and to the damage that intentional failures of justice can do to a criminal justice system's moral credibility within the community.

Statutes of limitation, the entrapment defense, the legality principle, and various kinds of immunities, such as governmental and diplomatic, are all examples of rules that give serious offenders the opportunity to go free without liability or punishment. Each of these doctrines promotes or protects a legitimate interest and most of them deserve to be kept in some form. But many of them could be formulated or applied in ways that take fuller account of the importance of avoiding the kind of gross failures of justice that occurred in *Eyler* and *Ignatow*.[33]

For example, some states require that all felony prosecutions must be brought within three years of the offense.[34] Thus an offender can go free as long as he can avoid police scrutiny for that period. Of course, for any number of reasons it might take longer than that to track down an offender and some victims might need that much time to sufficiently recover from an offense to be able to help police. In one case, for example, a woman named Laurie Kustudick was brutally raped, beaten, and burned by a man named Herbert Howard. She was so traumatized by the attack that she couldn't assist police in their investigation. Howard was a suspect, based on statements given by other people, but the police had insufficient evidence to prosecute him. After working with a therapist, the victim was finally able to deal with her attack—to recall details and have the mental strength to talk with police about it. She quickly identified Howard from a photograph array, independent of the statements of the other witnesses, and the cumulative evidence became compelling. Howard could not be prosecuted for the brutal rape, however, because the statute of limitations had expired. He walked free. (The case prompted the State of Illinois to reform its statute of limitations.)

Even if a case is quite old, evidence against an offender can be extremely reliable, as with showing a DNA match to semen left by a rapist. A jurisdiction that understands the importance of doing justice ought to consider longer terms of limitation, especially for offenses where victims may take time to recover. Some jurisdictions seem to understand this and have provided longer limitation periods, with a few imposing limitation periods only for misdemeanors.[35] The reforms do not *require* that old offenses be prosecuted, and in fact older cases—"cold cases," as they are now popularly called—are harder to prosecute beyond a reasonable doubt. But longer statute of limitation periods can at the very least give prosecutors the opportunity to bring the case if evidence is available to clearly prove it.

For another example, the entrapment defense in many states gives a defense when an offender commits the offense "in response to" police conduct that would "create a substantial risk that such an offense will be committed by persons other than those who are ready to commit it." The defendant need not be such a person; he can be a career criminal searching for an opportunity to commit the offense. But this person will get an entrapment defense nonetheless.[36] It is in many ways analogous to the exclusionary rule: barring conviction as a means of deterring police conduct, specifically, sting operations that do not meet strict court requirements. For example, the Reno, Nevada, police had a problem with robberies of drunk customers who had left their casinos. To stop the robberies they had an undercover police officer pretend to be a passed out drunk on the sidewalk, with a few cash bills visible in his pocket.[37] If making such cash visible created a risk that someone who was not "ready to commit" the offense would take it, then the thief would get an entrapment defense even if he were a professional thief out looking for a theft opportunity.

In other words, like the exclusionary rule, the entrapment defense is being used as a means of trying to control police conduct not directly, such as by sanctioning or disciplining police who violate the legal rules, but by hurting society in letting blameworthy offenders go free no matter how clear their guilt. The entrapment defense was originally created by the courts, just as the exclusionary rule was, but has since been codified in many American jurisdictions. Not surprisingly, it is a uniquely American rule; the rest of the world rejects the American application of it.[38]

In Italy, entrapment is grounds for criminal liability against a police officer but it does not relieve the offender of his liability. The German form of entrapment allows it to be used as a mitigating factor to reduce punishment only if there has been coercion, but does not allow entrapment as a defense.[39] The Australian courts reject altogether the notion of using the entrapment defense to control police conduct.[40] Even where it is used to control police it is commonly presented in a way that makes its crime control costs more apparent. In Canada, for example, it is considered only by the judge and only after a conviction for the offense. This is at least a more honest and upfront approach, making it clear to all that the offender is guilty of an offense, rather than the American approach, which lets offenders pretend they are innocent.[41]

It is as important for a criminal justice system to *do justice* as it is for the system to *avoid injustice*. The commitment to giving deserved punishment, no more and no less, is not only the right thing to do on moral grounds—it also is the smart thing to do on crime-control grounds. Only then can the criminal justice system maintain its moral credibility with the community and harness the powerful forces of social and normative influence.

CHAPTER ELEVEN

COLLAPSE

Escobar's Colombia

PABLO ESCOBAR WAS BORN IN 1949 ON THE OUTSKIRTS OF MEDEL-lin, Colombia, a region famous for organized smuggling of gold and emeralds. As a teenager he was known to dress well, play soccer, eat fast food, watch movies, and listen to popular music. He dropped out of school early and became a hustler, partnering with his cousin Gustavo Gaviria. Marijuana use became a daily habit.[1]

Escobar began his criminal career by selling contraband cigarettes and fake lottery tickets. His crimes grew more sophisticated as he approached adulthood. He stole cars to strip them for parts, and saved enough money to begin bribing officials to re-paper the stolen cars so he could sell them intact. Escobar then began demanding money from people in exchange for *not* stealing their cars. Eventually, kidnapping for ransom became Escobar's specialty. He sometimes even kidnapped his associates. As Jaime, another of his cousins, recalled, "Kidnapping was the base of all Escobar's crimes in Medellin. Drugs was not his most important business. It was his most profitable, but not the one that he dedicated himself to."[2]

From the beginning Escobar differentiated himself from other young gangsters by his ruthlessness. The men above him were eliminated. Even when the families of his kidnapping victims paid their ransoms, he often killed the victims. As his influence increased, Escobar hired *sicarios*, or hit men, whom he found in the urban slums. These indigent men had few employment options and were easily persuaded by Escobar's offers of money and power. He equipped them with the latest weapons, phony police uniforms, and vehicles to move freely through Medellin, terrorizing anyone who got in their way.

Marijuana had been the foundation of Colombian drug smuggling, but as Escobar came into power the cocaine trade took over because it was more profitable. In the 1970s American Peace Corps volunteers were introduced to cocaine while working in South America and started small operations smuggling it back to the United States.

In 1976, twenty-six-year-old Escobar married fifteen-year-old Maria Victoria Henao Vallejo. Two months after the wedding, Escobar was arrested by two agents of the Departamento Administravo de Seguridad (DAS) upon returning from an operation in Ecuador. The agents found thirty-nine kilos of cocaine concealed in a spare tire. Potentially facing a long prison sentence, Escobar tried to bribe the judge, who refused the offer. Escobar then hired the judge's brother as his attorney, forcing the judge to recuse himself from the case. The next judge accepted Escobar's bribe. When an appellate judge later reinstated the indictment, the arresting DAS agents were killed. Escobar's strategy was "plata o plomo"—silver or lead, cash or bullets.

By the beginning of the 1980s Escobar was shipping four to five thousand kilos of cocaine a month. One of his close associates summed up Escobar's approach this way: "He was a gangster, pure and simple. Everybody, right from the start, was afraid of him."[3] In 1981 Escobar bought everyone in his family a house for Christmas. By 1982 *Forbes* magazine declared him the richest man in the world. Medellin was a region of serious poverty, so Escobar was able to buy the undying loyalty of the residents through a variety of charitable projects at what was to him little cost: constructing churches, hospitals, and housing for the poor; starting little league sports teams, building soccer stadiums, and developing world-class soccer teams; and a wide variety of other investments that promoted local loyalty. With his *sicarios* ruling the streets, Escobar easily won the congressional seat for the region. This was particularly useful because congressmen had immunity from criminal prosecution. Escobar was on a roll, and his goal was to become president of Colombia.

24. Arrest photo of
Pablo Escobar, 1976.

Escobar's election was awkward for the Colombian Congress. His money had backed many politicians, but none of those who had accepted his money wanted him to be sitting next to them in the public's view. Two men from an opposition party, Rodrigo Lara Bonilla and Luis Carlos Galan, spearheaded a movement to expose Escobar as a narco-trafficker and have him banned from political office. The revelations about his activities increasingly damaged his public reputation and eventually led Escobar to resign from Congress and abandon his political ambitions.

Within months of Escobar's resignation, Lara Bonilla, minister of justice, began a fight against the corrupting influence of the drug traffickers. He filed papers that would have Escobar and his associates extradited to the United States, where they had been charged with serious drug smuggling offenses. By attaching tracking devices on supply shipments, Bonilla's agents were able to locate *Tranquilandia*, a massive drug production facility. the facility had by then made Escobar and his Medellin cartel $12 billion. Within two months of the seizure Bonilla was killed. Escobar, fearing extradition, declared a "war against the state."[4]

Escobar and the top Medellin cartel leaders fled to Panama. Before he had been in Panama for even a week, the former president of Colombia, who was currently its attorney general, visited Escobar and his associates to broker a deal under which Escobar—and his money—would return to Colombia with amnesty and immunity from extradition. But the deal was not implemented because several key players in the government still wanted to rid the country of Escobar rather than appease him.

For a time, Escobar was welcome in Panama. He paid the chief of the Panamanian defense forces, Gen. Manuel Noriega, US$5 million to provide protection and to cover up his drug activities. Escobar began to feel less safe, however, when it became clear that Noriega was also being paid by the United States and began to threaten Escobar's drug laboratories. Escobar moved briefly to Nicaragua but felt no safer there, so he returned to Colombia. He was under the threat of extradition but felt his chances of fighting extradition were better if he stayed on his home turf rather than trust men such as Noriega, who could be bought by the Americans.

In Escobar's absence Colombia had begun extraditing narco-traffickers to the United States. Facing this reality, Escobar united his Medellin cartel members and created a clandestine organization called the Extraditables. The group used kidnapping and assassination to pursue their goal of stopping the extraditions, targeting anyone with influence over the process including judges, police, journalists, politicians, and army officers. To enhance the terror, the Extraditables often sent letters to their potential victims. The letter to one judge read in part:

> We are not going to ask or beg or seek compassion, because we do not need it VILE WRETCH. We are going to DEMAND a favourable decision. . . . We will not accept stupid excuses of any kind; we will not accept that you go sick; we will not accept that you go on holiday; and we will not accept that you resign. . . . We swear before God and the life of our children that if you fail us or betray us, you will be a dead man!!![5]

The Colombian Supreme Court was scheduled to hear legal challenges to the extradition treaty on November 6, 1985. That day, fifty armed men took over the Palace of Justice. During the operation, one hundred people were killed, including twelve judges. One of Escobar's hit men later explained, "Pablo wins because the justice system is brutally beaten, Pablo wins because they destroyed the evidence that was there, Pablo wins because he shows that the country is vulnerable."[6] A new Supreme Court was appointed to take the place of those who had been assassinated, but all of the judges now understood the consequences for them were they to approve the extradition treaty. On December 12, 1986, the court declared the treaty to be null and void.

When the president re-signed the treaty back into law, Escobar increased pressure on the legislators with murder, bribery, and kidnapping. Violence enveloped Colombia more widely. The Extraditables killed police, intimidated judges, and bombed businesses that advertised in unfriendly newspapers. The group was being fought, but it was winning the war with the state.

In 1989 the campaign for the next president was in full swing. Galan, the source of Escobar's difficulties in Congress, was the lead candidate. He was gunned down. Two other candidates were also killed. A fourth candidate, César Gaviria, was scheduled to fly to a campaign event but had to change his plans at the last minute. The plane he was scheduled to take, carrying 107 passengers, was blown up midflight. Escobar claimed responsibility for the bombing.

Escobar also initiated a round of high-profile kidnappings, going after the political and public elite. In August 1990 former president Julio César Turbay's daughter, Diana Turbay, a journalist, and her film crew were seized. Then Francisco Santos, the son of a powerful media mogul who was also a confidant of the president, was taken hostage. Relatives of the recently dead presidential candidate Galan were also taken. In January of 1991 hostages began to be executed. Eventually the political class of the country gave in: in June of 1991 a new constitution was passed by Congress that expressly prohibited native-born Colombians from being extradited.

WE SEE IN PABLO ESCOBAR'S COLOMBIA THE SAME DYNAMIC OF lost criminal justice credibility as seen in the United States during Prohibition. People became disillusioned with the system's underlying corruption and its failure to punish offenders. Though violence had previously been a problem in Colombia, it exploded in the 1980s and 1990s. Kidnappings increased from 258 in 1985 to nearly 2,000 in 1990 and over 3,700 by 2000. The murder rate rose 122 percent between 1981 and 1990, from 36 per 100,000 inhabitants to 80.[7] The homicide rate in Colombia was three times that of Brazil and Mexico and fifty times that of a typical European country. In Medellin, where Escobar was headquartered, the violence began increasing in the late 1970s, as did the increase in drug trafficking, and more than tripled by the early 1990s. There were 400 murders per 100,000 inhabitants in the early 1990s, more than ten times the already-ghastly average in the rest of Colombia.

It was not only violent crimes and other crimes tied to drug trafficking that increased. As with Prohibition, other types of crimes also increased significantly, including car thefts, bank robberies, and even petty crimes. According to researchers, the increase in crime was not the result of changes in socioeconomic or demographic characteristics, such as poverty. Nor was it simply a direct effect of drug trafficking violence. In fact, over 80 percent of the homicides were due to everyday violence unrelated to drug trafficking. As a leading Colombian economics scholar put it, Escobar and other drug traffickers "transformed Colombia into a more-than-suitable place for the flowering of criminal activities of all sorts."[8] This is the same dynamic of Prohibition, during which non-Prohibition-related crime increased as the criminal justice system lost credibility.

Criminologists and economists explain the phenomenon in Colombia as a case of criminal "spillover." The drug traffickers and members of organized crime directly contribute to the crime rate by their own criminal activities, but they also indirectly contribute in other ways. For example, when traffickers are active in one area, law enforcement agencies are forced to pull resources away from other areas to focus efforts there, making it easier for others to commit crimes without getting caught. Additionally, in areas with high drug trafficking and organized crime, there generally is easier access to weapons, which enables other crimes.

Most significant, however, is that drug trafficking and its accompanying violence spurs "the creation of a 'culture' that favors easy money and violent escalation of conflicts over more traditional values."[9] This is a lethal version of the "broken windows" theory. As people see increased violence and criminality around them, it becomes that much easier for them to be violent in their own dealings with others. Each bit of criminality signals that others take less seriously others' violation of the society's norms against such criminality.

The dynamic creates a downward spiral. The increased criminality prompts both a loss of credibility with the community and a desensitization to criminality, which in turn contribute to a greater loss of credibility and greater desensitization, and so on. The criminal justice system's reputation within the community suffers and, as its reputation suffers, people are less inclined to assist it and defer to it, which means that they are less likely to resist the pressures and temptations of doing crime themselves.

The downward spiral of lost credibility and lost deference feeds on itself. As the system's reputation becomes worse, there is less incentive to stand by it and more justification to disparage it by subversion. The criminal justice official who might in another context have remained honest and devoted may now say, "Why should I risk myself and pass up great financial gain for such an obviously corrupt system?" As its reputation sinks, the system's vulnerability to further corruption increases, feeding the downward spiral. But the Colombia story goes beyond Prohibition's lost-credibility dynamic. It has its own lessons to teach.

AFTER THE CREATION OF THE NEW CONSTITUTION FORBIDDING extradition, Escobar wanted to get things back to normal. His conflict with authorities had made life uncomfortable for him—he had to remain in hiding and regularly change his whereabouts. He could not enjoy the good life that he had worked so hard to create. His drug business also was suffering. Its operations had been disrupted and he had been distracted from its management. But he had a plan that would fix all that.

Now that extradition was no longer a possibility, Escobar arranged to surrender, but on his own terms. The president issued a decree directing that if Escobar would plead guilty to something, the government would not prosecute him for anything else. Escobar agreed to serve a five-year prison sentence in a "prison" that he would build on his own land on a hill with a nice view overlooking the city of Medellin. No police were to be allowed at the facility. Escobar hired and paid the prison "guards." The cartel would pay the $250,000 per month cost of operating Escobar's "prison."

A 10,000-watt electric fence enclosed the compound, but the power switch was located in Escobar's "cell" so it seemed more a mechanism for keeping the police out rather than to keep Escobar in. Indeed, Escobar was regularly seen outside the "prison," including at nationally televised soccer games. When he attended games the police would block the intersections so Escobar's group would not get caught in traffic. He held his celebrations at a local nightclub. And the shopping at the prison was not so good, so at Christmastime Escobar shopped at the local mall.

Once safely in "prison," Escobar was free to manage his business without interruption. He started by getting his own house in order—by having associates whom he suspected of disloyalty killed. Many of his associates who survived the initial purge worried nonetheless that it was only a matter of time before Escobar might come for them. They sought help wherever they could get it. Some approached the government in the hope that by sharing information they might receive protection. The government, recently and increasingly humiliated, was buoyed by the possibility of such cooperation, but bureaucrats were also aware that history had shown that there were limits to what they could do against Escobar.

To intimidate possible defectors, Escobar had the bodies of some of the men he murdered burned in a fire large enough for the city below to see. This created a public uproar and further humiliated the government, which felt compelled to do something. The president, as a face-saving device, sent a young lawyer, Eduardo Mendoza, to officially investigate the situation at the "prison." "Prisoner" Escobar simply took Mendoza prisoner. While holding a loaded pistol, Escobar discussed with the official what the official's fate would be. Escobar decided he would not kill Mendoza but would simply keep him as a hostage. The "guards" did not intervene.

With this latest humiliation, the government felt that it had to do something. Word reached Escobar that his peaceful "prison" experience might soon be coming to an end. Unannounced, or so they thought, the government arrived at Escobar's compound to move him to a real prison, but he was not there. Escobar and several associates had simply walked out without any of the well-paid guards noticing.

Although he had secured an end to extradition, Escobar still feared a Drug Enforcement Agency–backed assassination or a kidnapping that would take him to the United States, perhaps in collusion with the government. When he later learned that the government had only planned to move him, not help assassinate or kidnap him, he offered to turn himself in. But the situation had changed. The government's willingness to move on the "prison" and its hesitancy to accept a new surrender had emboldened Escobar's former associates, who were now providing information in exchange for amnesty.

César Gaviria, the presidential candidate who narrowly escaped Escobar's plane bombing, was now president. He announced his intention to devote all of the resources of the Colombian government to bringing down Escobar. But, as before, this proved to be an elusive prize. Gen. Miguel Maza Marquez, head of the secret police in charge of the government's official hunt for Escobar, suffered seven assassination attempts. Maza walked away from each, but hundreds of innocent people were killed.

Given its previous losses in a war with Escobar, the government saw that it must do things differently to be effective. The government invited the elite Delta Force of the U.S. Army to help in the search for Escobar. The Delta Force tapped his phones and tracked his associates, yet Escobar remained elusive. The intelligence they provided triggered thousands of raids in fruitless attempts to locate Escobar, who had shown himself to be a master at staying hidden.

A second difference in the campaign against Escobar did change the game, however: the appearance of a group that was willing to play the game as Escobar played it while the government turned a blind eye and even helped in the operation. Both President Gaviria and the now disaffected Cali cartel members (whom Escobar had been killing) informally supported a new entity called Perseguidos por Pablo Escobar (People Persecuted by Pablo Escobar), known by its Spanish acronym, Los Pepes.

The tactics of Los Pepes mirrored those of Escobar: assassinations, kidnappings, tortures, and threats. The actions were not the wild gyrations of rogue gangsters but rather the carefully orchestrated strategy of a "Group of Six." The group was formed from and influenced by "men of the highest level of Colombian society, the cream of the crop!" according to one of their hit men.

In charge of operations was Carlos Castana, a former Escobar hit man, and his brother. From their years in service to it, they knew the intricacies of the Escobar organization, including its people and its methods, and they provided the Group of Six with names, positions, and locations of people to be targeted. The Cali cartel provided the money, which Los Pepes then used to buy further information, supplies, and betrayal. Carlos Castana explained the government's view of their extralegal killings: "We were tolerated by the attorney general, the police, the army, DAS and the Procuraduria, and even the president, César Gaviria Trujillo, never ordered us to be captured. Journalists applauded in silence and this is how it had to be."[10]

The Los Pepes program was to attack the families and the lawyers and to terrify the operatives and anyone who provided Escobar with help or protection. After an execution, Los Pepes would often leave a sign on the corpse that read:

Drug terrorist in the service of child-killer Pablo Escobar.
For Colombia, 'Los Pepes.'[11]

When Escobar's accountants betrayed him or succumbed to torture and gave up his financial secrets, he lost access to his vast wealth. Escobar had shown the power of the "silver or lead" model of business, and Los Pepes now adopted it. But they had the means to outdo Escobar in both money and terror.

Not all the killings were the work of Los Pepes. Because Los Pepes moved secretly, it was easy to shift blame to them for any attack on Escobar associates, making it possible for yet another new force to join in the fight: ordinary people taking revenge for Escobar's victimization of them and their families.

In his criminal life Pablo Escobar could have killed more than ten thousand people, so if I am from a poor family and I also have the means of shooting people and Pablo kills my dear beloved brother, I could be anybody in Medellin, any one of ten thousand people. How many enemies did he have? Times ten? That's a hundred thousand people. Enemies! And minimum 50 percent were people that had the guts to do something against Pablo Escobar.[12]

With his old support network compromised, Escobar was forced out on the run. He was compelled to construct a new, costly, and untested network that was not known to Castana; it. worked for a time but was of limited value because Escobar could not change out his own family, all of whom were well known. Los Pepes began hunting them. With information from the Medellin cartel members, Los Pepes had come to see Escobar's immediate family as his greatest weakness, so they were not harmed but they were forever in play. Just before Escobar's forty-fourth birthday the German government granted Escobar's wife and children asylum. The family was flown to Germany, where Escobar believed they were safe. Upon landing the family was denied the right to stay. It had all been another trap to show Escobar that his options were few. He celebrated his forty-fourth birthday with a bodyguard and one of his mother's cousins.

The Los Pepes terror campaign had a dramatic effect. It stripped Escobar of his power and support, just as his terror campaign had stripped the government of its power and support. Escobar's ability to maneuver and evade became increasingly restricted—fewer places to hide, fewer people willing to help. He could not easily communicate with others due to Delta Force's surveillance; he could not easily access his money or buy protection because of Los Pepes' attacks on his financial base. Thus hampered, he could no longer move fast enough to evade the Colombian Army.

On December 2, 1993, the news featured the killing that morning of the son of one of Escobar's cousins. The authorities were closing in. Escobar got into a taxi cab and drove around Medellin so he could make phone calls. He got out of the cab at a modest two-story house in the Los Olivos neighborhood of Medellin, near the soccer stadium. The American surveillance equipment tracked the source of the calls and soon located Escobar. They passed his approximate location to General Maza's son Hugo, who was leading one of the army search groups, called Centra Spike units.

The unit swept the neighborhood and Hugo Maza actually saw Escobar standing in a second-story window. The positive identification was all the team needed. Within minutes a sledgehammer was being used to break down the heavy metal door of the house. The single bodyguard inside tried to escape out a back window and was gunned down. Escobar kicked off his flip-flops and jumped out a second-story window onto a roof, but men were stationed all around the house and they opened fire. Soon his body lay face forward on the tile roof. Later examination revealed one bullet wound to his lower leg, one to his back below the shoulder blade, and one straight through his brain—in the right ear and out the left. A similar precision head shot was found through the brain of the bodyguard. Presumably both men were shot in the head after they had been knocked down by other wounds.

A search team member shouted the team's report into his radio: "Viva Colombia! We have just killed Pablo Escobar." The Colombian Army had fired the shots, but it was the extralegal tactics of Los Pepes that provided them with the unprotected target that had for so long eluded them and the Americans.

THE COLOMBIA STORY ILLUSTRATES THE DYNAMICS OF LOST CREDibility and decreased deference, similar to Prohibition, but it also makes an important new point. Recall from chapter 6 the resilience of the human inclination toward justice and against injustice. No matter how traumatic the experience in which this inclination might have to be sacrificed for survival, people naturally revert to it when conditions permit. This is true with both Prohibition and Colombia: at the individual level, people seem primed to return to justness. (The rise of Los Pepes may illustrate one part of this situation, that is, the desire to resist at all cost the oppression of Escobar—although that group's conduct in resisting went well beyond doing justice and into the realm of doing injustice.)

At a macro level the reversion picture is different. Once a society goes beyond a tipping point of lost deference and lost control, there may be no coming back, at least not by lawful methods. The downward spiral in Colombia pushed beyond the critical point; criminal elements gained sufficient influence to prevent any attempts to reform the system. Escobar repeatedly proved that, through corruption and intimidation—through "silver or lead"—he had gotten past the critical point of no (lawful) return. Can one blame the Colombians for capitulating to Escobar's demands? No. Presumably every rational liberal democracy would be willing to do the same. Colombians did what they had to do: they gave in to save innocent lives.

Once the point of lost control is passed, there are real limits to what a society can do to recover control. One possible approach, as seen in Colombia, is for the state to compromise its sovereignty to some extent by allowing a "big brother" to come in and use its superior strength to overwhelm the criminal elements. But not all democratic governments would be willing to so compromise, for both principled and nationalistic reasons. The approach also requires a "big brother" willing to undertake the risks and costs of such an intervention. It was the good fortune of Colombia that the United States saw Pablo Escobar's criminal enterprise as endangering U.S. interests because it helped create a U.S. willingness to intervene. This may not be the case with most other criminal enterprises that corrupt or intimidate governments. In any case, the U.S. intervention was by itself insufficient.

The only thing that did finally work in Colombia was for a group to take on the hateful methods of the oppressor: Los Pepes channeling Escobar. This eventually did bring Colombia back to a functioning democracy. What of the civil rights of Pablo Escobar's associates and their families, who were threatened and assassinated by Los Pepes? The attacks on them seem completely shameful conduct, yet many good and ethical people in Colombia held silent because they saw no other way out of the mess. In the long term, the only ethical way to deal with such an unconscionable plight is to never let it happen in the first place by never letting an Escobar or any such criminal force gain power.

Not everyone would agree, though. Many civil liberty absolutists presumably would never permit a government to undertake any liberty violations, no matter the cost. As D. H. Lawrence once wrote, "I do esteem individual liberty above everything. What is a nation for, but to secure the maximum liberty to every individual?"[13] And none other than Benjamin Franklin went further to famously remark, "Those who would give up essential liberty, to purchase a little temporary safety, deserve neither liberty nor safety."[14]

Presumably, then, these people and others like them would simply let their cherished democracy slip away, permanently, along with the civil liberties it provides. They would sacrifice long-term liberty and safety to promote short-term liberties. When a threat like Escobar arises, those who won't give up some liberty to purchase some safety deserve the hell that they may get, but the rest of us don't. Yet the absolutist view of civil liberties is common. It is standard fare in court opinions, for example.

> The efforts of the courts and their officials to bring the guilty to punishment, praiseworthy as they are, are not to be aided by the sacrifice of those great principles established by years of endeavor and suffering which have resulted in their embodiment in the fundamental law of the land.[15]

This grand view no doubt derives its value in helping people understand the importance of civil liberties, and one would want courts to trumpet such sentiments often. But one would also hope that the courts have enough sense to understand that these public-relations slogans have real-world limits. When push comes to shove, the courts must quietly do what is needed to protect the continuing strength of the liberal democracy and not allow it to be destroyed out of either ignorance or principle.

The larger point is that the most effective means of protecting civil liberties in the long term can mean balancing them against justice and security in the short term. The only way to prevent the downward spiral past the point of no (lawful) return is to never let criminal law enforcement slip below the point that damages the system's credibility to the point of triggering the downward spiral.

The problem is relevant to the conclusions of the previous chapter: a reexamination and reformulation of doctrines that predictably produce gross failures of justice is in order. The absolutists oppose any sort of compromise on civil liberties without regard for the crime-control consequences. If the crime-control costs of such doctrines are ignored then we invite the possibility that criminal elements can position themselves to subvert the system. This is dangerous business, for both crime control and civil liberties over the long term. Would absolutists really be this irrational? Many of our present failure-of-justice doctrines exist precisely because those creating the doctrines, typically the courts (but not always), refuse to take account of the costs of failures of justice and their effect on crime control.

It is undeniable that a civilized society must protect the rights of offenders, but it ought to also openly acknowledge that promoting those rights has a corresponding crime-control cost. Society's long-term success depends upon striking a proper balance between the two and recognizing that allowing criminal elements to gain strength can and does jeopardize the conditions that allow liberties to flourish. Once a mistake allows the rise of criminal influence, the road back is likely to be littered with correspondingly gross violations of civil liberty.

ONE MIGHT LOOK AT THE COLOMBIA STORY AND CONCLUDE THAT it is simply not relevant to the United States. Even before Escobar appeared, Colombia had a high level of corruption and violence and faced pressures and problems that the United States does not. But such a view reflects a dangerous complacency. It assumes that the current state of affairs in the United States is somehow the country's norm, when in fact it is not and has not been and it could easily be much different had we made a different set of decisions along the way. America's Prohibition story already illustrates this point. Upon enactment of the new law, U.S. society immediately began trending toward rampant corruption and crime as the criminal justice system's credibility began to slip. There is no reason to think that this could not happen again today under the right circumstances.

As a further illustration, consider the strength of U.S. organized crime (born in Prohibition) until quite recently.[16] It is easy to forget the serious levels of corruption and intimidation of local, state, and even national government that organized crime brought to bear during most of the past century.[17] We seem to have finally gotten control over it, but only through our own "special procedures" that many consider to be a perversion of the normal principles of criminal liability. RICO (Racketeer Influenced and Corrupt Organization) offenses are a strange breed and it is not always easy to determine or articulate the harm that the extremely complex RICO statutes prohibit.[18] The offending conduct may be something as simple as investing money or managing a company, but when such conduct is done within a certain context—for example, using funds derived from certain sources or maintaining a relationship with certain people who have engaged in certain conduct—it becomes unlawful.[19]

RICO statutes have been criticized as improperly broad in scope, both in the lack of a coherent definition of the criminal conduct and in providing evidentiary parameters that permit the introduction of character evidence and prior bad acts, both of which are normally carefully excluded from criminal adjudications.[20] But while RICO statutes may seem a bit odd by traditional standards, they were necessary since traditional criminal law had proved to be ineffective, in stopping organized crime's rise and breaking its power to subvert government.

While RICO rulings may have distended the law, they were a fix that did not break it, as Los Pepes had to do in Colombia. Nevertheless, the larger dynamic is the same: once criminal forces are allowed to undermine overall criminal justice, special measures may be required and one cannot always assume that civil liberties will be immune.

While it is hoped that powerful organized crime is behind us, new sources of threat have arisen that have the potential to endanger the society in ways that may prompt the need for extraordinary measures and thereby endanger civil liberties over the long term. Terrorism is a current example. While our current government may be less vulnerable to corruption than it was, it is still vulnerable to intimidation. We may be free from Pablo's carrot but not from his stick.

Just as the terroristic methods of Pablo Escobar in Colombia proved effective in gaining power and control, many countries in the world have been destabilized by the terror of suicide bombers and political assassinations. Governmental responses to terrorism have often been controversial among civil libertarians, but the lesson of Colombia and other ineffective-enforcement situations suggests that, with scrutiny, in the end antiterror measures may be the better path to a stable liberal democracy than letting organized terror gain power over government that cannot be countered except by an even greater intrusion on liberties.[21] When the unbearable terror threat comes—such as from a weapon of mass destruction (WMD)—we may have to give in, but the choices we make today will determine whether it will ever come.

At the very least we ought not consider in a vacuum the extent of liberties we can afford. What limitations should be put on intelligence data collection, on detainee questioning, on the authorization of drone strikes, on the prosecution and detention of members of terrorist organizations? All of these questions can raise important civil liberty issues but we cannot afford to consider them without taking account of the effect on court-terrorism efforts. The threat of WMDs are not so remote a possibility in today's world, where some states openly supporting terrorist groups willing to use them, such as Al Qaeda. Al Qaeda aside, does anyone doubt that all innumerable terrorist organizations in the world seek to acquire a WMD and would be anxious to use it once they got it? It seems only a matter of time before one terrorist group or another is successful in that effort, whether next year or next decade.

Absolutist civil libertarians must consider that the next 9/11 will cause its own rupture to civil liberties as society frantically scurries to avoid still another attack. We will think we have learned our lesson—again—albeit at the cost of thousands of lives each time. But the likelihood of such a disaster is being determined now, within the context of the balance we are presently striking between our liberties and our security. When the next avoidable disaster occurs, no doubt we will all regret it. But a significant responsibility for it will fall upon civil-liberty absolutists who today refuse to take account of the security costs at risk in striking a security-liberties balance.

THANKFULLY, GIVEN THE CURRENT HEALTH OF U.S. CRIMINAL justice and antiterrorism efforts, one can be optimistic that we will have limited occasions to compromise civil liberties over the short term in order to preserve them over the long term. But this may not always be true in the United States, and it is certainly not true today in most of the world. Instead we see a world in which government corruption and crime-control ineffectiveness invite criminal groups to take control and establish a base from which to launch serious threats against others.

Governmental corruption is endemic in many if not most other countries. The 2011 World Justice Project reports that 47 of the 66 countries in the survey (71 percent) have levels of corruption within their criminal justice systems that is greater than that of the United States.[22] In Afghanistan, for instance, a UN report shows that Afghan citizens are more concerned about corruption and public dishonesty than insecurity or unemployment. Surveys indicate that one in two Afghans had to bribe a public official in 2009, and the average bribe was $160. In total, Afghans paid out $2.5 billion in bribes that year, an amount equivalent to 23 percent of Afghanistan's total GDP.[23]

Few countries in the world have the right combination of resources and public-sector structural transparency that is needed to assure low corruption. A 2011 survey by Transparency International scored 183 countries on the degree of government corruption perceived by the public; on a scale of zero (very corrupt) to ten (very clean), more than two-thirds of the countries scored lower than five.[24]

Wherever governmental corruption remains active, the balance of crime control versus civil liberties requires a calculation that takes account of the special dangers to civil liberties of government slipping beyond the reach of normal methods for regaining control, e.g., the Columbia problem. Research indicates that terrorist organizations seek enclaves in countries where organized crime is most intertwined with the government. Organized crime sets the groundwork for governmental structures by which public servants do the bidding of, or ignore the bad deeds of, their crime-boss sponsors. It is not much of a leap for a local police chief to move from the payroll of a drug trafficker to the payroll of a terrorist.

In such circumstances the corrupt public sector has no incentive to use expanded crime-control powers to fight terrorism. Just like Mafia bosses, terrorists find protection at the expense of good governance.[25]

Research data supports the idea that corrupt governments do not effectively combat terrorism. The countries with the highest levels of perceived corruption are also the countries with higher occurrences of terrorism. All of the twenty-five countries with the greatest number of terror incidents between 2004 and 2010 have correspondingly high levels of perceived public corruption, and higher than that of the United States.[26] As with organized crime, terrorism puts government in danger of losing the battle for control.

This suggests another important modern lesson: something that may be a good balance of individual rights and enforcement effectiveness for the United States may not be a good balance for other countries that face a different threat level of corruption and intimidation. The rampant governmental corruption and limited effectiveness in controlling terror groups elsewhere means that many if not most countries are already too compromised to easily resist these influences. Indeed, some countries are so compromised that they presently can serve as bases for organized criminal and terror groups. Consider, for example, the case of Pakistan and its chief military intelligence agency, the Inter-Services Intelligence (ISI). According to former prime minister Benazir Bhutto, who was assassinated, the ISI exists as a "state within a state" that is beyond the reach of civilian control.[27] U.S. officials have accused the agency of supporting Afghan insurgents and organizing terrorist attacks against American interests.[28] Within Pakistan, the ISI is likely responsible for the violent suppression of criticism of the military which the civilian government is either unwilling or unable to stifle. The Pakistani Supreme Court convened a commission to investigate the 2011 kidnapping and murder of a journalist. Despite significant evidence, including emails from the slain journalist detailing threats received from ISI agents, the commission did not question a single ISI official as part of the investigation.[29] After the 2007 assassination of Ms. Bhutto, Pakistani police failed to conduct a meaningful investigation because they feared the ISI may have been involved.[30] In situations like this, the criminal justice system has little hope of holding branches of its own government accountable for potential acts of terror.

U.S. reformers ought to be careful about what they export to other countries, and reformers in other countries ought to be careful about what they import from the United States. What may be considered a proper crime control versus civil liberties balance for the United States may not be a proper balance for another country that stands in a different situation with regard to threats of corruption or intimidation. Yet Americans have urged the export of all manner of U.S. criminal law rules and practices that undermine the system's ability to do justice without regard to the other country's situation.[31] Such attempts at uncritically propagating American practice reflects classic absolutist civil-liberties thinking and illustrates another of its dangers.

Many countries, even other liberal democracies, have considered certain U.S. criminal law rules or practices and rejected them as inappropriate for their circumstances (see chapter 10).[32] This can be said of American exclusionary rules and the entrapment defense, both of which strike a questionable balance between promoting defendants' rights and doing justice.[33] The proper balance may depend upon the crime-threat context, which may well be quite different in different countries. Even other liberal democracies that stand in a threat situation similar to that of the United States, such as England, nonetheless reject some American practices not because they lack appropriate concern for civil liberties but rather because they seek a credible and effective criminal justice system that will mete out justice while preserving those liberties long-term.

CHAPTER TWELVE

TAKING JUSTICE SERIOUSLY

Five Proposals

WE HUMANS HAVE FLOURISHED AS A SPECIES PRIMARILY BECAUSE of our social nature and inclination to cooperation, but social cooperation is possible only when a group establishes norms against basic wrongdoing and exercises a system of punishment to enforce those norms. A punishment system itself does not provide the necessary foundation, however. It is only fairness in punishment that will achieve that goal—punishment that takes account of the wealth of factors that humans see as contributing to a violator's blameworthiness. Regular injustices or failures of justice tend to produce alienation and discord rather than cooperation.

Human nature compels our continuing concern for doing justice and avoiding injustice. But the desire for justice can be overborne by immediate circumstances. Yet, when conditions permit, a group commonly returns to a commitment to justice as if it were the human default. These are the conclusions suggested by the examination of how humans behave when beyond the influence of government or law and left to their own devices.

However, times have changed since these intuitions of justice were necessary for humans to survive. In an earlier age, a saber-toothed tiger might have found humans on the bill of fare. Today we lead safer and more comfortable lives, at least as far as animal predators are concerned, and have the means to create through government and law a society that does not rely upon group cooperation and justice that appears essential in absent-law situations.

The natural human interest in seeing justice done and avoiding injustice carries a basic wisdom about the essentials for social cooperation, even in a modern society. After 125,000 generations of human development, these are the realities that system designers must understand. People cannot easily be "reeducated" to no longer care about justice and injustice. Whether they like it or not, people who shape the organization of our modern world must accept the fundamental truth about human nature as it exists. Government has done much and can do more to educate and socialize humans toward views that promote social good, but there are limits to what can be done.

More important, there are limits on what *should* be done. Human success will always demand a high degree of social cooperation, which in turn will require the just punishment of wrongdoing. For humans, justice has become and will remain a fundamental value. Crime-control policies that harness our powerful inner voice of justice are the ones that will serve us best over the long term. But what does this all mean for our present society? What, if anything, should we do differently in our modern responses to serious wrongdoing? We offer five recommendations for change.

1. Purge the Criminal Justice System of Rules and Practices that Give Offenders More Punishment Than They Deserve

Doing injustice hurts crime control. Giving offenders the punishment they deserve and no more is morally correct, it provides a deterrent message to others, and it helps keep dangerous people out of mainstream society. Giving offenders more punishment than they deserve undermines the moral credibility of the criminal justice system, which hurts crime control effectiveness (chapter 8).

If an offender continues to be deemed dangerous at the conclusion of a deserved punishment and further restraint is needed, we should be open and honest about the effects of detaining the offender longer. Further detention should not be disguised as deserved punishment for past wrongdoing and it must be openly acknowledged as purely preventive. But the different justifications for further restraint—that is, prediction, not punishment—should require different terms and conditions for such restraint. Only the least intrusive restraint on liberty consistent with public safety ought to be permitted. If only incarceration can provide the needed protection, then the conditions of incarceration should be nonpunitive. Periodic review ought to be required to confirm continuing dangerousness. Some minimum assessment of the seriousness of threatened harm ought to be required and perhaps tied to the extent of the restraint being sought. Some minimum likelihood of future offending and some minimum reliability in prediction ought to be required, perhaps tied to the seriousness of the harm threatened. Note that all of these logical limitations on preventive detention are short-circuited under our current practice of cloaking preventive detention under the guise of criminal justice (see chapter 9).

A range of rules and practices have already been discussed that we know regularly impose more punishment than is deserved: three-strikes statutes (as in *Rummel*—the air-conditioning fraud case); the felony murder rule (as in *Holle*—life without parole for lending his car keys); tripling penalties for a prior criminal record (as in *Almond*—fifteen years for shooting his TV); decreasing the age at which juveniles can be tried as adults; and grading incomplete offenses the same as the completed offense (such as equating attempted rape and rape, or attempted serious wounding and actual serious wounding) (chapter 9). Other legal doctrines that have been shown to produce significantly higher levels of punishment than community views would support include abolishing or narrowing the insanity defense; very stiff penalties for drug offenses; regulatory offenses that make minor breaches of a governmental regulations, not just a civil law breach but also a crime; and so-called strict liability offenses that do not require proof that the defendant had any culpable state of mind (that is, proof that he knew or should have known the circumstances that made his conduct criminal).

Current criminal law's tendency to mete out injustice is more pervasive than just these controversial doctrines and others like them. Indeed, most modern American criminal codes are riddled with offense provisions that improperly grade offenses far more seriously than they are viewed within the community. For example, in Pennsylvania, which is viewed as having a more fair criminal code than most states, illegally selling a friend a copy of a CD carries the same penalty as robbery and stalking.[1] Displaying obscene material carries the same statutory penalty for a second offense as a second offense for forcible rape (twenty-five years). A pawn shop owner who buys what he knows is a stolen stereo is subject to the same penalty as someone who commits forcible rape. Locking a seventeen-year-old in her room for half an hour carries the same statutory penalty as chaining a fourteen-year-old to a wall for a month (ten years). These are only a few of hundreds of examples documented in a study of that state's code. People recognize overpunishment when they see it. Studies have compared the various state criminal codes' assessments of an offense's seriousness to what residents feel is proper. In New Jersey, for example, opening a bottle of ketchup at the supermarket and placing it back on the shelf without purchasing it is graded by New Jersey residents as similar in seriousness to public fighting, a petty disorderly persons offense with a maximum sentence of thirty days—but under the New Jersey criminal code the ketchup move carries a penalty of five years.[2] Watching a dogfight is punishable with the same maximum sentence, five years, as actually organizing weekly dogfights.

Some other examples can begin to look like jokes. New Jersey residents felt that obscuring hair loss medication with a fake label so that others won't know what it is deserves a maximum sentence of thirty days. Under the New Jersey law, however, that bit of vanity carries a maximum sentence of five years, which is the same penalty as possession of a weapon for unlawful purposes. Again, these are just a few of hundreds of examples of irrationalities documented in a study of that state's code.

In Kentucky, a parent whose child dies because he or she failed to properly buckle the child in her car seat is subject to the same penalty as a parent who intentionally kills the child. Stealing $301 has the same penalty as stealing $5,000,000. Possessing another's identity information with the intent to use it in a later theft is graded more seriously than the theft of any amount of money.[3]

In Illinois, a college student who takes another's lunch money from his pocket is subject to the same penalty as a person who commits kidnapping or criminal sexual assault. Unlawfully eavesdropping on another's conversation is graded as more serious than unlawfully videotaping them undressing at home. And the list goes on and on.[4]

One of the authors was commissioned by two of these states, Illinois and Kentucky, to help draft a new criminal code and analyze the internal consistency of offense grading in the two other states, Pennsylvania and New Jersey. We give examples of criminal code irrationalities from these states only because we know their statutes. None of these states stand out as noticeably worse than other states. On the contrary, they are noticeably better than many if not most states.[5] In a study of all fifty-two American criminal codes done by one of the authors several years ago, these four states were not unusually bad but rather were representative of the range of quality among the codes' "accuracy in grading liability and punishment." Indeed, Kentucky was tied for ninth and Illinois was ranked sixteenth on this measure. Irrationalities that are this bad or worse are common in every state code in the United States. And federal criminal law is the worst of all. (Despite several attempts, the federal government never codified its criminal law into a modern code, as most states did during the 1960s and 1970s.) Every jurisdiction needs a systematic review of all aspects of that jurisdiction's criminal law to determine which rules and practices most seriously conflict with the community's judgments of justice, and then a reform process that will revise these most troublesome provisions.

2. Purge the Criminal Justice System of Rules and Practices that Subvert Having Justice Done

Equally important to building the moral credibility of the criminal law itself by correct application of the law is the elimination of rules and practices that predictably produce failures of justice. Not every offender can get the punishment he deserves. People understand that. No one wants to live in the kind of police state that would be required for such absolute control. We have federal and state constitutions that set important limits on the power of government, and those limits ought to be respected. But what the criminal justice system must do is make it clear that, within appropriate boundaries, everything will be done to assure that justice prevails.

Justice must not be used as currency to be traded in the furtherance of other less-compelling interests (see chapter 10).

Motivation counts heavily in building reputation. Failures are forgiven if there is an understandable reason for them and the system is working hard to always do its best. But the adoption of rules and practices that appear to show an indifference to the importance of doing justice is counterproductive and extremely damaging to the system's reputation. Some reputation-damaging doctrines already mentioned include: the exclusionary rule; the double jeopardy rule; short statutes of limitation; and the entrapment defense (chapter 10). But these are only some examples of a wide range of criminal justice rules and practices that guarantee a continuing string of serious failures of justice. If a criminal justice system is to have moral credibility among the community it governs, leaders and the rules they establish must make clear that they will do everything possible to avoid failures of justice for serious wrongdoing.

3. See the Big Picture: Set Punishment According to Offender's Blameworthiness as Compared to Other Offenders, through Modern Recodification and Sentencing Guidelines

We know from empirical studies that people are highly sensitive to relative blameworthiness among different offenders and will expect commensurate punishment. Even uneducated people have sophisticated and nuanced judgments on this. It is not that people have in mind a fixed absolute amount of punishment for a particular offense, but rather that they feel strongly that greater punishment ought to be imposed on more serious wrongdoing. Societies may have different maximum penalties—say fifteen years, as in some Scandinavian countries, as compared to life or death in the United States—but they are likely to have the same rank order of offenses along their respective punishment continuums, at least for the core of wrongdoing (see chapter 4).

Unfortunately, it is common in our present system for legislatures to set the seriousness of an offense, and for judges to judge the blameworthiness of an offender, in isolation. Legislatures commonly create a new offense or penalty in reaction to a recent news event or an ongoing public debate about a crime problem. They want to show their constituents that they are responsive to their concerns, so they tend to exaggerate the statutory penalty for the "crime du jour." A legislature's focus tends to be on that "crime du jour" standing alone and it fails step back to put that crime in its proper place among all other existing offenses and penalties. Indeed, if any existing offense is considered at all, it is usually to be sure that the penalty for the new offense will be greater in order to dramatize to constituents how concerned the lawmakers are. A year later, when the heat of the press coverage and public debate has subsided, the penalty they set for that new offense will stick out as not in line with other offenses—and this will only serve to set a higher baseline that needs to be exceeded for the next "crime du jour" to come down the road.

This distorting process can be seen at work firsthand. It is not uncommon for good legislators who know that a crime bill is a bad idea—that it will accomplish nothing but create internal penalty inconsistency—to nonetheless vote for a bill because he or she cannot afford to be seen at the next election as unconcerned about crime. It is this common dynamic of distortion in American crime politics that has created the host of irrational penalty inconsistencies in criminal codes at work every day in legislatures throughout the country.

And the problem is getting worse. Illinois is typical. As most American states did during the 1960s and 1970s, it enacted a new comprehensive criminal code in 1972 based upon the American Law Institute's Model Penal Code. The new code replaced the mess of previously existing criminal statutes of 282 different offenses and suboffenses, which still today would fully cover 95 percent or more of the crimes committed. Between 1972 and 2010 the Illinois legislature has passed 2,331 additions and amendments to the state criminal law, and the rate of criminal law legislation is accelerating.[6] Criminal law legislation now rarely provides thoughtful, needed improvements; it is simply a vehicle for political posturing and maneuvering, effectively rendering American criminal codes increasingly irrational and internally inconsistent.

The failure to look at the bigger picture—to look at each case in the context of all others—also has a distorting effect when individual judges are given broad sentencing discretion. Judges sentence cases one at a time, so it is not their fault. Without guidance that provides the bigger picture, their sentencing judgments are not likely to reflect a comparison of the case at hand against all others. judge simply does not have available to him or her the kind of resources required to do a comprehensive comparative analysis. This broader perspective can be made available through sentencing commissions and sentencing guidelines that take account of the full range of offenses and the full range of offender characteristics. The guidelines need not be legally binding on judges to have an effect. It is enough that they give judges the critical information about how this offense and this offender compare to other offenses and other offenders in judging relative blameworthiness under the community's principles of justice.

The drafting of this kind of sentencing guidelines is a large project but is entirely feasible. PHR was one of the original commissioners of the United States Sentencing Commission, which drafted sentencing guidelines for all federal judges. With its considerable resources, the commission could have nicely done such a comparative project but it chose not to. (PHR was the only one of the seven members to dissent from the commission's promulgation of the present federal sentencing guidelines.) To be fair to the commission, at the time of its work (1985–1987) did not yet fully appreciate the level of sophistication and agreement among ordinary people's judgments of justice, the importance of the law's deference to these shared judgments in building the system's moral credibility, and the crime-control benefits of such moral credibility.

There are other good reasons to guide an individual sentencing judge's discretion, beyond giving access to the bigger picture. Most judges have their own sentencing philosophies and may well disagree with other judges about proper sentencing policies. Allowing these kinds of policy disagreements to affect an offender's sentence is to have an offender's punishment depend not on the offense committed or the capacities and character of the offender but rather on the good or bad luck in the sentencing judge assigned to the case. That kind of irrationality in sentencing can only further undermine the system's moral credibility among the community.

Accounting for blameworthiness also means ignoring factors that are inappropriate or irrelevant. For example, one might be tempted to think that taking account of community views means paying attention to news headlines, bloggers' rants, Twitter campaigns, or any knee-jerk responses out there. But the reason to pay attention to community views is to build the long-term moral credibility of the criminal justice system. Paying attention to the short-term heat of the moment only invites a perception that the criminal law is shifting and unreliable. The criminal justice system ought to see the truth of what justice requires, undistracted by current ravings, even if many in the public arena cannot rise above the current heat. When the heat passes and the community judges the criminal law over the long term, even those who were themselves caught up in the heat of the moment may not hesitate to criticize the system harshly for not rising above that passing heat. The lynch mob member who has regrets the next day—who sees in his heart that what was done was wrong—will still think badly of the others who participated in the lynching even though he too made the same mistake. The community will expect a morally credible criminal justice system to get it right even if they temporarily got it wrong.

Another reason the criminal justice system should not look to current political debates or current news coverage of a particular case is that such debates and news coverage inevitably distort by distracting judgments from the principles of justice that ordinary people hold in their hearts. People's judgments about a particular case in the news may be influenced by factors that we would all agree are inappropriate: race, religion, political affiliation, socioeconomic status, etc. We know from the empirical research that such inappropriate factors can color our judgments even when we do not realize that they do. We tend to be more sympathetic to people like ourselves and less sympathetic to people different from ourselves. A system that builds a reputation for moral credibility within the community is a system that the community can depend upon to ignore distorting factors and to look only at the factors that are truly relevant in judging an offender's blameworthiness. That is, we want the system to be unbiased even if we can't always live up to that ideal.

One of the beauties of empirical testing of people's judgments of justice is that it can exclude from consideration factors that we agree are inappropriate. The studies can include in their testing a wide range of offense and offender characteristics, yet exclude factors like race and religion to get to the ordinary person's undistorted principles of justice. Community views of justice teased out from such studies ought to be used to draft the provisions of the criminal code, to formulate articulated sentencing guidelines, and to govern the establishment of sentencing practices. But once these rules and practices are established, the general public ought not be able to influence the adjudication of individual cases in the news. Community views ought to control the rules but not the disposition of specific cases.

People's shared intuitions of justice say that similar offenders committing similar offenses ought to receive a similar amount of punishment (even if that amount is imposed in different ways). That equality of treatment can be assured only if all defendants are judged by the same liability and punishment rules rather than having individual cases influenced either by public opinion or by judicial idiosyncrasy.

4. Create or Designate a Public Body—a Justice Commission—to Promote Justice and Fight Injustice

The criminal justice system's moral credibility won't be built on its own. Too many things are working against it, such as the temptation increase deterrence or incapacitation through unjust means (see chapter 9); the temptation to sacrifice justice to promote some other goal, such as controlling police or prosecutions (chapter 10); or the natural distorting effect of government politics or public discourse (this chapter). The sad state of our current criminal justice system shows the result of the existing processes: regular and serious deviations from justice in both directions. Something more is needed if we want to change the dynamics in the future. That something is a credible body, a justice commission, that will promote both doing justice and avoiding injustice by working for legal and policy reforms. Many organizations now express views on criminal justice issues and on particular cases. On the left, organizations like the American Civil Liberties Union and the National Committee against Repressive Legislation (now the Defending Dissent Foundation) support policies that commonly attempt to avoid or minimize punishment. Organizations on the right, such as the National District Attorney's Association and the National Criminal Justice Association, tend to support policies that provide greater liability and punishment.[7] But everybody knows that every one of these organizations has a one-sided agenda and everyone easily dismisses their complaints as a product of that political view. A nonpartisan organization that is careful to fight injustice vigorously and promote justice universally is an organization that could, over time, gain influence across the political spectrum. The vigor displayed in fighting injustice might make liberals pause before condemning failures of justice, just as those condemnations could make conservatives take seriously its complaints of exaggerated punishment.

What kinds of things should such a justice commission do? Much can be done, for example, to encourage legislators to think longer term, to see the bigger picture described above in proposal 3. The commission could publicly comment on proposed or existing legislation, or even propose legislation itself that would promote justice and avoid injustice. If it earned credibility as an organization dedicated to assuring justice, the commission could provide useful political cover to legislators who know that a proposed "crime du jour" bill is a bad idea but are politically afraid to oppose it. Legislators could say, "The justice commission, which we all know to be devoted to having justice done, opposes this bill as unnecessary and out of balance, so I, too, oppose it, because I care about doing justice."

Such an organization, with appropriate funding, also could undertake the kind of comparative analyses of proposed penalties in existing criminal codes described earlier. Every criminal code in the United States needs such an analysis to identify offense-grading irrationalities. Simply knowing that an organization is ready to do such work and expose irrationalities might be all that is needed to prompt legislatures to undertake the comparative analysis themselves and to avoid the embarrassment of having it pointed out by others.

Such an organization also could conduct the empirical research needed to fill in the more-detailed understanding we need of ordinary people's judgments of justice. Present research gives us a good foundation—a rough sketch of the landscape—but a more refined picture is needed. This organization could encourage other institutions, such as the United States Sentencing Commission, to conduct similar research and foster expertise in the area. The needed organization might be governmental, but it need not be because its influence and moral authority will come not from its statutory definition but from the reputation it builds for scrupulously standing up for justice, nothing more and nothing less.

5. Regularly Ask Whether the Present Community Judgment Might Be Wrong

There are good crime control reasons, as well as good democracy reasons, for having the criminal law track the community's views of justice. The effect of this tracking, and the credibility that it brings, gives the system an ability to attract support and assistance, gain compliance with its demands, and promote the internalization of its norms (see chapter 8). However, there ought to be an important limitation on criminal law's tracking of the community's existing views: the community might be wrong and hold a view that is not particularly good for it. A different view might make for a better society. If criminal law were never allowed to deviate from community views, it could never help to change those views.

Some judgments of justice are not susceptible to change, at least using the kinds of methods that a liberal democracy would tolerate. Many intuitions relating to the core of wrongdoing are beyond easy manipulation, but beyond that core set of beliefs, community views are more malleable and criminal law itself, if it has earned moral credibility with the community, can be a powerful force in helping to change community views for the better.

The last several decades have seen a remarkable shift in societal views on such things as drunk driving, domestic violence, smoking in public places, hate crimes, insider trading, and white collar crime. These shifts came from a broad public conversation, but U.S. criminal law had at least some role to play in those public discussions. Of course, if it were able to speak with greater moral authority than our present system, it could have exerted more influence. The greater the criminal law's credibility among the community, the greater its ability to influence such public debates. A criminal law system seen as frequently "getting it wrong" is a system whose views are easily discounted. A criminal law system that has reputation for "getting it right" is a system whose criminalization of conduct or whose increasing the penalties on certain conduct will be taken as an influential statement that the conduct really is more condemnable than it was thought to be.

As the lesson of Prohibition teaches us (chapter 8), though, is that the laws cannot get too far out in front of the public in changing community views and some important limitations must be imposed upon such attempts to do so. First, criminal laws ought not deviate from community views unless there is a reasonable chance of changing them. Every deviation risks undercutting a law's moral credibility, at least temporarily. If community views shift as a result, the conflict and threat to credibility fade away. But the corollary is that a law ought not continue in conflict with community views if the law is not successful in shifting them. Even if the chance of success look promising at the start, if a reform effort is not making progress, it ought to be abandoned. The system ought not fritter away its "credibility chips" on a losing proposition because it will want and need those chips for other reform projects in the future.

A second operating principle is that this power of the criminal law system to lead rather than follow ought to be used sparingly. The "credibility chips" that it earns by tracking community views are precious and ought to be "spent" only to bring about changes in social norms that are the most important to the long-term well-being of society. While social reformers might be tempted to spend a system's credibility chips on many different laudable reform goals, credibility is a limited commodity that must be reserved for the most important reforms.

Finally, note that criminal law cannot and should not be expected to do all of the heavy lifting. Many other public institutions—political, religious, educational, social, and commercial—will have a voice in the larger public conversation by which community views are changed. It might even be possible to bring about changes without the involvement of the criminal law system at all; other public forces could change the community view on their own, and the law could follow. But, no doubt, a credible criminal law system can provide reformers with much-needed influence.

In fact, in a society as diverse as ours, criminal law may be the only society-wide institution that can speak to everyone. Traditional institutions of influence that shaped societal views—the older religious, social, educational, and ethnic organizations—have increasingly limited influence due to the splintering of a common social view as diversity grows. Criminal law is the one institution on which all of us depend for justice and safety and in which we vest the greatest power to intrude upon our personal lives.

The larger point here is that criminal law ought not always follow existing community views. If society is to improve itself, the criminal law can, selectively, be an enormously important force for positive change. But this influence is possible only if it has first earned a reputation within the community as a reliable moral authority, and that reputation is not possible unless the system is careful to avoid conflicts with the community's existing judgments of justice. The criminal justice system's enormous potential as an influential reformer depends on its ability to publicly commit itself to the goal of promoting justice and avoiding injustice.

POSTSCRIPT

What Are They Doing Now?

ONE ASPECT OF OUR SOCIAL NATURE AS HUMANS IS AN INTEREST in other humans. So to answer lingering curiosities that some readers will have, we bring you up to date on the people whose stories we have told here.

The exiles on Molokai Island improved their conditions slowly. For centuries people believed leprosy was a curse from God or an advanced stage of syphilis. But medical advances helped remove that stigma. It is now called Hansen's disease, named after Gerhard Hansen, who first isolated the leprosy bacteria. Only 5 percent of the world's population has the genetic makeup that renders them susceptible to the bacteria's effects. In the 1940s, drug treatments became available to fight the infection, making the disease rarely fatal. The Molokai inhabitants who responded to treatment and thus no longer had active bacilli in their blood, were allowed to leave Molokai. New cases of leprosy were usually treated with outpatient medications.[1] By the time Hawaii joined the United States in 1959, 139 of the 174 patients on Molokai had left the island. The exile policy ended in 1969.[2]

Some exiles wanted to stay on the island as permanent residents and, after some legal battles, were allowed to do so. As one long-term resident explained, it "[u]sed to be a devil's island, a gateway to hell, worse than a prison. Today it is a gateway to heaven. There is a spirituality to the place. All the sufferings of those whose blood has touched the land—the effect is so powerful even the rain cannot wash it away."[3] As of 2014, the facility remains open for the few remaining long-term residents, the youngest of whom is older than seventy. Father Damien was canonized by the Roman Catholic Church in 2009.

THE TWO-MAN EXPEDITION THAT MADE IT OUT OF THE ANDES after the plane crash to bring back rescuers had a dramatic story of their own. Recall that the expeditionaries had no ropes, tents, or maps to find their way. Nando Parrado recalls, "I had never felt so focused, so driven, so fiercely alive."[4] The other man, Roberto Cannessa, repeatedly wanted to turn back but Parrado would hardly stop to rest. They hiked for ten days and arrived in a green valley. The other man refused to go on. Suddenly they saw a grazing cow, which meant people were nearby. While they debated how to kill and eat the cow, Cannessa saw a rancher on the opposite side of a fast-moving river. Then came a moment of comedy. Parrado could not see the rancher because his vision at that point had become so poor, but Cannessa, whose vision was fine, was too weak to move, so Cannessa shouted directions to Parrado to guide him to the best yelling location and direction. Just as they gave up in despair, the rancher reappeared closer, then yelled to them. Over the roar of the river only one word was understood: "Mañana" (tomorrow). Indeed, when the men woke the next morning before dawn they saw three men sitting around a campfire across the river. The raging river made shouting useless, so one rancher tossed a note fastened to a rock to the dirty, bearded, emaciated men on the other side. The note read, "There is a man coming later that I told him to go. Tell me what you want." Upon receiving a note tossed back, the man threw the survivors a hunk of bread and left. After a few hours, a different rancher arrived on their side of the river. He gave the men some cheese and went off to tend his animals. By afternoon the men were fed, but they were anxious to start the rescue of their comrades back at the crash site. They were assured that earlier in the day a man had begun the ten-hour horseback ride to alert the authorities. Help would soon be on its way. The police arrived by evening and radioed authorities in Santiago for the helicopters that would be needed for the rescue in the Andes.

When the police asked the men to give the names of the survivors, the men hesitated. Two of the survivors had been so close to death that they feared their families might be told of their rescue only to learn soon after that they had in fact died. Before the helicopters arrived, the press did. The police then announced that the helicopters would not be coming that day because of thick fog, but just hours later the helicopters found a break in the fog and landed near the group. The air force commander, Carlos Garcia, showed the two survivors a map and had them point out the crash site location. But he was skeptical. He told the other pilots, "He's confused. They couldn't have crossed the Andes on foot! Impossible!"[5] Still doubtful, the commander began the rescue attempt three hours later.

As the three helicopters climbed to clear the last mountain, the air became thin, making it difficult to safely manage the machines. As they crossed the last mountain, the rush of air coming up the other side grabbed the machines and the pilots had to fight to prevent a crash. Commander Garcia thought the helicopters could continue but made each man on board state that he was volunteering to continue.

They did arrive safely at the crash site, exactly where Parrado had said it would be. The other survivors were shouting and waving wildly. Because the air was so thin, the helicopters could not land for fear they would be unable take off again. Hovering just above the snow, each copter discharged two rescuers and took on two survivors. The two gravely ill men were taken directly to a hospital. Not everyone was able to get off the mountain that night. For those left on it, one more night did not seem to matter. There was now food, warmth, and the knowledge that their ordeal was nearly over.

At day's end, alone in a hospital room, a safe and warm Parrado struggled to believe. "Breathe once more, we used to say on the mountain, to encourage each other in moments of despair. As long as you breathe, you are alive. In those days, each breath was almost an act of defiance. In my seventy-two days in the Andes, there had not been a single breath that wasn't taken with fear."

As people celebrated the men's survival, questions began to be asked: How could they have survived so long? The men acknowledged eating the dead.[6] One of the men asked a priest for forgiveness for the sin only to be told that no sin had been committed. The Catholic Church recognizes the necessity that had driven the survivors to eat the dead. The families of the dead and the families of those eaten seemed to understand that there were no good choices.

Parrado's father implored his son in his first days back, "Don't let this be the most important thing that happens to you. Look forward." He did. Parrado, who had lain in a coma after the crash with a broken skull yet lived to save them all, became a Formula One race car driver. He later retired to his father's business and married. Cannessa became a trusted doctor. Among the other crash survivors were doctors, farmers, managers, and fathers.

WHILE MOST PIRATES NEAR THE BAHAMAS ACCEPTED THE KING'S amnesty (chapter 2), some, including Blackbeard, perhaps the most famous of the pirates, were furious at the deal that had been made for amnesty.[7] They preferred to stay with piracy. However, they soon found themselves outgunned and outnumbered by Woodes Rogers's fleet. Blackbeard sailed north and negotiated a deal with Gov. Charles Eden of North Carolina; the governor made a fortune as Blackbeard's fence.[8] Unfortunately for Blackbeard, Alexander Spotswood, the governor of Virginia, was unhappy with the deal (perhaps out of jealousy) and also had local political problems from which he needed to divert public attention, so he took on the task of hunting down the famous holdout. Blackbeard was eventually decapitated in battle and his head hung from the mast of his ship.[9] Woodes Rogers, the privateer captain who brought force and the promise of amnesty to the Bahamas to end the age of piracy, became something of a trendsetter when he adopted much of the pirate code for his own ships.

The young colonies of North America were an attractive destination for many former pirates. Many of the novel democratic features of pirate governance were echoed in the legal structure of the colonies and, a generation later, in the new American government. Pirate regulations and American law both sought a separation of powers within government, clearly stated laws and punishment, equality among all members, and the subservience of the elected leaders to the public.

In 1776, when America declared independence from Britain, the

American navy was six ships strong. The English placed shipping embargoes on the breakaway colonies, and the United States adopted the British tradition of "letters of marque" that actually created pirates, or "privateers" (depending on which country was applying the label). The newly minted U.S. Constitution listed, and still lists, issuing *letters of marque and reprisal* in Section 8 as one of the enumerated powers of Congress, alongside the powers to tax and declare war. However, since the American Civil War, the United States has followed the terms of the 1856 Paris Declaration that forbids the practice.

The power of pirates, who act as water-based guerrilla fighters, is still evident in the Gulf of Aden. In 2010 alone, Somali pirate activities generated $12 billion of insurance claims.[10] As with the British-issued letters of marque under which privateers shared their loot with the sponsoring issuer, Somalis today can buy stock shares in piracy bands and share in the proceeds of their ventures.

THE IDEA OF PUNISHMENT-FREE COMMUNITIES STILL HOLDS appeal for many people, with many so-called intentional communities in existence. Most successful communes, like Black Bear Ranch, have struck compromises in their goals by working hard to use discourse and negotiation to settle disputes, with punishment as a backup when gentler measures fail. While some may claim to be free of punishment, they all have, at a minimum, a policy of expelling those who do not abide by the group's rules—exile being the ultimate punishment.

No communes attempt to have a rule-free life, as some in our stories tried to do. The reality of such an existence—hepatitis from unwashed bodies sitting on kitchen counters or goats destroying gardens—has made its unworkability obvious. They typically have a significant list of rules that members are obliged to follow or risk ejection. As of 2014, both Black Bear Ranch and Tolstoy Farm still exist. Drop City, which is now an empty goat pasture, will be remembered by architectural scholars as important and innovative for its novel building techniques and its focus on art as part of everyday life. Stephen Baer, the engineer who designed the radical structures on the property, now runs Zomeworks Corporation, a company incorporated in 1969 that produces passive solar energy products. Peter Rabbit now concedes that he was in fact the most prominent catalyst for the demise of Drop City.

WHEN THE GOLD RAN OUT IN CALIFORNIA, MANY OF THE MINERS (chapter 4) left for other ventures while the miners' laws often stayed and spread through the western half of the country. One Shasta County prospector of 1876, who followed the typical miner pattern, migrated to Montana, Nevada, New Mexico, and other states. By 1881, he was back in California. Everywhere he traveled, the informal laws were of a similar styling, including one man, one vote.[11] What worked for the miners worked for other groups. Cattlemen in California joined forces to protect their overlapping interests by adopting formal statements in 1868.[12] (It was possibly the decedents of these cattlemen who were part of Bob Ellickson's classic study of Shasta County ranchers and farmers, discussed in chapter 1.) The western states all eventually created formal governments, with voters often electing men they knew from their time in the mines or the communities that grew up to support the gold rush. The new governments relied heavily on popular voting and formalized that means of decision—the referendum system in California, for example. It was the men from the mining camps and communities who came to hold political force in California, New Mexico, and Colorado, and, again, what had worked in the camps worked in other contexts. As one writer put it, "Giants of debate and caucus these, whose first efforts to control their fellow-men were under the Mariposa oaks, or beneath the dome of Shasta."[13]

THE NUMBER OF PIONEERS WHO CROSSED THE CONTINENT ON the Oregon Trail (chapter 4) was never tallied, but a best guess suggests that 500,000 people migrated along that route.[14] The early destination of choice was most often Oregon, but the discovery of gold added a contingent of California-bound travelers. When the Mormons were driven out of Illinois, they escaped religious persecution by migrating along the Oregon Trail to Utah.

The most famous of the wagon trains was that of the Donner Party. Due to several mistakes, bad luck, and trouble with the local Native Indians, the Donners were late in advancing into the mountains. Trapped, they could do nothing but try to survive until spring. Thirty-nine of the eighty-one members of the group did not survive, despite several rescue attempts by others. Some members turned to killing and eating others in the group each time they became desperately hungry—a living food cupboard. When the transcontinental railroad opened in 1869, wagon train travel essentially stopped. The train took only eight days to travel the same distance and a ticket cost only $65, including the shipment of goods.

The people of the wagon trains added to the tradition of self-governance as they settled the west. Even before a formal government was established, they built a system by which groups peacefully resolved the points of tension that inevitably arose, and much of this tradition carried on to later times. For example, in 1841 Ewing Young died, leaving considerable wealth and no apparent heir. There was no system to probate his estate. At a meeting after his funeral, a probate government was proposed by those present, and Dr. Ira Babcock of Jason Lee's Methodist Mission was elected supreme judge. Eventually Babcock took on the role of a general leader to the community as well. Records show that he chaired two meetings in 1842 to discuss wolves and other similar animal concerns. This active group self-regulation continued with the formation of the Provisional Government of Oregon, a popularly elected government created on May 2, 1843, and remained in place until March 3, 1849, when the United States Territorial Government took over.

IN THE GERMAN EXTERMINATION CAMPS DURING WORLD WAR II (chapter 4), the prisoners knew that as the war's end drew near, the Germans intended to hide the atrocities of the camps in part by killing the remaining prisoners. In Auschwitz an uprising was planned to ensure that someone would remain alive to report what had happened there. Using corrupted guards, stolen weapons, and arson, the whole camp was brought down. Many died, but forty prisoners lived to share the truth.

In Buchenwald, the underground prison movement found a way to communicate with the outside world and guided Allied bomb attacks into the proper regions of the camp. The underground resistance organization in Buchenwald, w members held key administrative posts in the camp, saved many lives. They obstructed Nazi orders and delayed the attempts evacuation. On April 11, 1945, knowing that the Americans would be arriving before a counterattack could be waged, the starved and emaciated prisoners stormed the watchtowers seized control of the camp. Later that afternoon the U.S. forces entered Buchenwald. The Germans were unable to destroy the evidence of the atrocities.[15] By inmate manipulation and uprising, at least twenty thousand prisoners were spared last-minute death at the hands of their captors.

AT ATTICA STATE PRISON, WHERE A PRISON REVOLT OCCURRED in 1971 (chapter 5), the standoff between the authorities and the prisoners lasted four days. When Gov. Nelson Rockefeller refused to come to the scene and the last attempt at compromise was rejected by the prisoners, an order to take back the prison by force was issued. By the end of the assault, ten hostages and twenty-nine inmates were dead or dying and three hostages, eighty-five inmates, and several state troopers were wounded by gunfire from state police and correctional officers.[16] Medical care was denied the wounded inmates, and many of the prostrate and naked prisoners were beaten by angry guards and police.

Numerous investigations showed little justification for the brutality during the retaking. In the judicial inquiries that followed, the police and the prison authorities attempted to cover up their actions. Attica prosecutor Malcolm Bell quit his job and issued a report accusing the prosecution of failing to pursue the state police shooters who planned and executed what was essentially a massacre. Faced with the damning evidence provided by Bell, New York's governor, Hugh Carey, declared an end to all further attempts to understand Attica. No one—police or prisoners—answered for what occurred there.[17] A group of Attica survivors pursued civil cases, which were settled for $12 million—$8 million for the inmates and $4 million for the attorneys who had been working pro bono on the case. As of 2014 the state of New York still retains thousands of documents concerning Attica to which no one is permitted access.

FOR THE SURVIVORS OF THE *BATAVIA* (CHAPTERS 5, 7, AND 8), recall that at the end of their story the forces of Cornelisz were actively assaulting the Weibbe Hayes group. Cornelisz's gang possessed manufactured weapons and gunpowder; Hayes had only organization and guile at his disposal. Using slingshots, spears, and hand-built fortifications, the Hayes people captured Cornelisz but were slowly losing ground to the greater firepower of his mercenaries until the rescue sailing ship arrived.

Cornelisz had planned all along for his mutineers to take by force any rescue ship that appeared. Two men from Hayes's group rushed to warn the rescuers. Once on notice, the rescuers held all parties at bay while they sorted out what really happened and whose story to believe. The Dutch legal system of the time relied heavily on confessions rather than on physical evidence, and Cornelisz was not inclined to confess.[18] However, Dutch practice allowed torture, and under torture Cornelisz confessed early and often. But the law stipulated that such confessions did not apply if the person recanted after the torture stopped. Eventually Cornelisz stuck to enough of the story to justify a painful execution: "[F]irst cut off both his hands, and after that punish him on a gallows with a cord until death follows."[19] Other mutineers who were sentenced to death asked for and received the satisfaction of watching Cornelisz die first.[20] Several mutineers were given lesser punishments because of extenuating circumstances.[21]

The company representative in charge when the *Batavia* was lost was forgiven for the loss of the ship but was thought to be unreliable. He died within a year. The captain of the *Batavia*, who brought about the rescue with a daring feat of near-miraculous seamanship, nonetheless was held under some suspicion that he had once been a confederate of the evil Cornelisz in a never-executed plot to take the ship for private purposes. It apparently did not help him that he alone had made the rescue possible, that he had full power to execute such a taking but had not, or that he was never found guilty of anything. He was essentially left to rot in prison, where he died.

Steadfast Weibbe Hayes, the common soldier who rose to lead, received a handsome promotion and was commissioned as an officer. The soldiers who served alongside him were also promoted and given cash rewards.[22] The treasure that Cornelisz had sought to steal was recovered from the wreck and eventually made its way back to Holland.

THE NETSILIK PEOPLE'S STRUGGLES TO SURVIVE (CHAPTER 6) were relieved to some extent when their isolation ended in the 1900s. Canadian law began to be applied to the Netsilik, but Canadian law did not always translate well into the realities of Netsilik life. In one case, for example, a man killed his hunting partner and word of the killing made its way to the mounties, who came to investigate. The man cooperated fully, explaining the crime and showing the police where it had occurred. He was sentenced to jail, and while in jail he discovered that meals were brought to him regularly, heat was provided, he did not need to fashion his own clothing or weapons, and there was, he believed, a form of "magic" whereby you pushed a button and it became daylight. After this prisoner returned to his people, the mounties had a new problem of people turning themselves in for crimes in order to be sentenced to jail.

There existed some tension between the Netsilik and mainstream Canadians in judging blameworthiness. In one instance, a European trapper threatened a Netsilik group and demanded that they give him their dogs, which he needed for transport. They feared the trapper but could not afford the loss of the dogs, so they killed him. The Netsilik did not see this as criminal, but the killers were sentenced to jail by the Canadian courts, where the proceedings were held in English and without the assistance of a counsel who understood Netsilik culture and traditions.

Canada has worked to build a better relationship with the Netsilik and other Inuit peoples. In 1999 Nunavut ("Our Land") was made Canada's newest territory, carved out of land from the Northwest Territories. It is governed by the Inuit. Their traditional practices and Canadian law are being gradually integrated into a single body of written law. An Inuit law school, Akitsiraq, was established to help bridge the gap. One of its graduates became the first Inuk selected as a law clerk at the Supreme Court of Canada.

WHEN THE CRIMINAL TRIALS OF THE MEN ON PITCAIRN ISLAND were over (chapter 6), those found guilty were sentenced to time in prison which, recall, they had built themselves. The sentences were quite short. Brian Young, for example, who was convicted of five rapes and assorted other sexual crimes, was sentenced in January 2007 and released two years later. All of the men were freed in less than three years. Even while the men were serving their sentences they continued to work around the island. At night they slept in the jail (and used the island's only indoor plumbing). On Thursday nights, movies were played in the prison and most of the island came to watch. The women who testified at the trials remained the focus of anger for many in the community. Some saw the trials as a way to begin again, but others felt that the culture of abuse was too deeply ingrained to change. As one resident explained, "[T]here's no acknowledgment that anyone did anything wrong. They just see it as what blokes do, a bit of fun in their youth."[23] When the men were released from their time in jail, Britain banned children from visiting the island. The convicted sex offenders were soon back in positions of authority.

THE PEACE TREATY WITH THE MAROONS (CHAPTER 6) WAS VIO-lated by the British in 1795. The Maroons quickly reverted to their old way of life, and a majority returned to the mountains to wage a campaign of property theft and destruction, as before. During this conflict, known as the Second Maroon War, the British imported dogs to hunt and kill the Maroons. The dogs were effective, and yet it was still not possible for the British to control the elusive groups. A single Maroon with a match setting fire to a canefield send a year's profit up in smoke.

With continued devastation to the plantation economy, the British and the Maroons negotiated a second treaty. The second treaty was not violated, and the Maroons of Jamaica have continued as an autonomous people with a separate culture. The isolation used to their advantage by their ancestors has continued and their communities remain the most inaccessible on the island. There are five Maroon settlements: three in the Blue Mountains, one in Trelawney Town, and one in Accompong (the largest town) on the edge of Cockpit Country. In Accompong the Leeward Maroons are a community of about six hundred.

Col. Sydney Peddie, current chief of the twenty-member Maroon Council established under the original treaty, works to preserve Accompong as an authentic bastion of Maroon heritage and culture. The treaty gives the Maroons self-rule and they fly their own flag. Today's Maroons insist that they are not part of independent Jamaica and tend not to mix with the other people of the country. Tourists have become a source of revenue for the communities. Each year on January 6 a festival commemorates the treaty signing. In recognition of the Maroon culture's influence on greater Jamaica, the famous Maroon leader Queen Nanny was given the title of National Heroine in 1975. Her image appears on the Jamaican $500 banknote.

FOR THE MEN LOADED ONTO THE HELLSHIPS HEADED FOR JAPAN (chapter 7), death continued to stalk. While weapons transports were sometimes fraudulently marked as Red Cross ships, the prisoner transports were left unmarked and often targeted by Allied submarines and aircraft. More than twenty thousand Allied POWs died at sea from Allied attacks.

A life of slave labor awaited those who survived the journey to Japan. The men toiled in factories, worked in mines, and did farm labor.[24] Some groups refused to meet the Japanese work quotas knowing that met quotas would only be raised. But such tactics required group cooperation. Disobeying orders had to be a collective action to succeed. One group adopted a scheme in which every two hours they announced that it was break time. They simply put down their tools and rested for fifteen minutes. Even though the guards ranted and raved, the group hung tight; from then on, two hours of work yielded fifteen minutes of break time.

All the while, the Allies closed in around the Japanese regime. The prisoners knew their chance for revenge was coming. While the Japanese suddenly produced Red Cross packages filled with treats from home, many men still secretly plotted elaborate deaths for the cruelest guards. Then it happened—the atomic bomb. From some camps the prisoners saw the bomb over Nagasaki explode. American bombers then began to fly over the camps. The war was over and joy replaced the thirst for revenge.

THERE WERE FEW SURVIVORS, RECALL, AFTER THE WRECK OF THE *Invercauld* and the subsequent misadventures of the her crew (chapter 7). A Spanish ship on its way from China to Peru spotted them. As the rescue boat approached, the otherwise-inert captain suddenly came to life and explained that he alone would do the talking. The men were dropped off in Peru, where the two officers were provided with tickets home. Seaman Holding, who had saved their lives, was left behind but eventually earned his way home. He later moved to Canada, worked in the gold fields of Ontario, ran a hotel, and died at age ninety-three, having written a private account of the adventure, which was published after his death. The officers discussed their adventure as little as possible.[25]

FOR THE MEN OF THE *GRAFTON* RESCUE NEVER CAME, SO THEY rescued themselves. The ever-resourceful Raynal, the man who had been too sick to save himself at the time of the wreck, built a forge. Raynal and the stronger men used the forge to construct a seaworthy boat. Only three of the five could ride in the boat, so two remained on the island. Through ferocious storms the little boat survived and brought the desperate group to a fishing village with Maoris and Europeans. A dog spotted the boat and his barking drew attention. Soon a rescue mission was formed to recover the two men who had been left behind. While on the island, some of the rescue group thought they spotted distant smoke. The group conducted a search of the island and found a dead body, and concluded that someone else had been on the island at the same time. (The survivors of the *Invercauld* had never made an effort to look for their missing men.)

After a twenty-year absence, Raynal returned to France and moved in with his parents. His book, which recounted the fate of the *Grafton*, became a huge best seller. He worked in increasingly important government posts, lived frugally, and dabbled in engineering projects. By the time he died in 1864 at age eighty-six he was one of France's most celebrated intellectuals.[26]

AS WE SAW, U.S. PROHIBITION LASTED ONLY THIRTEEN YEARS (chapter 8), but the ramifications of the experiment continue today. Before Prohibition, Americans would have been surprised to learn that a policeman was "on the take." After thirteen years of Prohibition, official criminality was seen as commonplace. Organized crime rings matured into multinational organizations beyond the reach of the state and proponents of removing drug prohibitions use the alcohol prohibition example to bolster their argument, claiming that legalizing drugs will reduce organized crime and that ordinary crime might also decrease. Currently, drug crimes account for half of America's prison population in federal custody.[27] On the other hand, there is dramatically more public condemnation of drug use today than there was of alcohol use when Prohibition failed.

Alcohol regulation has replaced alcohol prohibition. Every state imposes the drinking age of twenty-one, alcohol sales have additional restrictions enacted on a state-by-state basis, and televised liquor ads are prohibited. Despite the regulations, though, alcoholism and drug abuse remain major social ills in America.

RYAN HOLLE, THE HUNGOVER TWENTY-YEAR-OLD WHO, WHEN awakened, allowed his roommate to borrow his car (chapter 9), remains in prison today, serving a life term without parole in the Graceville Correctional Facility. The men who planned and participated in the robbery and the man who did the killing all received the same sentence, as if all of them had the same degree of blameworthiness. Holle had intended to go to college for business. While in prison he has taken all the educational courses that are offered. He likes reading science fiction and is regularly visited by his family. Holle appeared before the Florida Clemency Review Board on December 10, 2014. After an impassioned speech by the victim's father, Governor Rick Scott took the case off the agenda without a vote.

WILLIAM RUMMEL'S SUPREME COURT APPEAL TO REDUCE HIS sentence of life in prison (chapter 9) began attracting national media attention. The television news magazine *60 Minutes* aired a segment on his case in the winter of 1980. The local prosecutor's office bristled under the spotlight. Even after the Supreme Court rejected Rummel's appeal, the attention generated around the case continued.

Two months after the Supreme Court's ruling, U.S. District Judge D. W. Suttle ordered the state to give Rummel a new trial. Suttle ruled that Rummel's trial attorney, William B. Chenault III, provided ineffective counsel at the 1973 trial, noting that Chenault attempted virtually no investigation of the facts. The district attorney, still weary from the nationwide publicity of Rummel's case, offered Rummel a deal: if he pled guilty to felony theft over $50, the state would recommend an eight-year prison sentence, which would allow Rummel to go free because he had already served almost that much time. On November 15, surrounded in court by national news media, Rummel pled guilty to the theft offense and received a seven-year sentence backdated to 1973. He was released from custody five hours later. "I am ready to go out and work. And I intend to stay free for the rest of my life." As of this writing, he has.

LARRY EYLER, WHO RECEIVED A DEATH SENTENCE FOR TORTURing and killing Danny Bridges (chapter 10), hired a new lawyer and appealed to the Illinois Supreme Court, arguing that it was his housemate Little who had brought Danny to the apartment and murdered him. The appeal was denied. Eyler changed representation again and his new lawyer, Kathleen Zellner, cut a deal with the state attorney's office in Indiana. In exchange for a promise from the state attorney's office not to pursue the death penalty in Indiana, Eyler agreed to give a full confession to Steven Agan's murder, in which he claimed Little participated. The two were indicted for the murder. Eyler pled guilty, and on December 28, 1990, exactly eight years after Agan's body was found, Eyler was sentenced to sixty years in prison. On April 11, 1991, Eyler testified as the main prosecution witness against Little. He testified that Little used a camera to take photographs of the murder and took turns in stabbing and torturing Agan. The jury did not find Eyler believable and acquitted Little. Zellner also tried to make a deal with the Illinois state attorney's office: in exchange for commuting the death sentence to life imprisonment, Eyler would confess to twenty unsolved murders (and name his accomplices in some of the murders).

Jack O'Malley, Cook County state attorney, rejected the offer, calling it "extortion of the most venal and gruesome nature," adding that he would not let Eyler benefit from being a mass murderer and accusing him of exploiting the victims' families' agony.[28] Eyler's appeal of his conviction and death penalty was pending before the Illinois Supreme Court when he died of AIDS while still in prison in March of 1994.[29]

BY THE TIME THE PHOTOGRAPHS OF MEL IGNATOW TORTURING and killing Brenda Schaefer were discovered in the ceiling of Ignatow's former residence (chapter 10), recall that he could only be convicted of perjury (an option that would not have been available had he chosen not to testify). In an effort to relieve overcrowding, Ignatow was released from federal prison after serving only five years and three months.[30]

After Schaefer's disappearance, her boss, Dr. William Spalding, had written to Ignatow that he had hired "a gang of Cubans" to execute Ignatow unless he revealed where he had hidden Schaefer's body. The attempt to scare Ignatow into confessing did not yield a confession, but it brought Ignatow back to court, this time claiming to be a victim. Ignatow sued Dr. Spalding for making terroristic threats against him. He won his case and collected a judgment of $300. After Ignatow's torture-murder photographs were discovered, however, it became apparent that Ignatow had perjured himself to get victory over Dr. Spalding because he had denied accusations that he and Schaefer were together on the night of the murder. The state used this trial testimony to pursue their own perjury case against Ignatow, who maintained that the charges were politically motivated. Ignatow was convicted in Kentucky state court in December 2001 of being a "persistent felon" and of perjury. He was released in 2006. Ignatow died alone in his apartment in September 2008 when he fell and cut open his head on a glass coffee table and bled to death. The coffee table was the same one to which he had tied Brenda Schaefer while he sodomized her.[31]

ON DECEMBER 16, 1997, FOUR YEARS AFTER THE DEATH OF PABLO Escobar (chapter 11), Colombia's extradition provision was put back into force. While Escobar's death had confirmed the destruction of the Medellin drug cartel, it did not end Colombia's drug business—it simply caused it to fragment. Younger operators realized that the large organizations were more vulnerable to sustained attack. They formed smaller, more controllable groups and began specializing in particular aspects of the cocaine trade. One group handled the transportation of coca paste from the fields to the labs, while another managed the labs and another moved the final product from Colombia to Mexico. Colombian Marxist guerrilla groups, such as FARC, have in large part left behind their political origins and now operate instead as well-organized and well-armed drug organizations that are paid by traffickers to protect the fields and labs in remote areas. Colombian right-wing paramilitary groups are also thought to control fields, labs, and some of the smuggling routes.

Generations of Colombians have grown up under one compromised political regime after another. Without ever having known good government, the people of Colombia still seem to believe it is achievable. Antanas Mockus resigned his professorship in math and philosophy and ran for mayor of Bogotá, the capital of Colombia. He had no political background but people voted for him *because* of his inexperience. Entrenched politicians were viewed as dishonest while Mockus offered hope. Mayor Mockus used inexpensive social pressure—such as mimes who mocked people for jaywalking or silently teased cabbies who clogged intersections—to restore a sense of civil order in Bogotá. He had "thumbs-up" and "thumbs-down" cards printed and distributed around the city so that average citizens could use to cards to actively—and peacefully—bring attention to antisocial or prosocial behavior. For a passerby who helped a mom lift a stroller onto a bus: thumbs-up. For hooligans hassling an old lady: thumbs-down. People loved the cards and used them frequently. One result is that in Bogotá, seven thousand community security groups were formed.

Reformers organized "community police" to overcome the conventional view of police corruption. Police officers were given long-term assignments to a specific neighborhood, which helped integrate them into the community.[32] Local security councils were also set up to interface between communities and local police.[33] The unconventional measures triggered a new era of safety and trust in public officials. In 1992 only 17 percent of the population claimed to trust the police, but the level of trust increased to 75 percent by 2006. Bogota had more than 81 murders for every 100,000 inhabitants in 1992. That number dropped to just over 16 per 100,000 inhabitants in 2012.[34] Bogota today has a murder rate roughly below that of Chicago, where the rate is 19 per 100,000.[35]

NOTES

1. WHAT IS OUR NATURE

1. Madison, *The Federalist*, 319.
2. Hobbes, *Leviathan* , chapter 13.
3. "And because the condition of man (as hath been declared in the precedent chapter) is a condition of war of every one against every one; in which case everyone is governed by his own reason; and there is nothing he can make use of, that may not be a help unto him, in preserving his life against his enemies." Hobbes, *Leviathan*, 86–87.
4. Hobbes, *Leviathan*, 178.
5. "Hobbes is off the mark." Ellickson, *Order without Law*, 10..
6. Robinson et al., "Report on Offense Grading in New Jersey"); John S. Baker, "Revisiting the Explosive Growth of Federal Crimes," The Heritage Foundation, June 16, 2008, http://www.heritage.org/research/reports/2008/06/revisiting -the-explosive-growth-of-federal-crimes; John C. Coffee, "Does 'Unlawful' Mean 'Criminal'?"193, 216.
7. Jennifer L. Truman and Michael Planty, "Criminal Victimization, 2011," U.S. Department of Justice, 2011, http://bjs.ojp.usdoj.gov/content/pub/pdf/cv11 .pdf, 1, highlights; "Global Study on Homicide 2013: Trends, Contexts, Data," United Nations Office on Drugs and Crimes 2013, ed. Enrico Bisogno et al., www.unodc.org/documents/gsh/pdfs/2014_global_homicide_book_web.pdf.

2. COOPERATION

1. "The 16 Most Dangerous Jobs in America, No. 11: Police and Sheriff's Patrol Offi- cers," *Business Insider*, http://www.businessinsider.com/most-dangerous-jobs -in-america-2013–8#no-11-police-and-sheriffs-patrol-officers-6; Steven Greenhut, "Firefighter: One of Nation's Safest Jobs,"http://calwatchdog.com /2013/01/23/firefighter-one-of-nations-safest-jobs/; "Census of Fatal Occu- pational Injuries Summary, 2012," U.S. Bureau of Labor Statistics, http:// www.bls.gov/news.release/cfoi.nr0.htm.

2. The factual narrative is drawn from these sources: Dutton, *Samaritans of Molokai;* Gugelyk and Bloombaum, *Ma'i Ho'oka'awale, The Separating Sickness;* London, *The Cruise of the Snark;* "Collected Historical Documentation Concerning the Early Years of the Molokai Settlement," The University of Hawaii Archives; Moblo, *A Land Set Apart;* Stevenson, *Father Damien, an Open Letter;* and Tayman, *The Colony.*

3. The factual narrative is drawn from these sources: Lopez, *They Lived on Human Flesh* ; Parrado and Rause, *Miracle in the Andes;* and Read, *Alive.*

4. Hobbes, *Leviathan,* 84.

5. Nietzsche, *Beyond Good and Evil;* Thoreau, *Journal,* 356.

6. Rahn and Transue, "Social Trust and Value Change," 545, 547–48.

7. Wuthnow, *Acts of Compassion,* 19–20.

8. Shinn and Jackson, *Mining Camps,* 119.

9. Birenbaum, *Hope Is the Last to Die,* 71–75.

10. Anonymous, *A Woman in Berlin,* 34.

11. Miller and Ratner, "The Disparity between the Actual and Assumed Power of Self-Interest," 53, 60; Gintis et al., "Explaining Altruistic Behavior in Humans," 153; Camerer, *Behavioral Game Theory;* Fehr and Gintis, "Human Motivation," 43, 45.

12. Dawes and Thaler, "Anomalies," 187.

13. Gibbons, *The First Human,* 89. See also Leonard Jeffries, "Africa: Birthplace of Humanity," Africawithin.com, http://www.africawithin.com/jeffries/africa _birthplace.htm; Hart and Sussman, *Man the Hunted;* Hart and Sussman, "The Influence of Predation"; Rob Dunn, "The Top Ten Deadliest Animals of Our Evolutionary Past," Smithsonian.com, http://www.smithsonianmag.com /science-nature/The-top-Ten-Deadliest-Animals-of-Our-Evolutionary-Past .html#ixzz2Em4IRXkJ.

14. Moll and Tomasello, "Cooperation and Human Cognition." 639–48. See also Bowles and Gintis, "The Origins of Human Cooperation": "[A] small number of strong reciprocators, who punish defectors without regard for the probability of future repayment, could dramatically improve the survival chances of human groups."

15. Hobbes, *Leviathan,* 178.

16. Tattersall, "Cooperation, Altruism, and Human Evolution," 17.

17. Moll and Tomasello, "Cooperation and Human Cognition," 639–48.

18. Des Pres, *The Survivor,* 144.

19. Des Pres, *The Survivor,* 144–46.

20. The factual narrative is drawn from these sources: Antoine, *Voices Rising*; Felicity Barringer, "Police and Owners Begin to Challenge Looters," *New York Times*, September 1, 2005; Julian Borger, "Mayor Issues SOS as Chaos Tightens Its Grip," *Guardian*, September 2, 2005; Brinkley, *The Great Deluge*; John Burnett, "More Stories Emerge of Rapes in Post-Katrina Chaos," NPR, June 9, 2009, accessed September 13, 2011, www.npr.org/templates/story/story.php?storyId=5063796; Jim Dwyer, "Fear Exceeded Crime's Reality in New Orleans," *New York Times*, September 29, 2005; Sheri Fink, "The Deadly Choices at Memorial," *New York Times*, August 30, 2009; Nicole Gelinas, "A Perfect Storm of Lawlessness," *City Journal*, September 1, 2005; Alec Gifford, "40 Rapes Reported In Hurricane Katrina, Rita Aftermath," wdsu.com, December 23, 2005, accessed December 18, 2013, http://www.wdsu.com/40-Rapes-Reported-In-Hurricane-Katrina-Rita-Aftermath/-/9854144/10967084/-/b3i2ea/-/index.html; Montana-LeBlanc, *Not Just the Levees Broke*.

21. Brinkley, *The Great Deluge*, 475-76.

22. The factual narrative is drawn from these sources: Cordingly, *Under the Black Flag*, 22-23; Woodard, *The Republic of Pirates*, 30; Burg, *Sodomy and the Pirate Tradition*, 164.

3. PUNISHMENT

1. Doyle, "Radical Critique of Criminal Punishment," 7, 21-22.

2. Garland, *Punishment and Modern Society*, 288-89.

3. Miller, *The Sixties Communes*, 35.

4. Bouvard, *The Intentional Community Movement*, 87.

5. Gardner, *The Children of Prosperity*, 44.

6. The factual narrative is drawn from these sources: Matthews, *Drop City*; Miller, *The Sixties Communes*; Doyle, "A Radical Critique of Criminal Punishments," 7, 21-22; Garland, *Punishment and Modern Society*; Hedgepath, *The Alternative*; Curl, *Memories of Drop City*.

7. Hedgepath, *The Alternative*, 156.

8. Curl, *Memories of Drop City*, 152.

9. "Trofim Denisovich Lysenko," *Encyclopedia Brittanica*, last updated August 16, 2013, www.britannica.com/ebchecked/topic/353099/Trofim-Denisovich-Lysenko.

10. Miller, *The Sixties Communes*, 82.

11. The factual narrative is drawn from these sources: Berger, *The Survival of a Counterculture*; Monkerud, *Free Land*; Coyote, *Sleeping Where I Fall*.

12. Coyote, *Sleeping Where I Fall*, 148.

13. Coyote, *Sleeping Where I Fall*, 151.

14. Monkerud, *Free Land*, 142.

15. The factual narrative is drawn from these sources: Miller, "Roots of Communal Revival 1962-1966"; Kanter, *Commitment and Community*; Houriet, *Getting Back Together*.

16. Houriet, *Getting Back Together*, 206.

17. See Robinson and Darley, "Intuitions of Justice," 1, 13-16.

18. See Fehr and Gächter, "Cooperation and Punishment," 980; Fehr and Gintis, "Human Motivation and Social Cooperation," 43.

19. Fehr and Gächter, "Cooperation and Punishment"; Fehr and Gintis, "Human Motivation." Of course, only one per group needs to punish in order to prompt cooperation. Others had no need to do so once another person punished and prompted as needed. Hibbing and Alford, "Accepting Authoritative Decisions," 62. See also Frank, "Repression of Competition," 693, 694: "Those individuals that invest in policing their selfish neighbors gain by living in a more cooperative group in the second time period of interaction within groups"; Burnham and Johnson, "Biological and Evolutionary Logic," 113; Robinson, Kurzban, and Jones, "The Origins of Shared Intuitions of Justice," 1633, 1643-49; Bowles and Gintis, "The Origins of Human Cooperation," 7: "When the group is threatened with extinction or dispersal, say through war, pestilence, or famine, cooperation is most needed for survival. But the probability of one's contributions being repaid in the future decreases sharply when the group is threatened, since the probability that the group will dissolve increases, and hence the incentive to cooperate will dissolve. Thus, precisely when a group is most in need of prosocial behavior, cooperation based on reciprocal altruism will collapse. Such critical periods were common in the evolutionary history of our species. But a small number of strong reciprocators, who punish defectors without regard for the probability of future repayment, could dramatically improve the survival chances of human groups. Moreover, humans are unique among species that live in groups and recognizing individuals, in their capacity to inflict heavy punishment at low cost to the punisher, as a result of their superior tool making and hunting ability. Indeed, and in sharp contrast to non-human primates, even the strongest man can be killed while sleeping by the weakest, at low cost to the punisher. A simple argument using Price's equation then shows that under these conditions, strong reciprocators can invade a population of self-regarding types, and can persist in equilibrium"; Reeve, "Queen Activation of Lazy," 147-48; Bekoff,

"Wild Justice, Cooperation, and Fair Play," 53, 62; Clutton-Brock and Parker, "Punishment in Animal Societies," 209, 212; Clutton-Brock, Albon, Gibson, and Guinness, "The Logical Stag," 211, 212; Clutton-Brock, Green, Hiraiwa-Hasegawa, and Albon, "Passing the Buck," 281, 287–88; Reiter, Stinson, and Le Boeuf, "Northern Elephant Seal Development," 337, 344; Reiter, Panken, and Le Boeuf, "Female Competition and Reproductive Success," 670, 676.

20. At least one person per group must be punishing, but nowhere is the number given. Fehr and Gintis, "Human Motivation and Social Cooperation," 48. Of course, only one per group needs to punish in order to prompt cooperation. Others had no need to do so once another person punished and prompted as needed.

21. See Fehr and Gächter, "Cooperation and Punishment"; Fehr and Gintis, "Human Motivation and Social Cooperation."

22. The article talks about aggregate contributions from ten groups of four people per group. The average result among the groups is that punishment prompts cooperation of 83 percent. Fehr and Gintis, "Human Motivation and Social Cooperation," 48.

23. Fehr and Gintis, "Human Motivation and Social Cooperation," 45.

24. Hibbing and Alford, "Accepting Authoritative Decisions," 62.

25. Alford and Hibbing, "The Origin of Politics," 707, 709.

26. Bowles and Gintis, "The Origins of Human Cooperation."

27. Burnham and Johnson, "The Biological and Evolutionary Logic," 113; Bowles and Gintis, "The Origins of Human Cooperation." See also Frank, "Repression of Competition," 693, 694: "Those individuals that invest in policing their selfish neighbors gain by living in a more cooperative group in the second time period of interaction within groups"; and Robinson, Kurzban, and Jones, "The Origins of Shared Intuitions of Justice," 1633, 1643–49.

28. Reeve, "Queen Activation of Lazy Workers," 147–48.

4. JUSTICE

1. The factual narrative is drawn from these sources: DeVoto, *The Year of Decision*; Williams, *History of the San Francisco Committee of Vigilance*; Shinn and Jackson, *Mining Camps*; Delavan, *Notes on California and the Placers*, 51; Senkewicz, *Vigilantes and the Gold Rush*.

2. DeVoto, *The Year of Decision*, 218–24.

3. Williams, *History*, 41.

4. Williams, *History*, 62.

5. Williams, *History*, 63.

6. Howard Shinn was raised in gold rush California and worked as a journalist. He eventually went east to study at Johns Hopkins University. His book is his dissertation for Johns Hopkins. "Shinn's *Mining Camps*," 66, Dorothy Sloan-Books, item 68, accessed December 18, 2013, http://www.dsloan.com/Auctions/A12/68WebA12.htm.

7. Williams, *History*, 76.

8. Williams, *History*, 77.

9. Shinn, *Mining Camps*, 125.

10. Williams, *History*, 69.

11. Shinn, *Mining Camps*, 125.

12. Shinn, *Mining Camps*, 194.

13. Shinn, *Mining Camps*, 194

14. Shinn, *Mining Camps*, 196.

15. Shinn, *Mining Camps*, 161.

16. Senkewicz, *Vigilantes*, 14.

17. Williams, *History*, 105.

18. Williams, *History*, 107.

19. Williams, *History*, 119.

20. Williams, *History*, 143.

21. Williams, *History*, 144.

22. Joe Hosey, "Wife of Man Killed by Drunk Driver Blasts Sentence and System," *Joliet Patch*, June 28, 2013, http://joliet.patch.com/groups/police-and-fire/p/wife-of-man-killed-by-drunk-driver-blasts-sentence-system.

23. Dave Forbes, *Mountain Xpress*, November 20, 2009, http://www.mountainx.com.

24. Tom Sherwood, "Bicyclist Disappointed in Hit-and-Run Sentence," NBC *Washington*, April 4, 2013, http://www.nbcwashington.com/news/local/Bicyclist-Disappointed-in-Hit-and-Run-Sentence-201514801.html.

25. Bob Segall, "13 Investigates: Violent Criminals Released Too Soon?" wthr.com, October 25, 2012, http://www.wthr.com/story/19919959/violent-criminals-released-too-soon.

26. Julie Shaw, "Parents of Man Who Died after '08 Subway Attack Are Angered by Pending Release of One Assailant," Philly.com, July 2, 2010, http://articles.philly.com/2010-07-02/news/24966557 1 subway-attack-fatal-asthma-attack-state-prison.

27. Glenn Beck, "Don't Mess with Texas: Home Intruder Shot 2 Killed; Criminal's Family Thinks He Should Have Been Warned," *Glenn Beck*, February 21, 2013, http://www.glennbeck.com/2013/02/21/don't-mess-

with-texas-home-intruder-shot-criminals-family-thinks-he-should-have
-been-warned/.

28. Mirta Ojito, "Kidnapping Victim Angered at Her Abductors' Sentences," *New York Times*, April 10, 1997.

29. Police Officers Association of Michigan, "Detroit Police Officer Upset with 'Lenient' Sentence against Shooter," Police Officers Association of Michigan, http://www.poam.net/the-police-beat/2012/detroit-police -officer-upset-with-lenient-sentence-against-shooter/.

30. Cynthia Jones, "Nashua Rape Victim Feels Cheated," *Telegraph*, May 8, 1982.

31. Vogel, "Evolution of the Golden Rule," 1128-29, 1131.

32. Alford and Hibbing, "The Origin of Politics," 707, 709.

33. Bolton and Zwick, "Anonymity versus Punishment in Ultimatum Bargaining," 95, 100. Finding some merit in the punishment hypothesis: "A player's preference for more money is modified by a preference for disagreement over amounts he perceives as small relative to his playing partner's share."

34. Fehr and Fischbacher, "Third-Party Punishment and Social Norms," 63, 85. "In this paper, we studied the enforcement mechanisms behind social norms, finding that a large percentage of subjects are willing to enforce distribution and cooperation norms even though they incur costs and reap no economic benefit from their sanctions and even though they have not been directly harmed by the norm violation. Thus, third party sanctions provide a further important example for the notion of strong reciprocity."

35. Fehr and Fischbacher, "The Nature of Human Altruism," *Nature* 425 (2003): 785.

36. Fehr and Fischbacher, "Third-Party Punishment," 73.

37. Marlowe and Berbesque, "More 'Altruistic' Punishment in Lower Society," 587-90. "In a cross-cultural project, three experimental economics games were played in societies ranging from foragers to city dwellers. . . . The cross-cultural games project revealed that higher levels of punishment were significantly associated with higher levels of cooperation. . . . [T]he level of third-party punishment varied greatly across the 12 societies in the cross-cultural project. . . . Second-party punishment may be sufficient to explain the cooperation observed in many small-scale human societies. It is only once a society becomes larger, more stratified, with more anonymity that cheating becomes more tempting and more difficult to monitor. These are the conditions that promote third-party punishment. As societies grow larger, they face more pressing collective-action problems such as defence of territory, distribution of communal food stores or prevention of theft. Political

hierarchy emerges first with big men, then chiefs and then monarchs to solve collective-action problems. This may first be dealt with by vigilantes but as societies grow even larger and more complex it is more likely that they will have an institutionalized system of third-party punishment involving police, judges and jailers. . . . We suggest that strong reciprocity based on third-party punishment is not a human universal, i.e. it is less common among egalitarian foragers than among stratified agricultural societies. Third-party punishment increases in agricultural societies because solving collective-action problems becomes more important as populations grow larger and more complex."

38. Rilling et al., "A Neural Basis for Social Cooperation," 395.

39. De Quervain et al., "The Neural Basis of Altruistic Punishment,"1254, 1258. "[H]igh caudate activation seems to be responsible for a high willingness to punish, which suggests that caudate activation reflects the anticipated satisfaction from punishing defectors. Our results therefore support recently developed social preference models, which assume that people have a preference for punishing norm violations, and illuminate the proximate mechanism behind evolutionary models of altruistic punishment."

40. Aron et al., "Reward, Motivation, and Emotion Systems," 327.

41. See, e.g., Warr, Meier, and Erickson, "Norms, Theories of Punishment," 75, 90. "[O]ur findings indicate that the perceived seriousness of offenses is the central (and perhaps only) criterion for fixing punishments. . . . [T]he fact that respondents rely on perceived seriousness *to the exclusion* of perceived frequency surely places the burden of proof on the utilitarian theorists." See also Carlsmith, Darley, and Robinson, "Why Do We Punish?" 284; Darley, Carlsmith, and Robinson, "Incapacitation and Just Deserts," 659; Carlsmith, "The Roles of Retribution and Utility," 437; and Robinson, *Intuitions of Justice*, part 3.

42. The factual narrative is drawn from these sources: Kogan, *Theory and Practice of Hell*; Bachner, *My Darkest Years*; Cymlich and Strawczynski, *Escaping Hell in Treblinka* ; Bondy, "Problems of Internment Camps," 453; Des Pres, *Survivor*; Hackett, *The Buchenwald Report*; Hesse, *Persecution and Resistance of Jehovah's Witnesses*; and Jackman, "Survival in the Concentration Camps," 23.

43. The factual narrative is drawn from these sources: Breverton, *Black Bart Roberts*; Leeson, *The Invisible Hook*; Konstam, *History of Pirates*; Konstam, *Privateers and Pirates*; Haring, *The Buccaneers in the West Indies*; Exquemelin and Sonnenschein, *The Buccaneers of America*; Johnson and Cordingly, *History of the Robberies and Murders*; Rogers, *Cruising Voyage*; and Woodard, *Republic of Pirates*.

44. Breverton, *Black Bart*, 29.

45. The journal of a pioneer of 1862 recounted: "Yesterday passed the grave of a man murdered on the 6th inst., by a person who up to that time was his traveling companion. To-day we passed the tomb of his murderer. He was caught, tried and shot the next day." Hewitt, *Notes by the Way*, 19.

46. Holmes and Duniway, *Covered Wagon Women*.

47. Killing or expelling the violator is possible, but given that it would weaken the group's overall strength, it may well be seen as a sanction of last resort.

48. Robinson, Kurzban, and Jones, "The Origins of Shared Intuitions of Justice," 1633, 1636.

49. Brosnan, "Nonhuman Species' Reactions," 153, 181.

50. Brosnan and de Waal, "Monkeys Reject Unequal Pay," 297, 298; Brosnan and de Waal, "Reply to "Animal Behavior," 140.

51. Brosnan and de Waal, "Reply."

52. Brosnan, "Nonhuman Species' Reactions," 177; Brosnan, Schiff, and de Waal, "Tolerance for Inequity," 253, 255.

53. Packer, "Reciprocal Altruism in Papio Anubis," 441, 442.

54. Flack and de Waal, "Any Animal Whatever,"1, 12; de Waal and Luttrell, "The Similarity Principle," 215.

55. See Seyfarth and Cheney, "Grooming, Alliances and Reciprocal Altruism," 541, 542.

56. De Waal, "Food Sharing and Reciprocal Obligations," 433.

57. Melis, Hare, and Tomasello, "Chimpanzees Recruit1297, 1299.

58. De Waal, "Food Sharing and Reciprocal Obligations," 433, 452.

59. Hauser, "Costs of Deception," 1237; Hauser and Marler, "Food-Associated Calls," 206.

60. de Waal, "Food Sharing," 456. See also de Waal, *Good Natured*, 160. The author concludes such behavior "suggests a sense of justice and fairness."

61. De Waal, *Chimpanzee Politics*, 207.

62. Flack and de Waal, "Any Animal Whatever," 8; Silk, "The Patterning of Intervention," 318.

63. De Waal, *Good Natured*, 157–58.

64. De Waal, *Good Natured*, 157–58.

65. De Waal, *Good Natured*, 157–59.

66. De Waal, *Chimpanzee Politics*. See also Flack and de Waal, "Any Animal Whatever," 9: "Monkeys and apes appear capable of holding received services in mind, selectively repaying those individuals who performed the favours. They seem to hold negative acts in mind as well, leading to retribution and revenge."

67. De Waal, *Good Natured,* 159. See also Flack and de Waal, "Any Animal Whatever," 9, describing similar behavior among monkeys and apes.
68. Clutton-Brock and Parker, "Punishment in Animal Societies," 209, 211.
69. Flack and de Waal, "Any Animal Whatever," 19-24; Hauser, "Costs of Deception," 108-9 ("We can safely assume that these intuitions evolved prior to or during our life as hunter-gatherers. ... In such small-scale societies, fairness was most likely an effective proxy for judging punishable acts."); and de Waal, *Good Natured,* 218 ("The fact that the human moral sense goes so far back in evolutionary history that other species show signs of it plants morality firmly near the center of our ... nature").
70. Flack and de Waal, "Any Animal Whatever," 3.
71. De Waal, *Good Natured,* 39. See also Joyce, *The Evolution of Morality,* 140-42 (explaining the evolution of fairness); Brosnan, "Fairness in Monkeys,"; Brosnan, "Nonhuman Species' Reactions," 160-61; Brosnan and de Waal, "Reply"; De Waal, "The Chimpanzee's Sense of Social Regularity," 335, 345-49.
72. See, e.g., Kohlberg, *Essays on Moral Development,* ; Kohlberg, "From Is to Ought." See also Colby and Kohlberg, *The Measurement of Moral Judgment,* vol. 1, and Colby and Kohlberg, *The Measurement of Moral Judgment,* vol. 2. This view parallels Piaget's views on development. See generally Kohlberg, *Psychology of Moral Development* (linking cognitive and moral development).
73. His view might be summarized as: (quotations from Lawrence Kohlberg, *Psychology of Moral Development,* vol. 1, 165, are used for the stage name and description because it is difficult to gloss these ideas. Emphasis in the description original.) Kohlberg argued that people universally progressed from lower to higher stages of moral development. He did not argue that everyone reached the highest stage, "universal ethical principle orientation." The early stages, the "preconventional" stages, commonly from ages five through ten, are essentially about self-interest. The intermediate "conventional" levels, commonly ages ten through fourteen, in contrast, reflect an awareness of the benefits of having a positive reputation as a moral agent and of fulfilling one's duties in the context of social exchange. The highest level, the "postconventional" stages, commonly from ages fourteen onward, includes a genuine interest in others' welfare, a respect for others' rights, and a recognition of universal moral principles. More recent approaches to Kohlberg's model maintain the idea that stages are reached in sequence, but instead of one stage "replacing" another, each stage is seen as supplementing the logic of previous stages. Krebs and Denton, "Toward a More Pragmatic Approach to Morality," 629, 633. On this view, a person who has reached

Stage 4 will still use Stage 3 reasoning in circumstances where doing so is useful or desirable.

Level (age range)	Stage	Description of Moral Behavior
Preconventional (5–10)	Obedience/ Punishment	Conform to norms because of potential for punishment by authority figures.
	Individualism/ Exchange	Do what is "good" (i.e., feels good) for the self. This includes beneficial exchanges with others.
Conventional (10–14)	Good/Bad	Behave so as to elicit approval from others.
	Law and Order	Behave so as to discharge one's duty as part of the social order.
Postconventional (14–adult)	Social Contract	Acting in a way that benefits others because of rationally based laws/norms in a society. Individual rights and utilitarianism.
	"Universal ethical principle orientation"	"Right is defined by the decision of conscience in accord with self-chosen ethical principles appealing to logical comprehensiveness, universality, and consistency."

74. Nucci, *Education in the Moral Domain*, 81.

75. The first evolutionary perspective on Kohlberg's work of which we are aware appears in Alexander, *The Biology of Moral Systems*, 131–39.

76. "There is considerable cross-cultural evidence that children and adults across a wide range of the world's cultures conceptualize prototypical moral issues pertaining to fairness and others' welfare in ways very similar to children and adults in Western contexts, and differentiate such issues from prototypical matters of convention." Nucci, *Education*, 95–96.

77. *See* Kohlberg, "Current Statement on Some Theoretical Issues," 491. See also Darley and Shultz, "Moral Rules," 525, 537.

78. Darley and Shultz, "Moral Rules," 552.

79. See Judith Smetana, "Preschool Children's Conceptions of Moral and Social Rules," *Child Development* 52 (1981): 1333-1334.

80. Smetana, "Toddlers' Social Interactions," 1767.

81. Smetana et al., "Preschool Children's Judgments," 202, 210 (internal citations omitted).

82. Smetana et al., "Preschool Children's Judgments."

83. We take "innate" ideas to be those ideas that develop reliably in each member of the species given the broad range of plausible environments in which the organism develops. That is, an idea is innate if it does not rely on very general processes such as induction or social transmission for its acquisition.

84. Newman, *Comparative Deviance*, 115.

85. Newman, *Comparative Deviance*, 140, 141. (See table 12, pp. 142-43.) See also Newman at 135-48, discussing variability deriving from differences in views regarding how particular acts should be controlled or punished. People from different cultures might share the intuition that an act is wrong, and even acts' relative seriousness, but differ in how punishment should be imposed, whether by the state, family, or some other source. This discussion highlights the importance of assessing intuitions regarding seriousness as distinct from preferred punishments meted out by the state. While the former might be correlated strongly with the latter in some contexts, it will be less so in others.

86. Robinson and Darley, "Intuitions of Justice," 1. See also Robinson, Kurzban, and Jones, "The Origins of Shared Intuitions of Justice," 1633.

87. Robinson and Darley, "Intuitions of Justice," 3-4.

88. Robinson and Kurzban, "Concordance and Conflict," 1829.

89. Another complication for this kind of argument—that the groups' conduct is simply an expression of norms previously instantiated by governmental law—is what we know about the limits of laypersons' knowledge of governmental law. It is more likely intuitions of justice shared by humans across cultures, rather than governmental law that is accountable for the shared norm of justice, for example. Indeed, in the context of doing criminal law, people appear to assume that the law is as they think it should be. Robinson, *Distributive Principles of Criminal Law*, 26. A related complication is found in the fact that we know governmental law has a limited ability on its own to create internalized norms. The U.S. Prohibition experience is an obvious illustration. Governmental law may play a role in the larger public conversation by which community norms are shaped, but they have a limited ability to create them simply by legal enactment. Robinson, "Criminalization Tensions."

1. The factual narrative is drawn from these sources: Leys, *The Wreck of the Batavia*; Dash, *Batavia's Graveyard*; Drake-Brockman, *Voyage to Disaster* ; "The *Batavia*," The Grey Company, http://members.iinet.net.au/~bill/batavia .html; W. Ernest L. Wears, "Disastrous Voyage of the Vessel Batavia to the East Indies," Koninklijke Bibliotheeek (1836), www.kb.nl/galerie/australie/3 /Pelsaert%20Eng%20geheel.pdf.

2. Leys, *The Wreck of the Batavia,* 26.

3. Others have talked in more detail about the "member exit problem" for groups. See, e.g., Hoffman, "The Neuroeconomic Path of the Law," 1667, 1673–74.

4. Similarly, in Jamestown Colony under John Smith, a man who would not work was not given food, a person who disobeyed orders was placed in chains, and a person found guilty of theft of stores was killed. Price, *Love and Hate in Jamestown*, 108. The Netsilik Eskimos also had the punishment fit the crime. Insufficient sharing of stores might prompt a public scolding by the older women of the group, while excluding others from a hunting area might prompt a community-authorized beating, and taking another's wife might merit being killed. Balikci, *The Netsilik Eskimo*, 185; van den Steenhoven, *Legal Concepts among the Netsilik*, 28–61.

5. Read, *Alive*, 216.

6. Scott, "Journal of a Trip to Oregon," University of Oregon: CATE, July 15, 1852, http://cateweb.uoregon.edu/duniway/notes/DiaryProof1.html. For another example, during Hurricane Katrina, several well-organized, otherwise lawful groups participated in planned looting expeditions and took up residence in public buildings yet were never prosecuted for their offenses. Stephen Kiehl, "Some Stay to Save; Some Come to See," *Baltimore Sun*, September 11, 2005. Similarly, at Memorial Hospital, patients were given lethal injections of morphine so that they might die peaceful, painless deaths. A New Orleans grand jury declined to indict the doctor on second-degree murder charges, and the case faded from view. Sheri Fink, "The Deadly Choices at Memorial," *New York Times*, August 30, 2009. In one of the wagon train cases, the president of the group has commanded that the teams not cross a stream until direction is given for them all to cross together. When one team moves to do so in violation of the order, men are sent with instructions to shoot the violators if they will not stop. However, when the violators are confronted yet will not stop, the men sent decline to shoot them. Coffman, *Blazing a Wagon Trail to Oregon*, 38. On Pitcairn Island an outsider by the name of Joshua Hill had been elected to be head of the island council. He runs an ever more tyrannical government

on the island, including flogging one man for an adultery act that occurred before Hill was even on the island. When Hill tries to get the community to help him sanction two women guilty of spreading rumors about himself, he ends the meeting with a prayer. No one but Hill says "amen." Shortly after the prayer, Hill sentences a twelve-year-old to death for stealing yams. The child's father is commanded to kill her; he refuses. Hill attacks the father with a sword. Hill is disarmed, the father unharmed, and Hill finds his authority on the island has disappeared. Young, *Mutiny of the Bounty and the Story of Pitcairn Island*, 78.

7. Comstock, *The Life of Samuel Comstock*, 87–93.

8. Shinn and Jackson, *Mining Camps*, 179.

9. Shinn and Jackson, *Mining Camps*, 119.

10. Robinson, *Distributive Principles*, 73–95, 109–34.

11. Robinson, *Distributive Principles*, 135–212.

12. Elkind and Dabek, "Personal Injury and Property Damage," 518, 519.

13. Interestingly, the youngest group of children (average age roughly five and a half) thought that unintentional personal injury was more serious than intentional property damage, suggesting the importance of personal injury. This pattern was not found in the older children. While very young children focus on either intention *or* harm, older children (age four and five) use both harm *and* intention when making decisions about punishment. In other words, children have sophisticated views on desert and possess the ability to weigh multiple factors by age seven. Elkind and Dabek, "Personal Injury and Property Damage," 521. There is evidence that even three-year-olds take intentions into account when making judgments about actors. See Nelson, "Factors Influencing Young Children's Use," 823, 828–29.

14. See Darley et al., "Intentions and Their Contexts," 66, finding evidence in children as young as six that judgments regarding punishment vary depending on relevant circumstances, such as provocation; Furnham and Jones, "Children's Views," 18, 25–27. See also Wainryb, "Understanding Differences in Moral ," 840, 847, stating that new information can modify judgments of wrongness considerably among people aged eleven to twenty-one.

15. Wainryb and Ford, "Young Children's Evaluations ," 484.

16. Wainryb and Ford, "Young Children's Evaluations," 484.

17. See, e.g., Nucci and Weber, "Social Interactions in the Home," 1438, 1445: "[C]hildren differentiate personal issues from matters of moral or conventional regulation."; and Smetana, "Toddlers' Social Interactions," 1767, 1774: "[T]oddlers initiate responses to moral transgressions . . . [and are] more likely

to respond to moral than conventional transgressions with emotional reactions, physical retaliation, and increasingly with age, statements regarding the harm or injury caused."

18. Wicker, *A Time to Die*, 16.

19. The factual narrative is drawn from these sources: Bell, *The Turkey Shoot*; Useem and Kimball, *State of Siege*; "A Year Ago at Attica," *Time*, September 25, 1972; Akil Al-Jundi, "I Would Do It Any Day, Again!," *Revolutionary Worker #1118*, September 16, 2001, accessed September 15, 2011, http://www.revcom.us/a/v23/1110–19/1118/attica_interview.htm; Anonymous, "Episodes from the Attica Massacre," 34; Tom Wicker, *A Time to Die: The Attica Prison Revolt* (Bison Book, 1978); "Attica Revisited," *Talking History*, accessed September 15, 2011, www.talkinghistory.org/attica/; Brooks, "How Can We Sleep," 159; Deutsch, Cunningham, and Fink, "Twenty Years Later," 13; Featherstone, *Narratives*; Bruce Jackson, "Attica: An Anniversary of Death," *Artvoice*, September 9, 1999; Lynch, "Attica."

20. Wicker, *A Time to Die*, 23.

21. Wicker, *A Time to Die*, 229–230.

22. Bell, *The Turkey Shoot*, 37.

23. Benaquisto and Freed, "The Myth of Inmate Lawlessness," 481.

24. The factual narrative is drawn from these sources: Breverton, *Black Bart Roberts*; Leeson, *The Invisible Hook*; Konstam, *History of Pirates*; Haring, *The Buccaneers in the West Indies*; Exquemelin and Sonnenschein, *The Buccaneers of America*; Johnson and Cordingly, *A General History*; Rogers, *Cruising Voyage Round the World*; and Woodard, *The Republic of Pirates*.

25. Leeson, *Invisible Hook*, 15.

26. Leeson, *Invisible Hook*, 14–16.

27. Leeson, "An-arrgh-chy," 1049, 1060.

28. Leeson, *Invisible Hook*, 60.

29. John Phillips, "John Phillips' Articles 1724," *Pirate Documents*, https://www.piratedocuments.com/Articles/john_phillips_articles_1724.htm.

30. Robinson, *Criminal Law*, 615.

31. Model Penal Code: Sentencing (American Law Institute, April 11, 2003), 37.

32. Ristroph, "Desert, Democracy, and Sentencing Reform," 1293. See also Braman, Kahan, and Hoffman, "Some Realism," 1531, 1532–33, arguing that "while individuals do hold deep and abiding intuitions regarding wrongdoing and responses to it, these intuitions depend on social constructs that are demonstrably plastic."

33. Robinson, Goodwin, and Reisig, "The Disutility of Injustice," 1940.

34. These complaints are based in part on a failure to appreciate the specific demands of desert and of people's intuitions about it. The confusion arises in part from the failure to distinguish two distinct judgments: setting the endpoint of the punishment continuum and, once that endpoint has been set, ordinally ranking cases along that continuum. Every society must decide what punishment it will allow for its most egregious case, be it the death penalty or life imprisonment or fifteen years. Once that endpoint is set, the distributive challenge that desert must guide is to determine who should be punished how much. That process requires only an ordinal ranking of offenders according to their relative blameworthiness. The result is a specific amount of punishment for a particular offense, but that amount of punishment is not the product of some magical connection between that violator's offense and the corresponding amount of punishment. Rather, it is the specific amount of punishment needed to *set the offender's violation at its appropriate ordinal rank* according to blameworthiness, relative to all other offenses. If the endpoint were changed, the appropriate punishment for each offender would change accordingly.

35. See, for example, the impressive nuance repeatedly shown by subjects in the eighteen studies reported in Robinson, *Intuitions of Justice* , part 3.

36. See, e.g., Robinson, *Intuitions of Justice, part 3* ; Robinson and Kurzban, "Concordance and Conflict," 1829, 1854–65; Robinson et al., "Competing Theories of Blackmail," 291, 335–47; Robinson and Darley, "Objectivist Versus Subjectivist," 409; Robinson and Darley, "Testing Competing Theories of Justification," 1095; Robinson et al., "Extralegal Punishment Factors," 737.

37. Robinson, *Intuitions of Justice,* part 3 .

38. Robinson, *Intuitions of Justice,* chapters 12–16.

39. Robinson et al., "Extralegal Punishment Factors," 737n36.

40. Durham , "Public Opinion," 1, 2.

6. SURVIVAL

1. The factual narrative is drawn from these sources: Steenhoven, *Legal Concepts*; Rasmussen, *The Netsilik Eskimos*; Burch, *The Eskimos*; Graburn, "Eskimo Law," 45; Laugrand, Oosten, and Rasing, *Interviewing Inuit Elders*; Briggs, *Never in Anger*; Balikci, *The Netsilik Eskimo* (; De Poncins, *Kabloona.*

2. Steenhoven, *Legal Concepts*, 37.

3. The factual narrative is drawn from these sources: Maude, "History of Pitcairn Island," ; Henry E. Maude, "History of Pitcairn Island," Pacific Union College, accessed December 18, 2013, http://library.puc.edu/pitcairn/pitcairn/history

.shtml; Young, *Mutiny of the Bounty* ; Marks, *Lost Paradise*; "Pitcairn: The Island of Fear," *The Independent (Australia),* November 19, 2006; William Prochnau, "Pitcairn Woman Tells of Island Sex Culture," *Reuters*, October 1, 2004; Parker, "Trials and Tribulations,"

4. Maude, "History of Pitcairn Island," 96.

5. The names of the girls are pseudonyms that were used by Kathy Marks in *Lost Paradise*.

6. Marks, *Lost Paradise*, 45.

7. Marks, *Lost Paradise*, 42.

8. Marks, *Lost Paradise*, 250.

9. The factual narrative is drawn from these sources: Campbell, *The Maroons of Jamaica*, ; Carey, *The Maroon Story*; Dallas, *History of the Maroons*; Gottlieb, *The Mother of Us All*; Harris, *The Chieftainess*; Deborah Gabriel, "Jamaica's True Queen: Nanny of the Maroons," Jamaicans.com, http://jamaicans.com/articles/primearticles/queennanny.shtml; "Nanny of the Maroons," *Wikipedia*, http://en.wikipedia.org/wiki/Nanny_of_the_Maroons; Price, *Maroon Societies*; http://www.itzcaribbean.com/history_jamaica_queen_nanny.php; "Caribbean History: Queen Nanny of the Jamaican Maroons," *Itzcaribbean*, http://www.itzcaribbean.com/history_jamaica_queen_nanny.php; Thalia S. Stone, "Black Women Do Not Lack Heroines or Role Models," *The Dread Library*, www.uvm.edu/~debate/dreadlibrary/stone.html; C. L. G. Harris, "The Maroons and Moore Town," *Smithsonian Center for Folklife and Cultural Heritage*, http://www.folklife.si.edu/resources/maroon/educational_guide/60.htm; "The Maroons," *Jamaica 50*, www.jamaica50.com/html/the_maroons.html; Zips, *Black Rebels*

10. See Darley et al., "Incapacitation and Just Deserts," 659.

11. Darley et al., "Incapacitation and Just Deserts," 671–675.

7. SUBVERSION

1. The factual narrative is drawn from these sources: Daws, *Prisoners of the Japanese*; Gilpatrick, *Footprints in Courage*; Gordon and Llamzon, *Horyo*; Holmes, *Four Thousand Bowls of Rice*; Jackson and Norton, *I Am Alive!*; Jacobsen, *We Refused to Die*; Kerr, *Surrender and Survival*; Knox, *Death March*; Lawton, *Some Survived*; Levering, *Horror Trek*; Whitecross, *Slaves of the Son of Heaven*; Sides, *Ghost Soldiers*; "Report on American Prisoners of War Interned by the Japanese in the Philippines: Camp O'Donnell: Provost Marshal Report 19 Nov. 1945," *Mansell*, http://www.mansell.com/pow_resources/camplists/philippines/odonnell/provost_rpt.html.

2. *Paying Homage to a Special Group of Veterans, Survivors of Bataan and Corregidor*, 107th Cong, 1st Sess, 147 Cong Rec H 11980–11985, 11981 (June 26, 2001) (statement of Rep. Rohrabacher).

3. Levering, *Horror Trek*, 99.

4. "After the Fall of Bataan," Militaria, *History and Security*, militariaatbp.blogspot .com.

5. Daws, *Prisoners of the Japanese*, 110.

6. Norman and Norman, *Tears in the Darkness*, 292.

7. Knox, *Death March*, 223.

8. Knox, *Death March*, 339.

9. Knox, *Death March*, 339.

10. Knox, *Death March*, 340.

11. Daws, *Prisoners of the Japanese*, 297.

12. Daws, *Prisoners of the Japanese*, 299.

13. Lawton, *Some Survived*, 157.

14. Lawton, *Some Survived*, 158.

15. Whitecross, *Slaves of the Son of Heaven*, 21.

16. Tayman, *The Colony*, 43.

17. Tayman, *The Colony*, 43.

18. Tayman, *The Colony*, 51.

19. Tayman, *The Colony*, 51.

20. Tayman, *The Colony*, 85.

21. Tayman, *The Colony*, 96.

22. Tayman, *The Colony*, 95.

23. Norman Fulkerson, "Saint Damien: A Hero Who Died on the Battlefield," *The American Society for the Defense of Tradition, Family and Property*, http://www.tfp .org/tfp-home/articles/saint-damien-a-hero-who-died-on-the-battlefield-of -honor.html.

24. The factual narrative is drawn from these sources: Allen, *Wake of the Invercauld*; Musgrave, *Castaway on the Auckland* ; Druett, *Island of the Lost*; Raynal, *Wrecked on a Reef*; Smith, *The Castaways*; Ingram, *New Zealand Shipwrecks*.

25. Raynal, *Wrecked on a Reef*, 95.

26. Druett, *Island of the Lost*, 84.

27. Weyrauch, "The Experience of Lawlessness," 415, 430.

28. Also ironically, the new age of interconnectedness has for many produced greater insolation rather than greater interaction. The advent of social media may make it easier to connect with people but less likely that human groups will actually form for cooperative action. Indeed, we live in an age

in which a person can be a complete hermit with little loss of comfort or amenities.

8. CREDIBILITY

1. Sunday and Sunday, *The Sawdust Trail*, 68.

2. The factual narrative is drawn from these sources: Sunday and Sunday, *The Sawdust Trail*; Behr, *Prohibition*; Bergreen, *Capone*; Mendelson and Mello, *Alcohol*; Allsop, *The Bootleggers*, 204; Shoenberg, *Mr.*; Cashman, *Prohibition*, 2.

3. Vivian M. Baulch, "How Billy Sunday Battled Demon Rum in Detroit," *Jesus Is Savior*, http://www.jesus-is-savior.com/Great%20men%20of%20god/sunday -demon_rum.htm.

4. Behr, *Prohibition*, 57.

5. Behr, *Prohibition*, 80.

6. Behr, *Prohibition*, 97.

7. Behr, *Prohibition*, 160.

8. Behr, *Prohibition*, 139.

9. "William Hale Thompson," *Wikipedia*, http://en.wikipedia.org/wiki/William _Hale_Thompson.

10. Allsop, *The Bootleggers*, 217.

11. Allsop, *The Bootleggers*, 209.

12. Allsop, *The Bootleggers*, 245–46: "Changes in consumption during Prohibition were modest given the change in price. This suggests that legal deterrents had little effect on limiting consumption outside of their effect on price. Social pressure and respect for the law did not go far in reducing consumption during Prohibition."

13. Allsop, *The Bootleggers*, 242: "[T]he inability to restrict the illegal trade and the inevitable accompanying corruption eventually led to widespread public disenchantment with Prohibition."

14. See, e.g., Miron, "Violence and the U.S. Prohibitions," 78.

15. Miron, "Violence and U.S. Prohibitions."; See also Miron and Zweibel, "Alcohol Consumption"; Jensen, "Prohibition, Alcohol, and Murder," 18, 19-20 ("[T] he perception that Prohibition failed may stem from potential side effects. Prohibition allegedly led to a shift in consumption to more harmful beverages, exposed people to toxic alcohol, and established an economic base for organized crime"); and Asbridge and Weerasinghe, "Homicide in Chicago," 355.

16. Asbridge and Weerasinghe, "Homicide in Chicago," 357, 361: "Alcohol-related homicides" include "homicides where the offender, victim or both had

consumed alcohol prior to the homicide, as well as homicides that occurred in drinking establishments or where connected with the production, sale or distribution of alcoholic beverages."

17. Asbridge and Weerasinghe, "Homicide in Chicago," 361.

18. Abadinsky, *Organized Crime*, 90, quoting Andrew Sinclair).

19. "The Wickersham Report," *Outlook*, January 28, 1931, http://www.unz.org/Pub /Outlook-1931jan28-00130.

20. Minnesota Fats and Fox, *The Bank Shot*, 21–22.

21. The scenarios are reported at Robinson, Goodwin, and Reisig, "The Disutility of Injustice," 1940, 2031–32, appendix C.

22. Kelling and Wilson, "The Police and Neighborhood Safety," 3: "[A]t the community level, disorder and crime are usually inextricably linked, in a kind of developmental sequence. Social psychologists and police officers tend to agree that if a window in a building is broken and left unrepaired, all the rest of the windows will soon be broken. This is as true in nice neighborhoods as in rundown ones. . . . [O]ne unrepaired broken window is a signal that no one cares, and so breaking more windows costs nothing."

23. Keizer, Lindenberg, and Steg, "The Spreading of Disorder," 1681: "[W]hen people observe that others violated a certain social norm or legitimate rule, they are more likely to violate other norms or rules, which causes disorder to spread."

24. Corman and Mocan, "Carrots, Sticks, and Broken Windows," 235.

25. Braga and Bond, "Policing Crime," 577.

26. Braga and Bond, "Policing Crime," 592.

27. Braga and Bond, "Policing Crime," 596.

28. Braga and Bond, "Policing Crime," 597. The factual narrative on the division of Berlin is drawn from these sources: Ghouas, *The Conditions, Means, and Methods* Johnson, *Training Socialist Citizens*, 33; Naimark, *The Russians in Germany*, 168–69; Andrews, "One Hundred Miles of Lives," 24; Ouimet, *The Rise and Fall of the Brezhnev Doctrine*; Currie, *Constitution*; Clark and Wildner, "Violence and Fear of Violence," 373.

29. Andrews, "One Hundred Miles," 24.

30. Ian Johnson, "Crime Soars in Eastern Germany, but the Judges Can't Be Trusted," *Baltimore Sun*, November 26, 1990.

31. Ray Moseley, "Berlin Wall Is Down, but German Crime Up," *Chicago Tribune*, July 7, 1991, http://articles.chicagotribune.com/1991-07-07/news /9103170487_1_nazis-neo-police-in-eastern-germany.

32. Rohrschneider and Schmitt-Beck, "Trust in Democratic Institutions," 35, 42. Only 14.9 percent of East Germans trusted the national parliament, compared to 28.4 percent of West Germans.

33. Horst Entorf and Hannes Spengler, "Is Being Soft on Crime the Solution to Rising Crime Rates? Evidence from Germany," IZA Discussion Paper No. 3710 (2008), 39, fig. 1.

34. Source for 1995 figures (using Google Translate): "Polizeiliche Kriminalstatistik," BKA Statisk (1995), https://www.bka.de/nn_196810/SharedDocs/Downloads/DE/Publikationen/PolizeilicheKriminalstatistik/pksJahrbuecher/pks1995.html?_nnn=true, 18; Source for 2002 figures: "Police Crime Statistics," BKA Statistik (2002), http://www.bka.de/nn_194552/EN/Publications/PoliceCrime Statistics/policeCrimeStatistics_node.html?_nnn=true , 13.

35. Nadim, *Pakistan*, 95.

36. The factual narrative is drawn from these sources: Nadim, *Pakistan*, 95; Nadim, "Impact of Lawlessness"; "100 Corrupt Pakistani Police Officers Take Oath Never to Receive Bribes," *Maverick Pakistanis*, August 2, 2010, www.maverick pakistanis.com.

37. Nadim, *Pakistan*, 219.

38. "Criminals Will Be Shot on Sight, Says DIG Operations," *Pakistan Today*, June 10, 2011, http://www.pakistantoday.com.pk/2011/06/10/city/lahore/criminals -will-be-shot-on-sight-says-dig-operations/.

39. Nadeem, *Political Economy*, 224.

40. Nadeem, *Political Economy*, 227.

41. Nadeem, *Political Economy*, 235.

42. Nadeem, *Political Economy*, 211.

43. Nadeem, *Political Economy*, 225.

44. Demleitner, "Organized Crime and Prohibition," 613, 622–23.

45. Editorial, "The U.S. Prohibition Experiment: Myths, History and Implications," *Addiction* 92 (1997): 1405, 1406; and Demleitner, "Organized Crime."

46. Demleitner, "Organized Crime," 623–24: "The new breed of gangster was considered the equivalent of a businessman who succeeded in building a stable and affluent organization. . . . No longer did politicians employ organized crime to get elected but organized crime either financially supported desirable candidates or promoted candidates it had previously selected. This development was another indication of the evolution of true criminal organizations, the increased cooperation among them, and the syndication of organized crime."

1. The factual narrative is drawn from these sources: *Ryan Joseph Holle v. Secretary*, Florida Department of Corrections, Case 3:11-cv-00436-LC-EMT Document 16, United States District Court Northern District of Florida Pensacola Division, *Memorandum of Law in Opposition to Respondent's Motion to Dismiss Petitioner's Habeas Corpus Petition as Untimely*, filed May 16, 2012; *Ryan Joseph Holle v. Secretary*, Florida Department of Corrections, Case 3:11-cv-00436-LC-EMT Document 26, United States District Court Northern District of Florida Pensacola Division, *Petitioner's Objections to the Magistrate Judge's Report and Recommendation to Grant Respondent's Motion to Dismiss Petitioner's Habeas Corpus Petition as Untimely and to Deny Petitioner a Certificate of Appealability*, filed July 9, 2012; *Ryan Joseph Holle, v. Secretary*, Florida Department of Corrections, Case 3:11-cv-00436-LC-EMT Document 27, United States District Court Northern District of Florida Pensacola Division, *Answer to Petition to Dismiss*, filed July 13, 2012; *Ryan Joseph Holle v. Secretary*, Florida Department of Corrections, Case 3:11-cv-00436-LC-EMT Case 3:11-cv-00436-LC-EMT Document 24, United States District Court Northern District of Florida Pensacola Division, *Report and Recommendation*, filed July 27, 2012; *Ryan Joseph Holle v. Secretary*, Florida Department of Corrections, Case 3:11-cv-00436-LC-EMT, Trial Record Transcript, Case 03-1056 E-F, August 4, 2004; *Florida v. Ryan Holle*, in the Circuit Court of the First Circuit in and for Escambia County, Florida, Jury Instructions, Case 03-1056 E-F, August 4, 2004; *State of Florida v. Ryan Holle*, Case 03-1056, Order Dismissing Defendant's Pro-se Motions—For Habeas Corpus, Bond, Discovery, and Speedy Trial, May 6, 2003; Ryan Holle, Escambia Sheriff's Office, Warrant/OTTIC Served, ECS003ARR008313, April 8, 2003; Heather Leigh Holle, Transcript of Recorded Statement, Escambia Sheriff's Office, Complaint #ECS0030FF5707, March 10, 2003; Charles H. Miller, Transcript of Recorded Statement, Escambia Sheriff's Office, Complaint #ECS0030FF5707, March 11, 2003; Sarah Robinson, Questions presented to and answers received from Sylvia Garnet [Holle's mother], email reply to authors, August 15, 2012.

2. The Florida statutes themselves provided that a person cannot be an accomplice of another unless he consciously intends to assist the other's crime. The law as interpreted by Florida courts is that "Under Florida law, in order to be convicted as a principal for a crime physically committed by someone else, a defendant must both intend that the crime be committed and do some act to assist the other person in actually committing the crime." *Brown v. Crosby*, 249 F. Supp. 2d 1285, 1318 (S.D. Fla. 2003). Relevant portion of Florida

criminal code re: accomplice liability: Fla. Stat. Ann. § 777.011 (West 2012): "Whoever commits any criminal offense against the state, whether felony or misdemeanor, or aids, abets, counsels, hires, or otherwise procures such offense to be committed, and such offense is committed or is attempted to be committed, is a principal in the first degree and may be charged, convicted, and punished as such, whether he or she is or is not actually or constructively present at the commission of such offense." Relevant portions of Florida criminal code re: felony murder rule: Fla. Stat. Ann. § 782.04 (3): "When a human being is killed during the perpetration of, or during the attempt to perpetrate, any: . . . (d) Robbery, (e) Burglary . . . (m) Home-invasion robbery . . . the person perpetrating or attempting to perpetrate such felony commits murder in the second degree, which constitutes a felony of the first degree, punishable by imprisonment for a term of years not exceeding life or as provided in —."

3. Ohio § 2921.22 is one of the few statutes we could find that seems even close, and it does not apply to future plans but only to past or ongoing felonies: "no person, knowing that a felony has been or is being committed, shall knowingly fail to report such information to law enforcement authorities."

4. Robinson, *Intuitions of Justice*, part 3.

5. *Heacock v. Virginia*, 323 S.E.2d 90, 93 (Va. 1984). His sentence is actually eighty years imprisonment, but forty years of the sentence are suspended.

6. Robinson, Goodwin, and Reisig, "The Disutility of Justice," 1940, 1970, table 3 scenario H, compared to scenario 7.

7. *Louisiana v. Moore*, 2006-KA-1979, 2 (La. App. 1 Cir. March 28, 2007); 2007 WL 914637, at *1.

8. Robinson, Goodwin, and Reisig, "The Disutility of Justice," 1970, table 3 scenario J, compared to scenario 9.

9. Tomkovicz, "Endurance of the Felony-Murder Rule," 1429, 1459.

10. *See* Haw. Rev. Stat. § 707-701 (LexisNexis 2008); Ky. Rev. Stat. Ann. § 507.020 (LexisNexis 2008).

11. § 125.25 Murder in the second degree: A person is guilty of murder in the second degree when: 3. Acting either alone or with one or more other persons, he commits or attempts to commit robbery, burglary, kidnapping, arson, rape in the first degree, sodomy in the first degree, sexual abuse in the first degree, aggravated sexual abuse, escape in the first degree, or escape in the second degree, and, in the course of and in furtherance of such crime or of immediate flight therefrom, he, or another participant, if there be any, causes the death of a person other than one of the participants; except that in any prosecution

under this subdivision, in which the defendant was not the only participant in the underlying crime, it is an affirmative defense that the defendant:

(a) Did not commit the homicidal act or in any way solicit, request, command, importune, cause or aid the commission thereof; and

(b) Was not armed with a deadly weapon, or any instrument, article or substance readily capable of causing death or serious physical injury and of a sort not ordinarily carried in public places by law-abiding persons; and

(c) Had no reasonable ground to believe that any other participant was armed with such a weapon, instrument, article or substance; and

(d) Had no reasonable ground to believe that any other participant intended to engage in conduct likely to result in death or serious physical injury.

12. Jurisdictions that allow broad application of the rule: Arkansas, Ark. Code Ann. § 5-10-102(a)(1) (2008); Delaware, Del. Code Ann. tit. 11, § 636 (2008); Georgia, Ga. Code Ann. § 16-5-1 (2008); Missouri, Mo. Rev. Stat. § 565.021.1(2) (2007); New Hampshire, N.H. Rev. Stat. Ann. § 630:1-a, b (2008); New Mexico, N.M. Stat. Ann. § 30-2-1-A(2) (LexisNexis 2008); Oklahoma, Okla. Stat. Ann. tit. 21 § 701.7 (2007); Pennsylvania, 18 Pa. Cons. Stat. § 2502(b); Texas, Tex. Penal Code Ann. § 19.02(b)(3) (Vernon 2003); Washington, Wash. Rev. Code. Ann. § 9A.32.030(1)(c), 9A.32.050(1)(b) (LexisNexis 2008). Jurisdictions that impose limits on the application of the rule: Alabama, Ala. Code. § 13A-6-2(a)(3) (LexisNexis 2008); Alaska, Alaska Stat. § 11.41.110(a)(3) (2008); Arizona, Ariz. Rev. Stat. § 13-1105(A)(2) (LexisNexis 2008); California, Cal. Penal Code § 1-8-1-189 (Deering 2007); Colorado, Colo. Rev. Stat. § 18-3-102(1)(b) (2007); Connecticut, Conn. Gen. Stat. § 53a-54c (2008); District of Columbia, D.C. Code Ann. § 22-2101 (LexisNexis 2008); Florida, Fla. Stat. Ann. § 782.04(2)-(3) (Westlaw 2012); Idaho, Idaho Code Ann. § 18-4003(d) (2008); Illinois, 720 Ill. Comp. Stat. Ann. 5/9-1§ 9-1(a),(b) (LexisNexis 2008); Indiana, Ind. Code Ann. § 35-42-1-1 (LexisNexis 2008); Iowa, Iowa Code § 707.2.2-3 (2008); Kansas, Kan. Stat. Ann. § 21-3401(b) (2006); Louisiana, La. Rev. Stat. Ann.§ 14:30 (2008); Maine, Me. Rev. Stat. Ann. tit. 17-A, § 202 (2008); Maryland, Md. Code Ann. Crim. Law § 2-201 (LexisNexis 2008); Massachusetts, Mass. Ann. Laws ch. 265, § 1 (LexisNexis 2008); Michigan, Mich. Comp. Laws Serv. § 750.316(1)(b) (LexisNexis 2008); Minnesota, Minn. Stat. Ann. § 609.18-19 (2007); Mississippi, Miss. Code Ann. § 97-3-19(1)(c) (2008); Montana, Mont. Code Ann. § 45-5-102(1)(b) (2007); Nebraska, Neb. Rev. Stat. Ann. § 28-303(2) (2008); Nevada, Nev. Rev. Stat. Ann. § 200.030(1) (b) (LexisNexis 2007); New Jersey, N.J. Rev. Stat. 2C:11-3.a(3) (2008); New York, N.Y. Penal Law § 125.27.1(a)(vii) (Consol. 2008); North Carolina, N.C.

Gen. Stat. § 14-17 (2008); North Dakota, N.D. Cent. Code § 12.1-16-01(1)(c) (2008); Ohio, Ohio Rev. Code Ann. § 2903.01(B) (LexisNexis 2008); Oregon, Ore. Rev. Stat. § 163.115(b) (2007); Rhode Island, R.I. Gen. Laws § 11-23-1 (2008); South Carolina, S.C. Code Ann. § 16-3-10 (2007); South Dakota, S.D. Codified Laws § 22-16-4; Tennessee, Tenn. Code Ann. § 39-13-202(a)(2-3) (2008); United States, 18 U.S.C. § 1111; Utah, Utah Code Ann § 76-5-203(1)(d) (2008); Vermont, Vt. Stat. Ann. tit. 13, § 2301 (2007); Virginia, Va. Code Ann. § 18.2-32 (2008); West Virginia, W. Va. Code Ann. § 61-2-1 (LexisNexis 2008); Wisconsin, Wis. Stat. Ann. § 940.03 (2007); Wyoming, Wyo. Stat. Ann. § 6-2-101(a) (2007).

13. Appellant's brief, *Holle v. State of Florida*, Case 1D04-3707, 1; see also Florida, Fla. Stat. Ann. § 782.04(3)(d)-(e) (Westlaw 2012).

14. Bagaric, "In Defence of a Utilitarian Theory," 109.

15. Robinson, *Distributive Principles* , chaps. 3, 4.

16. See Anup Malani, "Does the Felony-Murder Rule Deter? Evidence from the FBI Crime Data," *New York Times,* December 3, 2007, http://www.nytimes.com /packages/pdf/national/malani.pdf.

17. Anup Malani, "Does the Felony-Murder Rule Deter? Evidence from the FBI Crime Data," *New York Times,* December 3, 2007, http://www.nytimes.com/packages /pdf/national/malani.pdf, 23.

18. Anup Malani, "Does the Felony-Murder Rule Deter? Evidence from the FBI Crime Data," *New York Times,* December 3, 2007, http://www.nytimes.com/packages /pdf/national/malani.pdf, 19.

19. Ultimately, the study seems to suggest that the felony murder rule does have an effect on conduct—yet at least some of its effect is to *increase* the social damage, rather than decrease it as the lawmakers intended. In any case, changes in conduct that amount to small fractions of a percent, as reported in the study, are hardly a ringing case for the overall efficacy of basing criminal law formulation on an explicit deterrence justification, even at the sacrifice of desert. The study's results also illustrate another good reason not to rely upon deterrence analysis in the formulation of criminal law rules: the complexity of the dynamics of deterrence and our lack of information about those factors that are needed to accurately predict an effect. If anything, the study seems to argue against the usefulness of formulating the felony murder rule in order to affect crime rates—even before one considers the additional costs of such a rule in terms of desert.

20. The felony murder does not seem to exist in non—common law (civil law) nations. For example, France Criminal Code § 221-1 requires "willful" causation

of death for murder liability, and § 121-3 states that no criminal liability can be found "in the absence of an intent" to commit the crime. Similarly, German Criminal Code §§ 211 and 212 imply that homicide must be intentional or purposeful to qualify as murder, or else the punishment is mitigated. See *Legislationonline*, http://legislationline.org/documents/section/criminal -codes, for an easy way to click on a specific country's criminal code. Regarding England and Wales see Homicide Act of 1957, 5 & 6 Eliz. 2, chapter 11, § 1, http://www.legislation.gov.uk/ukpga/Eliz2/5-6/11). Regarding Northern Ireland see Criminal Justice Act (Northern Ireland), 1966, c. 2 § 8, http://www.legislation.gov.uk/apni/1966/20/section/8). Regarding Republic of Ireland see Criminal Justice Act, 1964, sec. 4 (Act No. 5/ 1964) (Ir.), http://www.irishstatutebook.ie/1964/en/act/pub/0005/print.html#sec4. Regarding Canada see *R. v. Martineau*, (1990) 2 S.C.R. 633 (Can.) holding that mens rea must be proven in order to convict for murder, thus abrogating section 213(a) of Canada's Criminal Code which provided for "constructive murder," the equivalent of U.S. felony murder rules).

21. The factual narrative is drawn from these sources: Indictments of William J. Rummel, October 2, 1969 (Passing as True a Forged Instrument); Indictments of William Rummel, dated December 1, 1964 (Fraudulent Use of a Credit Card), October 2, 1968 (Passing as True a Forged Instrument), November 29, 1972 (Worthless Check passed with a value over $50); Motion to Waive Reading of Indictment, February 23, 1972; Indictment for Check Fraud, November 20, 1972; *Rummel v. Estelle, Director, Texas Department of Corrections*, 587 F.2d 651 (5th Circuit 1978); Brief for the Respondent, Supreme Court of the United States, *Rummel v. Estelle*, October 1979; U.S. Supreme Court Brief—Criminal DA of Bexar County, Tx., October 1979; *Rummel v. Estelle, Corrections Director*, 445 U.S. 263 (1980); *Rummel v. Estelle, Director, Texas Department of Corrections*, 498 F. Supp. 793 (W.D. Tx. 1980).

22. Jim Mann, "Courts to Review Tough Texas Law," *San Antonio Express-News*, September 9, 1979.

23. Robinson, Goodwin, and Reisig, "Disutility of Justice," 1970, table 3 scenario F, compared to scenario 5.

24. Jim Mann, "Courts to Review Tough Texas Law," *San Antonio Express News*, September 9, 1979, 14A.

25. See Mann, "Courts to Review." Rummel claimed that his life sentence was so disproportionate to the seriousness of his offense as to be cruel and unusual and hence unconstitutional. His claim was rejected by the Supreme Court

on March 19, 1980. The court held, in a 5 to 4 vote, that it was not so grossly disproportionate as to violate the Eighth Amendment, and that grading criminal offenses and prescribing punishments was "largely within the discretion of the punishing jurisdiction." *Rummel v. Estelle, Corrections Officer*, 445 U.S. 263, 285 (1980). There is no hard-and-fast test for "gross disproportionality" in sentencing. However, the Supreme Court has suggested factors to be considered in determining whether a punishment violates the proportionality principle of the Eighth Amendment. A 5-4 court in *Solem v. Helm* invalidated a sentence of life without possibility of parole, where Helm had committed seven felonies which the court described as "minor" and nonviolent Helm had convictions inter alia for three burglaries and multiple DUIs, and was sentenced under a South Dakota habitual offender statute. The court identified a three-part test for proportionality: "In sum, a court's proportionality analysis under the Eighth Amendment should be guided by objective criteria, including (i) the gravity of the offense and the harshness of the penalty; (ii) the sentences imposed on other criminals in the same jurisdiction; and (iii) the sentences imposed for commission of the same crime in other jurisdictions." *Solem v. Helm*, 463 U.S. 277, 292 (1983).

Eight years later, the court decided *Harmelin v. Mich.*, 501 U.S. 957 (1991), refusing to set aside a sentence of life without possibility of parole for a first-time conviction of possessing 672 grams of cocaine. The lead opinion by Scalia attempted to overturn Solem and entirely reject the proportionality principle for noncapital offenses, but the controlling rule set down in Kennedy's concurrence affirmed Solem. Kennedy clarified that the Eighth Amendment does not require strict proportionality, but forbids "gross disproportionality." *Harmelin*, 501 U.S. at 1001. Kennedy read Solem to say that courts need not always perform an intrajurisdictional comparative analysis; rather, they may do so if it is helpful in confirming the court's inference of gross proportionality. Id. at 1004–05. The court has reiterated that a combination of the Solem/Harmelin analysis was the proper gauge of proportionality. See *Ewing v. California*, 538 U.S. 11, 23 (2003), refusing to find constitutionally disproportionate a sentence of twenty-five-to-life for a grand larceny that was aggravated by California's "three-strike" recidivist statute. All of the cases cited here draw heavily on the *Rummel* decision.

26. *Almond v. United States*, 854 F. Supp. 439, 441 (W.D. Va. 1994).
27. Robinson and Cahill, *Law without Justice,* 132–33.
28. Ristroph, "Desert, Democracy, and Sentencing Reform," 1293, 1315–16.

29. Michael Vitiello argues that the three-strikes laws, widely implemented from 1993 to 1996, marked a paradigm shift away from retributivism in U.S. penal philosophy. Vitiello, "Three Strikes," 395, 425.

30. See Clark, Austin, and Henry, "Three Strikes and You're Out,". See also James Austin, John Clark, Patricia Hardyman, and D. Alan Henry Henry, "Three Strikes and You're Out: The Implementation and Impact of Strike Laws, National Institute of Justice," 2000, https://www.ncjrs.gov/pdffiles1/nij/grants/181297.pdf; and Elsa Chen, "Impact of Three Strikes and Truth in Sentencing on the Volume and Composition of Correctional Populations," National Institute of Justice, 2001, https://www.ncjrs.gov/pdffiles1/nij/grants/187109.pdf.

31. See Austin et al., "Three Strikes and You're Out: The Implementation and Impact." Another possible explanation for the lack of impact is that, in virtually all jurisdictions that enacted three-strikes laws, there had already been a statute in place providing for enhanced sentencing of repeat offenders.

32. Model Sentencing Act art. 1, §1 comment (National Council on Crime and Delinquency 1st ed. 1962), reprinted in Rector, "A Revolutionary Revision," 337, 346.

33. According to a 2008 *New York Times* article, it cost an average of $23,876 to imprison someone in 2005, the most recent year for which data were available. But state spending varies widely, from $45,000 a year in Rhode Island to $13,000 in Louisiana. The California Legislative Analyst's Office put the 2008–2009 cost of incarceration at $47,102 per inmate per year. Adam Liptak, "1 in 100 U.S. Adults behind Bars, New Study Says," *New York Times*, February 28, 2008, http://www.nytimes.com/2008/02/28/us/28cnd-prison.html.

34. See Robinson, "Punishing Dangerousness," 1429, 1450, and note 79.

35. See Zimring et al., *Punishment and Democracy*; Males and Macallair, "Striking Out," 65; see also Vitiello, "Punishment and Democracy," 257, 268–80 (reviewing book by Zimring et al., supra, and discussing its data). For more on the effects of three-strikes laws see Beres and Griffith, "Habitual Offender Statutes," 55, 69 ("One survey of parolees showed that at ages seventeen or less more than 75% of parolees were rearrested within three years of their release. By ages twenty-five to twenty-nine, the number dropped to 65% and at ages forty-five and older only 40.3% were rearrested"); Beres and Griffith, "Do Three Strikes Laws Make Sense?" 103, 135 ("The average career of an active offender is estimated to last between five and ten years. The peak ages for criminal activity are the late teens and early twenties. Only a small portion of offenders continue to commit offenses after the age of forty"); Spelman,

Criminal Incapacitation, 14 (noting that criminal career lasts between five and ten years); Blumstein, "Prisons" (noting that peak criminal activity is during teen years).

36. See Shepherd, "Fear of the First Strike," 159, 159 (using county-by-county data to find greater deterrent effect from three-strikes legislation, claiming that during the first two years it deterred approximately eight murders; 3,952 aggravated assaults; 10,672 robberies; and 384,488 burglaries); Ardaiz, "California's Three Strikes Law," 1, 3-7 (arguing that three strikes deters criminals from committing further crimes and achieves the goals of rehabilitation, retribution, and incapacitation); Janiskee and Erher, "Crime, Punishment and Romero," 39, 43, 53 (critiquing the Zimring study, supra note 52, and concluding that the decline in the crime rate was sharper after the three-strikes law). See also Jones, "Why the Three Strikes Law Is Working," 23 (article by secretary of state for California, who was involved in drafting the three-strikes legislation, concluding the law has been effective in deterring crime). Cf. Greenwood et al., "Estimated Benefits" (projecting that the California three-strikes law would result in 338,000 fewer crimes, at a cost of $16,300 per serious crime prevented).

37. See, e.g., U.S.S.G. § 4A1.1 *et seq.*; United States Sentencing Commission, Guidelines Manual, §3E1.1 (November 2007), chapter 5, part A (Sentencing table) (1997) (setting guideline sentence as function of "Offense Level" and "Criminal History Category"); Ariz. Stat. § 16-90-801(b)(1); Del. Stat. tit. 11, § 6580(c)(1); Wash. Stat. § 9.94A.010(1).

38. U.S. Sentencing Guidelines Manual 289 (1999).

39. In *Almond v. United States*, 854 F. Supp. 439, 444-445 (W.D. Va. 1994), the court considered Almond's argument that Section 4A1.2(e) of the US Sentencing Guidelines (USSG) should preclude the additional punishment of the "career criminal" statute, Section 924(e). The court rejected Almond's argument, because the commentary to Section 4 of the USSG explicitly states that Section 924(e) supersedes the § 4A1.2(e) time limits.

40. *Almond*, 854 F. Supp. at 445 ("It is the reluctant opinion of the court that Almond's sentence under § 924(e), although unfairly harsh on its face given Almond's conduct and record, was lawful."); and at 447, "Congress can change current laws and the President of the United States may grant a federal convict clemency even in the face of current law, but, regrettably, under current law this court cannot grant Mr. Almond the relief he seeks."

41. Between 1992 and 1995, forty-one states passed laws making it easier to try juveniles as adults. Sickmund, Snyder, and Poe-Yamagata, *Juvenile Offenders*

and *Victims 1997*, 30. Twenty-nine states now allow the prosecution of ten-year-olds for at least one offense. See Snyder and Sickmund, *Juvenile Offenders and Victims: A National Report*, 88. Some of these states require juvenile court judges to agree to the transfer of juveniles to adult court, others leave the decision to transfer to prosecutorial discretion, and still others require the transfer for certain offenses; see 85–89. See generally Klein, "Dennis the Menace or Billy the Kid," 371, 401–9 (discussing the problems that result when children are tried as adults). According to a recent Justice Department report, "every state now has at least one provision to transfer juveniles to adult courts." Strom, *Profile of State Prisoners*, 1. As of 1997 twenty-eight states had statutes that automatically excluded certain types of offenders from juvenile court jurisdiction, fifteen states permitted prosecutors to file some juvenile cases in adult criminal courts directly, and forty-six states allowed juvenile court judges to send cases to adult courts at their discretion. Idem at 2. As a result of such changes, the number of minors under age eighteen sent to prison rose from 18 per 1,000 violent crime arrestees in 1985, to 33 per 1,000 arrestees in 1997. Idem at 5 tbl.4. Legislative histories provide further evidence of the incapacitative rationale underlying these reforms. The report for the 1994 California legislation, for example, explains the need for lowering the age of criminal prosecution from sixteen to fourteen by noting that "the public is legitimately concerned that crimes of violence committed by juveniles are increasing in number and in terms of the level of violence" and concluding that the legislation "is a rational response to the legitimate public desire to address what is a serious problem." A.B. 560, 1993–1994 Leg., Reg. Sess. (Cal. 1994) (enacted). The Congressional Research Service similarly summarizes the rationale for such state legislation: "locking up dangerous kids so that they will not commit further crimes." Juveniles in the Adult Criminal Justice System: An Overview: Pub. No. 95–1152 GOV (Congressional Research Service, 1995), 5. Federal legislation that the House passed and that is pending in the Senate would reduce the age of presumptive adult prosecution to fourteen and would allow prosecution at thirteen for violent offenses and drug offenses. The "Background and Need for the Legislation" section of the bill indicates that "[i]n America today no population poses a larger threat to public safety than juvenile criminals." H.R. Rep. No. 105–86 (1997), 14.

42. See, e.g., Model Penal Code § 5.05(1) (attempt to commit first-degree felony is excepted).

43. See Robinson, *Intuitions of Justice, part 3*, Study 1 at 14–28 and study 3 at 33–42. Moral theorists, on the other hand, are divided on this issue, making this

one of the few areas (and perhaps the only major one) we discuss in which some retributivists and desert utilitarians might disagree as to the dictates of "desert." See chapter 1 note 7 and accompanying text.

44. As the drafters explain, "The theory of this grading system may be stated simply: To the extent that sentencing depends upon the antisocial disposition of the actor and the demonstrated need for a corrective sanction, there is likely to be little difference in the gravity of the required measures depending on the consummation or the failure of the plan." Model Penal Code § 5.05(1) (1985) commentary at 490 . Similarly, the drafters explain, "The primary purpose of punishing attempts is to neutralize dangerous individuals." Model Penal Code § 5.01 commentary at 323 (1985); see also ibid., 298, 299, 331. For other examples of Model Penal Code concern for dangerousness, see Robinson, *Criminal Law*, 647–48.

10. FAILURE

1. The factual narrative is drawn from these sources: *People of the State of Illinois v. Larry W. Eyler*, Case 83 CF 1585, "Report of Proceedings," February 3, 1984; *People of the State of Illinois v. Larry W. Eyler*, Case 83 CF 1585, "Supplemental Memorandum in Support of Defendant's Motions to Suppress," February 1, 1984; *People of the State of Illinois v. Larry W. Eyler*, Case 83 CF 1585, "Supplemental Memorandum in Opposition to Defendant's Motion to Suppress," February 1, 1984; *People of the State of Illinois v. Larry W. Eyler*, Case 84-126, (North Eastern Reporter, 2nd Series, October 25, 1989), 268–92; John O'Brien, "The Eyler Legacy: 21 Deaths," *Chicago Tribune*, March 9, 1994; Sarah Talalay, "Eyler Dies in Prison," *Chicago Tribune*, March 7, 1994; John O'Brien, "Call Helped Link Eyler to Slayings," *Chicago Tribune*, December 16, 1990; Jon O'Brien, "Professor Who Lived with Eyler Charged in '82 Torture Killing," *Chicago Tribune*, December 19, 1990; George Papajohn, "Eyler Sentenced to 60 Years for '82 Indiana Killing," *Chicago Tribune*, December 29, 1990; Kolarik and Klatt, *Freed to Kill*; *Eyler v. Babcox*, 582 F. Supp. 981 (N.D. Ill. 1983); *People v. Eyler*, 477 N.E.2d 774 (Ill. App. 1985); *Eyler v. Illinois*, 498 U.S. 881 (1990); Anastaplo, "Lawyers, First Principles," 353.

2. The latest Supreme Court opinion on the good faith exception is *Herring v. United States*, 555 U.S. 135 (2009). The opinion explains that the "benefits of deterrence must outweigh the costs" to society in order to trigger the exclusionary rule. As such, the good faith exception is applied in circumstances where the court finds little or no deterrence value because the police misdeeds were the result of a negligent mistake, rather than a deliberate disregard of the law.

3. The sheriff of Lake County, Robert Babcox, was at a public event and saw the judge. When someone brought up the case, Babcox started yelling at the judge, "You freed the son-of-a-bitch; you freed him to kill. You had the evidence to stop him and you knew it." Kolarik and Klatt, *Freed to Kill*, 258.

4. Justice Harry Blackmun in *Janis* explained the purpose of the Fourth Amendment exclusionary rule: "The 'prime purpose' of the rule, if not the sole one, is to deter future unlawful policy conduct." *United States v. Janis*, 428 U.S. 433, 446 (1976).

5. *Herring v. United States*, 555 U.S. 135, 141 (2009) (stating that the Fourth Amendment does not always require that the exclusionary rule apply when there has been a Fourth Amendment violation); *United States v. Calandra*, 414 U.S. 338, 348 (1974) ("the rule is a judicially created remedy designed to safeguard Fourth Amendment rights generally through its deterrent effect, rather than a personal constitutional right of the party aggrieved"); Milhizer, "Debunking Five Great Myths," 211, 214–24 (arguing that the Supreme Court requires the exclusionary rule not because it is constitutionally mandated, but because it is necessary to deter Fourth Amendment violations).

6. Kaplan, "Limits of the Exclusionary Rule," 1027, 1031–32.

7. As to the Fourth Amendment rule, see *Arizona v. Evans*, 514 U.S. 1, 10 (1995) (noting that "the Fourth Amendment contains no provision expressly precluding the use of evidence obtained in violation of its commands"); *United States v. Leon*, 468 U.S. 897, 905 (1984) (rejecting "[l]anguage in the opinions of this Court and of individual Justices [that has] sometimes implied that the rule is a necessary corollary of the Fourth Amendment"); *United States v. Calandra*, 414 U.S. 338, 347 (1974) (exclusionary rule is a "judicially created remedy, rather than a personal constitutional right"). As to the rule for *Miranda*, see *Dickerson v. United States*, 530 U.S. 428, 120 S. Ct. 2326 (2000).

8. Some fifteen years after *Mapp v. Ohio*, 367 U.S. 643 (1961), extended the Fourth Amendment exclusionary rule to the states, the Supreme Court itself acknowledged that "[n]o empirical researcher . . . has yet been able to establish with any assurance whether the rule has a deterrent effect." *United States v. Janis*, 428 U.S. 433, 452 n.22 (1976). One recent study provides statistics regarding the number of convictions prevented by the exclusionary rule and suggests that the rule has not been an effective deterrent to police misconduct. See L. Perrin et al., "If It's Broken," 669, 734–36.

9. Bowers and Robinson, "Perceptions of Fairness and Justice," 211.

10. *Herring v. United States*, 555 U.S. 135 (2009).

11. Payne and Guastaferro, "Mind the Gap," 93, 99.

12. Bilz, "Dirty Hands or Deterrence?" 141, 155–57.

13. *Herring v. United States*, 555 U.S. 135 (2009).

14. *Bivens v. Six Unknown Federal Narcotics Agents*, 403 U.S. 388, 415 (1971) (Burger, J., Dissenting).

15. Pizzi, "The Need to Overrule Mapp v. Ohio," 679 (comparing the exclusionary rules in Canada, New Zealand, Ireland, and England to the American rule); Wilkey, "The Exclusionary Rule,"215, 216 ("one proof of the irrationality of the exclusionary rule is that no other civilized nation in the world has adopted it"); Pitler, "Independent State Search," 1, 171 (arguing that no other country has a rule identical to the American rule, though a few have a limited, discretionary form); Bradley, "The Exclusionary Rule in Germany," 1032, 1034 (arguing that Germany's limited version of the exclusionary rule serves the purpose of protecting privacy interests rather than deterrence); Starr and Maness, "Is the Exclusionary Rule a Good Way," 373, 388 (noting that only Australia and Spain apply the rule for deterrence purposes, although the rules are applied discretionarily).

16. *R. v. Harrison*, 2008 Court of Appeal for Ontario 85.

17. Van Kessel, "Suspect as a Source," 1, 29.

18. Van Kessel, "Suspect as a Source," 29.

19. *P. J. and J. H. v. The United Kingdom*, European Court of Human Rights, 25 September 2001, at para. 76.

20. *People of the State of Illinois v Larry W. Eyler*, Case 84-126 (1985), 291.

21. The factual narrative is drawn from these sources: The facts of the *Ignatow* case are derived from Hill, *Double Jeopardy*; Elinor J. Brecher, "Brenda Schaefer: "That Woman Who Disappeared"; How Could This Ordinary Person with No Apparent Enemies—a Doctor's Office Assistant Who Lived with Her Parents—Just Simply Vanish?" *Courier-Journal*, March 5, 1989; Susan Craighead, "Attorney's Slip of the Tongue Led to Break in Schaefer Case," *Courier-Journal*, March 1, 1990; Susan Craighead, "Family Urge Bond Be Set at Affordable Level," *Courier-Journal*, February 1, 1990; Susan Craighead, "Police Focused Investigation on Ignatow from Start, Files Show," *Courier-Journal*, February 13, 1990; Todd Murphy, "Ignatow Witness Pleads Guilty to Evidence Tampering," *Courier-Journal*, December 3, 1991; Mary O'Doherty, "Threatening-Letter Trial Begins for Missing Woman's Boss," *Courier-Journal*, August 9, 1989; Clay Ryce, "Schaefer's Boss Is Charged in Threat against Her Fiancé," *Courier-Journal*, March 26, 1989; Leslie Scanlon, "Bizarre Murder Case Enters New Stage with Jury Selection," *Courier-Journal*, December 4, 1991; Leslie Scanlon, "Schaefer Wasn't Going to Wed Ignatow,"

Courier-Journal, December 14, 1991; Leslie Scanlon, "Shore-Inlow to Tell Jury Her Side of Schaefer Case," *Courier-Journal,* December 17, 1991; Leslie Scanlon, "I Did Not Kill Her; Ignatow's Ex-Lover Admits Helping Dig Hole for Victim," *Courier-Journal,* December 18, 1991; Leslie Scanlon, "Ignatow Confesses to Killing Schaefer," *Courier-Journal,* October 3, 1992; Leslie Scanlon, "Ignatow's Defense Rests without His Testimony in Murder Trial," *Courier-Journal,* December 21, 1991; Elinor J. Brecher, "Brenda Schaefer: That Woman Who Disappeared"; How Could This Ordinary Person with No Apparent Enemies—a Doctor's Office Assistant Who Lived with Her Parents—Just Simply Vanish?" *Courier-Journal,* March 5, 1989; Leslie Scanlon, "Ignatow's Lawyer Blames Shore-Inlow; Former Girlfriend Described as Jealous," *Courier-Journal,* December 10, 1991; Leslie Scanlon, "Kenton Jury Acquits Ignatow in Death of Fiancé Schaefer," *Courier-Journal,* December 22, 1991; Leslie Scanlon, "No Evidence Links Ignatow with Murder, Jurors Say," *Courier-Journal,* December 23, 1991; Cary B. Willis, "FBI Recorded Murder Suspect in Brenda Schaefer Case," *Courier-Journal,* February 6, 1990; Cary B. Willis, "Ignatow Lawyer Says Release of Tape Should Rule Out Death," *Courier-Journal,* February 7, 1990; Cary B. Willis, "Top Schaefer-Case Suspect Talks to Federal Grand Jury," *Courier-Journal,* October 17, 1989; Andrew Wolfson, "Court Won't Hear Ignatow Perjury Appeal; 2001 Conviction for Lying about Schaefer Stands," *Courier-Journal,* April 21, 2004; Andrew Wolfson, "Finding Evidence in Home a Fluke," *Courier-Journal,* October 3, 1992; Deborah Yetter, "Federal Grand Jury Indicts Ignatow on Perjury Charge," *Courier-Journal,* January 9, 1992; Deborah Yetter, "Textbook Example; Ignatow Fits Profile of Sexual Sadist," *Courier-Journal,* October 11, 1992.

22. Brecher, "Brenda Schaefer,"

23. Scanlon, "No Evidence Links Ignatow."

24. Scanlon, "No Evidence Links Ignatow."

25. *Heath v. Alabama,* 474 U.S. 82, 89 (1985) (explaining that the dual sovereign doctrine permits prosecution of the same offense in both state and federal court because "the States are separate sovereigns with respect to the Federal Government because each State's power to prosecute is derived from its own 'inherent sovereignty,' not from the Federal Government."); Paul G. Cassell, "The Rodney King Trials: Civil Rights Prosecutions and Double Jeopardy: The Rodney King Trials and the Double Jeopardy Clause: Some Observations on Original Meaning and the ACLU's Schizophrenic Views of the Dual Sovereign Doctrine," *UCLA Law Review* 41 (1994): 693, 695-697 (explaining double jeopardy in the context of the Rodney King trials).

26. Double jeopardy also does not apply when circumstances are such that the defendant is never actually "in jeopardy" of conviction in the first trial. For example, if the defendant bribes the judge in exchange for acquittal in the first trial, then the outcome was never in doubt and retrial is permitted. *Aleman v. Judges of the Circuit Court*, 138 F.3d 302, 308–309 (7th Cir. 1998).

27. David S. Rudstein, "Prosecution Appeals of Court-ordered Midtrial Acquittals: Permissible under the Double Jeopardy Clause?" (working paper, Chicago-Kent College of Law, 2012), 7, 9, http://works.bepress.com/david_rudstein/23 (the author lists dozens of countries that have a relaxed double jeopardy rule). "Some modern nations have no double jeopardy concept at all." J. Sigler, *Double Jeopardy: The Development of a Legal and Social Policy* (Cornell University Press, 1969), 152.

28. See Criminal Justice Act 2003, Part 10: Retrial for Serious Offences, §§ 76(4), 78(1) http://www.legislation.hmso.gov.uk/acts/acts2003/30044−k.htm#75.

29. Nyssa Taylor, Note and Comment, "England and Australia Relax the Double Jeopardy Privilege for Those Convicted of Serious Crimes," *Temple International and Comparative Law Journal* 19 (2005): 189.

30. See Law Commission, "Report 70: Acquittal Following Perversion of the Course of Justice," Law Commission (2001), 16, http://www.lawcom.govt.nz. Those changes were included in a Criminal Procedure Bill, along with a proposal to modify the jury unanimity requirement to allow conviction based on an 11–1 vote, which was introduced to Parliament in 2004. The bill proposed the insertion of section 374A and 378F to the Crimes Act of 1961. The changes were approved by Parliament in 2008. The Law Reform Commission of Hong Kong, Double Jeopardy Sub-Committee, "Consultation Paper: Double Jeopardy," GovHK, 3, 43, http://www.gov.hk/en/residents/government /publication/consultation/docs/2010/DoubleJeopardy.pdf; See Diana McCurdy, "Verdict of Public Hits the Courts," *New Zealand Herald*, June 26, 2004; Lesley Deverall, "Changes to the Law to Allow for Majority Verdicts in Court and Changing the Double Jeopardy Rules Have Been Introduced into Parliament; Majority Verdicts Bill Introduced," *IRN News*, June 23, 2004.

31. See Law Commission, "Report 70," 16. http://www.lawcom.govt.nz. Those changes were included in a Criminal Procedure Bill, along with a proposal to modify the jury unanimity requirement to allow conviction based on an 11–1 vote, which was introduced to Parliament in 2004. The Bill proposed the insertion of section 374A and 378F to the Crimes Act of 1961. The changes were approved by Parliament in 2008. The Law Reform Commission of Hong

Kong, "Double Jeopardy," 3, 43. See McCurdy, "Verdict of Public"; Deverall, "Changes to the Law."

32. Rajendra Ramlogan, "The Human Rights Revolution in Japan: A Story of New Wine in Old Skins?" *Emory International Law Review* 8 (1994): 127, 209; Daniel H. Foote, "The Benevolent Paternalism of Japanese Criminal Justice," *California Law Review* 80 (1992): 317, 341; A. H. J. Swart, "The Netherlands," in *Criminal Procedure Systems in the European Community,* ed. Christine Van Den Wyngaert (Bloomsbury Professional, 1993), 279, 314.

33. For a discussion of each, see Robinson and Cahill, *Law without Justice,* 137–55, 159–70.

34. See, e.g., Alabama 15-3-1.

35. See, e.g., Kentucky 500.050.

36. See Robinson and Cahill, *Criminal Law,* 430–31.

37. See Hawkins case, Robinson, *Criminal Law Case Studies,* 153–56.

38. Adam Liptak, "U.S. Is Alone in Rejecting All Evidence If Police Err," *New York Times,* July 19, 2008, http://www.nytimes.com/2008/07/19/us/19exclude.html ?pagewanted=all&_r=0.

39. Ross, "Impediments to Transnational Cooperation," 569, 577; Ross, "The Place of Court Surveillance," 493, 539.

40. Re Australia: "[J]udicial oversight of entrapment in Australia is extremely thin. This is consistent with the Australian judicial attitudes toward the admissibility of confessional material. Australian courts reject the role of regulating police conduct and tend to focus far more on the reliability of the material presented to them." Marcus and Waye, "Australia and the United States," 27, 78.

41. Re Canada: "[T]he entrapment defense in Canada is generally litigated after the accused has been convicted on the merits and it is the judge and not the jury who decides whether the entrapment defense has been established. This approach recognizes the objective nature of the defense and requires judicial reasons for decisions whether to accept or reject the entrapment defense. At the same time, litigating entrapment after a verdict makes clear to judges the crime control costs of finding that the accused has established entrapment." Roach, "Entrapment and Equality," 1455, 1461–62.

11. COLLAPSE

1. The factual narrative is drawn from these sources: Eldredge, *Ending the War on Drugs*; Godson, *Menace to Society*; Harris, *Political Corruption* ; "High Judge Fighting Drug Traffic Is Slain in Colombia," *Chicago Sun-Times,* August 1, 1986;

Mark Uhlig, "As Colombian Terror Grows, the Press Becomes the Prey," *New York Times,* May 24, 1989; Bowden, *Killing Pablo*; Collett Merrill, "Colombians Strike: Violence Spreads Death Toll Rises after Killing of Leftist Political Leader," *Washington Post*, October 14, 1987; "Gang Murders Cop Who Fought Medellin Cartel," *Miami Herald,* August 19, 1989; Penny Lernoux, "The Minister Who Had to Die: Colombia's Drug War," *Nation*, June 16, 1984; Nelson and Mollison, *The Memory of Pablo Escobar*; Mazur, *The Infiltrator*; Escobar and Fisher, *The Accountant's Story*; Kirk, *More Terrible Than Death*; Gaviria, "Increasing Returns," 1.

2. Nelson and Mollison, *The Memory of Pablo Escobar*, 45.

3. Bowden, *Killing Pablo*, 23.

4. Nelson and Mollison, *The Memory of Pablo Escobar*, 68.

5. Nelson and Mollison, *The Memory of Pablo Escobar,* 85.

6. Nelson and Mollison, *The Memory of Pablo Escobar,* 90.

7. Sanchez et al., "Conflict, Violence, and Crime in Colombia," 126.

8. Gaviria, "Increasing Returns," 21.

9. Gaviria, "Increasing Returns," 20.

10. Nelson and Mollison, *The Memory of Pablo Escobar*, 224.

11. Nelson and Mollison, *The Memory of Pablo Escobar*, 223.

12. Nelson and Mollison, *The Memory of Pablo Escobar*, 227.

13. Lawrence, "Letter to Thomas Dunlop," July 12, 1916.

14. Benjamin Franklin, "Pennsylvania Assembly: Reply to the Governor," Benjamin Franklin Papers, November 11, 1755, http://franklinpapers.org/franklin/framed Volumes.jsp?vol=6&page=238a.

15. *Weeks v. United States*, 34 S.Ct. 341, 344 (1914) (overturned by *Mapp v. Ohio*).

16. Anderson, *The Business of Organized Crime*, chapter 5.

17. Anderson, *The Business of Organized Crime*, 10; Abadinsky, *Organized Crime,* 9th ed., sec. 5.

18. 18 U.S.C. §§ 1961–1968.

19. See 18 U.S.C. §§ 1957, 1961, 1962.

20. Lynch, "RICO," 661, pt. 1–4; Robinson and Cahill, *Criminal Law*, 2nd ed., § 12.4.

21. Haque, "Government Responses to Terrorism," 170.

22. See WJP factor 8.5, Mark David Agrast, et al., eds., "The World Justice Project: Rule of Law Index 2011," *World Justice Project*, http://worldjusticeproject.org/sites /default/files/WJP_Rule_of_Law_Index_2011_Report.pdf.

23. "Corruption in Afghanistan: Bribery as Reported by the Victims," United Nations Office on Drugs and Crime, http://www.unodc.org/documents

/data-and-analysis/Afghanistan/Afghanistan-corruption-survey2010
-Eng.pdf.

24. "2011—A Crisis in Governance: Protests That Marked 2011 Show Anger at Corruption in Politics and Public Sector," *Transparency International*, December 1, 2011, http://cpi.transparency.org/cpi2011/press/.

25. Thachuk, "Corruption and International Security," 143, 148–49.

26. Source for number of terror incidents: RAND Database of Worldwide Terrorism Incidents, http://smapp.rand.org/rwtid/search.php. Source for levels of perceived public corruption: "Corruption Perceptions Index 2011," *Transparency International*, http://cpi.transparency.org/cpi2011/.

27. "A Conversation with Benazir Bhutto," Council on Foreign Relations, August 15, 2007, http://www.cfr.org/pakistan/conversation-benazir-bhutto/p14041.

28. Source for "U.S. officials accuse": Mark Mazzetti and Eric Schmitt, "Pakistanis Aided Attack in Kabul, U.S. Officials Say," *New York Times*, August 1, 2008.

29. "Pakistan: Shahzas Commission Results Marred by Free Ride for ISI," Human Rights Watch, January 20, 2012, http://www.hrw.org/news/2012/01/30/pakistan-shahzad-commission-results-marred-free-ride-isi.

30. "Report of the United Nations Commission of Inquiry into the Facts and Circumstances of the Assassination of Former Pakistani Prime Minister Mohtarma Benazir Bhutto," United Nations, April 15, 2010, 63, http://www.un.org/News/dh/infocus/Pakistan/UN_Bhutto_Report_15April2010.pdf.

31. For example, one American argued to the International War Crime Project: "[A]fter studying various international versions of the exclusionary rule, I further recommend that the ICTR adapt Rule 66 to shadow the United States' version of the exclusionary rule. My conclusion is based upon the fact that the American exclusionary rule allows a multitude of remedies to the injured party while providing the most constitutionally/statutorily prescribed structure and demand for compliance on the part of its police authority." Benjamin Snyder, "When, If Ever, Will an Illegal Arrest Result in Dismissal of the Charges and, If an Illegal Arrest Does Not Result in Dismissal of the Charges, What, If Any, Remedies Will Exist for an Illegal Arrest?" (New England School of Law, International War Crimes Project, Rwanda Genocide Prosecution, Memorandum for the Office of the Prosecutor, April 28, 2000).

32. Adam Liptak, "U.S. Is Alone in Rejecting All Evidence If Police Err," *New York Times,* July 19, 2008, www.nytimes.com/2008/07/19/us/19exclude.html?pagewanted=all (American nondiscretionary exclusionary rule rejected by all other countries, including Canada, Australia, England, and European Court of Human Rights).

33. See, e.g., Dolinger, "The Influence of American Constitutional Law," 803, 827 (rejecting the American exclusionary rule for fear it will lead to the release of dangerous criminals and have an adverse effect on public safety); Blum, "Doctrines without Borders," 2131, 2135-39 (the Israeli Supreme Court ruled that the most suitable rule for the Israeli justice system is a discretionary exclusionary rule, which allows courts the discretion to exclude evidence in appropriate cases and repay injustices caused by police misconduct); Cladwell and Chase, "The Unruly Exclusionary Rule," 45 (England, Canada, Australia, and New Zealand adopted a discretionary exclusionary rule that does not mandate automatic exclusion). For more on the exclusionary rule, see Robinson and Cahill, *Law without Justice*, chapter 7.

12. TAKING JUSTICE SERIOUSLY

1. See Paul H. Robinson, "Report on Offense Grading in Pennsylvania" (working paper, University of Pennsylvania Law School, Public Law Research Paper No. 10-01, 2009), 32, 34, 52, http://papers.ssrn.com/sol3/papers.cfm?abstract_id=1527149.

2. Paul H. Robinson et al., "Report on Offense Grading in New Jersey" (working paper, University of Pennsylvania Law School, Public Law Research Paper No. 11-03, 2011), 3-5, http://papers.ssrn.com/sol3/papers.cfm?abstract_id=1737825.

3. Paul H. Robinson, "Final Report of the Kentucky Penal Code Revision Project of the Criminal Justice Council" (Final Report of the Kentucky Penal Code Revision Project, 2003), http://papers.ssrn.com/sol3/papers.cfm?abstract_id=1526674.

4. Paul H. Robinson and Michael T. Cahill, "Final Report of the Illinois Criminal Code Rewrite and Reform Commission" (University of Pennsylvania Law School, Public Law Research Paper No. 09-40, 2003), http://ssrn.com/abstract=1523384.

5. Robinson et al., "The Five Worst," 1.

6. Robinson et al., "The Modern Irrationalities," 709.

7. See ACLU: American Civil Liberties Union, https://www.aclu.org/; Defending Dissent Foundation, defendingdissent.org; National District Attorneys Association, ndaa.org; National Criminal Justice Association, ncja.org.

13. POSTSCRIPT

1. Tayman, *The Colony*, 269.

2. Tayman, *The Colony*, 281.

3. Tayman, *The Colony*, 315.

4. Parrado and Rause, *Miracle in the Andes*, 197.

5. Parrado and Rause, *Miracle in the Andes*, 227.

6. Read, *Alive*, 347.

7. Rogers, *Cruising Voyage Round the World*, 229.

8. Woodard, *The Republic of Pirates*, 248–60.

9. Woodard, *The Republic of Pirates,* 296.

10. "By the Numbers: How Much Does Somali Piracy Cost?" gCaptain, http://gcaptain.com/somali-piracy-cost-report/.

11. Shinn, *Mining Camps*, 293–95.

12. Anderson and Hill, "An American Experiment in Anarcho-Captialism.

13. Shinn, *Mining Camps*, 294.

14. "Trail Facts: Frequently Asked Questions," Oregon-California Trails Association, http://www.octa-trails.org/learn/trail_facts.php#howmanyemigrants.

15. "Buchenwald," *Holocaust Encyclopedia*, http://www.ushmm.org/wlc/en/article .php?ModuleId=10005198.

16. Wicker, *A Time to Die*, 286.

17. "Attica Timeline," *Attica Is All of Us*, http://atticaisallofus.org/?page_id=506.

18. Dash, *Batavia's Graveyard*, 194.

19. Dash, *Batavia's Graveyard*, 198.

20. Dash, *Batavia's Graveyard,* 203.

21. Dash, *Batavia's Graveyard,* 209.

22. Dash, *Batavia's Graveyard,* 244.

23. Marks, *Lost Paradise*, 290.

24. Gordon and Llamzon, *Horyo*, 187.

25. Cummins, *Cast Away*, 67–68.

26. Druett, *Island of the Lost*, 257.

27. The U.S. Department of Justice, "Prisoners in 2009," *Bureau of Justice Statistics Bulletin*, December 2010, 33, http://bjs.ojp.usdoj.gov/content/pub/pdf/p09 .pdf.

28. Zellner also seeks a retrial in the Bridges murder case. She accuses Schippers of professional misconduct, alleging that he received $16,875 from Little as payment for Eyler's legal fees, though Eyler told him that Little was the actual killer. Thus, she claims Schippers had a conflict of interest at the trial and Eyler did not receive proper representation.

29. Sarah Talalay, "Eyler Dies in Prison," *Chicago Tribune*, March 7, 1994.

30. "Mel Ignatow, 70," Google Groups, https://groups.google.com/forum /?fromgroups#!topic/alt.obituaries/jSUvRwmKgvA%5B1-25%5D.

31. "Irony Is a Bitch," . . . *And the Adventure Continues,* http://schlub28.blogspot.com /2008/09/irony-is-bitch.html.

32. Source for "community police": Charo Quesada, "The People's Police," *IDBAmerica,* http://www.iadb.org/idbamerica/index.cfm?thisid=2817.

33. Source for "local security councils": Alys Willman and Megumi Makisaka, "Interpersonal Violence Prevention," The World Bank: World Development Report 2011 (2011), 45.

34. Source for 1992 figure: "Seguridad, ciudadanía y políticas públicas en Bogota," Institute for Research and Debate on Governance, http://www.institut -gouvernance.org/en/conference/fiche-conference-36.html; Source for 2012 figure: "Bogotá registra la cifra más baja de homicidios en 27 años," BBC Mundo, http://www.bbc.co.uk/mundo/ultimas_noticias/2012/09/120910_ultnot _bogota_baja_homicidios_msd.shtml.

35. Sources for figures: "Crime Rates by Type," U.S. Census Bureau, http://www.census .gov/compendia/statab/2012/tables/12s0309.pdf. Victoria Rossi, "Bogota Homicides Reach 27-Year Low after Gun Ban," September 12, 2012, *InSight Crime,* http://www.insightcrime.org/news-briefs/gun-ban-bogota-homicide, accessed on December 20, 2013.

GLOSSARY

The following words and phrases are intended by the authors to have the following meanings:

Adjudication. Adjudication is the legal process by which a judge or jury reviews the evidence and arguments of the opposing parties to come to a decision—in the criminal context, the decision will be to convict or dismiss.

Blameworthiness. Refers to the degree of moral blame a person deserves for a violation. In the context of criminal law, an offender's blameworthiness depends upon a wide variety of factors, including the seriousness of the offense, his culpable state of mind at the time of committing the offense, and his capacity to have avoided the violation.

Culpable state of mind. Generally, proof of a criminal offense requires proof that the offender at the time of committing the offense had a particular state of mind as to the circumstances, his conduct, and its consequences. In the United States, the common levels of culpable states of mind are: "intentionally" (or "purposely"), "knowingly," "recklessly," and "negligently." In the context of homicide, for example, a person "intentionally" kills another if he hopes or wants to cause the death and "knowingly" kills another if he is practically certain that his conduct will cause the death (even if he does not particularly want to cause it). These killings typically are both murder. One "recklessly" kills another if he is aware that his conduct creates a substantial risk of causing the death, usually treated as the offense of manslaughter. One "negligently" kills another if he was not aware of the risk of death but should have been aware. This typically is punished as the offense of negligent homicide. For an example of such definitions, see the American Law Institute's Model Penal Code Section 2.02.

Denatured alcohol. Denatured alcohol or methylated spirits is ethanol that has additives to make it poisonous, extremely bad tasting, foul smelling, or nauseating, in order to discourage recreational consumption.

Desert. That which is deserved or merited; a just punishment or reward. In the criminal context, an offender's desert is punishment based upon the degree of his moral blameworthiness for his offense. (See *Blameworthiness*.)

Deviation from desert. In this volume, this phrase refers to imposing criminal liability or punishment that is either more or less than an offender deserves.

Double jeopardy bar. The Fifth Amendment to the U.S. Constitution provides, "No person shall . . . be subject for the same offence [sic] to be twice put in jeopardy of life or limb." This provision, known as the Double Jeopardy Clause, prohibits state and federal governments from reprosecuting a person for an offense after the person has been tried and convicted or acquitted for it. Each of the fifty states offers similar protection through its own constitution and statutes.

Entrapment defense. The entrapment defense to a criminal charge is available in most states if it is established that the government agent or official originated the idea of the crime and induced the accused to engage in it when he was not previously disposed to do so. It is not available for inducement by a private party. So-called "sting" operations by police are otherwise legal.

Exclusionary rule. The exclusionary rule is a legal principle in the United States, created by the courts, that allows evidence collected or analyzed in violation of the defendant's constitutional rights to be excluded from use at trial without regard to its reliability or the effect of its exclusion on the prosecution. The rule was adopted to deter police from violating suspects' constitutional rights.

Excuse defense. An excuse defense to a criminal offense is one based upon a claim that, while the offender committed the harm or evil of the offense without justification, he ought not be blamed for it because of the dysfunctions he suffered at the time of committing the offense. Common excuse defenses include insanity, involuntary intoxication, duress, immaturity, involuntary act, and some forms of reasonable mistake. See, for example, the American Law Institute's Model Penal Code Sections 4.01, 2.08(4), 2.09, 4.10, 2.01(2). (Compare to *Justification defense*.)

Felony murder rule. The felony murder rule is a legal doctrine present in a majority of American jurisdictions that broadens the crime of murder in two ways. First, when an offender kills a person even accidentally during commission of a felony, the offense is murder. Second, it makes any accomplice in the felony liable for murder for any death that occurs in furtherance of the felony.

General deterrence. Deterrence is the use of a threat of official punishment to discourage people from offending. When the threat is aimed at the general population, it is termed *general deterrence* (as opposed to *special deterrence*, where the threat is aimed at the offender being sentenced).

Grand jury. A grand jury is a legal body empowered to conduct official proceedings to investigate potential criminal conduct and to determine whether sufficient evidence exits to justify bringing a criminal charge. A grand jury may compel the production of documents and may compel the sworn testimony of witnesses to appear before it.

Habitual-offender statutes. A habitual offender is a person who is convicted of a new crime and who was previously convicted of a crime. Many states have laws targeting habitual offenders, providing for enhanced punishment for a subsequent offense. Such statutes are typically designed to provide greater deterrence of a new offense by a past offender and to gain control of a repeat offender for a longer period of time in order to prevent another offense.

Inchoate offense. An inchoate offense is one that is incomplete, such that the harm or evil of the offense does not occur. A person may be held criminally liable for conduct short of a completed offense if it was his intention that the offenses be committed and he acted toward that commission (the offenses of attempt), he agreed with another person that one of them would commit the offense (the offenses of conspiracy), or he solicited another person to commit the offense (the offenses of solicitation).

Intentional. See *Culpable state of mind*.

"Joyriding" offense. To joyride is to drive around in a stolen vehicle with no particular goal; a ride taken solely for pleasure. At English common law, joyriding was not theft because the intention to "permanently deprive" the owner of the vehicle is not present. Instead, most jurisdictions create a separate offense of "taking without consent" or unauthorized use.

Justification defense. A justification defense to a criminal offense is one based upon the claim that what the person did was the right thing to do in the situation, commonly because it avoided a greater harm or evil than the harm or evil of the offense committed. Common justification defenses include lesser evils (necessity), self-defense, defense of others, defense of property, law enforcement authority, authority of persons with special responsibility, and general public duty. See, for example, the American Law Institute's Model Penal Code Article 3. (Compare to *Excuse defense*.)

Knowing. See *Culpable state of mind*.

Legality principle. Fundamental rule of criminal law that nothing is a crime unless it is clearly forbidden in law, preferably by a clear and specific written statute.

Negligent. See *Culpable state of mind*.

Petit jury. A jury, usually of twelve persons, empaneled to observe a trial and, in a criminal case, to acquit or convict the defendant pursuant to the direction of the court on points of law (called "jury instructions"). Compare to *Grand jury*.

Preventive detention. The confinement in a secure facility of a person who has not been found guilty of a crime, but who is thought to be dangerous. Persons held in preventive detention commonly include the mentally ill and those suffering a contagious disease, but also sometimes a person thought likely to commit a future criminal offense, such a persistent sexual predators.

Reckless. See *Culpable state of mind*.

RICO offenses. Refers to the Racketeer Influenced and Corrupt Organizations Act (18 U.S.C. §§ 1961–1968), commonly referred to as the RICO Act. The act was an attempt to reach the leaders of organized crime, who had previously insulated themselves from criminal liability, although they ran large organizations built upon criminal activity. RICO made it a serious offense to commit certain defined offenses within a certain period of time or to benefit from or control the proceeds from the activities related to these offenses. The purpose of the RICO Act was stated as "the elimination of the infiltration of organized crime and racketeering into legitimate organizations operating in interstate commerce."

Strict liability. Refers to an offense that is defined to not require proof of a culpable state of mind. Strict liability often applies to vehicular traffic offenses. In a speeding case, for example, whether the defendant knew that the posted speed limit was being exceeded is irrelevant. The prosecutor would need to prove only that the defendant was operating the vehicle in excess of the speed limit. Strict liability is sometimes used for more serious offenses, but its use there can be controversial. Compare to *Culpable state of mind*.

***Terry* stop.** In the United States, a *Terry* stop is a brief detention of a person by police on reasonable suspicion of involvement in criminal activity but short of probable cause to arrest. The name derives from the U.S. Supreme Court decision in *Terry v. Ohio* 392 U.S. 1 (1968), authorizing such stops and also allowing police to do a limited search of the suspect's outer garments for weapons if they have a reasonable and articulable suspicion that the person detained may be "armed and dangerous." When a search for weapons is authorized, the procedure is known as a "stop and frisk."

United States Sentencing Commission. The commission is an independent agency within the judicial branch of the federal government of the United States responsible for articulating sentencing guidelines for the U.S. federal courts. The commission promulgates the U.S. Sentencing Guidelines, which replaced the prior system of indeterminate sentencing that allowed trial judges to give sentences ranging from probation to the maximum statutory punishment for the offense.

Utilitarianism. Stripped down to its essentials, utilitarianism holds that the correct course of action in any situation is the one that produces the greatest balance of benefits over harms for everyone affected. In the context of criminal law and punishment , utilitarianism has been taken to support the imposition of punishment that will most effectively deter or incapacitate a potential offender, even if the punishment is more (or less) than is deserved.

BIBLIOGRAPHY

PUBLISHED WORKS

Abadinsky, Howard. *Organized Crime*. 2nd ed. Chicago: Nelson-Hall, 1985.

———. *Organized Crime,* 9th ed. Boston: Cengage Learning, 2009.

Agrast, Mark David et al., eds. *The World Justice Project: Rule of Law Index 2011*. The World Justice Project, 2011, http://worldjusticeproject.org/sites/default/files /WJP_Rule_of_Law_Index_2011_Report.pdf.

Alexander, Caroline. *The Bounty: The True Story of the Mutiny on the "Bounty."* New York: Viking, 2003.

Alexander, Richard. *The Biology of Moral Systems*. Piscataway NJ: Aldine Transaction, 1987.

Alford, John, and John Hibbing. "The Origin of Politics: An Evolutionary Theory of Political Behavior." *Perspectives on Politics* 2 (2004).

Allen, Madelene Ferguson. *Wake of the Invercauld: Shipwrecked in the Sub-Antarctic: A Great-Granddaughter's Pilgrimage.* Montreal: McGill-Queen's University Press, 1997.

Allsop, Kenneth. *The Bootleggers: The Story of Chicago's Prohibition Era.* New York: Random House, 1968.

Anastaplo, George. "Lawyers, First Principles, and Contemporary Challenges: Explorations." *Northern Illinois University Law Review* 19 (1999).

Anderson, Annelise Graebner. *The Business of Organized Crime: A Cosa Nostra Family*. Stanford CA: Hoover Institution Press, 1979.

Anderson, Terry, and P. J. Hill. "An American Experiment in Anarcho-Capitalism: The Not So Wild, Wild West." Boseman: Department of Economics, Montana State University, 1989.

Andrews, Molly. "One Hundred Miles of Lives: The Stasi Files as People's History of East Germany." *Oral History* 26 (1998).

Anonymous. "Episodes from the Attica Massacre." *Black Scholar* 4 (1972).

Anonymous. *A Woman in Berlin: Eight Weeks in a Conquered City, A Diary*. London: Picador, 2005.

Antoine, Rebeca, and the Katrina Narrative Project. *Voices Rising: Stories from the Katrina Narrative Project*. Omaha: UNO Press, 2008.

Ardaiz, James A. "California's Three Strikes Law: History, Expectations, Consequences." *McGeorge Law Review* 32 (2000).

Aron, Arthur, et al. "Reward, Motivation, and Emotion Systems Associated with Early-Stage Intense Romantic Love." *Journal of Neurophysiology* 94 (2005).

Asbridge, Mark, and Swarna Weerasinghe. "Homicide in Chicago from 1890 to 1930: Prohibition and Its Impact on Alcohol- and Non-Alcohol-Related Homicides." *Addiction* 104 (2009).

Bachner, James. *My Darkest Years: Memoirs of a Survivor of Auschwitz, Warsaw and Dachau*. Jefferson NC: McFarland, 2007.

Bagaric, Mirko. "In Defence of a Utilitarian Theory of Punishment: Punishing the Innocent and the Compatibility of Utilitarianism and Rights." *Australian Journal of Legal Philosophy* 24 (1999).

Balikci, Asen. *The Netsilik Eskimo*. Copenhagen, Denmark: Natural History Press, 1970.

Behr, Edward. *Prohibition: Thirteen Years that Changed America*. New York: Arcade, 1996.

Bejarano, Jesus Antonio. "Violence, Security, and Economic Growth in Colombia, 1985–1995." *Colombian Economic Journal* 1 (2003).

Bekoff, Mark. "Wild Justice, Cooperation, and Fair Play." In *The Origins and Nature of Sociality*, ed. Robert W. Sussman and Audrey R. Chapman, 451–52. Piscataway NJ: Aldine Transaction, 2004.

Bell, Malcolm. *The Turkey Shoot: Tracking the Attica Cover-Up*. New York: Grove, 1985.

Benaquisto, Lucia, and Peter J. Freed. "The Myth of Inmate Lawlessness: The Perceived Contradiction between Self and Other in Inmates' Support for Criminal Justice Sanctioning Norms." *Law and Society Review* 30 (1996).

Beres, Linda S., and Thomas D. Griffith. "Do Three Strikes Laws Make Sense? Habitual Offender Statutes and Criminal Incapacitation." *Georgetown Law Review* 87 (1998).

———. "Habitual Offender Statutes and Criminal Deterrence." *Connecticut Law Review* 34 (2002).

Berger, Bennett M. *The Survival of a Counterculture*. Oakland CA: University of California Press, 1981.

Bergreen, Laurence. *Capone: The Man and the Era*. New York: Simon and Schuster, 1994.

Bilz, Kenworthy. "Dirty Hands or Deterrence? An Experimental Examination of the Exclusionary Rule." *Journal of Empirical Legal Studies* 9 (2012).

Birenbaum, Halina. *Hope Is the Last to Die: A Coming of Age under Nazi Terror.* Woodbridge CT: Twayne, 1971.

Blum, Binyamin. "Doctrines without Borders: The "New" Israeli Exclusionary Rule and the Dangers of Legal Transplantation." *Stanford Law Review* 60 (2008).

Blumstein, Alfred. "Prisons: A Policy Challenge." In *Crime: Public Policies for Crime Control*, ed. James Q. Wilson and Joan Petersilia, 451-82. Oakland CA: Institute for Contemporary Studies, 2002.

Bolton, Gary E., and Rami Zwick. "Anonymity Versus Punishment in Ultimatum Bargaining." *Games and Economic Behavior* 10 (1995).

Bondy, Curt. "Problems of Internment Camps." *Journal of Abnormal and Social Psychology* 38 (1943).

Bouvard, Marguerite. *The Intentional Community Movement: Building a New Moral World.* Port Washington NY: Kennikat National University Publications, 1975.

Bowden, Mark. *Killing Pablo: The Hunt for the World's Greatest Outlaw.* New York: Atlantic Monthly Press, 2001.

Bowers, Josh, and Paul H. Robinson. "Perceptions of Fairness and Justice: The Shared Aims and Occasional Conflicts of Legitimacy and Moral Credibility." *Wake Forest Law Review* 47 (2012).

Bowles, Samuel, and Herbert Gintis. "The Origins of Human Cooperation." In *The Genetic and Cultural Evolution of Cooperation*, ed. Peter Hammerstein, 429-43. Cambridge: MIT Press, 2003. http://www.umass.edu/preferen/gintis/dahlem .pdf.

Bradley, Craig. "The Exclusionary Rule in Germany." *Harvard Law Review* 96 (1983).

Braga, Anthony A., and Brenda J. Bond. "Policing Crime and Disorder Hot Spots: A Randomized Controlled Trial." *Criminology* 46 (2008).

Braman, Donald, Dan M. Kahan, and David Hoffman. "Some Realism about Punishment Naturalism." *University of Chicago Law Review* 77 (2010).

Breverton, Terry. *Black Bart Roberts: The Greatest Pirate of Them All.* Gretna LA: Pelican, 2004.

Briggs, Jean L. *Never in Anger: Portrait of an Eskimo Family.* Cambridge MA: Harvard University Press, 1971.

Brinkley, Douglas. *The Great Deluge: Hurricane Katrina, New Orleans, and the Mississippi Gulf Coast.* New York: Harper Perennial, 2007.

Brooks, Justin. "How Can We Sleep While the Beds Are Burning? The Tumultuous Prison Culture of Attica Flourishes in American Prisons Twenty-Five Years Later." *Syracuse Law Review* 47 (1996).

Brosnan, Sarah F. "Fairness in Monkeys." In *Encyclopedia of Animal Behavior*, ed. Marc Bekoff, 288-89. Westport CT: Greenwood, 2004.

———. "Nonhuman Species' Reactions to Inequity and Their Implications for Fairness." *Social Justice Research* 19 (2006).

Brosnan, Sarah F., and Frans B. M. de Waal. "Monkeys Reject Unequal Pay." *Nature* 425 (2003).

———. "Reply: Animal Behavior: Fair Refusal by Capuchin Monkeys." *Nature* 428 (2004).

Brosnan, Sarah F., Hillary C. Schiff, and Frans B. M. de Waal. "Tolerance for Inequity May Increase with Social Closeness in Chimpanzees." *Proceedings of the Royal Society B: Biological Sciences* 272 (2005).

Burch, Ernest S. *The Eskimos.* London: J. R. MacDonald, 1988.

Burg, Barry Richard. *Sodomy and the Pirate Tradition: English Sea Rovers in the Seventeenth-Century Caribbean.* New York: NYU Press, 1995.

Burnham, Terence C., and Dominic D. P. Johnson. "The Biological and Evolutionary Logic of Human Cooperation." *Analyse and Kritik* 27 (2005).

Camerer, Colin F. *Behavioral Game Theory—Experiments in Strategic Interaction.* Princeton: Princeton University Press, 2003.

Campbell, Mavis Christine. *The Maroons of Jamaica, 1655-1796: A History of Resistance, Collaboration, and Betrayal.* Boston: Bergin and Garvey, 1988.

Carey, Bev. *The Maroon Story: The Authentic and Original History of the Maroons in the History of Jamaica 1490-1880.* Baltimore MD: Agouti, 1997.

Carlsmith, Kevin M. "The Roles of Retribution and Utility in Determining Punishment." *Journal of Experimental Social Psychology* 42 (2006).

Carlsmith, Kevin M., John M. Darley, and Paul H. Robinson. "Why Do We Punish? Deterrence and Just Deserts as Motives for Punishment." *Journal of Personality and Social Psychology* 83 (2002).

Cashman, Sean Dennis. *Prohibition—The Lie of the Land.* New York: Free Press, 1989.

Cladwell, Harry M. and Carol A. Chase. "The Unruly Exclusionary Rule: Heeding Justice Blackmun's Call to Examine the Rule in Light of Changing Judicial Understanding about Its Effects Outside the Courtroom." *Marquette Law Review* 78 (1994).

Clark, David E., and Manfred Wildner. "Violence and Fear of Violence in East and West Germany." *Social Science and Medicine* 51 (2000).

Clark, John, James Austin, and D. Alan Henry. *Three Strikes and You're Out: A Review of State Legislation.* Washington DC: National Institute of Justice, 1997. https://www.ncjrs.gov/pdffiles/165369.pdf.

Clutton-Brock, T. H., and G. A. Parker. "Punishment in Animal Societies." *Nature* 373 (2005).

Clutton-Brock, T. H., D. Green, M. Hiraiwa-Hasegawa, and S. D. Albon. "Passing the Buck: Resource Defence, Lek Breeding and Mate Choice in Fallow Deer." *Behavioral Ecology and Sociobiology* (1988).

Clutton-Brock, T. H., S. D. Albon, R. M. Gibson, and F. E. Guinness. "The Logical Stag: Adaptive Aspects of Fighting in Red Deer (Cervus elaphus L.)." *Animal Behavior* 27 (1979).

Coffee, John C., Jr. "Does 'Unlawful' Mean 'Criminal'?: Reflections on the Disappearing Tort/Crime Distinction in American Law." *Boston University Law Review* 71 (1991).

Colby, Anne, and Lawrence Kohlberg. *The Measurement of Moral Judgment,* vol. 1. Cambridge: Cambridge University Press, 1987.

———. *The Measurement of Moral Judgment,* vol. 2. Cambridge: Cambridge University Press, 1987.

Coffman, Lloyd. *Blazing a Wagon Trail to Oregon: A Weekly Chronicle of the Great Migration of 1843.* Bend OR: Maverick Distributors, 1993.

Comstock, William. *The Life of Samuel Comstock: The Terrible Whaleman* 88. Boston: James Fisher, 1840.

Cordingly, David. *Under the Black Flag: The Romance and the Reality of Life among the Pirates.* New York: Random House, 2006.

Corman, Hope, and Naci Mocan. "Carrots, Sticks, and Broken Windows." *Journal of Law and Economics* 48 (2005).

Coyote, Peter. *Sleeping Where I Fall: A Chronicle.* Berkeley CA: Counterpoint, 1998.

Cummins, Joseph. *Castaway: Epic True Stories of Shipwreck, Piracy, and Mutiny on the High Seas.* New South Wales, Australia: Pier 9, 2008.

Curl, John. *Memories of Drop City: The First Hippie Commune of the 1960s and the Summer of Love, A Memoir.* iUniverse, 2006.

Currie, David P. *The Constitution of the Federal Republic of Germany.* Chicago: University of Chicago Press, 1994.

Cymlich, Israel, and Oscar Strawczynski. *Escaping Hell in Treblinka.* Jerusalem: Yad Vashem and The Holocaust Survivors' Memoirs Project, 2007.

Dallas, R. C. *History of the Maroons: From their Origin to the Establishment of their Chief Tribe at Sierra Leone; Including the Expedition to Cuba for the Procuring Spanish Chasseurs; and the State of the Island of Jamaica for the Last Ten Years; with a Succinct History of the Island Previous to that Period.* London: T. N. Longman and O. Rees, 1803.

Darley, John M., and Thomas R. Shultz. "Moral Rules: Their Content and Acquisition." *Annual Review of Psychology* 41 (1990).

Darley, John M., et al. "Incapacitation and Just Deserts as Motives for Punishment." *Law and Human Behavior* 24 (2000).

Darley, John M. et al. "Intentions and Their Contexts in the Moral Judgments of Children and Adults." *Child Development* 49 (1978).

Darley, John M., Kevin M. Carlsmith, and Paul H. Robinson. "Incapacitation and Just Deserts as Motives for Punishment." *Law and Human Behavior* 24 (2000).

Dash, Michael. "*Batavia's Graveyard: The True Story of the Mad Heretic Who Led History's Bloodiest Mutiny.* New York: Crown, 2002.

Dawes, Robyn M., and Richard H. Thaler. "Anomalies: Cooperation." *Journal of Economic Perspectives* 2 (1988).

Daws, Gavan. *Prisoners of the Japanese: POWs of World War II in the Pacific.* New York: W. Morrow, 1994.

Delevan, James. *Notes on California and the Placers: How to Get There, and What to Do Afterwards, By One Who Has Been There.* New York: H. Long & Brother, 1850.

Demleitner, Nora V. "Organized Crime and Prohibition: What Difference Does Legalization Make?" *Whittier Law Review* 15 (1994).

De Poncins, Gontran. *Kabloona.* London: Reynal and Hitchcock, 1941.

Des Pres, Terrence. *The Survivor: An Anatomy of Life in the Death Camps.* New York: Oxford University Press, 1980.

De Quervain, Dominique J. F., et al. "The Neural Basis of Altruistic Punishment." *Science* 305 (2004).

Deutsch, Michael E., Dennis Cunningham, and Elizabeth Fink. "Twenty Years Later—Attica Civil Rights Case Finally Cleared for Trial." *Social Justice* 18 (1991).

DeVoto, Bernard. *The Year of Decision 1846.* Boston: Little, Brown, 1943.

De Waal, Frans B. M. *Chimpanzee Politics: Power and Sex among Apes.* Baltimore: Johns Hopkins University Press, 1998.

———. "The Chimpanzee's Sense of Social Regularity and Its Relation to the Human Sense of Justice." *American Behavioral Scientist* 34 (1991).

———. "Food Sharing and Reciprocal Obligations among Chimpanzees." *Journal of Human Evolution* 18 (1989).

———. *Good Natured: The Origins of Right and Wrong in Humans and Other Animals.* Cambridge: Harvard University Press, 1997.

De Waal, Frans B. M, and Lesleigh M. Luttrell. "The Similarity Principle Underlying Social Bonding among Female Rhesus Monkeys." *Folia Primatologica* 46 (1986).

Dolinger, Jacob. "The Influence of American Constitutional Law on the Brazilian Legal System." *American Journal of Comparative Law* 38 (1990).

Doyle, James. F. "Radical Critique of Criminal Punishment." *Social Justice* 22 (1995).

Drake-Brockman, Henrietta. *Voyage to Disaster*. Perth: University of Western Australia Press, 1996.

Druett, Joan. *Island of the Lost: Shipwrecked at the Edge of the World*. Chapel Hill: Algonquin, 2007.

Durham, Alexis M., III. "Public Opinion Regarding Sentences for Crime: Does It Exist?" *Journal of Criminal Justice* 21 (1993).

Dutton, Charles J. *The Samaritans of Molokai: The Lives of Father Damien and Brother Dutton among the Lepers*. Ann Arbor MI: Dodd, Mead, 1932.

Eldredge, Dirk Chase. *Ending the War on Drugs: A Solution for America*. Bridgehampton NY: Bridge Works, 1998.

Elkind, David, and Ruth F. Dabek. "Personal Injury and Property Damage in the Moral Judgments of Children." *Child Development* 48 (1977).

Ellickson, Robert C. *Order without Law: How Neighbors Settle Disputes*. Cambridge: Harvard University Press, 1991.

Escobar, Roberto, and David Fisher. *The Accountant's Story: Inside the Violent World of the Medellín Cartel*. New York: Grand Central, 2009.

Exquemelin, Alexandre Olivier, and William Swan Sonnenschein. *The Buccaneers of America*. London: Allen and Unwin, 1684.

Eynikel, Hilde. *Molokai: The Story of Father Damien*. New York: Alba House, 1999.

Featherstone, Richard Andrew. *Narratives from the 1971 Attica Prison Riot: Towards a New Theory of Correctional Disturbances*. Lewiston NY: Edwin Mellon, 2005.

Fehr, Ernst, and Simon Gachter. "Cooperation and Punishment in Public Goods Experiments." *American Economic Review* 90 (2000).

Fehr, Ernst, and Herbert Gintis. "Human Motivation and Social Cooperation: Experimental and Analytical Foundations." *Annual Review of Sociology* 33 (2007).

Fehr, Ernst, and Urs Fischbacher. "The Nature of Human Altruism." *Nature* 425 (2003).

——. "Third-Party Punishment and Social Norms." *Evolution and Human Behavior* 25 (2004).

Ferguson Allen, Madelene. *Wake of the Invercauld: Shipwrecked in the Sub-Antarctic, A Great-Granddaughter's Pilgrimage*. Montreal: McGill-Queen's University Press, 1997.

Flack, Jessica C., and Frans B. M. de Waal. "'Any Animal Whatever': Darwinian Building Blocks of Morality in Monkeys and Apes." In *Evolutionary Origins of Morality: Cross-Disciplinary Perspectives*, ed. Leonard D. Katz. Exeter, UK: Imprint Academic, 2000.

Frank, Steven A. "Repression of Competition and the Evolution of Cooperation." *Evolution* 57 (2003).

Furnham, Adrian, and Steven Jones. "Children's Views Regarding Possessions and Their Theft." *Journal of Moral Education* 16 (1987).

Gardner, Hugh. *The Children of Prosperity: Thirteen Modern American Communes.* New York: St. Martin's Press, 1978.

Garland, David. *Punishment and Modern Society*. Chicago: University of Chicago Press, 1990.

Gaviria, Alejandro. "Increasing Returns and the Evolution of Violent Crime: The Case of Colombia." *Journal of Development Economics* 61 (2000): 1–25.

Ghouas, Nessim. *The Conditions, Means and Methods of the MfS in the GDR: An Analysis of the Post and Telephone Control.* New York: Cuvillier Verlag, 2004.

Gibbons, Ann. *The First Human: The Race to Discover Our Earliest Ancestors.* New York: Anchor, 2007.

Gilpatrick, Kristin. *Footprints in Courage: A Bataan Death March Survivors Story.* Middleton WI: Badger, 2002.

Gintis, Herbert, et al. "Explaining Altruistic Behavior in Humans." *Evolution and Human Behavior* 24 (2003).

Godson, Roy, ed. *Menace to Society: Political-Criminal Collaboration around the World.* Piscataway NJ: Transaction, 2003.

Gordon, Richard, and Benjamin S. Llamzon. *Horyo: Memoirs of an American POW.* St. Paul MN: Paragon House, 1990.

Gottlieb, Karla. *The Mother of Us All: A History of Queen Nanny.* Trenton NJ: Africa World Press, 2000.

Graburn, Nelson H. H. "Eskimo Law in Light of Self-and Group-Interest." *Law and Society Review* 4 (1969).

Greenwood, Peter, et al. "Estimated Benefits and Costs of California's New Mandatory-Sentencing Law." In *Three Strikes and You're Out: Vengeance As Public Policy*, ed. David Shichor and Dale K. Sechrest, 53–89. Santa Monica CA: Rand, 1996.

Gruter, Margaret. "The Origins of Legal Behavior." *Journal of Social and Biological Structures* 2 (1979): 43–51.

Gugelyk, Ted, and Milton Bloombaum. *Ma'i Ho'oka'awale, The Separating Sickness: Interviews with Exiled Leprosy Patients at Kalaupapa, Hawaii*. Honolulu: Social Science Research Institute, University of Hawaii, 1979.

Hackett, David A. *The Buchenwald Report*. Boulder: Westview, 1997.

Hammer, Jacob, and Thomas A. Rumer. *This Emigrating Company: The 1844 Oregon Trail Journal of Jacob Hammer*. Cleveland OH: A. H. Clark, 1990.

Hammerstein, Peter, ed. *The Genetic and Cultural Origins of Cooperation*. Cambridge: MIT Press, 2003.

Haque, Shamsul M. "Government Responses to Terrorism: Critical Views of Their Impact on People and Public Administration." *Public Administration Review* 62 (2002).

Haring, Clarence Henry. *The Buccaneers in the West Indies in the XVII Century*. Charleston SC: BiblioBazaar, 2009.

Harris, C. L. G. *The Chieftainess: Glimpses of Grandy Nanny*. Owens Cross Roads AL: Publishing Designs, 2009.

Harris, Robert. *Political Corruption in and Beyond the Nation State*. Florence KY: Routledge, 2003.

Hart, Donna, and Robert W. Sussman. *Man the Hunted: Primates, Predators, and Human Evolutions*. Boulder CO: Westview, 2005.

———. "The Influence of Predation on Primate and Early Human Evolution: Impetus for Cooperation." In *Origins of Altruism and Cooperation*, ed. Robert Sussman and Robert Cloninger, 25–30. New York: Springer Science + Business Media, 2011.

Hauser, Marc D. "Costs of Deception: Cheaters Are Punished in Rhesus Monkeys (Macaca mulatta)." *Proceedings of the National Academy of Sciences* 89 (1992).

Hauser, Marc D., and Peter Marler. "Food-Associated Calls in Rhesus Macaques (Macaca mulatta); 2: Costs and Benefits of Call Production and Suppression." *Behavioral Ecology* 4 (1993).

Hedgepath, William. *The Alternative: Communal Life in New America*. New York: Macmillan, 1970.

Hesse, Hans. *Persecution and Resistance of Jehovah's Witnesses during Nazi-Regime*. Bremen: Edition Temmen, 2001.

Hewitt, R. H. *Notes by the Way: Memoranda of a Journey across the Plains from Dundee, Ill., to Olympia, W. T., May 7 to November 3, 1862*. Washington DC: Office of the Washington Standard, 1863.

Hibbing, John R., and John R. Alford. "Accepting Authoritative Decisions: Humans as Wary Cooperators." *American Journal of Political Science* 48 (2004): 62–76.

Hill, Bob. *Double Jeopardy: Obsession, Murder, and Justice Denied*. New York: William Morrow, 1995.

Hobbes, Thomas. *Leviathan: Or The Matter, Forme and Power of a Common Wealth Ecclesiasticall and Civil*. Edited by J. C. A. Gaskin. London: 1651; rpt. Oxford University Press, 1996.

Hoffman, Morris B. "The Neuroeconomic Path of the Law." *Philosophical Transactions of the Royal Society B: Biological Sciences* 359 (2004).

Holmes, Kenneth L., and David C. Duniway, eds. *Covered Wagon Women: Diaries and Letters from the Western Trails, 1852: Journal of Abigail Jane Scott*. Lincoln: Bison Books, 1997.

Holmes, Linda. *Four Thousand Bowls of Rice: A Prisoner of War Comes Home*. Sydney: Allen and Unwin, 1993.

Houriet, Robert. *Getting Back Together*. New York: Coward, McCann, and Geoghegan, 1969.

Ingram, C. W. N. *New Zealand Shipwrecks—195 Years of Disaster at Sea.*, 7th rev. ed. Aukland, NZ: Hodder Moa Beckett, 1990.

Jackman, Norman. "Survival in the Concentration Camps." *Human Organization* 17 (1958).

Jackson, Charles R., and B. H. Norton. *I Am Alive!: A United States Marine's Story of Survival in a World War II Japanese POW Camp*. New York: Presidio, 2003.

Jacobsen, Gene Samuel. *We Refused to Die: My Time as a Prisoner of War in Bataan and Japan, 1942–1945*. Salt Lake City: University of Utah, 2004.

Janiskee, Brian P., and Edward J. Erher. "Crime, Punishment and Romero: An Analysis of the Case against California's Three Strikes Law." *Duquesne Law Review* (2000).

Jensen, Gary F. "Prohibition, Alcohol, and Murder: Untangling Countervailing Mechanisms." *Homicide Studies* 4 (2000).

Jensen, Keith. "Punishment and Spite, the Dark Side of Cooperation." *Philosophical Transactions of the Royal Society B* 365 (2010): 2635–50.

Johnson, Charles, and David Cordingly. *A General History of the Robberies and Murders of the Most Notorious Pirates*. Guilford CT: Globe Pequot, 2002.

Johnson, Molly Wilkinson. *Training Socialist Citizens: Sports and the State in East Germany*. Boston: Brill Academic, 2008.

Jones, Bill. "Why the Three Strikes Law Is Working in California." *Stanford Law Review* 11 (1999).

Joyce, Richard. *The Evolution of Morality*. Cambridge: MIT Press, 2006.

Kanter, Rosabeth Moss. *Commitment and Community: Communes and Utopias in Sociological Perspective*. Cambridge MA: Harvard University Press, 1972.

Kaplan, John. "The Limits of the Exclusionary Rule." *Stanford Law Review* 26 (1974).

Kavieff, Paul R. *The Violent Years: Prohibition and the Detroit Mobs*. Fort Lee NJ: Barricade, 2001.

Keizer, Kees, Siegwart Lindenberg, and Linda Steg. "The Spreading of Disorder." *Science* 332 (2008): 1681–85.

Kelling, George L., and James Q. Wilson. "The Police and Neighborhood Safety." *The Atlantic*, March 1982.

Kerr, E. Bartlett. *Surrender and Survival: The Experience of American POWs in the Pacific, 1941–1945*. New York: W. Morrow, 1985.

Kirk, Robin. *More Terrible Than Death: Drugs, Violence, and America's War in Colombia*. New York: Public Affairs, 2004.

Klein, Eric K. "Dennis the Menace or Billy the Kid: An Analysis of the Role of Transfer to Criminal Court in Juvenile Justice." *American Criminal Law Review* 35 (1998).

Knox, Donald. *Death March: The Survivors of Bataan*. Ann Arbor MI: Harcourt Brace Jovanovich, 1981.

Kogon, Eugen. *The Theory and Practice of Hell: The German Concentration Camps and the System behind Them*. New York: Farrar, Straus and Giroux, 1950.

Kohlberg, Lawrence. "Current Statement on Some theoretical Issues." In *Consensus and Controversy*, eds. Sohan Modgil and Celia Modgil, 485–546. Florence KY: Routledge, 1986.

———. *Essays on Moral Development*, vol. 1: *The Psychology of Moral Development*. New York: Harper and Row, 1981.

———. *Essays on Moral Development*, vol. 2: *The Psychology of Moral Development*. New York: Harper and Row, 1984.

———. "From Is to Ought: How to Commit the Naturalistic Fallacy and Get Away with It in the Study of Moral Development." In *Cognitive Development and Epistemology*, ed. Theodore Mischel, 151–235. Melbourne, Australia: Academic Press, 1971.

Kolarik, Gera-Lind, and Wayne Klatt. *Freed to Kill: The True Story of Larry Eyler*. Chicago: Chicago Review Press, 1990.

Konstam, Angus. *History of Pirates*. Guilford CT: Lyons, 1999.

———. *Privateers and Pirates: 1730–1830*. Oxford, UK: Osprey, 2001.

Krebs, Dennis L., and Kathy Denton. "Toward a More Pragmatic Approach to Morality: A Critical Evaluation of Kohlberg's Model." *Psychological Review* 112 (2005).

Laugrand, Frederic, Jarich Oosten, and Wim Rasing. *Interviewing Inuit Elders: Perspectives on Traditional Law*. Atviat, NU: Nunavut Arctic College, 1999.

Law Commission Report 70: Acquittal Following Perversion of the Course of Justice. Wellington, NZ: Law Commission, 2001.

Lawton, Manny. *Some Survived*. Chapel Hill NC: Algonquin, 1984.

Leeson, Peter. "An-arrgh-chy: The Law and Economics of Pirate Organization." *Journal of Political Economics* 115 (2007).

———. *The Invisible Hook: The Hidden Economics of Pirates*. Princeton: Princeton University Press, 2009.

Levering, Robert W. *Horror Trek: A True Story of Bataan, the Death March and Three and One-Half Years in Japanese Prison Camps*. Dayton OH: Horstman, 1948.

Leys, Simon. *The Wreck of the Batavia: A True Story*. New York: Thunder's Mouth, 2005.

London, Jack. *The Cruise of the Snark*. New York: Macmillan, 1911. Electronic, accessed September 13, 2011, http://carl-bell-2.baylor.edu/~bellc/jl/TheLepers OfMolokai.html.

Lopez, Enrique Hank. *They Lived on Human Flesh*. New York: Pocket Books, 1973.

Lynch, Gerard E. "RICO: The Crime of Being a Criminal." *Columbia Law Review* 87 (1987): 661-764.

Lynch, Theresa Catherine. "Attica: A Monstrous Credibility Gap." PhD dissertation, University of New Hampshire, 2006.

Lyons, John. "Curse of the Bounty." *The Australian*, April 29, 2008.

Madison, James. *The Federalist*. New York: Penguin, 1987.

Males, Mike, and Dan Macallair. "Striking Out: The Failure of California's 'Three Strikes and You're Out' Law." *Stanford Law and Policy Review* 11 (2000).

Marcus, Paul, and Vicki Waye. "Australia and the United States: Two Common Criminal Justice Systems Uncommonly at Odds." *Tulane Journal of International and Comparative Law* 12 (2004).

Marks, Kathy. *Lost Paradise: From Mutiny of the Bounty to a Modern-Day Legacy of Sexual Mayhem, the Dark Secrets of Pitcairn Island Revealed*. New York: Free Press, 2009.

Marlowe, Frank, and J. Colette Berbesque. "More 'Altruistic' Punishment in Larger Societies." *Proceedings: Biological Sciences* 275 (2008): 587-92.

Matthews, Mark. *Drop City: America's First Hippie Commune*. Norman: University of Oklahoma Press, 2010.

Maude, H. E. "History of Pitcairn Island." In *Introduction to the Pitcairnese Language*, ed. A. S. C. Ross and A. W. Moverley, 45-101. London: Andre Deutsch, 1946.

Mazur, Robert. *The Infiltrator: My Secret Life inside the Dirty Banks behind Pablo Escobar's Medellín Cartel*. New York: Little, Brown, 2009.

Melis, Alicia P., Brian Hare, and Michael Tomasello. "Chimpanzees Recruit the Best Collaborators." *Science* 311 (2006).

Mendelson, Jack, and Nancy Mello. *Alcohol: Used and Abused in America*. New York: Little, Brown,1985.

Miller, Dale, and Rebecca Ratner. "The Disparity between the Actual and Assumed Power of Self-Interest." *Journal of Personality and Social Psychology* 74 (1998).

Miller, Timothy. *The Sixties Communes: Hippies and Beyond*. Syracuse NY: Syracuse University Press, 1999.

———. "Roots of Communal Revival 1962-1966." *The Farm*, http://www.thefarm.org /lifestyle/root2.html.

Milhizer, Eugene. "Debunking Five Great Myths about the Fourth Amendment Exclusionary Rule." *Military Law Review* 211 (2012).

Minnesota Fats and Tom Fox. *The Bank Shot and Other Great Robberies: The Uncrowned Champion of Pocket Billiards, Describes His Game and How It Is Played*. Guilford CT: Lyons, 2006.

Miron, Jeffrey. "Violence and the U.S. Prohibitions of Drugs and Alcohol." *American Law and Economics Review* 1 (1999).

Miron, Jeffery A., and Jeffery Zwiebel. "Alcohol Consumption during Prohibition." *Economics of Drugs* 81 (1991): 242-47.

Moblo, Pennie. "A Land Set Apart: Disease, Displacement, and Death at Makanalua, Moloka'i." PhD dissertation, University of Hawaii, 2004.

Moll, Henrike, and Michael Tomasello. "Cooperation and Human Cognition: The Vygotskian Intelligence Hypothesis." *Philosophical Transactions: Biological Sciences* 362 (2007).

Mollison, James, and Rainbow Nelson. *The Memory of Pablo Escobar*. London: Chris Boot, 2007.

Monkerud, Don. *Free Land: Free Love: Tales of a Wilderness Commune*. Aptos CA: Black Bear Mining, 2000.

Montana-LeBlanc, Phyllis. *Not Just the Levees Broke: My Story During and After Katrina*. New York: Atria, 2008.

Musgrave, Thomas. *Castaway on the Auckland Isles A Narrative of the Wreck of the Grafton*. London: H. T. Dwight, 1865.

Nadim, Sayyid Azhar Hassan. "Impact of Lawlessness on Economic Development and Role of Effective Policing: A Case Study of Pakistan 1969-1993." Master's thesis, University of Punjab, 1997. http://eprints.hec.gov.pk/1907/1/1834.htm.

———. *Pakistan: The Political Economy of Lawlessness*. Oxford, UK: Oxford University Press, 2002.

Naimark, Norman M. *The Russians in Germany: A History of the Soviet Zone of Occupation, 1945-1949.* Cambridge MA: Harvard University Press, 1995.

Nelson, Sharon A. "Factors Influencing Young Children's Use of Motives and Outcomes as Moral Criteria." *Child Development* 51 (1980).

Newman, Graeme. *Comparative Deviance: Perception and Law in Six Cultures.* New York: Elsevier, 1976.

Nietzsche, Friedrich. *Beyond Good and Evil.* Translated by Walter Kaufman. Cambridge, UK: Cambridge University Press, 1986.

Norman, Michael, and Elizabeth Norman. *Tears in the Darkness: The Story of the Bataan Death March and Its Aftermath.* New York: Farrar, Straus and Giroux, 2009.

Nucci, Larry. *Education in the Moral Domain.* Cambridge: Cambridge University Press, 2001.

Nucci, Larry, and Elsa K. Weber. "Social Interactions in the Home and the Development of Young Children's Concepts of the Personal." *Child Development* 66 (1995).

Ouimet, Matthew J. *The Rise and Fall of the Brezhnev Doctrine in Soviet Foreign Policy.* Chapel Hill: University of North Carolina Press, 2003.

Packer, C. "Reciprocal Altruism in Papio Anubis." *Nature* 265 (1977).

Parker, Laura. "Trials and Tribulations Trouble in Paradise." *Vanity Fair*, January 2008.

Parrado, Nando, and Vince Rause. *Miracle in the Andes: Seventy-Two Days on the Mountain and My Long Trek Home.* New York: Crown, 2006.

Payne, Brian K., and Wendy P. Guastaferro. "Mind the Gap: Attitudes about Miranda Warnings among Police Chiefs and Citizens." *Journal of Police and Criminal Psychology* 24 (2009): 93.

Perrin, Timothy, et al. "If It's Broken, Fix It: Moving Beyond the Exclusionary Rule." *Iowa Law Review* 83 (1998).

Pitler, Robert M. "Independent State Search and Seizure Constitutionalism: The New York State Court of Appeals' Quest for Principled Decisionmaking." *Brooklyn Law Review* 62 (1996).

Pizzi, William T. "The Need to Overrule Mapp v. Ohio." *University of Colorado Law Review* 82 (2011): 679-738. Price, David A. *Love and Hate in Jamestown: John Smith, Pocahontas, and the Start of a New Nation.* New York: Knopf, 2003.

Price, Richard, ed. *Maroon Societies: Rebel Slave Communities in the Americas.* Baltimore: Johns Hopkins University Press, 1979.

Rahn, Wendy, and John Transue. "Social Trust and Value Change: The Decline of Social Capital in American Youth, 1976-1995." *Political Psychology* 19 (1998).

Rasmussen, Knud. *The Netsilik Eskimos: Social and Spiritual Culture*. Copenhagen, Denmark: Gyldendal, 1931.

Raynal, Francois. *Wrecked on a Reef; or, Twenty Months Among the Auckland Isles*. London: Nelson and Sons, 1874.

Read, Piers Paul. *Alive: Sixteen Men, Seventy-Two Days, and Insurmountable Odds—The Classic Adventure of Survival in the Andes*. New York: Harper Perennial, 2005.

Rector, Milton G. "A Revolutionary Revision of American Penal Law." *Crime and Delinquency* 9 (1963).

Reeve, Hudson K. "Queen Activation of Lazy Workers in Colonies of the Eusocial Naked Mole-Rat." *Nature* 358 (1992).

Reiter, Joanne, Kathy J. Panken, and Burney J. Le Boeuf. "Female Competition and Reproductive Success in Northern Elephant Seals." *Animal Behavior* 29 (1981).

Reiter, Joanne, Nell Lee Stinson, and Burney J. Le Boeuf. "Northern Elephant Seal Development: The Transition from Weaning to Nutritional Independence." *Behavioral Ecology and Sociobiology* 3 (1978).

Rilling, J. K., et al. "A Neural Basis for Social Cooperation." *Neuron* 35 (2002).395.

Ristroph, Alice. "Desert, Democracy, and Sentencing Reform." *Journal of Criminal Law and Criminology* 96 (2006).

Roach, Kent. "Entrapment and Equality in Terrorism Prosecutions: A Comparative Examination of North American and European Approaches." *Mississippi Law Journal* 80 (2011).

Robinson, Paul H. "Criminalization Tensions: Empirical Desert, Changing Norms, and Rape Reform." In *The Structures of the Criminal Law*, eds. R. A. Duff et al., 186–202. New York: Oxford University Press, 2011.

———. *Criminal Law* § 12.1. New York: Aspen, 1997.

———. *Criminal Law Case Studies*, 4th ed. St. Paul MN: West, 2009.

———. *Distributive Principles of Criminal Law: Who Should Be Punished How Much?* New York: Oxford University Press, 2008.

———. "Final Report of the Kentucky Penal Code Revision Project of the Criminal Justice Council." Final Report of the Kentucky Penal Code Revision Project, 2003, http://ssrn.com/abstract=1526674.

———. *Intuitions of Justice and the Utility of Desert*, part 3. New York: Oxford University Press, 2013.

———. "Natural Law and Lawlessness: Modern Lessons from Pirates, Lepers, Eskimos, and Survivors." *University of Illinois Law Review* 2013, no. 2.

———. "Punishing Dangerousness: Cloaking Preventive Detention as Criminal Justice." *Harvard Law Review* 114 (2001).

———. "Report on Offense Grading in Pennsylvania." Working paper, University of Pennsylvania Law School, Public Law Research Paper No. 10-01, 2009, 32, 34, 52. http://ssrn.com/abstract=1527149.

Robinson, Paul H., and John M. Darley. "Intuitions of Justice: Implications for Criminal Law and Justice Policy." *Southern California Law Review* 81 (2007): 1-67.

———. "Objectivist Versus Subjectivist Views of Criminality: A Study in the Role of Social Science in Criminal Law Theory." *Oxford Journal of Legal Studies* 18 (1998).

———. "Testing Competing Theories of Justification." *North Carolina Law Review* 76 (1998): 1095-1143.

Robinson, Paul H., and Michael T. Cahill. *Criminal Law*, 2nd ed. Fredrick MD: Wolters Kluwer Law and Business, 2012.

"Final Report of the Illinois Criminal Code Rewrite and Reform Commission." University of Pennsylvania Law School, Public Law Research Paper No. 09-40, 2003, http://ssrn.com/abstract=1523384.

———. *Law without Justice: Why Criminal Law Doesn't Give People What They Deserve.* New York: Oxford University Press, 2005.

Robinson, Paul H., and Robert Kurzban. "Concordance and Conflict in Intuitions of Justice." *Minnesota Law Review* 91 (2007).

Robinson, Paul H., Goeffrey P. Goodwin, and Michael Reisig. "The Disutility of Justice." *New York Law Review* 85 (2010): 1940-2033.

Robinson, Paul H., Robert Kurzban, and Owen D. Jones. "The Origins of Shared Intuitions of Justice." *Vanderbilt Law Review* 60 (2007): 1633-88.

Robinson, Paul H., et al. "Competing Theories of Blackmail: An Empirical Research Critique of Criminal Law Theory." *Texas Law Review* 89 (2010).

Robinson, Paul. H., et al. "Extralegal Punishment Factors: A Study of Forgiveness, Hardship, Good-Deeds, Apology, Remorse, and Other Such Discretionary Factors in Assessing Criminal Punishment." *Vanderbilt Law Review* 65 (2012).

Robinson, Paul H., et al. "Report on Offense Grading in New Jersey." Working paper, University of Pennsylvania Law School, Public Law Research Paper No. 11-03, 2011, 3-5, http://ssrn.com/abstract=1737825.

Robinson, Paul H., et al. Report on Offense Grading in Pennsylvania, December 2010.

Robinson, Paul H., et al. "The Five Worst (and Five Best) American Criminal Codes." *Northwestern University Law Review* 95 (2000): 1-89.

Robinson, Paul H., et al. "The Modern Irrationalities of American Criminal Codes: An Empirical Study of Offense Grading." *Journal of Criminal Law and Criminology* 100 (2010): 709-64.

Rogers, Woodes. *Cruising Voyage Round the World*. A. Bell and B. Lintot, 1712.

Rohrschneider, Robert, and Rudiger Schmitt-Beck. "Trust in Democratic Institutions in Germany: Theory and Evidence Ten Years after Reunification." *German Politics* 11 (2002).

Ross, Jacqueline E. "Impediments to Transnational Cooperation in Undercover Policing: A Comparative Study of the United States and Italy." *American Journal of Comparative Law* 52 (2004).

———. "The Place of Court Surveillance in Democratic Societies: A Comparative Study of the United States and Germany." *American Journal of Comparative Law* 55 (2007).

Sanchez, Fabio, et al. "Conflict, Violence, and Crime in Colombia." In *Understanding Civil War*, vol 2: *The World Bank*. Edited by Paul Collier and Nicholas Sambanis. Washington DC: World Bank, 2005.

Shoenberg, Robert J. *Mr. Capone: The Real and Complete Story of Al Capone*. New York: First Quill, 1993.

Scott, Abigail Jane. *Journal of a Trip to Oregon*. http://cateweb.uoregon.edu/duniway /notes/DiaryProof1.html, last accessed September 12, 2011.

Senkewicz, Robert M. *Vigilantes and the Gold Rush*. Redwood City CA: Stanford University Press, 1985.

Seyfarth, Robert M., and Dorothy L. Cheney. "Grooming, Alliances, and Reciprocal Altruism in Vervet Monkeys." *Nature* 308 (1984).

Shepherd, Joanna M. "Fear of the First Strike: The Full Deterrent Effect of California's Two- and Three-Strikes Legislation." *Journal of Legal Studies* 31 (2002).

Shinn, Charles Howard, and Joseph Henry Jackson. *Mining Camps: A Study in American Frontier Government*. Scribner's, 1884; rpt. New York: Scribner's Sons, 1884; rpt. Harper Torchbooks, 1965.

Sickmund, Melissa, Howard N. Snyder, and Eileen Poe-Yamagata. *Juvenile Offenders and Victims: 1997 Update on Violence*. Washington DC: National Center for Juvenile Justice, 1997.

Sides, Hampton. *Ghost Soldiers: The Forgotten Epic Story of World War II's Most Dramatic Mission*. New York: Doubleday, 2001.

Silk, Joan B. "The Patterning of Intervention among Male Bonnet Macaques: Reciprocity, Revenge, and Loyalty." *Current Anthropology* 33 (1992).

Smetana, Judith G. "Toddlers' Social Interactions Regarding Moral and Conventional Transgressions." *Child Development* 55 (1984): 1767–76.

Smetana, Judith G., et al. "Preschool Children's Judgments about Hypothetical and Actual Transgressions." *Child Development* 64 (1993).

Smith, Andrew. *The Castaways: A Narrative of the Wreck and Sufferings of the Officers and Crew of the Ship "Invercauld," of Aberdeen, on the Auckland Islands.* Aberdeen, Scotland: A. Brown, 1866.

Snyder, Howard N., and Melissa Sickmund. *Juvenile Offenders and Victims: A National Report.* Washington DC: National Center for Juvenile Justice, 1995.

Spelman, William. *Criminal Incapacitation* 14 (Plenum, 1994).

Starr, Kenneth, and Audrey Maness. "Is the Exclusionary Rule a Good Way of Enforcing Fourth Amendment Values?: Reasonable Remedies and (or?) the Exclusionary Rule." *Texas Tech Law Review* 43 (2010).

Stevenson, Robert Louis. *Father Damien, an Open Letter to the Reverend Dr. Hyde of Honolulu.* London: Chatto and Windus, 1914. Electronic, accessed September 13, 2011, www.gutenberg.org/files/281/281-h/281-h.htm.

Strom, Kevin J. *Profile of State Prisoners Under Age 18, 1985–97.* Washington DC: Bureau of Justice, 2000.

Sunday, Billy, and William A. Sunday. *The Sawdust Trail: Billy Sunday in His Own Words.* Iowa City: University of Iowa Press, 2005.

Sussman, Robert, and Robert Cloninger, eds. *Origins of Altruism and Cooperation.* New York: Springer Science and Business Media, 2011.

Talalay, Sarah. "Eyler Dies in Prison." *Chicago Tribune*, March 7, 1994.

Tattersall, Ian. "Cooperation, Altruism, and Human Evolution." In *Origins of Altruism and Cooperation*, edited by Robert Sussmann and Robert Cloninger. New York: Springer Science and Business Media, 2011.

Tayman, John. *The Colony: The Harrowing True Story of the Exiles of Molokai.* New York: Scribner, 2006.

Thachuk, Kimberley. "Corruption and International Security." *SAIS Review* 25 (2005).

Thoreau, Henry David. Tomkovicz, James J. "The Endurance of the Felony-Murder Rule: A Study of the Forces that Shape Our Criminal Law." *Washington and Lee Law Review* 51 (1994).

Useem, Bert, and Peter Kimball. *States of Siege: U.S. Prison Riots, 1971–1986.* New York: Oxford University Press, 1989.

Van den Steenhoven, Geert. *Legal Concepts among the Netsilik Eskimos of Pelly Bay.* Ottawa, Canada: Ottawa Department of Northern Affairs and National Resources, 1959.

Van Kessel, Gordon. "Suspect as a Source of Testimonial Evidence: A Comparison of the English and American Approaches." *Hastings Law Journal* 38 (1986): 1–152.

Vitiello, Michael. "Punishment and Democracy: A Hard Look at Three Strikes' Overblown Promises." *California Law Review* 90 (2002).

———. "Three Strikes: Can We Return to Rationality?" *Journal of Criminal Law and Criminology* 87 (1997).

Vogel, Gretchen. "The Evolution of the Golden Rule." *Science* 303 (2004).

Wainryb, Cecilia. "Understanding Differences in Moral Judgments: The Role of Informational Assumptions." *Child Development* 62 (1991).

Wainryb, Cecilia, and Sherrie Ford. "Young Children's Evaluations of Acts Based on Beliefs Different from Their Own." *Merrill-Palmer Quarterly* 44 (1998).

Warr, Mark, Robert F. Meier, and Maynard L. Erickson. "Norms, Theories of Punishment, and Publicly Preferred Penalties for Crimes." *Sociological Quarterly* 24 (1983).

Weyrauch, Walter O. "The Experience of Lawlessness." *New Criminal Law Review* 10 (2007): 415-40.

Whitecross, Roy H. *Slaves of the Son of Heaven: The Personal Story of an Australian POW, 1942-1945.* St. Kilda East, Australia: Kangaroo, 2000.

Wicker, Tom. *A Time to Die: The Attica Prison Revolt.* New York: Quadrangle, 1995.

Wilkey, Malcom. "The Exclusionary Rule: Why Suppress Valid Evidence?" *Judicature* 62 (1978).

Williams, Mary Floyd. *History of the San Francisco Committee of Vigilance of 1851: A Study of Social Control on the California Frontier in the Days of the Gold Rush.* Oakland: University of California Press, 1921.

Woodard, Colin. *The Republic of Pirates: Being the True and Surprising Story of the Caribbean Pirates and the Man Who Brought Them Down.* New York: Harcourt, 2007.

Wuthnow, Robert. *Acts of Compassion.* Princeton NJ: Princeton University Press, 1991.

Young, Rosalind Amelia. *Mutiny of the Bounty and the Story of Pitcairn Island, 1790-1894.* Nampa ID: Pacific Press, 1894.

Zimring, Franklin E., et al. *Punishment and Democracy: Three Strikes and You're Out in California.* New York: Oxford University Press, 2001.

Zips, Werner. *Black Rebels: African-Caribbean Freedom Fighters in Jamaica.* Princeton NJ: Markus Wiener, 1999.

COURT CASES

Florida v. Ryan Holle, in the Circuit Court of the First Circuit In and for Escambia County, Florida, Jury Instructions, Case 03-1056 E-F, August 4, 2004.

Indictment for Check Fraud, November 20, 1972. *Rummel v. Estelle*, Director, Texas Department of Corrections, 587 F.2d 651 (5th Circuit 1978).

Indictments of William Rummel, December 1, 1964 (Fraudulent Use of a Credit Card); October 2, 1968 (Passing as True a Forged Instrument); and November 29, 1972 (Worthless Check Passed with a Value over $50).

Indictments of William J. Rummel, October 2, 1969 (Passing as True a Forged Instrument).

Motion to Waive Reading of Indictment, February 23, 1972.

People of the State of Illinois v. Larry W. Eyler, Case No 83 CF 1585, "Report of Proceedings," February 3, 1984.

People of the State of Illinois v. Larry W. Eyler, Case No 83 CF 1585, "Supplemental Memorandum in Opposition to Defendant's Motion to Suppress," February 1, 1984.

People of the State of Illinois v. Larry W. Eyler, Case No 83 CF 1585, "Supplemental Memorandum in Support of Defendant's Motions to Suppress," February 1, 1984.

People of the State of Illinois v. Larry W. Eyler, No 84-126, (North Eastern Reporter, 2nd Series, October 25, 1989), 268-92.

Ryan Joseph Holle v. Secretary, Florida Department of Corrections, Case 3:11-cv-00436-LC-EMT Document 16, United States District Court Northern District of Florida Pensacola Division. *Memorandum of Law in Opposition to Respondent's Motion to Dismiss Petitioner's Habeas Corpus Petition as Untimely.* Filed May 16, 2012.

Ryan Joseph Holle v. Secretary, Florida Department of Corrections, Case 3:11-cv-00436-LC-EMT Case 3:11-cv-00436-LC-EMT Document 24, United States District Court Northern District of Florida Pensacola Division. *Report and Recommendation.* Filed July 27, 2012.

Ryan Joseph Holle v. Secretary, Florida Department of Corrections, Case 3:11-cv-00436-LC-EMT Document 26, United States District Court Northern District of Florida Pensacola Division. *Petitioner's Objections to the Magistrate Judge's Report and Recommendation to Grant Respondent's Motion to Dismiss Petitioner's Habeas Corpus Petition as Untimely and to Deny Petitioner a Certificate of Appealability.* Filed July 9, 2012.

Ryan Joseph Holle v. Secretary, Florida Department of Corrections, Case 3:11-cv-00436-LC-EMT Document 27, United States District Court Northern District of Florida Pensacola Division. *Answer to Petition to Dismiss.* Filed July 13, 2012.

Ryan Joseph Holle v. Secretary, Florida Department of Corrections, Case 3:11-cv-00436-LC-EMT , Trial Record Transcript, Case 03-1056 E-F, August 4, 2004.

Rummel v. Estelle, Director, Texas Department of Corrections, 498 F. Supp. 793 (W.D. Tx. 1980).

U.S. Supreme Court Brief—Criminal DA of Bexar County, Texas, October 1979. *Rummel v. Estelle*, Corrections Director, 445 U.S. 263 (1980).

INDEX

Page numbers in italic indicate illustrations

insider-trading, 250
intentional defined, 315
intuitions of justice, 74, 76–77, 79–80, 87, 89, 95, 97, 99–102, 167–69, 180–81, 195, 214, 239–40, 278; shared, 139, 171–72, 240–48
Inuit, *105*
the *Invercauld*, 128–30, *129*, 132, 265

Jamaica: early history of, 111; Maroons in, 111–12, *112*, 114, 133
Japan: and Japanese prisoners, 112, *119*, 264; during World War II, 122; World War II prisons in, 116–24, *119*; and World War II society, 116–17
Jentch, Hans-Joachim, 156
Joy Fest (at Drop City), 35–36
joyriding, 97; offense defined, 315
justice: commitment to, 113–15; communal value of, 61; compromises on, 103, 111–13; failure of, 61, 81, 195, 213–18; intuitions of, 69–70; promotion of, 248; social value of, 87, 94–95, 217–18; subversions to, 243–44; when undermined, 232–33
justice commission, 248
justice system, moral credibility of, 247
justification defense defined, 315

Kallweit, Richard, 35
Kaplan, John, 199
Kentucky, 207, 242–43, 268
King, Rodney, 213–14
King, Stephen, 64
Klein, Richard, 40

knowing defined, 315
Kohlberg, Lawrence, 74–75
Kushnir-Kushnarev, Gregory, 67
Kustudick, Laurie, 216

law: in ancient Egypt, 24; formation of, 134–35; as ineffective for controlling crime, 8; internalization of, 78–79; as source of authority, 118, 123–28, 135, 152–53; as source of order, 17, 30, 53, 58, 150–51
Lawrence, D. H., 232
leadership: effects of, 132–33, 135; failure of, 126–27, 129–30; unofficial, 123–28, 130
legal skepticism, 8
legality principle, 215; defined, 315
Leland, Henry, 140
leper colony, 12–14, *13*
Little, David, 189, 194, 203–5, 267
Los Pepes cartel, 227–31, 234
Love, Frank, 190–93

Maclaren, Alick, 130, *132*
Madison, James, 5
Maroons, 112, 263–64. *See also* Jamaica; Queen Nanny
Mason, Richard, 53
McKoski, Raymond, 195
Medellín Cartel, 268–69
medicinal whiskey. *See* Prohibition
Mendoza, Eduardo, 226
Miller, Charles, 164–67
Minnesota Fats, 149
Minority Report (film), 183
Miranda rule, 201
Mockus, Antanas, 269

Model Penal Code, 98, 173, 245
Model Sentencing Act, 182–83
Molokai HI, 12–15, 13, 19, 21, 25, 120, 124–26, 253
Moore, Jerry, 172, 176
moral authority, 251–52
moral blameworthiness. *See* blameworthiness
moral credibility, 243–44, 247
moral development, 74–78, 90–91, 101
moral theory, universalist, 74–80, 101–2
Musgrave, Thomas, 131

Nadeem, Azhar Hassan, 159–61
Nagasaki, Japan, 264
Nassau, Bahamas, 27
National Criminal Justice Association, 248
National District Attorney's Association, 248
natural selection. *See* evolution
negligent defined, 316
Netsilik, 105, 110, 262–63; and King William Land, 78, 101, 114–15
New Jersey, 242–43
Nietzsche, Friedrich, 18
Noriega, Manuel, 222
Northwest Territories, Canada, 262
Nunuvut, Canada, 262

occupational death rates, 11
Oglesby, Richard, 57
O'Malley, Jack, 267
Oregon Trail, 68–70, 258

Pakistan, 237; Gujranwala Range in, 159
Parrado, Nando, 17, 19, 254–56

Pavlakovic, John, 193–94
Pearl Harbor, attack on, 116
Peddie, Sydney, 264
Pennsylvania, 241–43
Pensacola FL, 164
Peter Rabbit, 34, 47, 81, 258
petit jury, 58; defined, 316
Philippines: Bataan Peninsula, 117; World War II society in, 116–20
Pineapple Primary (1928), 146
pirates, 27, 29, 67–68, 77, 88, 95, 133, 256–57
Pitcairn Island, 108–10, 109, 114, 263
police corruption, 269
Polk, James, 52
popular tribunals, 55–58
preschool brawl (Los Angeles), 3, 134
preventive detention, 181–85, 240–41
prisoner justice, 66–67, 70–72, 92–94
Privitiera, Michael, 93–94, 95, 112–13
procedural justice, 196–200; social costs of, 213–16
Prohibition, 142, *143*, 151, 161–63, 223–25, 233, 251, 265–66; and 18th Amendment, 140–49; in Chicago, 146–47; in New York, 143; origins of, 140–41; repeal of, 161–62; and Volstead Act, 140–49
Pryor, Frederic, 156
public goods experiments, 21, 46–48
punishment: and abolitionist movement, 39; among animals, 49, 73–74; and antipunishment theory, 32, 36–37, 42, 46, 51; and avoiding injustice, 103; coercive sanctions as, 33; and communal values, 70–74; continuum of, 100; and desert, 97–98, 104, 107, 114,